THOMSON
COURSE TECHNOLOGY
Professional ■ Trade ■ Reference

SOURCE CODE FOR ALL GAMES INCLUDED ON CD

PHP 5/MySQL® Programming

for the absolute beginner™

NO EXPERIENCE REQUIRED

"This series shows that it's possible to teach newcomers a programming language and good programming practices without being boring."

—Lou Grinzo, reviewer for *Dr. Dobb's Journal*

Premier Press™

ANDY HARRIS, Series Editor

PHP 5/MySQL Programming

for the absolute beginner

ANDY HARRIS

THOMSON
COURSE TECHNOLOGY
Professional ■ Technical ■ Reference

ISBN: 1-59200-494-6
Library of Congress Catalog Card Number: 2004108011
Printed in Canada
04 05 06 07 08 WC 10 9 8 7 6 5 4 3

THOMSON
COURSE TECHNOLOGY™
Professional ■ Technical ■ Reference

Thomson Course Technology PTR,
a division of Thomson Course Technology
25 Thomson Place
Boston, MA 02210
http://www.courseptr.com

SVP, Thomson Course Technology PTR:
Andy Shafran

Publisher:
Stacy L. Hiquet

Senior Marketing Manager:
Sarah O'Donnell

Marketing Manager:
Heather Hurley

Manager of Editorial Services:
Heather Talbot

Acquisitions Editor:
Mitzi Koontz

Senior Editor:
Mark Garvey

Associate Marketing Managers:
Kristin Eisenzopf and
Sarah Dubois

Project Editor:
Scott Harris/Argosy Publishing

Technical Reviewer:
Arlie Hartman

Thomson Course Technology PTR Market Coordinator:
Amanda Weaver

Copy Editor:
Tonya Cupp

Interior Layout Tech:
Shawn Morningstar

Cover Designer:
Mike Tanamachi

CD-ROM Producer:
Arlie Hartman

Indexer:
Maureen Shepherd

Proofreader:
Jan Cocker

To Heather, Elizabeth, Matthew, and Jacob,
and to all those who have called me Teacher.

Acknowledgments

First I thank Him from whom all flows.

Heather, you always work harder on these books than I do. Thank you for your love and your support. Thank you Elizabeth, Matthew, and Jacob for understanding why Daddy was typing all the time.

Thanks to the Open Source community for creating great free software like PHP and MySQL. Also, thanks to the phpMyAdmin team and the SQLite team for developing such terrific software and making it freely available.

Thank you, Stacy Hiquet, for your continued support and encouragement on this and other projects.

Thanks, Scott Harris. You did a great job of juggling all those balls around.

Thanks to Tonya Cupp for drastically improving the readability of the manuscript.

Arlie Hartman, thank you for technical editing and for putting together the CD-ROM.

Thanks to J. Wynia (www.phpgeek.com) for technical editing. Thanks also to Jason for use of PHPTriad on the CD-ROM.

Special thanks to those who worked on the first edition. Your hard work is the foundation for something even better.

Thank you to the many members of the Premier/Course team who worked on this book.

A *huge* thanks goes to my CSCI N399 and N452 Server-Side Web Development classes and the many people who sent in comments and advice from the first edition. Thank you for being patient with my manuscript, for helping me spot many errors, and for providing invaluable advice. I learned as much from you as you did from me.

About the Author

Andy Harris began his teaching career as a high-school special education teacher. During that time, he taught himself enough computing to do part-time computer consulting and database work. He began teaching computing at the university level in the late 1980s as a part-time job.

Since 1995 he has been a full-time lecturer in the Computer Science Department of Indiana University/Purdue University–Indianapolis, where he manages the Streaming Media Lab and teaches classes in several programming languages. His primary interests are PHP, Java, Microsoft languages, Perl, JavaScript, Web Data, virtual reality, portable devices, and streaming media. He has written numerous books on these and other technology topics.

Contents at a Glance

Contents

Introduction

Computer programming has often been seen as a difficult and arcane skill. Programming languages are difficult and complicated, out of the typical person's reach. However, the advent of the World Wide Web has changed that to some extent. It's reasonably easy to build and post a Web page for the entire world to see. The language of the Web is reasonably simple, and numerous applications are available to assist in the preparation of static pages. At some point, every Web author begins to dream of pages that actually do something useful. The simple HTML language that builds a page offers the tantalizing ability to build forms, but no way to work with the information that users type into these forms.

Often, a developer has a database or some other dynamic information they wish to somehow attach to a Web page. Even languages such as JavaScript are not satisfying in these cases. The CGI interface was designed as an early solution to this problem, but CGI itself can be confusing and the languages used with CGI (especially Perl) are very powerful, but confusing to beginners.

PHP is an amazing language. It is meant to work with Web servers, where it can do the critical work of file management and database access. It is reasonably easy to learn and understand, and can be embedded into Web pages. It is as powerful as more difficult languages, with a number of impressive extensions that add new features to the language.

In this book, I teach you how to write computer programs. I do not expect you to have any previous programming experience. You learn to program using the PHP language. Although PHP itself is a very specialized language (designed to enhance Web pages), the concepts you learn through this language can be extended to a number of other programming environments.

Whenever possible, I use games as example programs. Each chapter begins by demonstrating a simple game or diversion. I show you all the skills you need to write that game through a series of simple example programs. At the end of the chapter I show the game again, this time by looking at the code, which at that point you will understand. Games are motivating and often present special challenges to the programmer. The concepts presented are just as applicable in real-world applications.

This second edition adds new features and includes updates from the previous edition of the book. Specifically, it includes new chapters on object-oriented programming (OOP) and XML, as well as examples on using PHP to create content management systems. I've updated the code to reflect improvements in PHP 5.0, including the improved object model and XML tools, and the new SQLite data access tools.

Programming is not a skill you can learn simply by reading about it. You have to write code to really understand what's going on. I encourage you to play along at home. Look at the code on the accompanying CD. Run the programs yourself. Try to modify the code and see how it works. Make new variations of the programs to suit your own needs.

Exploring the PHP Environment

Web pages are interesting, but on their own they are simply documents. You can use PHP to add code to your Web pages so they can do more. A scripting language like PHP can convert your Web site from static document to an interactive application. In this chapter you learn how to add basic PHP functionality to your Web pages. You also learn how to do these things:

- Download and install Apache
- Download and install PHP
- Configure Apache to recognize PHP 5.0
- Configure PHP to run extensions used in this book (including MySQL and XML)
- Ensure PHP is on your system
- Run a basic diagnostic check of your PHP installation
- Add PHP code to a Web page

Introducing the Tip of the Day Program

Your first program probably won't win any Web awards, but it takes you beyond what you can do with regular HTML. Figure 1.1 illustrates the Tip of the Day page, which offers friendly, helpful advice.

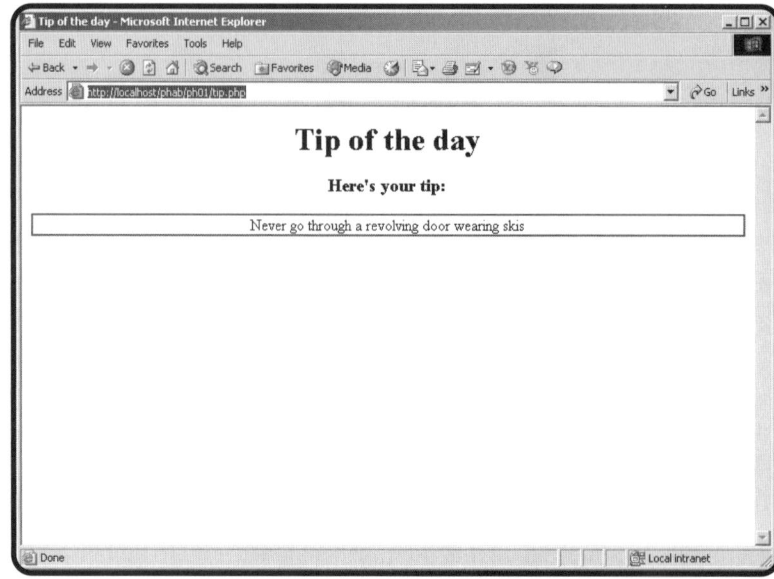

FIGURE 1.1

The tip of the day might look simple, but it is a technological marvel. It features HTML, cascading style sheets, and PHP code.

You could write this kind of page without using a technology like PHP, but the program is a little more sophisticated than it might look on the surface. The tip isn't actually embedded in the Web page at all, but it is stored in a completely separate file. The program integrates this separate file into the HTML page. The page owner can change the tip of the day very easily by editing the text file that contains the tips.

In the Real World

The Tip of the Day page illustrates one of the hottest concepts in Web programming today: the content management system. This kind of structure allows programmers to design a Web site's general layout, but isolates the contents from the page design. The page owners (who might not know how to modify a Web page directly) can easily change a text file without risk of exposing the code that holds the site together. You'll learn how to build a full-blown content management system in chapter 8, "XML and Content Management Systems."

You should begin by reviewing your HTML skills. Soon enough, you're going to be writing programs that write Web pages, so you need to be very secure with your HTML coding. If you usually write all your Web pages with a plain text editor, you should be fine. If you tend to rely on higher-end tools like Microsoft FrontPage or Macromedia Dreamweaver, you should put those tools aside for a while and make sure you can write solid HTML by hand. You should know how to build standard Web pages using modern standards (HTML 4.0 or XHTML), including form elements and cascading style sheets (CSS). If you need a refresher, please see Appendix A, which is stored on the CD that accompanies this book.

Programming on the Web Server

The Internet is all about various computers communicating with each other. The prevailing model of the Internet is the notion of clients and servers. You can understand this better by imagining a drive-through restaurant. As you drive to the little speaker, a barely intelligible voice asks for your order. You ask for your cholestoburger supreme and the teenager packages your food. You drive up, exchange money for the meal, and drive away. Meanwhile, the teenager waits for another customer to appear. The Internet works much like this model. Large permanent computers called *Web servers* host Web pages and other information. They are much like the drive-through restaurant. Users drive up to the Web server using a Web browser. The data is exchanged and the user can read the information on the Web browser.

What's interesting about this model is the interaction doesn't have to stop there. Since the client (user's) machine is a computer, it can be given instructions. Commonly, the JavaScript language stores special instructions in a Web page. These instructions (like the HTML code itself) don't mean anything on the server. Once the page gets to the client machine, the browser interprets the HTML code and any other JavaScript instructions.

While much of the work is passed to the client, there are some disadvantages to this client-side approach. Programs designed to work inside a Web browser are usually greatly restricted in the kinds of things they can do. A client-side Web program usually cannot access the user's printer or disk drives. This limitation alone prevents such programs from doing much of the most useful work of the Internet, such as database connectivity and user tracking.

The server is also a computer; it's possible to write programs designed to operate on the server rather than the client. This arrangement has a number of advantages:

- Server-side programs run on powerful Web server computers.
- The server can freely work with files and databases.
- The code returned to the user is plain HTML, which can be displayed on any Web browser.

Installing PHP and Apache

PHP is only interesting when it runs on a computer configured as a Web server. One way or another, you need access to a computer with at least three components on it: PHP, a Web server (such as Apache or Microsoft IIS), and some sort of database management system (usually MySQL).

Using an Existing Server

If you're lucky, you already may have access to a Web server that has PHP and some other useful programs installed. Once you start building professional Web sites, investigate using a commercial Web server so you don't have to deal with the headaches of server administration and security yourself (unless, of course, you really like that kind of thing). The advantage of using a prebuilt server is primarily avoiding the entire messy process of setting up your own server. The disadvantage is you're stuck with the configuration that your server administrator decides upon.

Ultimately, you need to have access to some sort of Web server so people can see your programs. It might make sense to do all your programming directly on the server you'll use to disseminate your work. If you already have a Web site stored on a server, check to see if your server offers PHP support. A surprising number of services offer PHP/MySQL support for little or no extra money.

There are some free PHP servers around, but they don't tend to stay up for long and they usually have some sort of advertisements or other strings attached. Still, it's possible to find a free host that will support PHP. To find a suitable hosting service, do a Google search on **free PHP hosting**. You have many choices if you're willing to pay a monthly fee for service. With a little digging, you can easily find full-featured services for less than $10 a month. If you want to be able to do all the projects in this book, look for a server that supports PHP 5.0 and MySQL. It is also useful if the service supports phpMyAdmin, a database management system described in chapter 9, "Using MySQL to Create Databases."

Installing Your Own Development Environment

Even if you have access to an online Web server, you may want to build a practice server for development. This approach has many advantages:

- You can control exactly how the server you install is configured. You can tune it so all the options you want are turned on, and things you don't need are disabled. (I describe how to do this later in this chapter in the section called "Telling Apache about PHP.")
- You can test your programs without exposing them to the entire world. When you install a local server, you usually do not expose it to anyone but yourself. That way people won't snoop around your work until you're ready to expose it.
- It's easier to configure development environments to work with local servers than to work with remote ones.
- You don't have to be connected to the Web while you work. This is especially important if you don't have a high-speed connection.

However, installing a Web server (and its related programs) is not as simple as installing commercial applications. There are a *lot* of variables and many things that can go wrong. However, with patience, you should be able to do it.

You need several components to build your own PHP development system. PHP development is often done with either a system called *LAMP* (Linux, Apache, MySQL, and PHP) or *WAMP* (Windows, Apache, MySQL, and PHP).

If you're running Linux, there's a good chance everything is already installed on your system and you need only configure and turn things on. For that reason, I'm presuming for this discussion that you're working on a Windows XP system. Please look at the various Help documents that come with the software components for assistance installing with other operating systems.

To get your system up and running, you need the following components.

A Web Server

The Web server is software that allows a computer to host Web pages. The most popular Web server as of this writing is *Apache*, an open-source offering which runs on Windows, Linux, and just about every other operating system. The Web server lets you write and test programs running from your local computer exactly the same way they will be seen on the Internet.

The PHP Environment

The PHP environment is a series of programs and library files. These programs are unusual because the user never runs them directly. Instead, a user requests a PHP program from a Web server and the server calls upon PHP to process the instructions in the file. PHP then returns HTML code, which the user sees in the browser. This book was written using PHP 5.0, although most of the code works well on earlier versions of PHP.

A Database Environment

Interacting with databases is one of PHP's most powerful uses. For that reason, you need at least one database engine installed with your system. For this book, you use MySQL and SQLite. I cover the installation and use of these packages more fully in chapter 9 and appendix B on the CD ROM, because you won't need them until then.

An Editor

Have some sort of editor to manipulate your code. You can use Notepad, but you probably want something more substantial. A number of freeware and commercial PHP editors are available. For this book, I used emacs (a powerful UNIX-based text editor that can be somewhat mystifying for beginners) and Maguma Studio. The latter is a commercial editor with a very impressive free version.

Installing Apache

According to the industry-standard Netcraft (www.netcraft.com) survey, 67 percent of the world's servers are running Apache as of March 2004. You might already have Microsoft's Internet Information Server (IIS) installed on your machine. If so, you can use it, but you have to read the documentation to see how to make sure IIS communicates with PHP. (The installation notes that come with PHP explain how to run PHP on an IIS Web server.)

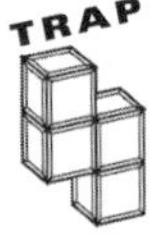

I know of several people who have had good luck running PHP on the IIS server, but I've had problems. Things got especially messy when I tried to run both IIS and Apache on the same system. IIS would tend to shut down Apache with little warning. If there's not an urgent need to run IIS, I'd stick with Apache on my PHP server. In my office, we actually run PHP on a Linux server and run IIS with .NET on its own Windows-based server.

The Apache Web server is extremely stable and relatively easy to use once it's installed. The code for this book was tested on Apache 1.3.23, 1.3.29, and 2.0.

Installing Apache Files

Apache is available on the CD that accompanies this book. You can also go directly to the Apache Web site to load a more recent version or get installation help.

Install Apache to your system as the first step of building your WAMP development environment. If you have any trouble, read the excellent documentation at http://httpd.apache.org/docs/windows.html.

When prompted for a domain name, use `localhost` for a local installation. This allows access to this practice server from your local machine only. Once you know things are working well, you can enter a different domain name.

Testing Your Server

Now see if Apache is installed correctly.

1. Use a file manager to look for the `Apache` directory.
2. Find a program called `apache.exe`.

   If you don't find it there, look in the `bin` directory.
3. Run `apache.exe`.

   A DOS window starts.

While configuring your system, *do not close this DOS window!* If you do, Apache will close down and work incorrectly. After testing this console version of Apache, you run it as a service, which runs in the background. (I'll explain that shortly.) If you've installed Apache 2.0, it automatically installs as a service.

4. Fire up your Web browser and type in one of the following URLs: http://localhost/ or http://127.0.0.1/.

   Apache doesn't show you much when it's running, but it adds a powerful new capacity to your computer. The 127.0.0.1 address actually works better for me, because IE sometimes "helpfully" takes me to a search engine when I type in `localhost`. Either address indicates the main page of the machine you're currently on. If you've turned Apache on correctly, you should see a page that looks something like Figure 1.2.

When Apache is up and running, you can reach it through the `localhost` address. Of course, if your computer has a domain name registered and if you've turned off any firewalls, others can reach it as well.

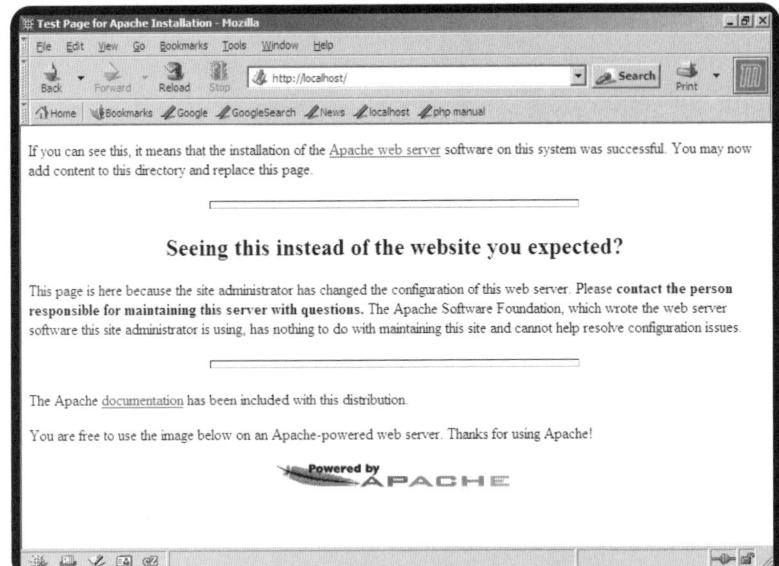

FIGURE 1.2

The default page for Apache proves a local server is running.

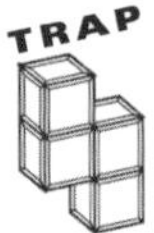

While you're getting started, I recommend not allowing external access.

To make a new home page for your computer, look for a directory called `htdocs` under your Apache installation.

Apache is configured to automatically display a file called `index.html` if the file exists. On live servers, I usually have an `index.html` page so the user gets a nice HTML page when she goes to a particular directory. However, for my own development server, I usually take out the index page so I can see a directory listing and navigate the `htdocs` directory through the server.

Starting Apache as a Service

You can run Apache as an executable program, but it's preferable to start it as a *service.* Services are background processes that automatically restart whenever the computer is restarted. Services don't usually have a graphic interface, but they sometimes have icons in the task bar.

To run Apache as a service, activate services from the control panel (on my machine the path is `Control Panel/Administrative Tools/Services`). Figure 1.3

shows the services control panel. Use this panel to turn your various services on or off. Note that if you change your server's configuration, you must turn it off, then back on before your server recognizes the changes.

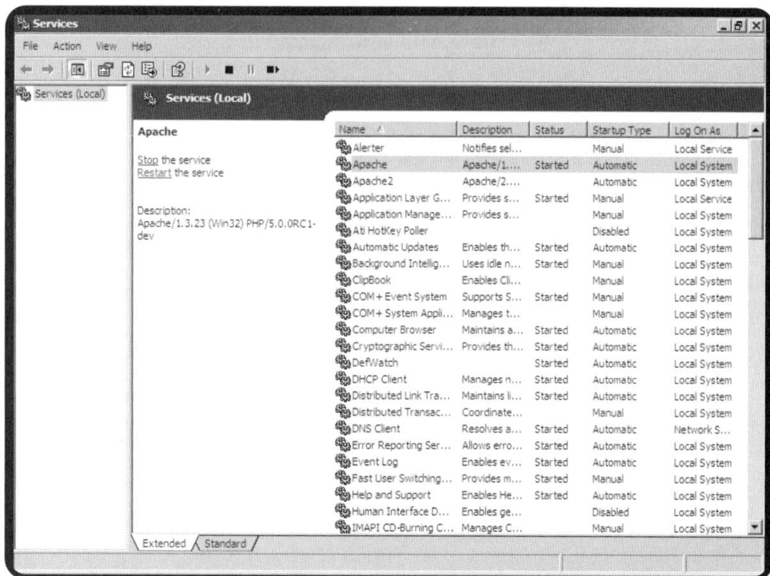

FIGURE 1.3

This control panel starts and stops Apache.

The newest versions of Apache seem to launch themselves as services automatically. If this happens, great. Don't worry about the DOS window I mentioned; it won't be there. The most important thing is whether you get a page when your browser is pointed at `localhost`. If so, you have a functioning Web server.

Configuring Apache

Apache is configured through a series of heavily commented text files. Look in the `conf` directory of your Apache directory for a file called `httpd.conf`. This is the main configuration file for Apache. You shouldn't have to change this file much, but this is the file to modify if you want, for example, to add a domain name.

After installing PHP, change `httpd.conf` to tell Apache where it can find PHP. Stay tuned—I show you how to do that once PHP is installed.

Running Your Local Server

The Apache directory has an `htdocs` subdirectory. Any files you want displayed on your local server must be in this directory or its subdirectories.

You might normally double-click a file in your file manager to display it in a browser, or you may drag it to the browser from your file-management system. This works for plain HTML files, but it bypasses the local server. That means PHP programs will not work correctly. PHP code must be called through a formal `http` call, even if it's `localhost`. All PHP code will be in an `htdocs` directory's subdirectory, unless you specifically indicate in your `httpd.conf` file that you want another directory to be accessible to your Web server.

Installing PHP

The PHP environment is a series of programs and library files. These programs are unusual because the user never runs them directly. Instead, a user requests a PHP program from a Web server and the server calls upon PHP to process the instructions in the file. PHP then returns HTML code, which the user sees in the browser.

Is This Appropriate for Beginners?

To tell you the truth, I think installation of Apache, PHP, and MySQL is a big headache. It isn't easy to get right. It's best if you can find a way to skip all this stuff and begin programming on a working server. If you cannot rely on somebody else to set up the server for you, the rest of the chapter will guide you through the process. I'm sorry that you have to start with a really messy process. Even if you have access to a server that supports PHP, it's not a bad idea to look through the rest of this chapter. You need to know how to check the configuration as well as how to change it (if you're allowed).

Downloading the PHP Program

The examples in this book use PHP 5.0, which is available on the accompanying CD. You can also go to http://www.php.net to get the PHP Windows binaries. You can install PHP wherever you wish, but I installed it to an Apache subdirectory so all my PHP programs are in proximity.

1. See `install.txt` in the PHP directory. This is a very important document. Be sure to look at it carefully and follow its instructions.
2. Find the numerous `.dll` files in the PHP directory.
3. Make sure the `.dll` files are in the same directory as `PHP.exe`.

   When you tell Apache how to find PHP, it will also find these important files.

4. Find a file called `php.ini-recommended`.
5. Copy it to your `C:\windows` directory.
6. Rename the new file `php.ini`.

Later on you edit this file to configure Apache, but you need to install PHP first.

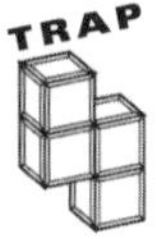

The `install.txt` document suggests the `php.ini` file goes in `C:\winnt`. I found that worked fine with PHP version 4, but version 5 requires the file to be in `C:\windows` (at least, that was the case on my machine). If your configurations are not taking hold, check this file's location. You should also be able to put the file in your `Apache` directory—but if you do, that's the only version you should have. If you get strange behavior, check to see that you don't have an extra copy of `php.ini` floating around somewhere.

Later in this chapter, I show you how to change this file so the programs contained in this book run without problems. For now, though, be sure that PHP is running.

Telling Apache about PHP

1. Open the Apache configuration file in your text editor.

   Remember, this file is called `httpd.conf` and it's probably in the `conf` directory of your Apache installation.
2. Find a section containing a series of `loadmodule` directives.

   If you're using PHP version 5, you must specifically tell Apache where to find it.
3. After all the other `loadmodule` commands, add the following code:

   ```
   LoadModule php5_module c:/apache/php5apache.dll
   ```
4. Modify the code so it points to wherever the `php5apache.dll` file was installed in your system:
5. Scroll down until you see a series of `AddModule` commands.
6. Add the following code to `httpd.conf` to add the module:

   ```
   AddModule mod_php5.c
   ```
7. Add the following line to the end of the file:

   ```
   AddType application/x-httpd-php .php
   ```
8. Save `httpd.conf` and restart Apache to ensure the changes are permanent.

Adding PHP to Your Pages

Now that you've got PHP installed, it's time to add some code.

See that PHP is installed and run a quick diagnostic check to see how it is configured. You should do this whether you're installing your own Web server or using an existing server for your programs.

The easiest way to determine if PHP exists on your server is this: Write a simple PHP program and see if it works. Here's a very simple PHP program that greets the user and displays all kinds of useful information about the development system.

Adding PHP Commands to an HTML Page

```
<html>
<head>
<title>Hello in PHP</title>
</head>
<body>
<h1>Hello in PHP</h1>

<?
print "Hello, world!";
phpInfo();
?>

</body>
</html>
```

Since this is the first PHP code you've seen in this book, I need to go over some basic concepts.

A page written in PHP begins much like an ordinary HTML page. Both are written with a plain text editor and stored on a Web server. What makes a PHP program different is the embedded `<script>` elements. When the user requests a PHP page, the server examines the page and executes any script elements before sending the resulting HTML to the user.

The `<? ?>` sequence is the easiest way to indicate PHP code, but it isn't always the best way. You can also indicate PHP code with a longer version, like this: `<?php ?>`. This version works better when your code is interpreted as XML. You can also specify your code with normal HTML tags much like JavaScript: `<script language = "php"></script>`. Some PHP servers are configured to prefer one type of script tag over another so you may need to be flexible. However, all these variations work in exactly the same way.

A PHP program looks a lot like a typical HTML page. The difference is the special `<?   ?>` tag, which specifies the existence of PHP code. Any code inside the tag is read by the PHP interpreter and then converted into HTML code. The code written between the `<?` and `?>` symbols is PHP code. I added two commands to the page. Look at the output of the program shown in Figure 1.4. You might be surprised.

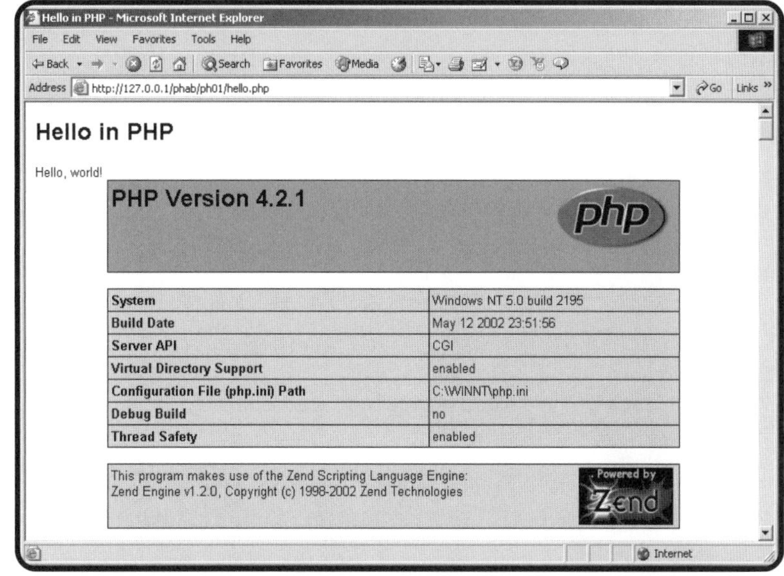

FIGURE 1.4

The page mixes HTML with some other things.

Examining the Results

This page has three distinct types of text.

- `Hello in PHP` is ordinary HTML. I wrote it just like a regular HTML page, and it was displayed just like regular HTML.
- `Hello, world!` was written by the PHP program embedded in the page.
- The rest of the page is a bit mysterious. It contains a lot of information about the particular PHP engine being used. It actually stretches on for several pages. The `phpInfo()` command generated all that code. This command displays information about the PHP installation.

It isn't that important to understand all the information displayed by the `phpInfo()` command. It's much more critical to appreciate that when the user requests the `hello.html` Web page, the text is first run through the PHP interpreter. This program scans for any PHP commands, executes them, and prints HTML code in place of the original commands. All the PHP code is gone by the time a page gets to the user.

For proof of this, point your browser at `hello.php` and view the source code. It looks something like this:

```
<html>
<head>
<title>Hello in PHP</title>
</head>
<body>
<h1>Hello in PHP</h1>

Hello, world!<!DOCTYPE HTML PUBLIC "-//W3C//DTD HTML 4.01 Transitional//EN">
<html>
<head><style type="text/css"><!--
a { text-decoration: none; }
a:hover { text-decoration: underline; }
h1 { font-family: arial, helvetica, sans-serif; font-size: 18pt; font-
weight: bold;}
h2 { font-family: arial, helvetica, sans-serif; font-size: 14pt; font-
weight: bold;}
body, td { font-family: arial, helvetica, sans-serif; font-size: 10pt; }
th { font-family: arial, helvetica, sans-serif; font-size: 11pt; font-weight:
  bold; }
//--></style>
<title>phpinfo()</title></head><body><table border="0" cellpadding="3"
  cellspacing="1" width="600" bgcolor="#000000" align="center">
<tr valign="middle" bgcolor="#9999cc"><td align="left">
<a href="http://www.php.net/"><img src="/phab/ph01/hello.php?=PHPE9568F34-
  D428-11d2-A769-00AA001ACF42" border=0 align="right" alt="PHP Logo"></a>
  <h1>PHP Version 4.2.1</h1>
```

Note that I showed only a small part of the code generated by the `phpInfo()` command. Also, note that the code details might be different when you run the program on your own machine. The key point is that the PHP code that writes `Hello, World!` (`print "Hello, World!"`) is replaced with the actual text Hello, World! More significantly, a huge amount of HTML code replaces the very simple `phpInfo()` command.

A small amount of PHP code can very efficiently generate large and complex HTML documents. This is one significant advantage of PHP. Also, by the time the document gets to the Web browser, it's plain-vanilla HTML code, which can be read easily by any browser. These two features are important benefits of server-side programming in general, and of PHP programming in particular.

As you progress through this book, you learn about many more commands for producing interesting HTML, but the basic concept is always the same. Your PHP program is simply an HTML page that contains special PHP markup. The PHP code is examined by a special program on the server. The results are embedded into the Web page before it is sent to the user.

Configuring Your Version of PHP

If you're running your own server, you probably want to tweak your version of PHP so it works cleanly. I have a number of suggestions for configuration that provide a relatively friendly environment for beginning programs. In particular, think about the following elements.

Safe Mode

This mode is a master setting that allows you to choose between ease of programming and server safety. For beginners, I recommend setting safe-mode to OFF while working on your own Web server. As you move to a production server, you will usually have safe mode set to ON, which requires you to be a little more careful about some elements. (However, most of these are advanced settings you won't need to worry about yet. The most important reason to have safe mode off right now is to allow access to the `register_globals` directive that is described next.)

Register Globals

The `register_globals` parameter determines whether PHP automatically transfers information from web forms to your program. (It's okay if that doesn't mean much to you yet.) This feature is useful for beginning programmers, but can be a security risk.

As you get more comfortable (after chapter 5, when I show you some alternatives to `register_globals`) you can turn off this variable to protect your code from some potential problems. To change this variable's value, simply type `on` or `off` as the value for `register globals`. As with any change to `php.ini`, restart your Web server to ensure the changes have taken hold.

Search in `php.ini` for a line that looks like this:

```
register_globals = On
```

Windows Extensions

PHP comes with a number of extensions that allow you to modify its behavior. You can add functionality to your copy of PHP by adding new modules. To find the part of `php.ini` that describes these extensions, look for `windows extensions` in the `php.ini` file.

You'll see some code that looks like this:

```
;Windows Extensions

;extension=php_bz2.dll
;extension=php_ctype.dll
;extension=php_cpdf.dll
;extension=php_curl.dll
;extension=php_cybercash.dll
;extension=php_db.dll
;extension=php_dba.dll
;extension=php_dbase.dll
;extension=php_dbx.dll
;extension=php_domxml.dll
;extension=php_dotnet.dll
;extension=php_exif.dll
;extension=php_fbsql.dll
;extension=php_fdf.dll
;extension=php_filepro.dll
;extension=php_gd.dll
;extension=php_gettext.dll
;extension=php_hyperwave.dll
;extension=php_iconv.dll
;extension=php_ifx.dll
;extension=php_iisfunc.dll
;extension=php_imap.dll
;extension=php_ingres.dll
;extension=php_interbase.dll
;extension=php_java.dll
;extension=php_ldap.dll
;extension=php_mbstring.dll
;extension=php_mcrypt.dll
;extension=php_mhash.dll
;extension=php_mssql.dll
```

```
;extension=php_oci8.dll
;extension=php_openssl.dll
;extension=php_oracle.dll
;extension=php_pdf.dll
;extension=php_pgsql.dll
;extension=php_printer.dll
;extension=php_sablot.dll
;extension=php_shmop.dll
;extension=php_snmp.dll
;extension=php_sockets.dll
;extension=php_sybase_ct.dll
;extension=php_xslt.dll
;extension=php_yaz.dll
;extension=php_zlib.dll

;;;;; I added gd2 extension
extension=php_gd2.dll

;;; I added ming support
extension=php_ming.dll

;;;;;I added mysql extension
extension=php_mysql.dll
```

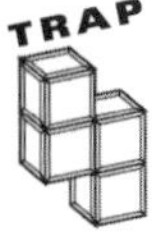

The `php.ini` file that comes with PHP 5.0 has a note that says `mySQL` support is built in. I found this was *not* the case in my installation. Run the `phpInfo()` command (in the `Hello.php` program described earlier, for example) to see exactly which extensions are active in your installation. If you don't see an extension that you need, you can add it yourself.

Most of the extensions begin with a semicolon. This character acts like a comment character and causes the line to be ignored. To add a particular extension, simply eliminate the semicolon at the beginning of the line. I usually put a comment in the code to remind myself that I added this extension.

I added the `php_mysql.dll` extension. This allows support for the MySQL database language used in the second half of this book. Add support for that library by removing the semicolon characters from the beginning of the `mysql` line.

You can determine whether PHP added support for MySQL by looking again at the results of the `phpInfo()` **function. If exposing the** `php_mysql.dll` **extension didn't work on its own, you may have to locate the** `libmysql.dll` **file and move it to the** `C:\Windows` **directory.**

I also added support for two graphics libraries that I occasionally use. The `gd2` library allows me to build and modify graphics, and `ming` allows me to create Flash movies. Don't worry about exposing these files until you're comfortable with basic PHP programming. However, when you're ready, it's really nice to know that you can easily add to the PHP features by supporting new modules.

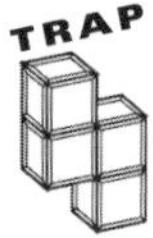

Some of the documentation that came with version 5.0 of PHP indicated that MySQL support is built in and doesn't need to be added through the configuration file. (In fact, this information is inside the configuration file as a comment.) When I ran `phpInfo()`**, I found that MySQL support was *not* built in, so I added it through the extension command. The sad truth is you can't always trust the documentation.**

Take a look at the `extension_dir` variable in `php.ini` to see where PHP expects to find all your extension files. Any `.dll` file in that directory might be an extension. You can also download new extensions and install them when you are ready to expand PHP's capabilities.

Because of space limitations, I was unable to include information on graphics programming in PHP in this book. However, you can always check on my PHP Web site (http://shelob.cs.iupui.edu:18011/n342) for examples and tutorials on these techniques.

Creating the Tip of the Day Program

Way back at the beginning of this chapter, I promised that you would be able to write the featured Tip of the Day program. This program requires HTML, CSS, and one line of PHP code. The code shows a reasonably basic page:

```
<html>
<head>
<title>Tip of the day</title>
</head>

<body>
<center>
```

```
<h1>Tip of the day</h1>

<div style = "border-color:green; border-style:groove; border-width:2px">
<?
readfile("tips.txt");
?>
</div>


</center>
</body>
</html>
```

The page is basic HTML. It contains one `div` element with a custom style setting up a border around the day's tip. Inside the `div` element, I added PHP code with the `<?` and `?>` devices. This code calls one PHP function called `readFile()`. The `readFile()` command takes as an argument the name of some file. It reads that file's contents and displays them on the page as if it were HTML. As soon as that line of code stops executing (the text in the `tips.txt` file has been printed to the Web browser), the `?>` symbol indicates that the PHP coding is finished and the rest of the page will be typical HTML.

Summary

You've already come a very long way. You've learned or reviewed all the main HTML objects. You installed a Web server on your computer. You added PHP. You changed the Apache configuration to recognize PHP. You saw how PHP code can be integrated into an HTML document. You learned how to change the configuration file for PHP to incorporate various extensions. Finally, you created your first page, which includes all these elements. You should be proud of your efforts already. In the next chapter you more fully explore the relationship between PHP and HTML and learn how to use variables and input to make your pages do interesting things.

CHALLENGES

1. Create a Web-based version of your resume, incorporating headings, lists, and varying text styles.
2. Modify one of your existing pages so it incorporates CSS styles.
3. Install a practice configuration of Apache, PHP, and MySQL (or some other package).
4. Build a page that calls the `phpInfo()` command and run it from your Web server. Ensure that you have a reasonably recent version of PHP installed on the server.

2 Using Variables and Input

In chapter 1, "Exploring the PHP Environment," you learn the foundations of all PHP programming. If you have your environment installed, you're ready to write some PHP programs. Computer programs are ultimately about data. In this chapter you begin looking at the way programs store and manipulate data in variables. Specifically, you learn how to:

- Create a variable in PHP
- Recognize the main types of variables
- Name variables appropriately
- Output the values of variables in your scripts
- Perform basic operations on variables
- Read variables from an HTML form

Introducing the Story Program

By the end of this chapter you'll be able to write the program, called `Story`, featured in Figures 2.1 and 2.2.

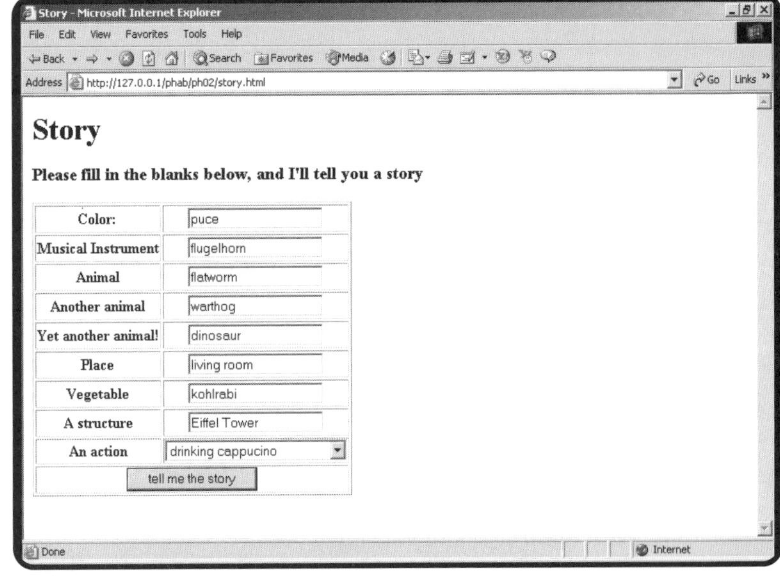

FIGURE 2.1

The program begins by asking the user to enter some information.

The program asks the user to enter some values into an HTML form and then uses those values to build a custom version of a classic nursery rhyme. The `Story` program works like most server-side programs. It has two distinctive parts: a form for user input, and a PHP program to read the input and produce some type of feedback. First, the user enters information into a plain HTML form and hits the submit button. The PHP program doesn't execute until after the user has submitted a form. The program takes the information from the form and does something to it. Usually, the PHP program returns an HTML page to the user.

FIGURE 2.2

I hate it when the warthog's in the kohlrabi.

Using Variables in Your Scripts

The most important new idea in this chapter is the notion of a variable. A *variable* is a container for holding information in the computer's memory. To make things easier for the programmer, every variable has a name. You can store information in and get information out of a variable.

Introducing the Hi Jacob Program

The program featured in Figure 2.3 uses a variable, although you might not be able to tell simply by looking at the output.

You can't really see anything special about this program from the Web page itself (even if you look at the HTML source). To see what's new, look at the `hiJacob.php` source code.

```
<html>
<head>
<title>Hi Jacob</title>
</head>
<body>
<h1>Hi Jacob</h1>
```

```
<h3>Demonstrates using a variable</h3>

<?

$userName = "Jacob";

print "Hi, $userName";

?>
</body>
</html>
```

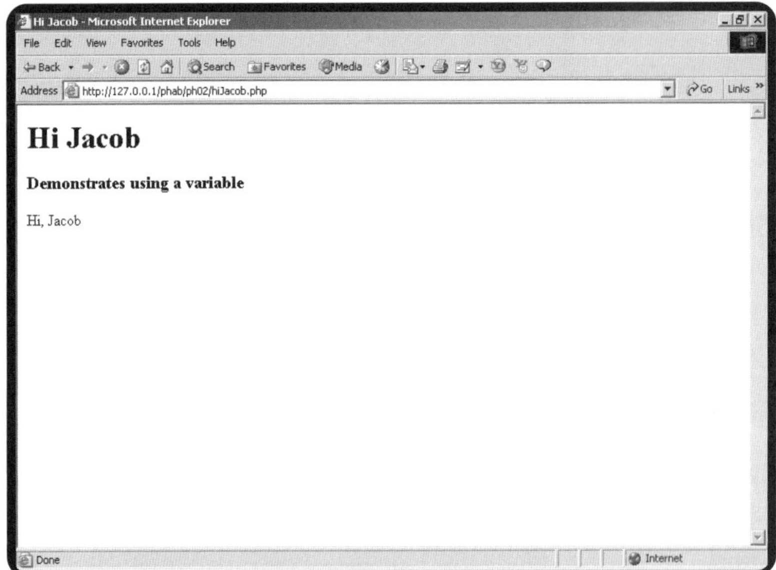

FIGURE 2.3

The word Jacob is stored in a variable in this page.

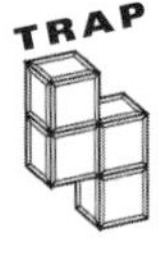

In regular HTML and JavaScript programming, you can use the Web browser's `view source` **command to examine your program code. For server-side languages, this is not sufficient; the view source document has no PHP at all. Remember that the actual program code never gets to your Web browser. Instead, the program is executed on the server and the program *results* are sent to the browser as ordinary HTML. Be looking at the actual PHP source code on the server when examining these programs. On a related note, you cannot simply use your browser's File menu to load a PHP page. Instead, run it through a server.**

The helloJacob page is mainly HTML with a small patch of PHP code in it. That code does a lot of very important work.

Creating a String Variable

The line `$userName = "Jacob";` does two major things. First, it creates a variable named `$userName`. Second, it will assign the value "Jacob" to the variable. In PHP, all variables begin with a dollar sign to distinguish them from other program elements. The variable's name is significant.

Naming Your Variables

As a programmer, you frequently get to name things. Experienced programmers have learned some tricks about naming variables and other elements.

- Make the name descriptive. It's much easier to figure out what `$userName` means than something like `$myVariable` or `$r`. When possible, make sure your variable names describe the kind of information they contain.
- Use an appropriate length. Your variable name should be long enough to be descriptive, but not so long that it becomes tedious to type.
- Don't use spaces. Most languages (including PHP) don't allow spaces in variable names.
- Don't use symbols. Most of the special characters such as #, *, and / already have meaning in programming languages. Of course, every variable in PHP begins with the $ character, but otherwise you should avoid using punctuation. One exception to this rule is the underscore (_) character, which is allowed in most languages, including PHP.
- Be careful about case. PHP is a case-sensitive language, which means that it considers `$userName`, `$USERNAME`, and `$UserName` to be three different variables. The convention in PHP is to use all lowercase except when separating words. (Note the uppercase `N` in `$userName`.) This is a good convention to follow, and it's the one I use throughout this book.
- Watch your spelling! Every time you refer to a variable, PHP checks to see if that variable already exists somewhere in your program. If so, it uses that variable. If not, it quietly makes a new variable for you. PHP will not catch a misspelling. Instead, it makes a whole new variable, and your program probably won't work correctly.

Assigning a Value to a Variable

The equals sign (=) is special in PHP. It does *not* mean *equals* (at least in the present context). The equals sign is used for assignment. If you read the equals sign as the word *gets,* you are closer to the meaning PHP uses for this symbol. For example, look at this line of code:

```
$userName = "Jacob"
```

It should be read as *The variable* `$userName` *gets the value* `Jacob`.

Usually when you create a variable in PHP, you also assign some value to it. Assignment flows from right to left.

The `$userName` variable has been assigned the value `Jacob`. Computers are picky about what type of information goes into a variable, but PHP automates this process for you by determining the data type of a variable based on its context. Still, it's important to recognize that `Jacob` is a text value, because text is stored and processed a little bit differently in computer memory than numeric data.

Computer programmers almost never refer to text as *text*. Instead, they prefer the more esoteric term *string*. The word string actually has a somewhat poetic origin, because the underlying mechanism for storing text in a computer's memory reminded early programmers of making a chain of beads on a string.

Printing a Variable's Value

The next line of code prints a message to the screen. You can print any text to the screen you wish. Text (also called *string data*) is usually encased in quotation marks. If you wish to print the value of a variable, simply place the variable name in the text you want printed. Examine the following line:

```
print "Hi, $userName";
```

It actually produces this output:

```
Hi, Jacob
```

It produces this because when the server encounters the variable `$userName`, it's replaced with that variable's value, which is `Jacob`. The PHP program output is sent directly to the Web browser, so you can even include HTML tags in your output, simply by including them inside the quotation marks.

The ability to print the value of a variable inside other text is called *string interpolation*. That's not critical to know, but it could be useful information on a trivia show or something.

Using the Semicolon to End a Line

PHP is a more formal language than HTML and, like most programming languages, has some strict rules about the syntax used when writing. Each unique instruction is expected to end with a semicolon. If you look at the complete code for the `helloJacob` program, you see that each line of PHP code ends with said semicolon. If you forget to do this, you get an error that looks like the one in Figure 2.4.

An instruction sometimes is longer than a single line on the editor. The semicolon goes at the end of the *instruction*, which often (but not always) corresponds with the end of the *line*. You'll see an example of this shortly as you build long string variables. In general, though, you end each line with a semicolon.

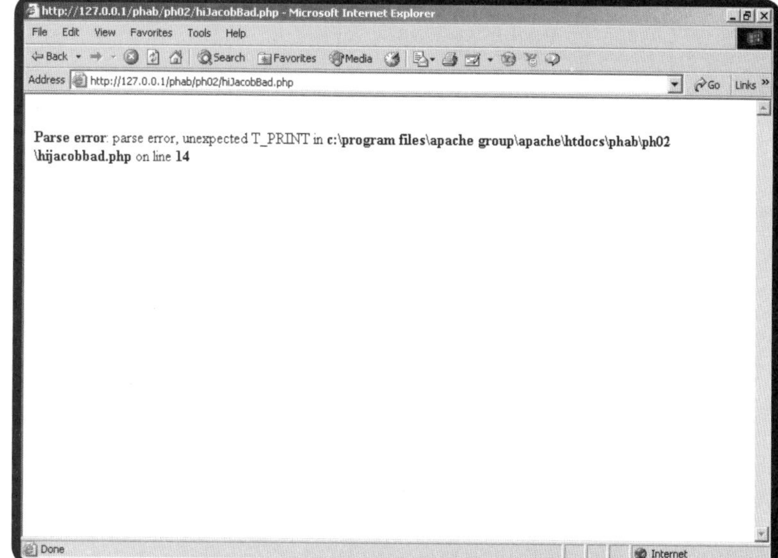

FIGURE 2.4

This error occurs if you go sans semicolon to the end of every line.

Don't panic if you get an error message or two. Errors are a completely normal part of programming. Even experienced programmers expect to see many error messages while building and testing programs.

Usually the resulting error code gives you important clues about what went wrong. Make sure you look carefully at whatever line of code is reported. Although the error isn't always on that line, you can often get a hint. In many cases (particularly a missing semicolon), a syntax error indicates an error on the line that actually follows the real problem. If you get a syntax error on line 14, and the problem is a missing semicolon, the problem line is actually line 13.

Using Variables for More-Complex Pages

While the `Hello Jacob` program was interesting, there is no real advantage to using a variable. Check out another use for variables.

Building the Row Your Boat Page

Figure 2.5 shows the `Row Your Boat` page.

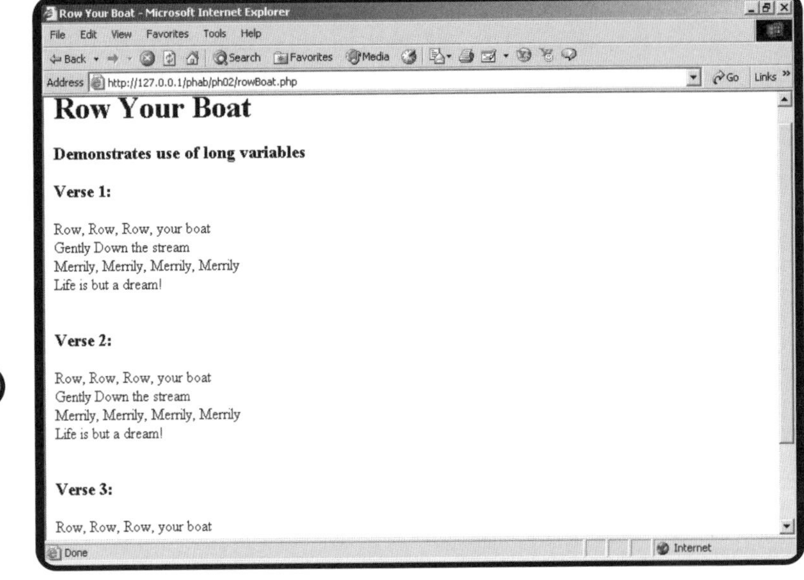

FIGURE 2.5

This program shows the words to a popular song. They sure repeat a lot.

I chose this song in particular because it repeats the same verse three times. If you look at the original code for the `rowBoat.php` program, you see I used a trick to save some typing:

```
<html>
<head>
<title>Row Your Boat</title>
</head>
<body>
<h1>Row Your Boat</h1>
<h3>Demonstrates use of long variables</h3>

<?

$verse = <<<HERE
```

```
Row, Row, Row, your boat<br>
Gently Down the stream<br>
Merrily, Merrily, Merrily, Merrily<br>
Life is but a dream!<br>
<br><br>
HERE;

print "<h3>Verse 1:</h3>";
print $verse;

print "<h3>Verse 2:</h3>";
print $verse;
print "<h3>Verse 3:</h3>";
print $verse;

?>

</body>
</html>
```

Creating Multi-Line Strings

You find yourself wanting to print several lines of HTML code at once. It can be very tedious to use quotation marks to indicate such strings (especially because HTML also often uses the quotation mark symbol). PHP provides a special quoting mechanism, which is perfect for this type of situation. The following line begins assigning a value to the `$verse` variable:

```
$verse = <<<HERE
```

The `<<<HERE` segment indicates this is a special multi-line string that ends with the symbol `HERE`. You can use any phrase you wish, but I generally use the word `HERE` because I think of the three less-than symbols as *up to.* In other words, you can think of the following as meaning *verse gets everything up to HERE.*

```
$verse = <<<HERE
```

You can also think of `<<<HERE` as a special quote sign, which is ended with the value `HERE`.

You can write any amount of text between `<<<HERE` and `HERE`. You can put variables inside the special text and PHP replaces the variable with its value, just like in ordinary (quoted) strings. The ending phrase (`HERE`) must be on a line by itself, and there must be no leading spaces in front of it.

You might wonder why the `$verse = <<<HERE` line doesn't have a semicolon after it. Although this is one line in the editor, it begins a multi-line structure. Technically, everything from that line to the end of the `HERE;` line is part of the same logical line, even though the code takes up several lines in the editor. Everything between `<<<HERE` and `HERE` is a string value.

The semicolon doesn't have any special meaning inside a string. At a minimum, you should know that a line beginning a multi-line quote doesn't need a semicolon, but the line at the end of the quote does.

Once the multi-line string is built, it is very easy to use. It's actually harder to write the captions for the three verses than the verses themselves. The `print` statement simply places the value of the `$verse` variable in the appropriate spots of the output HTML.

Working with Numeric Variables

Computers ultimately store information in on/off impulses. You can convert these very simple data values into a number of more convenient kinds of information. The PHP language makes most of this invisible to you, but it's important to know that memory handles string (*text*) differently than it does numeric values, and that there are two main types of numeric values, integers, and floating-point real numbers.

Making the ThreePlusFive Program

As an example of how PHP works with numbers, consider the `ThreePlusFive.php` program illustrated in Figure 2.6.

All the work in the `ThreePlusFive` program is done with two variables called `$x` and `$y`. (I know, I recommended that you assign variables longer, descriptive names, but these variables are commonly used in arithmetic problems, so these very short variable names are okay in this instance.) The code for the program looks like this:

```
<html>
<head>
<title>Three Plus Five</title>
</head>
<body>
<h1>Three Plus Five</h1>
<h3>Demonstrates use of numeric variables</h3>
```

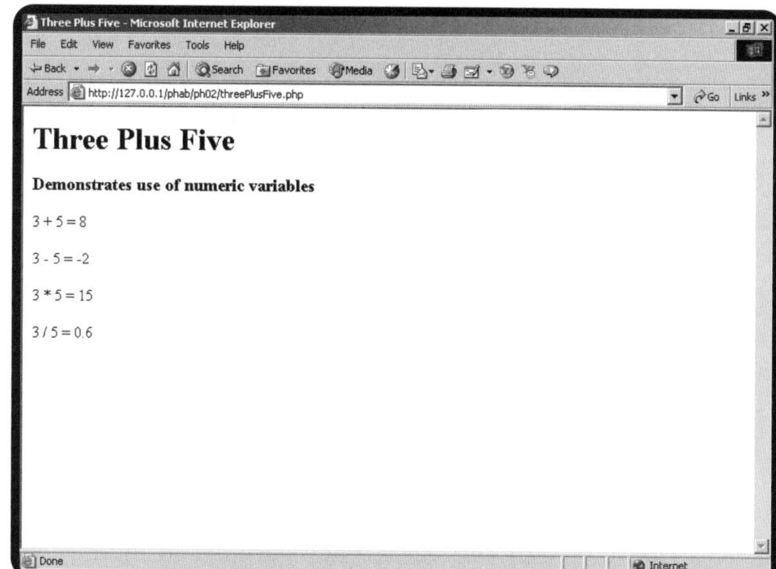

FIGURE 2.6

This program does basic math on variables containing the values 3 and 5.

```
<?
$x = 3;
$y = 5;

print "$x + $y = ";
print $x + $y;
print "<br><br>";

print "$x - $y = ";
print $x - $y;
print "<br><br>";

print "$x * $y = ";
print $x * $y;
print "<br><br>";

print "$x / $y = ";
print $x / $y;
print "<br><br>";

?>

</body>
</html>
```

Assigning Numeric Values

You create a numeric variable like any other variable in PHP: Simply assign a value to a variable. Notice that numeric values do not require quotation marks. I created variables called `$x` and `$y` and assigned appropriate values to these variables.

Using Mathematical Operators

For each calculation, I want to print the problem as well as its solution. This line prints out the values of the `$x` and `$y` variables with the plus sign between them:

```
print "$x + $y = ";
```

In this particular case (since `$x` is `3` and `$y` is `5`), it prints out this literal value:

```
3 + 5 =
```

Because the plus and the equals signs are inside quotation marks, they are treated as ordinary text elements. PHP doesn't do any calculation (such as addition or assignment) with them.

The next line does not contain any quotation marks:

```
print $x + $y;
```

It calculates the value of `$x + $y` and prints the result (`8`) to the Web page.

In the Real World

Numbers without any decimal point are called integers and numbers with decimal values are called real numbers. Computers store these two types differently, and this distinction sometimes leads to problems. PHP does its best to shield you from this type of issue.

For example, since the values `3` and `5` are both integers, the results of the addition, subtraction, and multiplication problems are also guaranteed to be integers. However, the quotient of two integers is often a real number. Many languages would either refuse to solve this problem or give an incomplete result. They might say that `3 / 5 = 0` rather than `0.6`. PHP tries to convert things to the appropriate type whenever possible, and it usually does a pretty good job.

You sometimes need to control this behavior, however. The `setType()` function lets you force a particular variable into a particular type. You can look up the details in the online Help for PHP (included in the CD that accompanies this book).

Most of the math symbols you are familiar with also work with numeric variables. The plus sign (+) is used for addition, the minus sign (-) indicates subtraction, the asterisk (*) multiples, and the forward slash (/) divides. The remainder of the program illustrates how PHP does subtraction, multiplication, and division.

Creating a Form to Ask a Question

It's very typical for PHP programs to be made of two or more separate documents. An ordinary HTML page contains a form, which the user fills out. When the user presses the `submit` button, the information in all the form elements is sent to a program specified by a special attribute of the form. This program processes the information from the form and returns a result, which looks to the user like an ordinary Web page. To illustrate, look at the `whatsName.html` page illustrated in Figure 2.7.

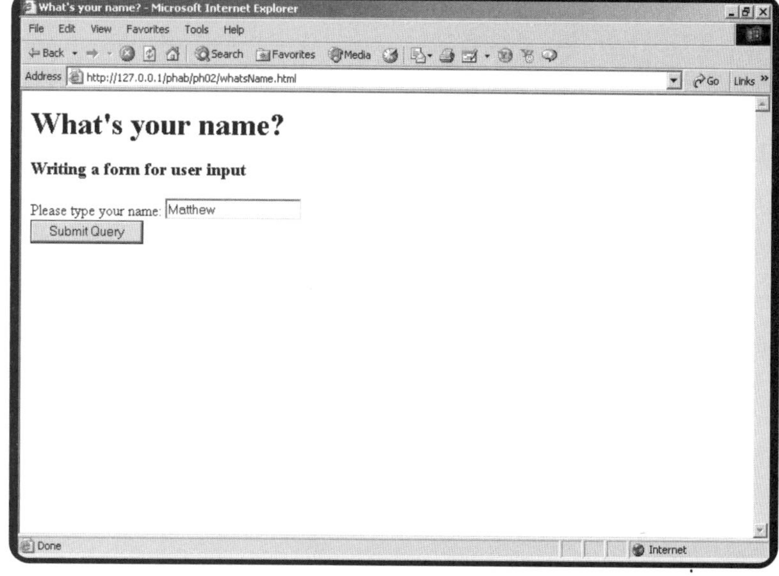

FIGURE 2.7

This ordinary HTML page contains a form.

The `whatsName.html` page does not contain any PHP at all. It's simply an HTML page with a form on it. When the user clicks the `Submit Query` button, the page sends the value in the text area to a PHP program called `hiUser.php`. Figure 2.8 shows what happens when the `hiUser.php` program runs.

It's important to recognize that two different pages are involved in the transaction. In this section you learn how to link an HTML page to a particular script and how to write a script that expects certain form information.

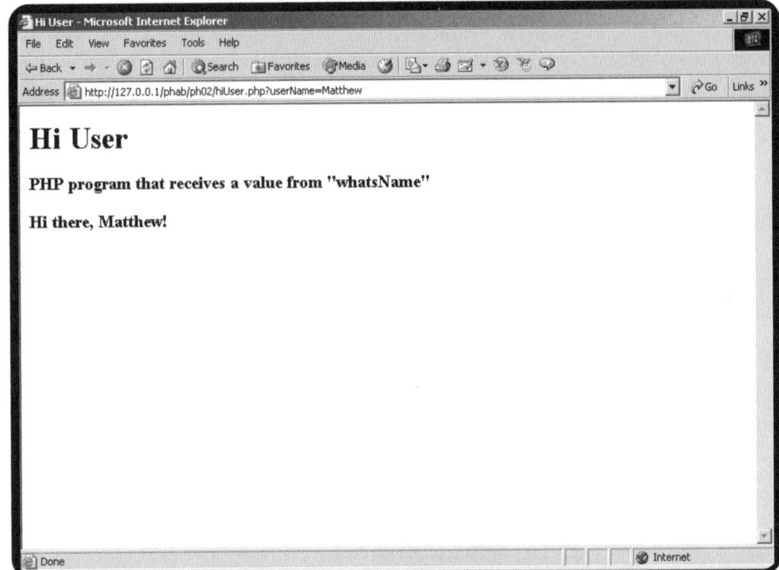

FIGURE 2.8

The resulting page uses the value from the original HTML form.

Building an HTML Page with a Form

Forms are very useful when you want to get information from the user. To illustrate how this is done, look at the `whatsName.html` code:

```
<html>
<head>
<title>What's your name?</title>
</head>
<body>
<h1>What's your name?</h1>
<h3>Writing a form for user input</h3>
<form method = "post"
      action = "hiUser.php">
Please type your name:
<input type = "text"
       name = "userName"
       value = "">
<br>
<input type = "submit">

</form>
</body>
</html>
```

There is only one element of this page that may not be familiar to you. Take a careful look at the `form` tag. It contains two new attributes. `action` is one of those attributes. The other, `method`, indicates how the data is sent to the browser.

`get` and `post` are the two primary methods. `post` is the most powerful and flexible, so it is the one I use most often in this book. However, you see some interesting ways to use `get` later in this chapter in "Sending Data without a Form."

Setting the Action Attribute to a Script File

The other attribute of the `form` tag is the `action` attribute. It determines the URL of a program, designed to read the page and respond with another page. The URL can be an *absolute* reference (which begins with `http://` and contains the entire domain name of the response program), or a *relative* reference (meaning the program is in the same directory as the original Web page).

The `whatsName.html` page contains a form with its `action` attribute set to `hiUser.php`. Whenever the user clicks the `submit` button, the values of all the fields (only one in this case) are packed up and sent to a program called `hiUser.php`, which is expected to be in the same directory as the original `whatsName.html` page.

Writing a Script to Retrieve the Data

The code for `hiUser.php` is specially built. The form that called the `hiUser.php` code is expected to have an element called `userName`. Take a look at the code for `hiUser.php` and see what I mean.

IN THE REAL WORLD

Some PHP servers have turned off the ability to automatically create a variable from a form. You might be able to convince your server administrator to turn on `register_globals` in the `PHP.INI` file. If not, here's a workaround: If your form has a field called `userName`, add this code to the beginning of the program that needs the value of that field:

```
$userName = $_REQUEST["userName"];
```

Repeat this code for every variable you wish to pull from the original form.

For a complete explanation of this code, skip to chapter 5, "Better Arrays and String Handling." In that chapter you also find a routine for automatically extracting all a form's fields, even if you don't know the field names.

```
<html>
<head>
<title>Hi User</title>
</head>
<body>
<h1>Hi User</h1>
<h3>PHP program that receives a value from "whatsName"</h3>

<?

  print "<h3>Hi there, $userName!</h3>";

?>

</body>
</html>
```

Like many PHP pages, hiUser.php is mainly HTML. The only thing that's different is the one print statement, which statement incorporates the variable $userName. The puzzling thing: no other mention of the variable anywhere in the code.

When a user submits a form to a PHP program, the PHP processor automatically creates a variable with the same name as every form element on the original HTML page. Since the whatsName.html page has a form element called userName, any PHP program that whatsName.html activates automatically has access to a variable called $userName. The value of that variable is whatever the user has entered into the field before pressing the submit button.

Sending Data without a Form

It can be very handy to send data to a server-side program without using a form. This little-known trick can really enhance your Web pages without requiring a lick of PHP programming. The Link Demo page (linkDemo.html) shown in Figures 2.9 and 2.10 illustrate this phenomenon.

Understanding the get Method

All the links in the linkDemo.html page use a similar trick. As you recall from earlier in the chapter, form data can be sent to a program through two different methods. The post method is the technique usually in your forms, but you've been using the get method all along, because normal HTML requests actually are get requests. The interesting thing is that you can send form data to any program that knows how to read get requests by embedding the request in your URL.

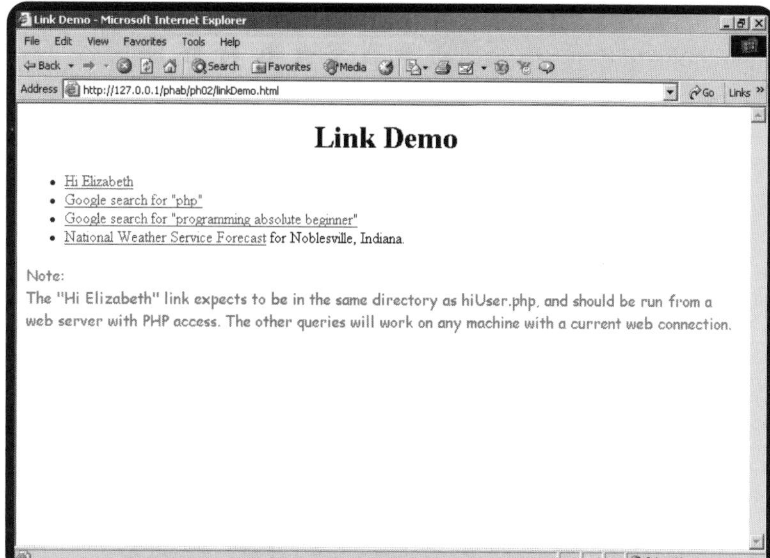

FIGURE 2.9

The links on this page appear ordinary, but they are unusually powerful.

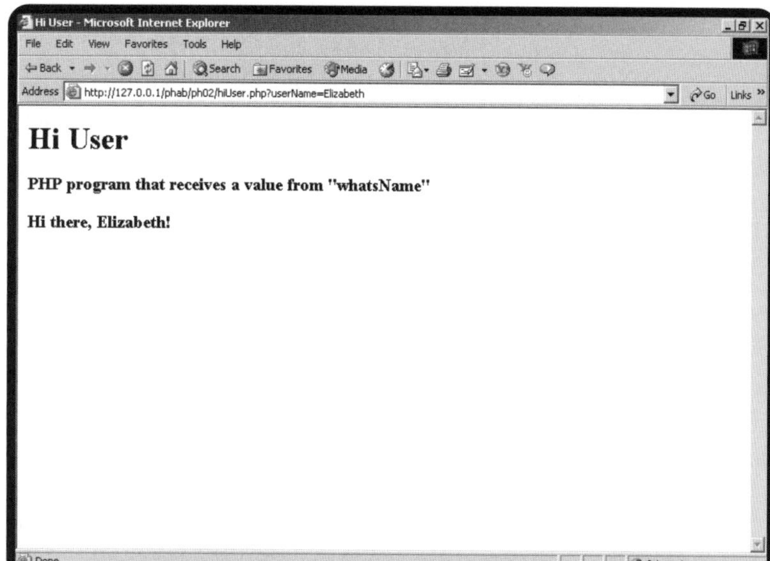

FIGURE 2.10

When I clicked the `Hi Elizabeth` link, I was taken to the `hiUser` program with the value `Elizabeth` automatically sent to the program!

As an experiment, switch the `method` attribute of `whatsName.html` so the form looks like this:

```
<form method = "get"
      action = "hiUser.php">
```

Run the page again. It works the same as before, but the URL of the resulting page looks like this (presuming you said the user's name is Andy):

```
http://127.0.0.1/phab/ph02/hiUser.php?userName=Andy
```

The get method stashes all the form information into the URL using a special code. If you go back to the whatsName page and put in Andy Harris, you get a slightly different result:

```
http://127.0.0.1/phab/ph02/hiUser.php?userName=Andy+Harris
```

The space between Andy and Harris was converted to a plus sign because space characters cause a lot of confusion. When form data is transmitted, it often undergoes a number of similar transformations. All the translation is automatic in PHP programming, so you don't have to worry about it.

Using a URL to Embed Form Data

If you understand how embedded data in a URL works, you can use a similar technique to harness any server-side program on the Internet (presuming it's set up to take get method data). When I examined the URLs of Google searches, I could see my search data in a field named q (for query, I suppose). I took a gamble that all the other fields would have default values, and wrote a hyperlink that incorporates a query. My link looked like this:

```
<li><a href = "http://www.google.com/search?q=php">
      Google search for "php"</a></li>
```

Whenever the user clicks this link, it sets up a get method query to Google's search program. The result is a nifty Google search. One fun thing you might want to do is figure out how to set up canned versions of your most common queries in various search engines, so you can get updated results with one click. Figure 2.11 illustrates what happens when the user clicks the Google search for "php" link in the linkDemo page.

Figure 2.12 shows the results of this slightly more complex search.

```
<li><a href =
   "http://www.google.com/search?q=programming for the absolute beginner">
    Google search for "programming absolute beginner"</a></li>
```

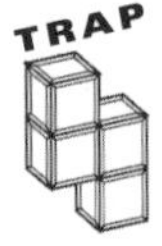

This approach has a down side. The program owner can change the program without telling you, and your link will no longer work correctly. Most Web programmers assume that their programs are called only by the forms they originally built.

The other thing to consider is that people can do this with your programs. Just because you intend for your program to be called only by a form, doesn't mean that's how it always works. Such is the vibrant nature of the free-form Internet.

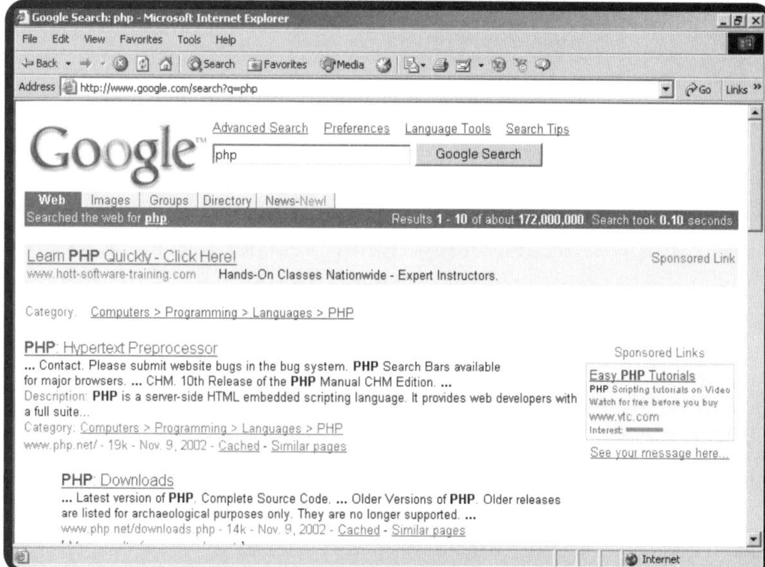

FIGURE 2.11

The link runs a search on www.google.com for the term `php`.

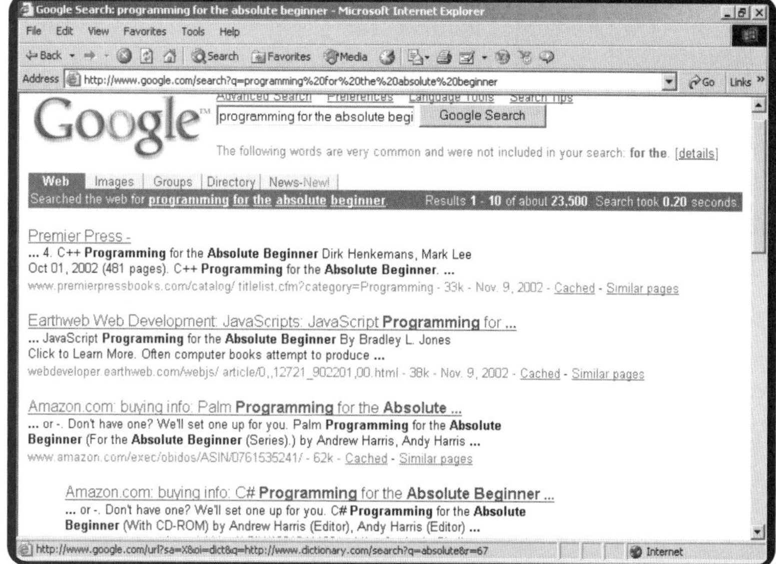

FIGURE 2.12

The Google search for `programming absolute beginner` shows some really intriguing book offerings!

Working with Multiple Field Queries

As one more practical example, the code for the `National Weather Service` link looks like this:

```
<li><a href =
"http://www.crh.noaa.gov/data/forecasts/INZ039.php?warncounty=INC057&city=
Noblesville">
National Weather Service Forecast</a>
for Noblesville, Indiana.
```

While this link looks a little more complex, it doesn't require any special knowledge. I simply searched the National Weather Service Web site until I found the automatically generated page for my hometown. When I looked at the URL that resulted, I was pleased (but not surprised) to see that the page was generated by a PHP script. (Note the `.php` extension in the URL.) I copied the link from my browser and incorporated it into `linkDemo.html`. The weather page is automatically created by a PHP program based on two inputs (the county and city names). Any time I want to see the local weather, I can recall the same query even though the request doesn't come directly from the National Weather Service. This is a really easy way to customize your Web page.

I've never actually seen the program, but I know the PHP program requires two fields because I looked carefully at the URL. The part that says `warncounty=INC057` indicates the state and county (at least that's a reasonable guess), and the `city=Noblesville` indicates the city within the county. When a form has two or more input elements, the ampersand (`&`) attaches them, as you can see in the National Weather Service example.

Reading Input from Other Form Elements

A PHP program can read the input from any type of HTML form element. In all cases, the `name` attribute of the HTML form object becomes a variable name in PHP. In general, the PHP variable value comes from the `value` property of the form object.

Introducing the borderMaker Program

To examine most of the various form elements, I built a simple page to demonstrate various attributes of cascading style sheet (CSS) borders. The HTML program is shown in Figure 2.13.

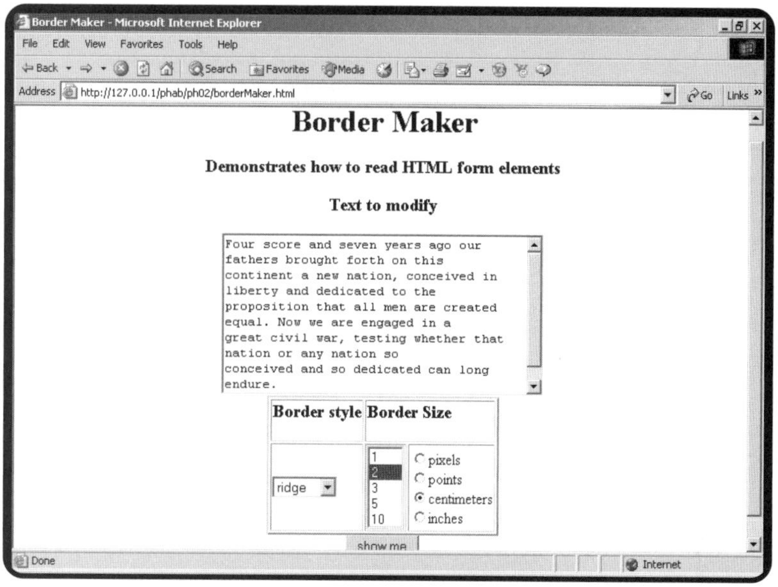

FIGURE 2.13

The borderMaker HTML page uses a text area, two list boxes, and a select group.

Building the borderMaker.html Page

The `borderMaker.html` page contains a very typical form with most of the major input elements in it. The code for this form is as such:

```
<html>
<head>
<title>Font Choices</title>
</head>
<body>
<center>
<h1>Font Choices</h1>
<h3>Demonstrates how to read HTML form elements</h3>

<form method = "post"
      action = "borderMaker.php">


<h3>Text to modify</h3>
<textarea name = "basicText"
          rows = "10"
          cols = "40">
Four score and seven years ago our fathers brought forth on this
```

```
continent a new nation, conceived in liberty and dedicated to the
proposition that all men are created equal. Now we are engaged in a
great civil war, testing whether that nation or any nation so
conceived and so dedicated can long endure.
</textarea>

<table border = 2>
<tr>
  <td><h3>Border style</h3></td>
  <td colspan = 2><h3>Border Size</h3></td>
</tr>

<tr>
<td>
<select name = borderStyle>
  <option value = "ridge">ridge</option>
  <option value = "groove">groove</option>
  <option value = "double">double</option>
  <option value = "inset">inset</option>
  <option value = "outset">outset</option>
</select>
</td>
<td>

<select size = 5
        name = borderSize>
  <option value = "1">1</option>
  <option value = "2">2</option>
  <option value = "3">3</option>
  <option value = "5">5</option>
  <option value = "10">10</option>
</select>
</td>

<td>
<input type = "radio"
       name = "sizeType"
       value = "px">pixels<br>
<input type = "radio"
       name = "sizeType"
```

```
        value = "pt">points<br>
<input type = "radio"
        name = "sizeType"
        value = "cm">centimeters<br>
<input type = "radio"
        name = "sizeType"
        value = "in">inches<br>
</td>
</tr>
</table>

<input type = "submit"
        value = "show me">

</form>

</center>
</body>
</html>
```

The `borderMaker.html` page is designed to interact with a PHP program called `borderMaker.php`, as you can see by inspection of the `action` attribute. Note that I added a `value` attribute for each `option` element, and the radio buttons all have the same name but different values. The `value` attribute becomes very important when your program is destined to be read by a program. Finally, the `submit` button is critical, because nothing interesting happens until the user submits the form.

I didn't include checkboxes in this particular example. I show you how checkboxes work in chapter 3, "Controlling Your Code with Conditions and Functions," because you need *conditional* statements to work with them. Conditional statements allow your programs to make choices.

Reading the Form Elements

The `borderMaker.php` program expects input from `borderMaker.html`. When the user submits the HTML form, the PHP program produces results like those shown in Figure 2.14.

In general, it doesn't matter what type of element you use on an HTML form. The PHP interpreter simply looks at each element's name and value. By the time the information gets to the server, it doesn't matter what type of input element was used. PHP

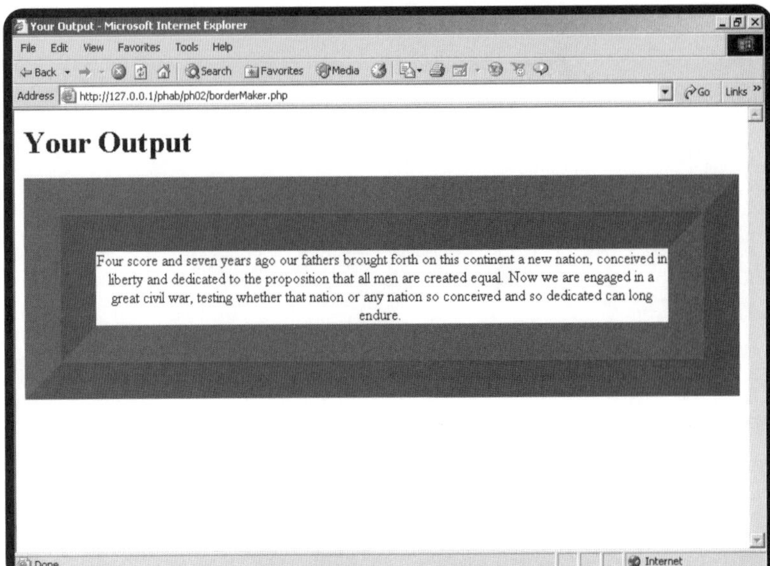

FIGURE 2.14

The `borderMaker.php` code reacts to all the various input elements on the form.

automatically creates a variable corresponding to each form element. The value of that variable is the value of the element. The code used in `borderMaker.php` illustrates:

```
<html>
<head>
<title>Your Output</title>
</head>
<body>
<h1>Your Output</h1>
<center>
<?
$theStyle = <<<HERE
"border-width:$borderSize$sizeType;
border-style:$borderStyle;
border-color:green"
HERE;

print "<div style = $theStyle>";
print $basicText;
print "</span>";

?>
</center>
```

```
</body>
</html>
```

In the case of text boxes and text areas, the user types in the value directly. In `borderMaker.html`, there is a text area called `basicText`. The PHP interpreter creates a variable called `$basicText`. Anything typed into that text box (as a default the first few lines of the *Gettysburg Address*) becomes the value of the `$basicText` variable.

Reading Select Elements

Recall that both drop-down lists and list boxes are created with the `select` object. That object has a `name` attribute. Each of the possible choices in the list box is an `option` object. Each `option` object has a `value` attribute.

The name of the `select` object becomes the variable name. For example, `borderMaker.html` has two select objects: `borderSize` and `borderStyle`. The PHP program can expect to find two corresponding variables: `$borderSize` and `$borderStyle`. Because the user has nowhere to type a value into a `select` object, the values it can return must be encoded into the structure of the form itself. The value of whichever option the user selected is sent to the PHP program as the value of the corresponding variable. For example, if the user chose `groove` as the border style, the `$borderStyle` variable has the value `groove` in it.

In the Real World

The options' value doesn't necessarily have to be what the user sees on the form. This "hidden value" is handy if you want to show the user one thing but send something else to the server. For example, you might want to let the user choose from several colors. In this case, you might want to create a list box that shows the user several color names, but the `value` property corresponding to each of the `option` objects might have the actual hexadecimal values. Similar tricks are used in online shopping environments, where you might let the user choose an item by its name but the value associated with that item might be its catalog number, which is easier to work with in a database environment.

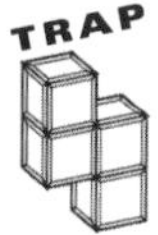

You can have multiple selections enabled in a list box. In that case, the variable contains a *list* of responses. While managing this list is not difficult, it is a topic for another chapter (chapter 4, "Loops and Arrays," to be specific). For now, concentrate on the singular list box style.

Reading Radio Groups

CSS allows the developer to indicate sizes with a variety of measurements. This is an ideal place for a group of radio buttons because only one unit of measure is appropriate at a time. Even though there are four different radio buttons on the `borderDemo.html` page with the name `sizeType`, the PHP program will only see one `$sizeType` variable. The `value` associated with whichever option is selected will become the value of the `$sizeType` variable. Note that like option elements, it is possible for the value of a radio button to be different than the text displayed beside it.

> **DECIDING ON A FORM ELEMENT**
>
> **You might wonder if all these form elements are necessary, since they all boil down to a name and value by the time they get to the PHP interpreter. The various kinds of user interface elements do make a difference in a few ways:**
>
> - **It's easier (for many users) to use a mouse than to type. Whenever possible, it is nice to add lists, checks, and options so the user can navigate your forms more quickly. Typing is often much slower than the kinds of input afforded by the other elements.**
> - **Interface elements (especially the drop-down list box) are extremely efficient in terms of screen space. You can pack a lot of choices on a small screen by using drop-downs effectively. While you might not think space is an issue, take a look at how many people are now surfing the Web with PDAs and cell phones.**
> - **Your life as a programmer is much easier if you can predict what the user will send. When users type things, they make spelling and grammar mistakes, use odd abbreviations, and are just unpredictable. If you limit choices whenever possible, you are less likely to frustrate users.**

Returning to the Story Program

The `Story` program introduced at the beginning of this chapter is an opportunity to bring together all the new elements you learned. The program doesn't introduce anything new, but it helps you see a larger context.

Designing the Story

Even though this is not an especially difficult program to write, you run into problems if you simply open your text editor and start blasting away. It really pays to plan ahead. The most important thinking happens before you write a single line of code.

In this situation, start by thinking about your story. You can write your own story or modify some existing text for humorous effect. I raided a nursery rhyme book for my story. Regardless of how you come up with a story, have it in place *before* you start writing code. I wrote the original unmodified version of "Little Boy Blue" in my text editor first so I could admire its artistic genius—and then mangle it beyond recognition.

As you look over the original prose, look for key words you can take out, and try to find a description that hints at the original word without giving anything away. For example, I printed my story, circled the word *blue* in the original poem, and wrote *color* on another piece of paper. Keep doing this until you've found several words you can take out of the original story. You should have a document with a bunch of holes in it, and a list of hints. Mine looked like Figure 2.15.

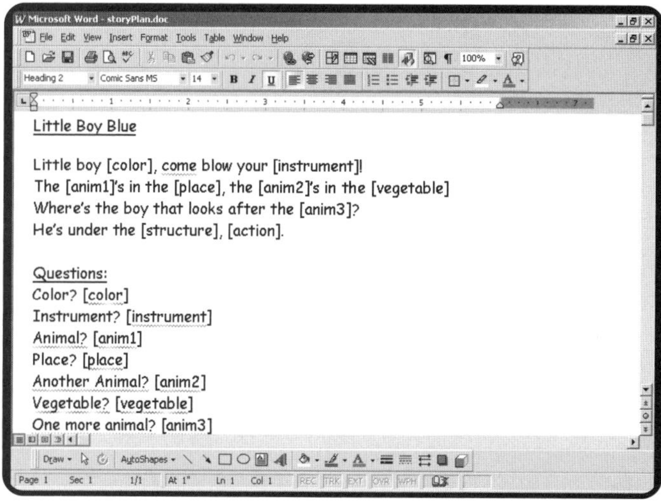

FIGURE 2.15

I thought through the story and the word list before writing any code.

IN THE REAL WORLD

Figure 2.15 shows the plan written as a Word document. Although things are sometimes done this way...(especially in a professional programming environment), I really wrote the plan on paper. I reproduced it in a cleaner format because you don't deserve to be subjected to my handwriting.

I usually plan my programs on paper, chalkboard, or dry erase board. I avoid planning programs on the computer, because it's too tempting to start programming immediately. It's important to make your plan describe what you wish to do in English before you worry about how you'll implement the plan. Most beginners (and a lot of pros) start programming way too early, and get stuck as a result. You see, throughout the rest of this chapter, how this plan evolves into a working program.

Building the HTML Page

With the basic outline from Figure 2.15, it becomes clear how the `Story` program should be created. It should have two parts. The first is an HTML page that prompts the user for all the various words. Here's the code for my version:

```
<html>
<head>
<title>Story</title>
</head>
<body>
<h1>Story</h1>
<h3>Please fill in the blanks below, and I'll tell
    you a story</h3>
<form method = "post"
      action = "story.php">

<table border = 1>
<tr>
  <th>Color:</th>
  <th>
    <input type = "text"
           name = "color"
           value = "">
  </th>
</tr>

<tr>
  <th>Musical Instrument</th>
  <th>
    <input type = "text"
           name = "instrument"
           value = "">
  </th>
</tr>

<tr>
  <th>Animal</th>
  <th>
    <input type = "text"
           name = "anim1"
```

```
            value = "">
    </th>
  </tr>

  <tr>
    <th>Another animal</th>
    <th>
      <input type = "text"
             name = "anim2"
             value = "">
    </th>
  </tr>

  <tr>
    <th>Yet another animal!</th>
    <th>
      <input type = "text"
             name = "anim3"
             value = "">
    </th>
  </tr>

  <tr>
    <th>Place</th>
    <th>
      <input type = "text"
             name = "place"
             value = "">
    </th>
  </tr>

  <tr>
    <th>Vegetable</th>
    <th>
      <input type = "text"
             name = "vegetable"
             value = "">
    </th>
  </tr>
```

```
<tr>
  <th>A structure</th>
  <th>
    <input type = "text"
           name = "structure"
           value = "">
  </th>
</tr>

<tr>
  <th>An action</th>
  <th>
    <select name = "action">
      <option value = "fast asleep">fast asleep</option>
      <option value = "drinking cappuccino">drinking cappuccino</option>
      <option value = "wandering around aimlessly">wandering around
aimlessly</option>
      <option value = "doing nothing in particular">doing nothing in
particular</option>
    </select>
  </th>
</tr>

<tr>
  <td colspan = 2>
    <center>
      <input type = "submit"
             value = "tell me the story">
    </center>
  </td>
</tr>
</table>

</form>
</body>
</html>
```

There's nothing terribly exciting about the HTML. In fact, since I had the plan, I knew exactly what kinds of things I was asking for and created form elements to ask each question. I used a list box for the last question so I could put in some interesting suggestions. Note that I changed the order a little bit just to throw the user off.

Check a few things when you're writing a page that connects to a script:

- Make sure you've added an `action` attribute.
- Ensure you've got the correct `action` attribute in the `form` tag.
- Make sure each form element has an appropriate `name` attribute.
- If you have radio or option objects, make sure each one has an appropriate value.
- Be sure there is a `submit` button somewhere in your form.
- Don't forget to end your form tag. Your browser may work fine if you forget to include `</form>`, but you don't know how the users' browsers will act.

Checking the Form

I actually wrote two different scripts to read this form. The first one simply checks each element to make sure it received the value I expected. Here's the first program, called `storySimple.php`:

```
<html>
<head>
<title>Little Boy Who?</title>
</head>
<body>
<h1>Little Boy Who?</h1>

<h3>Values from the story page</h3>

<table border = 1>
<tr>
  <th>Variable</th>
  <th>Value</th>
</tr>

<tr>
  <th>color</th>
  <td><? print $color ?></td>
</tr>

<tr>
  <th>instrument</th>
  <td><? print $instrument ?></td>
</tr>
```

```
<tr>
  <th>anim1</th>
  <td><? print $anim1 ?></td>
</tr>

<tr>
  <th>anim2</th>
  <td><? print $anim2 ?></td>
</tr>

<tr>
  <th>anim3</th>
  <td><? print $anim3 ?></td>
</tr>

<tr>
  <th>place</th>
  <td><? print $place ?></td>
</tr>

<tr>
  <th>vegetable</th>
  <td><? print $vegetable ?></td>
</tr>

<tr>
  <th>structure</th>
  <td><? print $structure ?></td>
</tr>

<tr>
  <th>action</th>
  <td><? print $action ?></td>
</tr>

</table>
<form>
</html>
```

I made this program as simple as possible, because I didn't expect to need it for long. It's simply a table with the name of each variable and its associated value. I did it this way to ensure that I get all the variables exactly the way I want them. There's no point in building the story if you don't have the variables working.

Building the Final Story

The story itself is very simple to build if you've planned and ensured that the variables are working right. All I had to do was write out the story as it was written in the plan, with the variables incorporated in the appropriate places. Here's the code for the finished `story.php` page:

```
<html>
<head>
<title>Little Boy Who?</title>
</head>
<body>
<center>

<h1>Little Boy Who?</h1>

<?

print <<<HERE
<h3>
Little Boy $color, come blow your $instrument!<br>
The $anim1's in the $place, the $anim2's in the $vegetable.<br>
Where's the boy that looks after the $anim3?<br>
He's under the $structure, $action.
</h3>
HERE;
?>

</center>

</body>
</html>
```

It might astonish you that the final program is quite a bit simpler than the test program. Neither is very complicated, but once you have created the story, set up the variables, and ensured that all the variables are sent correctly, the story program itself turns out to be almost trivial. Most of the `story.php` code is plain HTML. The only part that's in PHP is one long `print` statement, which uses the `print <<<HERE` syntax to print a long line of HTML text with PHP variables embedded inside. The story itself is this long concatenated text.

Summary

In this chapter you learn some incredibly important concepts: what variables are, and how to create them in PHP; how to connect a form to a PHP program with modifications to the form's `method` and `action` attributes; and how to write normal links to send values to server-side scripts. You built programs that respond to various kinds of input elements, including drop-down lists, radio buttons, and list boxes. You went through the process of writing a program from beginning to end, including the critical planning stage, creating a form for user input, and using that input to generate interesting output.

CHALLENGES

1. **Write a Web page that asks the user for his first and last name and then uses a PHP script to write a form letter to that person. Inform the user he might be a millionaire.**
2. **Write a custom Web page that uses embedded data tricks to generate custom links for your favorite Web searches, local news and weather, and other elements of interest to you.**
3. **Write your own story game. Find or write some text to modify, create an appropriate input form, and output the story with a PHP script.**

Controlling Your Code with Conditions and Functions

Most of the really interesting things you can do with a computer involve letting it make decisions. Actually, the computer only appears able to decide things. The programmer generates code that tells the computer exactly what to do in different circumstances. In this chapter, you learn how to control the flow of a program; specifically, how to:

- Create a random integer
- Use the `if` structure to change the program's behavior
- Write conditions to evaluate variables
- Work with the `else` clause to provide instructions when a condition is not met
- Use the `switch` statement to work with multiple choices
- Build functions to better manage code
- Write programs that can create their own forms

Examining the Petals Around the Rose Game

The `Petals Around the Rose` game, featured in Figure 3.1, illustrates all the new skills you learn in this chapter.

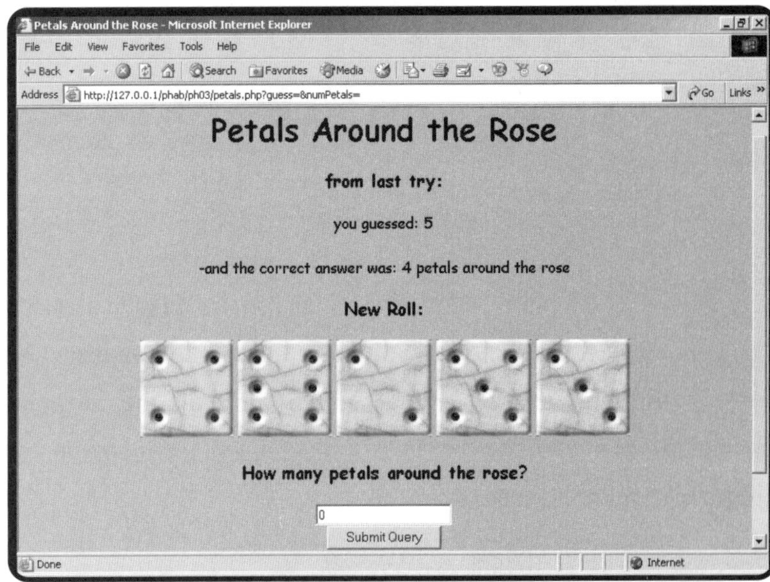

FIGURE 3.1

This is a new twist on an old dice puzzle.

The premise of the `Petals` game is very simple. The computer rolls a set of five dice and asks the user to guess the number of petals around the rose. The user enters a number and presses the button. The computer indicates whether this value is correct, and provides a new set of dice. Once the user understands the secret, it's a very easy game, but it can take a long time to figure out how it works. Try the game before you know how it's done.

Creating a Random Number

The dice game, like many other games, relies on random number generation to make things interesting. Most programming languages have at least one way to create random numbers. PHP's `rand` function makes it easy to create random numbers.

Viewing the Roll Em Program

The `Roll Em` program shown in Figure 3.2 demonstrates how the `rand` function can generate virtual dice.

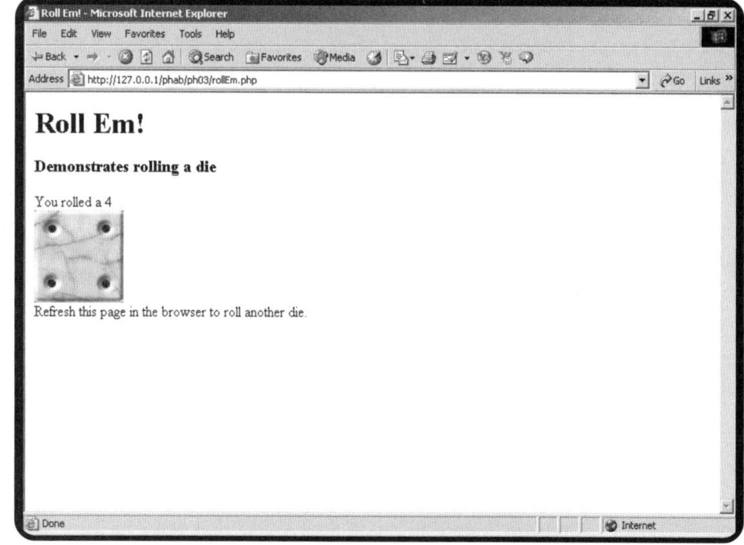

FIGURE 3.2

The die roll is randomly generated by PHP

The code for the `Roll Em` program shows how easy random number generation is:

```
<html>
<head>
<title>Roll Em!</title>
</head>
<body>
<h1>Roll Em!</h1>
<h3>Demonstrates rolling a die</h3>

<?
$roll = rand(1,6);
print "You rolled a $roll";
print "<br>";
print "<img src = die$roll.jpg>";
?>
<br>
Refresh this page in the browser to roll another die.

</body>
</html>
```

The rand function generates a random number between 1 and 6 (inclusive) and stores the resulting value in the $roll variable. The rand function expects two parameters: The first value is the lowest number and the second value represents the highest number.

Since I want to replicate an ordinary six-sided die, I told the rand function to return a value between 1 and 6. Since I knew that rand would return a value, I assigned that resulting value to the variable $roll. By the time the following line has finished executing, the $roll variable has a random value in it:

```
$roll = rand(1,6);
```

The lowest possible value is 1, the highest possible value is 6, and the value will not have a decimal part. (In other words, it will never be 1.5.)

If you're coming from another programming language, you might be surprised at the way random numbers are generated in PHP. Most languages allow you to create a random floating-point value between 0 and 1, and then requires you to transform that value to whatever range you wish. PHP allows—in fact, requires—you to create random integers within a range, which is usually what you want anyway. If you really want a value between 0 and 1, you can generate a random number between 0 and 1000 and then divide that value by 1000.

Printing a Corresponding Image

Notice the sneaky way I used variable interpolation in the preceding code. I carefully named my first image die1.jpg, the second die2.jpg, and so on. When I was ready to print an image to the screen, I used an ordinary HTML image tag with the source set to die$roll.jpg. If $roll is 3, the image shows die3.jpg.

Variable interpolation can be a wonderful trick if you know how the filenames are structured. You might recall from chapter 2, "Using Variables and Input," that *interpolation* is the technique that allows you to embed a variable in a quoted string by simply using its name.

Using the if Statement to Control Program Flow

One of the most interesting things computers do is appear to make decisions. The decision-making ability is an illusion. The programmer stores very specific instructions inside a computer, and it acts on those instructions. The simplest form of this behavior is a structure called the if statement.

In the Real World

The dice games in this chapter demonstrate the power of graphical images to make your programs more interesting and fun. You can get graphics for your programs a number of ways. The easiest is to find an existing image on the Web. Although this is technically very simple, many of the images on the Web are owned by somebody. Respect the intellectual property rights of the original owners. Get permission for any images you use.

Another alternative is to create the graphics yourself. Even if you don't have any artistic talent at all, modern software and technology make it quite easy to generate passable graphics. You can do a lot with a digital camera and a freeware graphics editor. Even if you hire a professional artist to do graphics for your program, you might still need to be able to sketch what you are looking for. This book's CD has a couple of very powerful freeware image-editing programs.

Introducing the Ace Program

You can improve the `Roll Em` program with an `if` structure. Enter the `Ace` program. Figure 3.3 shows the program when the program rolls any value except `1`.

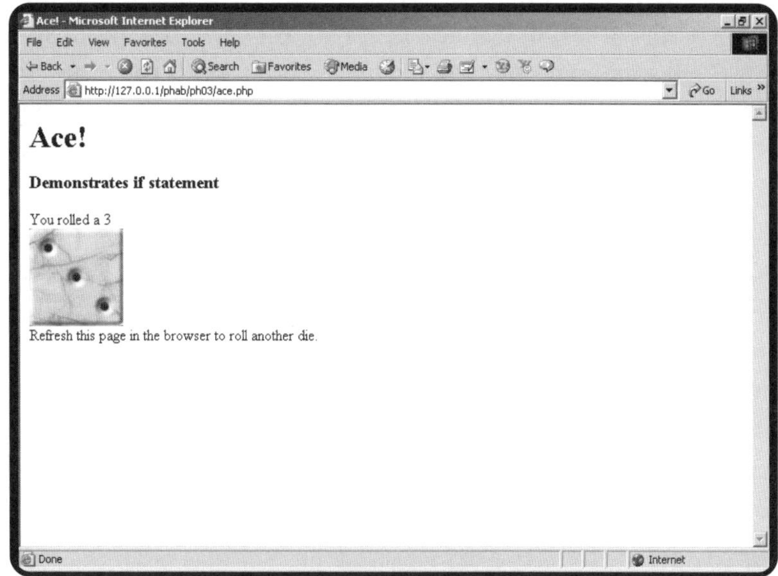

FIGURE 3.3

When the roll is not a 1, nothing interesting happens.

However, this program does something exciting (okay, moderately exciting), when it rolls a 1, as you can see from Figure 3.4.

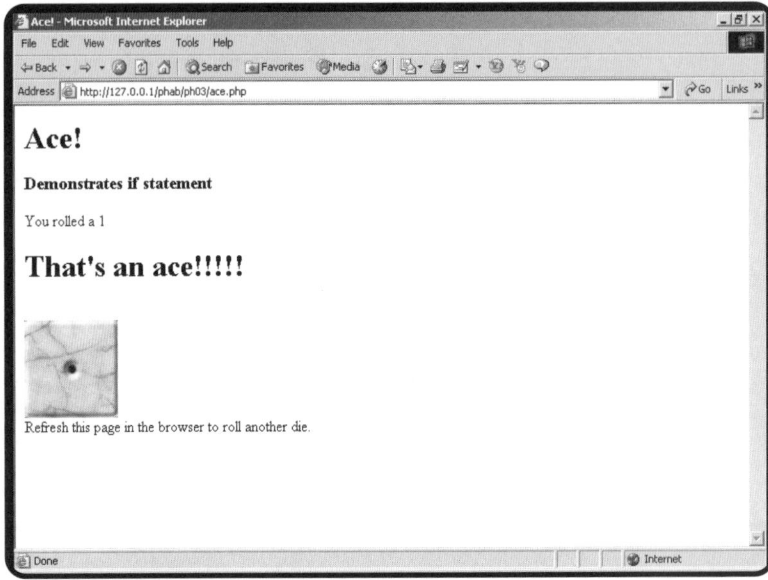

FIGURE 3.4

When a 1 appears, the user is treated to a lavish multimedia display.

Creating a Condition

On the surface, the behavior of the `Ace` program is very straightforward: It does something interesting only if the die roll is 1, and it doesn't do that interesting thing in any other case. While it is a simple idea, the implications are profound. The same simple mechanism in the `Ace` program is the foundation of all complicated computer behavior, from flight simulators to heart monitors. Take a look at the code for the `Ace` program and see if you can spot the new element:

```
<html>
<head>
<title>Ace!</title>
</head>
<body>
<h1>Ace!</h1>
<h3>Demonstrates if statement</h3>

<?
$roll = rand(1,6);
print "You rolled a $roll";

if ($roll == 1){
  print "<h1>That's an ace!!!!!</h1>";
} // end if
```

```
print "<br>";
print "<img src = die$roll.jpg>";
?>
<br>
Refresh this page in the browser to roll another die.

</body>
</html>
```

The secret to this program is the segment that looks like this:

```
if ($roll == 1){
  print "<h1>That's an ace!!!!!</h1>";
} // end if
```

The line that prints `"That's an ace!!!!!"` doesn't happen every time the program is run. It only happens if a certain condition is true. The `if` statement sets up a condition for evaluation. In this case, the condition is read *$roll is equal to 1.* If that condition is true, all the code between the left brace (`{`) and the right brace (`}`) evaluates. If the condition is not true, the code between the braces is skipped altogether.

A condition can be thought of as an expression that can be evaluated as true or false. Any expression that can return a true or false value can be used as a condition. Most conditions look much like the one in the `Ace` program. This condition checks the variable `$roll` to see if it is equal to the value `1`.

Note that equality is indicated by two equals signs (==).

This is important, because computer programs are not nearly as flexible as humans. We humans often use the same symbol for different purposes. While computer languages can do this, it often leads to problems. The single equals sign is reserved for *assignment*. You should read this line as *x gets five*, indicating that the value `5` is being assigned to the variable `$x`:

```
$x = 5;
```

This code fragment should be read as *x is equal to five,* as it is testing equality.

```
$x == 5;
```

It is essentially asking whether `x` is equal to `5`. A condition such as `$x == 5` does not stand on its own. Instead, it is used inside some sort of other structure, such as an `if` statement.

Exploring Comparison Operators

Equality (==) is not the only type of comparison PHP allows. You can compare a variable and a value or two variables using a number of comparison operators. Table 3.1 describes comparison operators.

TABLE 3.1 COMPARISON OPERATORS

Operator	Description
==	equal to
<	less than
>	greater than
<=	less than or equal to
>=	greater than or equal to
!=	not equal to

These comparison operators work on any type of data, although the results might be a little strange when you use these mathematical operators on non-numeric data. For example, if you have a condition like the following, you get the result `true`:

```
"a" < "b"
```

You get that result because alphabetically, the letter *a* is earlier than *b*, so it has a "smaller" value.

Creating an if Statement

An `if` statement begins with the keyword `if` followed by a condition inside parentheses. After the parenthesis is a left brace: {. You can put as many lines of code between the left brace and right brace as you wish. Any code between the braces is executed only if the condition is true. If the condition is false, program control flows to the next line after the right brace.

It is not necessary to put a semicolon on a line ending with a brace. It is customary to indent all the code between the left and right braces.

Code Style

The PHP processor ignores the spaces and carriage returns in your PHP code, so you might wonder if it matters to pay such attention to how code is indented, where the braces go, and so on. While the PHP processor doesn't care how you format your code, human readers do. Programmers have passionate arguments about how you should format your code.

If writing code with a group (for instance, in a large project or for a class), you are usually given a style guide you are expected to follow. When working on your own, the specific style you adopt is not as important as being consistent in your coding. The particular stylistic conventions I adopted for this book are reasonably common, relatively readable, and easily adapted to a number of languages.

If you don't have your own programming style, the one in this book is a good starting place. However, if your team leader or teacher requires another style, adapt to it. Regardless of the specific style guidelines you use, it makes lots of sense to indent your code, place comments liberally throughout your program, and use whitespace to make your programs easier to read and debug.

Do not put a semicolon at the end of the `if` line. The following code prints "`we must be near a black hole.`"

```
if ("day" == "night") ; {
print "we must be near a black hole";
} // end if
```

When the processor sees the semicolon following (`"day" == "night"`), it thinks there is no code to evaluate if the condition is true. The condition is effectively ignored. Essentially, the braces indicate that an entire group of lines are to be treated as one structure, and that structure is part of the current logical line.

Working with Negative Results

The `Ace` program shows how to write code that handles a condition. Much of the time, you want the program to do one thing if the condition is true, and something else if it's false. Most languages include a special variant of the `if` statement to handle exactly this type of contingency.

Demonstrating the Ace or Not Program

The `Ace or Not` program is built from the `Ace` program, but it has an important difference, as you can see from Figures 3.5 and 3.6.

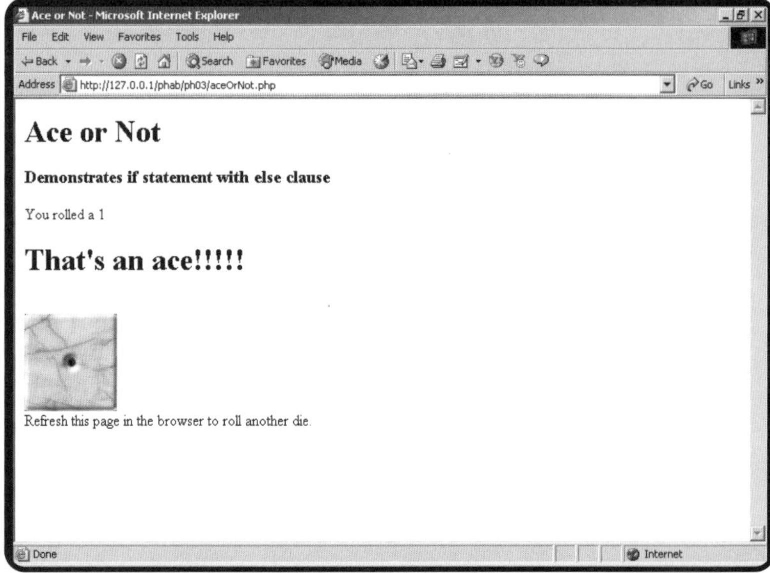

FIGURE 3.5

If the program rolls a 1, it still hollers out "`That's an ace!!!!!`"

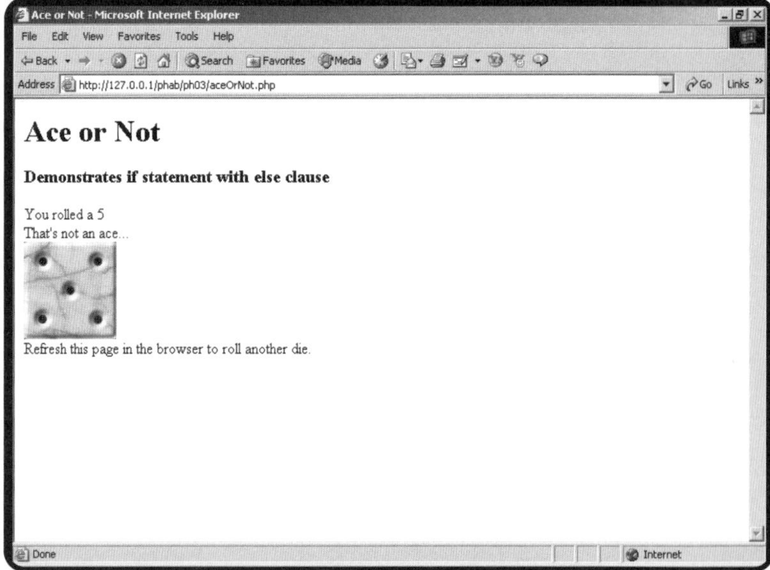

FIGURE 3.6

If the program rolls anything but a 1, it still has a message for the user.

The program does one thing when the condition is true and something else when the condition is false.

Using the else Clause

The code for the `Ace or Not` program shows how the `else` clause can allow for multiple behaviors based on different conditions:

```
<html>
<head>
<title>Ace or Not</title>
</head>
<body>
<h1>Ace or Not</h1>
<h3>Demonstrates if statement with else clause</h3>

<?
$roll = rand(1,6);
print "You rolled a $roll";
print "<br>";

if ($roll == 1){
  print "<h1>That's an ace!!!!!</h1>";
} else {
  print "That's not an ace...";
} // end if

print "<br>";
print "<img src = die$roll.jpg>";
?>
<br>
Refresh this page in the browser to roll another die.

</body>
</html>
```

The interesting part of this code comes near the `if` statement:

```
if ($roll == 1){
  print "<h1>That's an ace!!!!!</h1>";
} else {
  print "That's not an ace...";
} // end if
```

If the condition `$roll == 1` is true, the program prints "`That's an ace!!!!!.`" If the condition is *not* true, the code between `else` and the end of the `if` structure is executed instead.

Notice the structure and indentation. One chunk of code (between the condition and the `else` statement, encased in braces) occurs if the condition is true. If the condition is false, the code between `else` and the end of the `if` structure (also in braces) is executed. You can put as much code as you wish in either segment. Only one of the segments runs (based on the condition), but you are guaranteed that one *will* execute.

Working with Multiple Values

Often you find yourself working with more complex data. For example, you might want to respond differently to each of the six possible die rolls. The `Binary Dice` program illustrated in Figures 3.7 and 3.8 demonstrates just such a situation by showing the base two representation of the die roll.

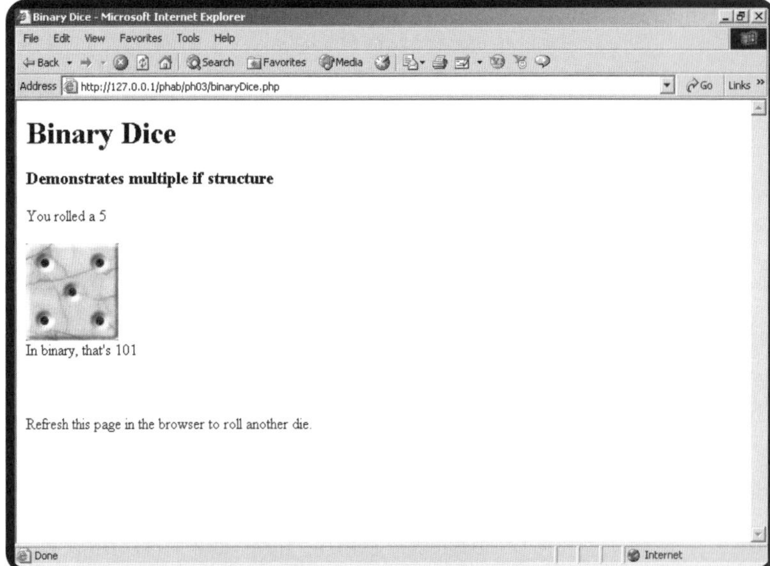

FIGURE 3.7

The roll is a 5, and the program shows the binary representation of that value.

Writing the Binary Dice Program

The `Binary Dice` program has a slightly more complex `if` structure than the others, because the binary value should be different for each of six possible outcomes.

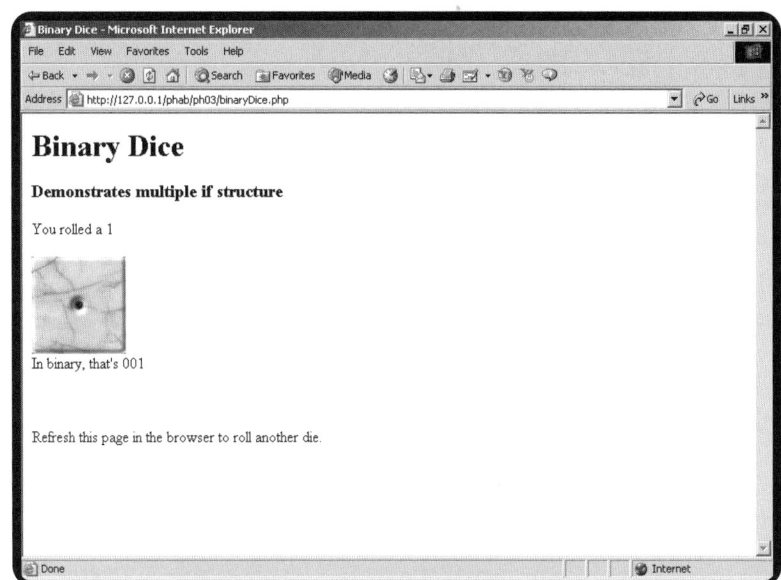

FIGURE 3.8

After rolling again, the program reports the binary representation of the new roll.

```
<html>
<head>
<title>Binary Dice</title>
</head>
<body>
<h1>Binary Dice</h1>
<h3>Demonstrates multiple if structure</h3>

<?
$roll = rand(1,6);
print "You rolled a $roll";
print "<br>";

if ($roll == 1){
  $binValue = "001";
} else if ($roll == 2){
  $binValue = "010";
} else if ($roll == 3){
  $binValue = "011";
} else if ($roll == 4){
  $binValue = "100";
} else if ($roll == 5){
  $binValue = "101";
```

```
} else if ($roll == 6){
  $binValue = "110";
} else {
  print "I don't know that one...";
} // end if

print "<br>";
print "<img src = die$roll.jpg>";
print "<br>";
print "In binary, that's $binValue";
print "<br>";
print "<br>";
print "<br>";

?>
<br>
Refresh this page in the browser to roll another die.

</body>
</html>
```

Using Multiple else if Clauses

The `Binary Dice` program has only one `if` structure, but that structure has multiple `else` clauses. The first condition simply checks to see if `$roll` is equal to `1`. If it is, the appropriate code runs, assigning the binary representation of `1` to the `$binValue` variable. If the first condition is false, the program looks at all the successive `if else` clauses until it finds a condition that evaluates to `TRUE`. If none of the conditions are true, the code in the `else` clause is executed.

You may be surprised that I even put an `else` clause in this code. Since you know the value of `$roll` must be between `1` and `6` and you checked each of those values, the program should never need to evaluate the `else` clause. Things in programming don't always work out the way you expect, so it's a great idea to have some code in an `else` clause even if you don't expect to ever need it. It's much better to get a message from your program explaining that something unexpected occurred than to have your program blow up inexplicably while your users are using it.

The indentation for a multiple-condition `if` statement is useful so you can tell which parts of the code are part of the `if` structure, and which parts are meant to be executed if a particular condition turns out to be true.

Using the switch Structure to Simplify Programming

The situation in the `Binary Dice` program happens often enough that another structure is designed for when you are comparing one variable to a number of possible values. The `Switch Dice` program in Figure 3.9 looks identical to the `Binary Dice` program as far as the user is concerned, except `Switch Dice` shows the roll's Roman numeral representation.

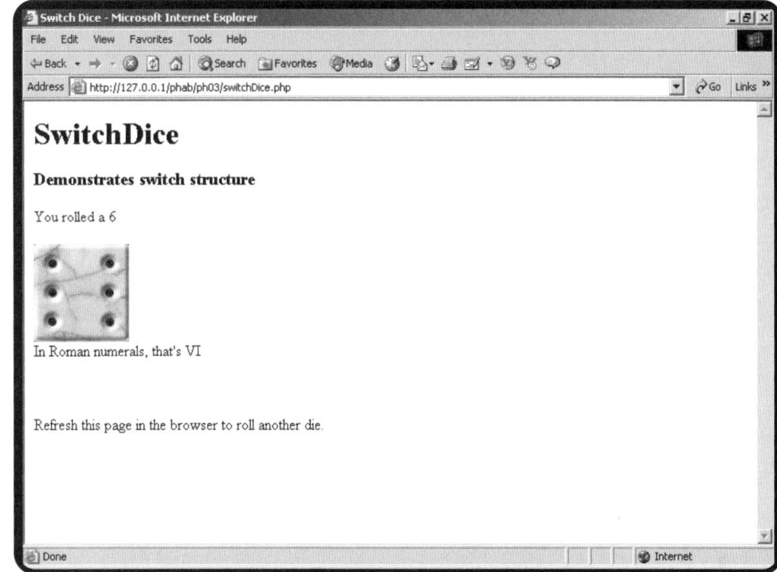

FIGURE 3.9

This version shows a die roll in Roman numerals.

While the outward appearance of the last two programs is extremely similar, the underlying code is changed to illustrate a very handy device called the `switch` structure. This device begins by defining an expression, and then defines a series of branches based on the value of that expression.

Building the Switch Dice Program

The `Switch Dice` program code looks different than the `Binary Dice` code, but the results are the same:

```
<html>
<head>
<title>Switch Dice</title>
</head>
<body>
```

```
<h1>SwitchDice</h1>
<h3>Demonstrates switch structure</h3>

<?
$roll = rand(1,6);
print "You rolled a $roll";
print "<br>";

switch ($roll){
  case 1:
    $romValue = "I";
    break;
  case 2:
    $romValue = "II";
    break;
  case 3:
    $romValue = "III";
    break;
  case 4:
    $romValue = "IV";
    break;
  case 5:
    $romValue = "V";
    break;
  case 6:
    $romValue = "VI";
    break;
  default:
    print "This is an illegal die!";
} // end switch


print "<br>";
print "<img src = die$roll.jpg>";
print "<br>";
print "In Roman numerals, that's $romValue";
print "<br>";
print "<br>";
print "<br>";
```

```
?>
<br>
Refresh this page in the browser to roll another die.

</body>
</html>
```

Using the switch Structure

The `switch` structure is optimal for when you have one variable to compare against a number of possible values. Use the `switch` keyword followed, in parentheses, by the name of the variable you wish to evaluate. A set of braces indicates that the next block of code focuses on evaluating this variable's possible values.

For each possible value, use the `case` statement, followed by the value, followed by a colon. End each case with a `break` statement, which indicates the program should stop thinking about this particular case and get ready for the next one.

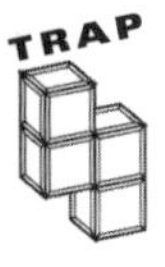

The use of the `break` statement is probably the trickiest part of using the `switch` statement—especially if you are familiar with a language such as Visual Basic, which does not require such a construct. It's important to add the `break` statement to the end of each case, or the program flow simply "falls through" to the next possible value, even if that value would not otherwise evaluate to true. As a beginner, you should always place the `break` statement at the end of each case.

The last case, which works just like the `else` clause of the multi-value `if` statement, is called `default`. It defines code to execute if none of the other cases is active; it's smart to test for a `default` case even if you think it is impossible for the computer to get to this default option. Crazy things happen. It's good to be prepared for them.

Combining a Form and Its Results

Most of your PHP programs up to now have had two distinct files. An HTML file has a form, which calls a PHP program. It can be tedious to keep track of two separate files. Use the `if` statement to combine both functions into one page.

The `Hi User` program shown in Figures 3.10 and 3.11 looks much like its counterpart in chapter 2, "Using Variables and Input," but it has an important difference. Rather than being an HTML page and a separate PHP program, the entire program resides in one file on the server.

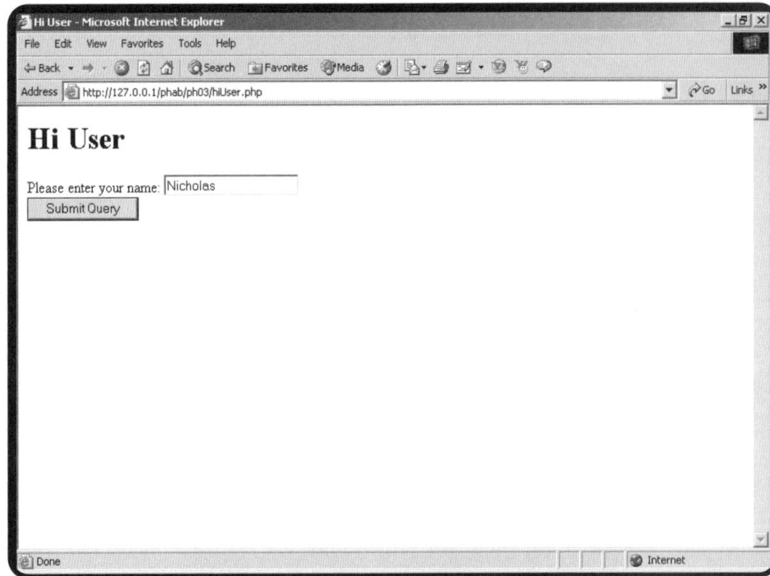

FIGURE 3.10

The HTML page is actually produced through the "Hi User" PHP code.

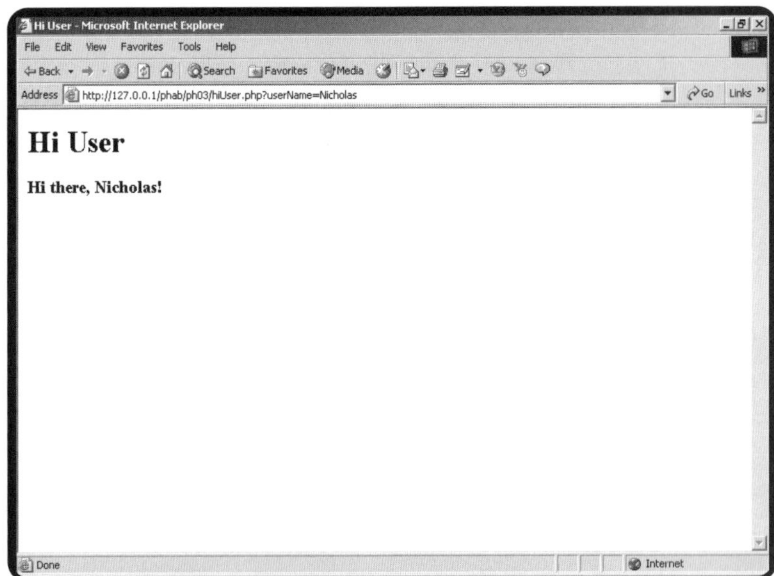

FIGURE 3.11

The result is produced by exactly the same "Hi User"program.

The code for the new version of `hiUser` shows how to achieve this trick:

```
<html>
<head>
<title>Hi User</title>
</head>
```

```
<body>
<h1>Hi User</h1>

<?

if (empty($userName)){
  print <<<HERE
  <form>
  Please enter your name:
  <input type = "text"
         name = "userName"><br>
  <input type = "submit">
  </form>
HERE;

} else {
  print "<h3>Hi there, $userName!</h3>";
} //end
?>

</body>
</html>
```

This program begins by looking for the existence of a variable called `$userName`. There is no `$userName` variable the first time the program is called, because the program was not called from a form. The `empty()` function returns the value `true` if the specified variable is empty; it returns `false` if it has a value. If `$userName` does not exist, `empty($userName)` evaluates as `true`. The condition `(empty($userName))` is generally true if this is the first time this page has been called. If it's true, the program should generate a form so the user can enter her name. If the condition is false, that means somehow the user has entered a name (presumably through the form) so the program greets the user with that name.

The key idea here is that the program runs *more than once*. When the user first links to `hiUser.php`, the program creates a form. The user enters a value on the form, and presses the `submit` button. This causes exactly the same program to be run again on the server. This time, though, the `$userName` variable is *not* empty, so rather than generating a form, the program uses the variable's value in a greeting.

Server-side programming frequently works in this way. It isn't uncommon for a user to call the same program many times in succession as part of solving a particular problem. You often use branching structures such as the `if` and `switch` statements to direct the program flow based on the user's current state of activity.

Responding to Checkboxes

Now that you know how to use the `if` structure and the `empty` function, you can work with checkboxes. Take a look at the following HTML code:

```
<html>
<head>
<title>Checkbox Demo</title>
</head>
<body>
<h1>Checkbox Demo</h1>

<h3>Demonstrates checkboxes</h3>

<form action ="checkDemo.php">

<h3>What would you like with your order?</h3>
<ul>
  <li><input type ="checkbox"
             name ="chkFries"
             value ="1.00">Fries
  </li>
  <li><input type ="checkbox"
             name ="chkSoda"
             value =".85">Soda
  </li>
  <li><input type ="checkbox"
             name ="chkShake"
             value ="1.30">Shake
  </li>
  <li><input type ="checkbox"
             name ="chkKetchup"
             value =".05">Ketchup
  </li>


</ul>

<input type ="submit">
</form>

</body>
</html>
```

This code generates the printout shown in Figure 3.12.

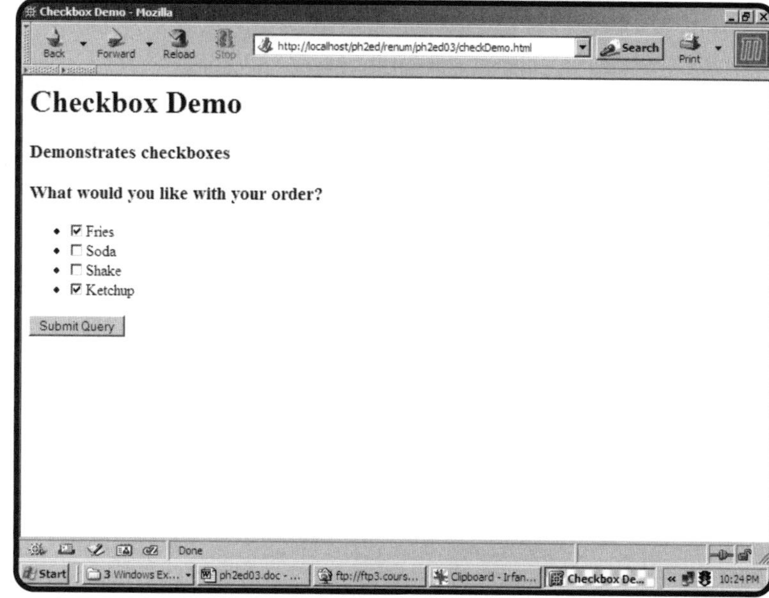

FIGURE 3.12

This page has a series of checkboxes.

When the user submits this form, it calls `checkDemo.php`, which looks like Figure 3.13.

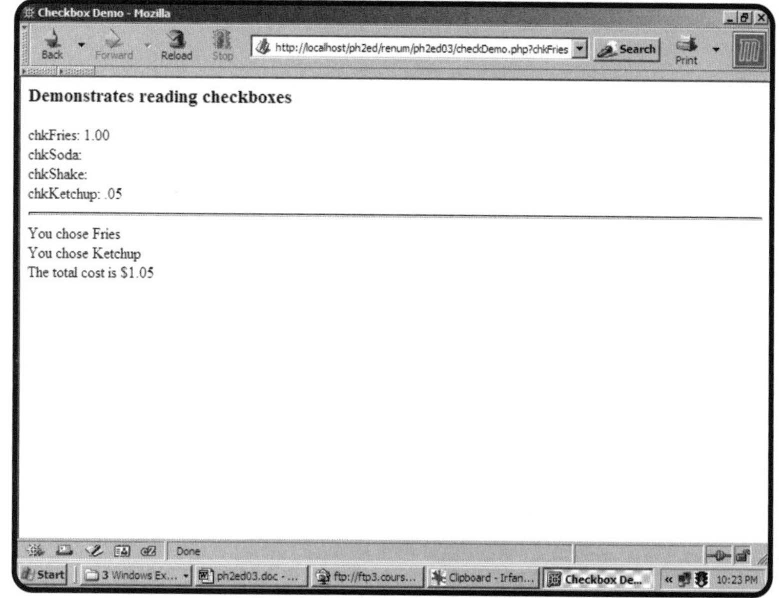

FIGURE 3.13

Notice that checkbox variables have a value or don't exist.

Checkboxes are a little different from other form elements, which consistently return a name/value pair. Checkboxes also have a name and a value, but the checkbox variable is sent to the server only if the box has been checked. As an example, compare Figures 3.12 and 3.13. You can see that only two of the checkboxes were selected. These checkboxes report values. If a checkbox isn't selected, its name and value are not reported to the program.

Take a look at the code for the `checkDemo.php` program to see how this works:

```
<html>
<head>
<title>Checkbox Demo</title>
</head>
<body>
<h3>Demonstrates reading checkboxes</h3>

<?

print <<<HERE

chkFries: $chkFries <br>
chkSoda: $chkSoda <br>
chkShake: $chkShake <br>
chkKetchup: $chkKetchup <br>
<hr>

HERE;

$total = 0;

if (!empty($chkFries)){
  print ("You chose Fries <br> \n");
  $total = $total + $chkFries;
} // end if

if (!empty($chkSoda)){
  print ("You chose Soda <br> \n");
  $total = $total + $chkSoda;
} // end if

if (!empty($chkShake)){
```

```
  print ("You chose Shake <br> \n");
  $total = $total + $chkShake;
} // end if

if (!empty($chkKetchup)){
  print ("You chose Ketchup <br> \n");
  $total = $total + $chkKetchup;
} // end if

print "The total cost is \$$total \n";

?>
</body>
</html>
```

The first part of the program simply prints out the expected variables. As you can see, if the checkbox has not been selected, the associated variable is never created. You can use the `empty()` function to determine if a checkbox has been checked. If the variable is empty, the corresponding checkbox was not checked. I used the negation operator (`!`) to check for the existence of a variable. The condition `(!empty($chkFries))` is `true` if `chkFries` was selected, and `false` otherwise. I tallied the values associated with all the selected checkboxes to get a grand total.

Using Functions to Encapsulate Parts of the Program

It hasn't taken long for your programs to get complex. As soon as the code gets a little bit larger than a screen in your editor, it gets much harder to track. Programmers like to break up code into smaller segments called *functions* to help keep everything straight. A function is like a miniature program. It is designed to do one job well. Look at Figure 3.14 for an example.

Examining the This Old Man Program

Song lyrics often have a very repetitive nature. The "This Old Man" song shown in Figure 3.14 is a good example. Each verse is different, but the chorus is always the same. You write each verse when you write the lyrics to such a song, but only write the chorus once. After that, you simply write "chorus." This works very much like functions in programming language. The code for the `This Old Man` program illustrates:

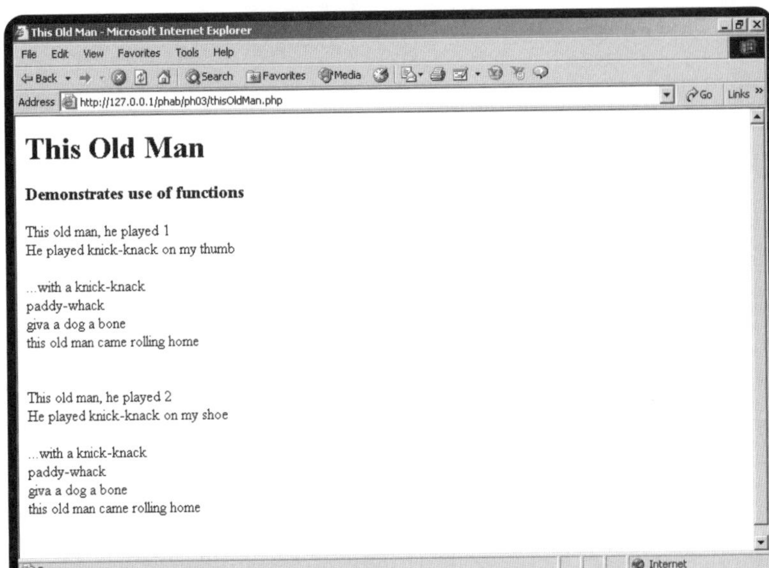

FIGURE 3.14

This song has a straightforward pattern: verse, chorus, verse, chorus.

```
<html>
<head>
<title>This Old Man</title>
</head>
<body>
<h1>This Old Man</h1>
<h3>Demonstrates use of functions</h3>
<?

verse1();
chorus();
verse2();
chorus();

function verse1(){
  print <<<HERE
  This old man, he played 1<br>
  He played knick-knack on my thumb<br><br>
HERE;
} // end verse1

function verse2(){
  print <<<HERE
```

```
  This old man, he played 2<br>
  He played knick-knack on my shoe<br><br>
HERE;
} // end verse1

function chorus(){
  print <<<HERE
  ...with a knick-knack<br>
  paddy-whack<br>
  give a dog a bone<br>
this old man came rolling home<br>
  <br><br>
HERE;
} // end chorus
?>
</body>
</html>
```

Careful examination of this code shows how it works. The main part of the program is extremely simple:

```
verse1();
chorus();
verse2();
chorus();
```

Creating New Functions

The `This Old Man` code appears to have some new PHP functions. I called the `verse1()` function, then the `chorus()` function, and so on. These new functions weren't shipped with PHP. Instead, I made them as part of the page. You can take a set of instructions and store them with a name. This essentially builds a new temporary command in PHP, so you can combine simple commands to do complex things.

Building a function is simple. Use the keyword `function` followed by the function's name and a set of parentheses. Keep the parentheses empty for now; you learn how to use this feature in the next section. Use a pair of braces (`{}`) to combine a series of code lines into one function. Don't forget the right brace (`}`) to end the function definition. It's smart to indent everything between the beginning and end of a function.

When you look at my code, note there's one line I never indent: the `HERE` token used for multi-line strings. The word `HERE` acts like a closing quotation mark and must be all the way to the left side of the screen, so it can't be indented.

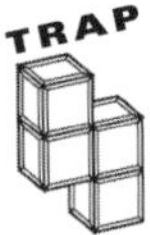

You can use any function name you like. Careful, though: If you try to define a function that already exists, you're bound to get confused. PHP has a large number of functions already built in. If you're having strange problems with a function, look at the Help to see if that function already exists.

The `chorus()` function is especially handy in this program because it can be reused. It isn't necessary to rewrite the code for the chorus each time, when you can simply call a function instead.

Using Parameters and Function Values

Functions are meant to be self-contained. This is good because the entire program can be too complex to understand. If you break the complex program into smaller functions, each function can be set up to work independently. When you work inside a function, you don't have to worry about anything outside the function. If you create a variable inside a function, that variable dies as soon as you leave the function. This prevents many errors that can otherwise creep into your code.

The bad side of functions being so self-contained is evident when you want them to work with data from the outside. You can accomplish this a couple of ways.

- Send a *parameter* to a function, which allows you to determine one or more values sent to the function as it starts.
- Give a function a *return* value.

The `param` program shown in Figure 3.15 illustrates another form of the "This Old Man" song. Although again the user might be unaware, some important differences exist between this more sophisticated program and the first `This Old Man` program.

Examining the Param.php Program

Notice that the output of Figure 3.15 is longer than that of 3.14, but the code that generates this longer output is shorter.

```
<html>
<head>
<title>Param Old Man</title>
</head>
```

FIGURE 3.15

While the output looks similar to Figure 3.14, the program that produced this page is much more efficient.

```
<body>
<h1>Param Old Man </h1>
<h3>Demonstrates use of function parameters</h3>
<?

print verse(1);
print chorus();
print verse(2);
print chorus();
print verse(3);
print chorus();
print verse(4);
print chorus();

function verse($stanza){
  switch ($stanza){
    case 1:
      $place = "thumb";
      break;
    case 2:
      $place = "shoe";
      break;
```

```
    case 3:
      $place = "knee";
      break;
    case 4:
      $place = "door";
      break;
    default:
      $place = "I don't know where";
  } // end switch

  $output = <<<HERE
  This old man, he played $stanza<br>
  He played knick-knack on my $place<br><br>
HERE;
  return $output;
} // end verse

function chorus(){
  $output = <<<HERE
  ...with a knick-knack<br>
  paddy-whack<br>
  give a dog a bone<br>
  this old man came rolling home<br>
  <br><br>
HERE;
  return $output;
} // end chorus

?>
</body>
</html>
```

Looking at Encapsulation in the Main Code Body

This code features a number of improvements over the previous version. First look at the main body of the code, which looks like this:

```
print verse(1);
print chorus();
print verse(2);
print chorus();
```

```
print verse(3);
print chorus();
print verse(4);
print chorus();
```

The program is to print the first verse, then the chorus, then the second verse, then the chorus, and so on. The details of how all these things are to be generated is left to the individual functions. This is an example of *encapsulation*. Encapsulation is good, because it allows you to think about problems in multiple levels. At the highest level, you're interested in the main ideas (print the verses and chorus) but you're not so concerned about the exact details. You use the same technique when you talk about your day: "I drove to work, had some meetings, went to lunch, and taught a class." You don't usually describe each detail of each task. Each major task can be broken down into its component tasks later. (If somebody asks, you could really describe the meeting: "I got some coffee, appeared to be taking notes furiously on my PDA, got a new high score on Solitaire while appearing to take notes, scribbled on the agenda, and dozed off during a presentation.")

Returning a Value: The chorus() Function

Another interesting thing about the code's main section code is the use of the `print()` function. In the last program, I simply said `chorus()` and the program printed the chorus. In this program, I did it a little differently. The `chorus()` function doesn't actually print anything to the screen. Instead, it creates the chorus as a big string and sends that value back to the program, which can do whatever it wants with it.

This behavior isn't new to you. Think about the `rand()` function. It always returns a value to the program. The functions in this program work the same way. Take another look at the `chorus()` function to see what I mean:

```
function chorus(){
  $output = <<<HERE
  ...with a knick-knack<br>
  paddy-whack<br>
  give a dog a bone<br>
  this old man came rolling home<br>
  <br><br>
HERE;
  return $output;
} // end chorus
```

I began the function by creating a new variable called `$output`. You can create variables inside functions by mentioning them, just like you can in the main part of the program. However, a variable created inside a function loses its meaning as soon as the function is finished. This is good, because it means the variables inside a function belong only to that function. You don't have to worry about whether the variable already exists somewhere else in your program. You also don't have to worry about all the various things that can go wrong if you mistakenly modify an existing variable. I assigned a long string (the actual chorus of the song) to the `$output` variable with the `<<<HERE` construct.

The last line of the function uses the `return` statement to send the value of `$output` back to the program. Any function can end with a `return` statement. Whatever value follows the keyword `return` is passed to the program. This is one way your functions can communicate to the main program.

Accepting a Parameter in the verse() Function

The most efficient part of the newer `This Old Man` program is the `verse()` function. Rather than having a different function for each verse, I wrote one function that can work for all the verses. After careful analysis of the song, I noticed that each verse is remarkably similar to the others. The only thing that differentiates each verse is what the old man played (which is always the verse number) and where he played it (which is something rhyming with the verse number). If I can indicate which verse to play, it should be easy enough to produce the correct verse.

Notice that when the main body calls the `verse()` function, it always indicates a verse number in parentheses. For example, it makes a reference to `verse(1)` and `verse(3)`. These commands both call the `verse` function, but they send different values (`1` and `3`) to the function. Take another look at the code for the `verse()` function to see how the function responds to these inputs:

```
function verse($stanza){
  switch ($stanza){
    case 1:
      $place = "thumb";
      break;
    case 2:
      $place = "shoe";
      break;
    case 3:
      $place = "knee";
      break;
```

```
    case 4:
      $place = "door";
      break;
    default:
      $place = "I don't know where";
  } // end switch

  $output = <<<HERE
  This old man, he played $stanza<br>
  He played knick-knack on my $place<br><br>
HERE;
  return $output;
} // end verse
```

In this function, I indicated `$stanza` as a parameter in the function definition. A parameter is simply a variable associated with the function. If you create a function with a parameter, you are required to supply some sort of value whenever you call the function. The parameter variable automatically receives the value from the main body. For example, if the program says `verse(1)`, the `verse` function is called and the `$stanza` variable contains the value `1`. I then used a `switch` statement to populate the `$place` variable based on the value of `$stanza`. Finally, I created the `$output` variable using the `$stanza` and `$place` variables and returned the value of `$output`.

You can create functions with multiple parameters. Simply declare several variables inside the parentheses of the function definition, and be sure to call the function with the appropriate number of arguments. Make sure to separate parameters with commas.

In the Real World

If you're an experienced programmer, you probably know other ways to make this code even more efficient. You return to this program as you learn about loops and arrays in the coming chapters.

Managing Variable Scope

You have learned some ways to have your main program share variable information with your functions. In addition to parameter passing, sometimes you want your functions to have access to variables created in the main program. This is especially true because all the variables automatically created by PHP (such as those coming from forms) are generated at the main level. You must tell PHP when you want a function to use a variable created at the main level. These program-level variables are also called *global* variables.

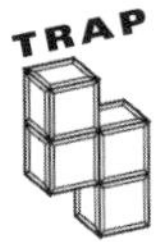

If you've programmed in another language, you're bound to get confused by the way PHP handles global variables. In most languages, any variable created at the main level is automatically available to every function. In PHP, you must explicitly request that a variable be global inside a function. If you don't do this, a new local variable with the same name (and no value) is created at the function level.

Looking at the Scope Demo

To illustrate the notion of global variables, take a look at the `Scope Demo`, shown in Figure 3.16.

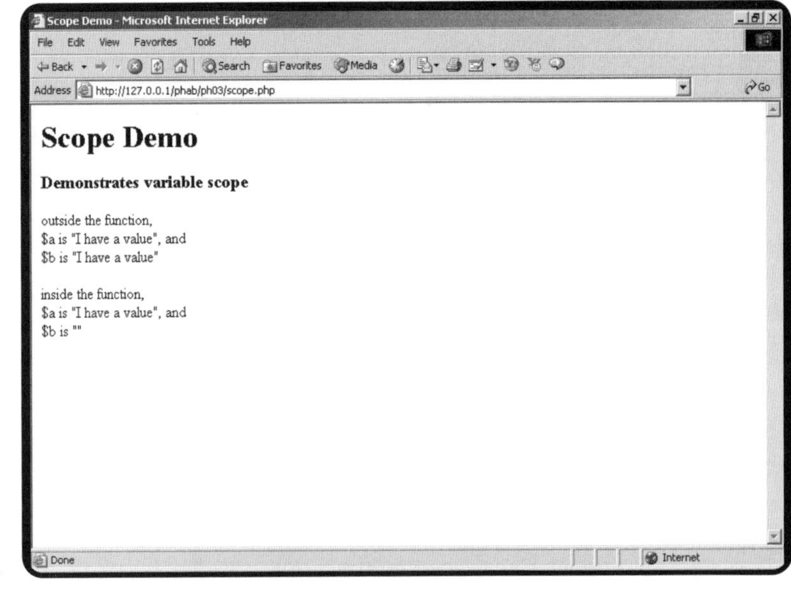

FIGURE 3.16

Variable $a keeps its value inside a function, but $b does not.

Take a look at the code for the `Scope Demo` and see how it works:

```
<html>
<head>
<title>Scope Demo</title>
</head>
<body>
<h1>Scope Demo</h1>
<h3>Demonstrates variable scope</h3>
```

```
<?

$a = "I have a value";
$b = "I have a value";

print <<<HERE
  outside the function, <br>
  \$a is "$a", and<br>
  \$b is "$b"<br><br>
HERE;

myFunction();

function myFunction(){

  //make $a global, but not $b
  global $a;

  print <<<HERE
    inside the function, <br>
    \$a is "$a", and<br>
    \$b is "$b"<br><br>
HERE;
} // end myFunction

?>

</body>
</html>
```

I created two variables for this demonstration: `$a` and `$b`. I gave them both the value `I have a value`. As a test, I printed out the values for both `$a` and `$b`.

Notice the trick I used to make the actual dollar sign show up in the quotation marks. When PHP sees a dollar sign inside quotation marks, it usually expects to be working with a variable. Sometimes (as in this case) you really want to print a dollar sign. You can precede a dollar sign with a backslash to have the sign appear. So, `print $a` **prints the value of the variable** `$a`**, but** `print \$a` **prints the value** `"$a"`**.**

Returning to the Petals Game

At the beginning of this chapter I show you the `Petals Around the Rose` game. This game uses all the skills you have learned so far, including the new concepts from this chapter. If you haven't already done so, play the game now so you can see how it works.

Here's the basic plan of the `Petals` game: Each time the page is drawn, it randomly generates five dice and calculates the correct number of petals based on a super-secret formula. The page includes a form that has a text area called `guess` for the user to enter the answer. The form also includes a hidden field called `numPetals`, which tells the program what the correct answer was.

CAN'T THE PROGRAM REMEMBER THE RIGHT ANSWER?

Since the program generated the correct answer in the first place, you might be surprised to learn that the right answer must be hidden in the Web page and then retrieved by the same program that generated it. Each contact between the client and the server is completely new.

When the user first plays the game, the page is sent to the browser and the connection is completely severed until the user hits the `submit` button. When the user submits the form, the `Petals` program starts over again. It's possible the user plays the game right before he goes to bed, then leaves the page on the computer overnight. Meanwhile, a hundred other people might use the program. For now, use hidden data to help keep track of the user's situation. Later in this book you learn some other clever methods for keeping track of the users' situations.

The `Petals` game doesn't introduce anything new, but it's a little longer than any of the other programs you've seen so far. I introduce the code in smaller chunks. All the code is shown in order, but not in one long code sample. Look on the CD for the program in its entirety.

Starting HTML

Like most PHP programs, the `Petals` game uses some HTML to set everything up. The HTML is pretty basic because PHP code creates most of the interesting HTML.

```
<HTML>
<head>
<title>Petals Around the Rose</title>
```

```
</head>
<body bgcolor = "tan">
<center>
<font face = "Comic Sans MS">
<h1>Petals Around the Rose</h1>
```

I decided on a tan background with a whimsical font. This should give the program a light feel.

Main Body Code

The main PHP code segment has three main jobs: print a greeting, print the dice, and print the form for the next turn. These jobs are (appropriately enough) stored in three different functions. One goal of encapsulation is to make the main code body as clean as possible. This goal is achieved in the `Petals` game.

```
<?

printGreeting();
printDice();
printForm();
```

All the real work is passed off to the various functions, which are described shortly. Even before you see the functions themselves, you have a good idea what each function does and a good sense of the program's overall flow. Encapsulating your code and naming your functions well makes your code much easier to read and repair.

The printGreeting() Function

The `printGreeting()` function prints one of three possible greetings to the user. If the user has never called this program before, the program should provide a welcome. If the user has been here before, she has guessed the number of petals. That guess might be correct (in which case a congratulatory message is appropriate) or incorrect, requiring information about what the correct answer was. The `printGreeting()` function uses a `switch` statement to handle the various options.

```
function printGreeting(){
  global $guess, $numPetals;
  if (empty($guess)){
    print "<h3>Welcome to Petals Around the Rose</h3>";
```

```
  } else if ($guess == $numPetals){
    print "<h3>You Got It!</h3>";
  } else {

    print <<<HERE

      <h3>from last try: </h3>
      you guessed: $guess<br><br>
      -and the correct answer was: $numPetals petals around the rose<br>
HERE;

  } // end if

} // end printGreeting
```

This function refers to both the `$guess` and `$numPetals` variables, which are automatically created. You can use one `global` statement to make more than one variable global by separating the variables with commas.

The `$guess` variable is empty if this is the first time the user has come to the program. If `$guess` is empty, I print a welcoming greeting. The user has guessed correctly if `$guess` is equal to `$numPetals`, so I print an appropriate congratulations. If neither of these conditions is true (which is most of the time), the function prints out a slightly more complex string indicating the user's last guess and the correct answer. This should give the user enough information to finally solve the riddle.

The `else if` structure turns out to be the easiest option for handling the three possible conditions I want to check.

The printDice() Function

After the program prints a greeting, it does the important business of generating the random dice. It's relatively easy to generate random dice, as you saw earlier in this chapter. However, I also wanted to be efficient and calculate the correct number of petals. To make the `printDice()` function more efficient, it calls some other custom functions.

```
function printDice(){
  global $numPetals;

  print "<h3>New Roll:</h3>";
  $numPetals = 0;
```

```
  $die1 = rand(1,6);
  $die2 = rand(1,6);
  $die3 = rand(1,6);
  $die4 = rand(1,6);
  $die5 = rand(1,6);

  showDie($die1);
  showDie($die2);
  showDie($die3);
  showDie($die4);
  showDie($die5);

  print "<br>";

  calcNumPetals($die1);
  calcNumPetals($die2);
  calcNumPetals($die3);
  calcNumPetals($die4);
  calcNumPetals($die5);

} // end printDice
```

The `printDice()` function is very concerned with the `$numPetals` variable, but doesn't need access to `$guess`. It requests access to `$numPetals` from the main program. After printing out the `"New Roll"` message, it resets `$numPetals` to `0`. The value of `$numPetals` is recalculated each time the dice are rolled.

I got new dice values by calling the `rand(1, 6)` function six times. I stored each result in a different variable, named `$die1` to `$die6`. To print out an appropriate graphic for each die, I called the `showDie()` function. I printed out a line break, then called the `calcNumPetals()` function once for each die.

The showDie() Function

The `showDie()` function is used to simplify repetitive code. It accepts a die value as a parameter and generates the appropriate HTML code for drawing a die with the corresponding number of dots.

```
function showDie($value){
  print <<<HERE
  <img src = "die$value.jpg"
       height = 100
```

```
        width = 100>
HERE;
} // end showDie
```

One advantage of using functions for repetitive HTML code is the ease with which you can modify large sections of code. For example, if you wish to change image sizes, change the `img` tag in this one function. All six die images are changed.

The calcNumPetals Function

The `printDice()` function also calls `calcNumPetals()` once for each die. This function receives a die value as a parameter. It also references the `$numPetals` global variable. The function uses a `switch` statement to determine how much to add to `$numPetals` based on the current die's value.

Here's the trick: The center dot of the die is the rose. Any dots around the center dot are the petals. The value `1` has a rose but no petals; `2`, `4`, and `6` have petals, but no rose; `3` has two petals; `5` has four. If the die roll is 3, `$numPetals` should be increased by `2`; if the roll is 5, `$numPetals` should be increased by `4`.

```
function calcNumPetals($value){

  global $numPetals;

  switch ($value) {
    case 3:
      $numPetals += 2;
      break;
    case 5:
      $numPetals += 4;
      break;
  } // end switch

} // end calcNumPetals
```

The `+=` code is a shorthand notation. The line shown here

```
$numPetals += 2;
```

is exactly equivalent to this line:

```
$numPetals = $numPetals + 2;
```

The first style is much shorter and easier to type, so it's the form most programmers prefer.

The printForm() Function

The purpose of the `printForm()` function is to print the form at the bottom of the HTML page. This form is pretty straightforward except for the need to place the hidden field for `$numPetals`.

```
function printForm(){
  global $numPetals;

  print <<<HERE

  <h3>How many petals around the rose?</h3>

  <form method = "post">
  <input type = "text"
         name = "guess"
         value = "0">
  <input type = "hidden"
         name = "numPetals"
         value = "$numPetals">
  <br>
  <input type = "submit">
  </form>
  <br>
  <a href = "petalHelp.html"
     target = "helpPage">
  give me a hint</a>
HERE;

} // end printForm
```

This code places the form on the page. I could have done most of the form in plain HTML without needing PHP for anything but the hidden field. However, when I start using PHP, I like to have much of my code in PHP. It helps me see the flow of things more clearly (print greeting, print dice, and print form, for example).

The Ending HTML Code

The final set of HTML code closes everything up. It completes the PHP segment, the font, the centered text, the body, and finally, the HTML itself.

```
?>
</font>
</center>
</body>
</html>
```

Summary

You learn a lot in this chapter. You learned several kinds of branching structures, including the `if` clause, `else` statements, and the `switch` structure. You know how to write functions, which make your programs much more efficient and easier to read. You know how to pass parameters to functions and return values from them. You can access global variables from inside functions. You put all these things together to make an interesting game. You should be very proud! In the next chapter you learn how to use looping structures to make your programs even more powerful.

CHALLENGES

1. **Write a program that generates 4-, 10-, or 20-sided dice.**
2. **Write a program that lets the user choose how many sides a die has and print a random roll with the appropriate maximum values. (Don't worry about using images to display the dice.)**
3. **Write a `Loaded Dice` program that half the time generates the value `1` and half the time generates some other value.**
4. **Modify the story game from chapter 2, "Using Variables and Input," so the form and the program are one file.**
5. **Create a Web page generator. Make a form for the page caption, background color, font color, and text body. Use this form to generate an HTML page.**

Loops and Arrays

You know all a program's basic parts, but your programs can be much easier to write and more efficient when you know some other things. In this chapter you learn about two very important tools, arrays and looping structures. *Arrays* are special variables that form lists. *Looping structures* repeat certain code segments. As you might expect, arrays and loops often work together. You learn how to use these new elements to make more interesting programs. Specifically, you do these things:

- Use the `for` loop to build basic counting structures
- Modify the `for` loop for different kinds of counting
- Use a `while` loop for more flexible looping
- Identify the keys to successful loops
- Create basic arrays
- Write programs that use arrays and loops
- Store information in hidden fields

Introducing the Poker Dice Program

The main program for this chapter is a simplified dice game. In this game, you are given $100 of virtual money. On each turn, you bet two dollars. The computer rolls five dice. You can elect to keep each die or roll it again. On the second roll, the computer checks for various combinations. You can earn money back for rolling pairs, triples, four or five of a kind, and straights (five numbers in a row). Figures 4.1 and 4.2 illustrate the game in action.

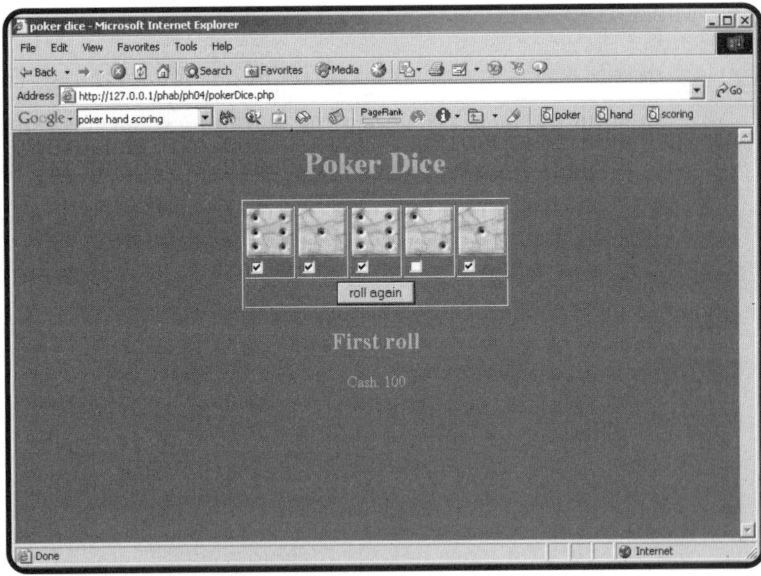

FIGURE 4.1

After the first roll, you can keep some of the dice by selecting the checkboxes underneath each die.

The basic concepts of this game are much like the ones you use in other chapters' programs. Keeping track of all five dice can get complicated, so this program uses arrays and loops to manage all the information.

Counting with the for Loop

You might want the computer to repeat some sort of action multiple times. Good thing computers excel at repetitive behavior. For example, take a look at the `simpleFor.php` program shown in Figure 4.3.

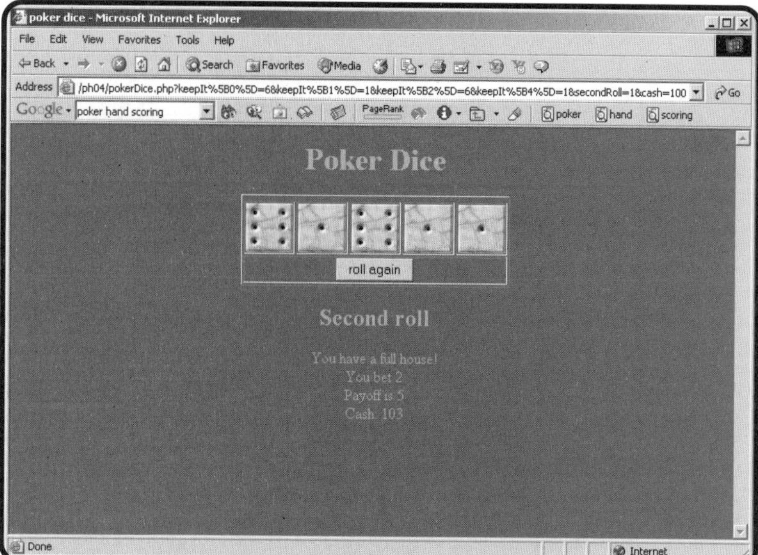

FIGURE 4.2

The player has earned back some money with a full house!

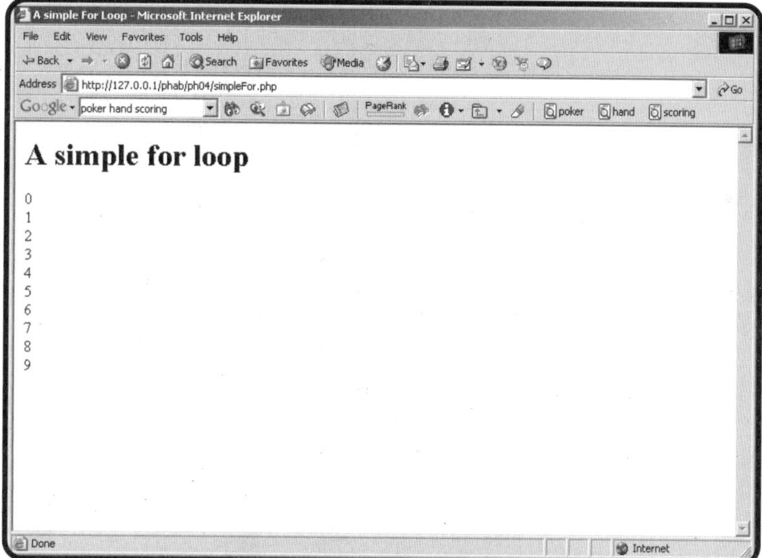

FIGURE 4.3

This program counts from zero to one using only one `print` statement.

While the output of the `simpleFor.php` program doesn't look all that interesting, it has a unique characteristic. It has only one `print` statement in the entire program, which is executed 10 different times. Take a look at the source code to see how it works:

```
<html>
```

```
<head>
<title>
A simple For Loop
</title>
</head>

<body>

<h1>A simple for loop</h1>

<?

for ($i = 0; $i < 10; $i++){
  print "$i <br>\n";
} // end for loop

?>

</body>
</html>
```

Each number is printed in the line that looks like this:

```
print "$i <br>\n";
```

This line can print only one value, but it happens 10 times. The key to this behavior is the `for` statement. The `for` structure has three main parts: a variable declaration, a condition, and an increment statement.

The `\n` character signifies a *newline* or carriage return. This means that the program's HTML source code places each number on a separate line. The `<br>` tag ensures that the HTML output also places each number on its own line. While carriage returns in the HTML source don't have much to do with how the output looks, I like my programs' code to be written as carefully as the stuff I build by hand.

Initializing a Sentry Variable

`for` loops usually involve an integer (non-decimal) variable. Sometimes the key variable in a loop is referred to as a *sentry variable,* because it acts like a gatekeeper to the loop. The first part of a `for` loop definition is a line of code that identifies and initializes the sentry variable to some starting value. In the simple `for` loop demo, the initialization segment looks like this:

```
$i = 0;
```

It specifies that the sentry variable be called `$i` and its starting value be `0`.

IN THE REAL WORLD

You might wonder why the sentry variable is called `$i`. Like most variables, it's best if sentry variables have a name that suits their purpose. Sometimes, however, a `for` loop sentry is simply an integer and doesn't have any other meaning. In those situations, an old programming tradition is often called into play.

In the Fortran language (one of the earliest common programming languages), all integer variables had to begin with the letters *i, j,* and a few other characters. Fortran programmers would commonly use *i* as the name of generic sentry variables. Even though most modern programmers have never written a line of Fortran code, the tradition remains. It's amazing how much folklore exists in such a relatively new activity as computer programming.

Computer programs frequently begin counting with zero, so I initialized `$i` to `0` as well.

Although the `$i = 0;` segment looks like (and is) a complete line of code, it is usually placed on the same line as the other parts of the `for` loop construct.

Setting a Condition to Finish the Loop

Getting a computer to repeat behavior is the easy part. The harder task comes when trying to get the computer to stop correctly. The second part of the `for` loop construct is a condition. When this condition is evaluated as `TRUE`, the loop should continue. The loop should exit as soon as the condition is evaluated to `FALSE`. In this case, I set the condition as `$i < 10`. This means that as long as the variable `$i` has a value less than `10`, the loop continues. As soon as the program detects that `$i` has a value equal to or larger than `10`, the loop exits. Usually a `for` loop's condition checks the sentry variable against some terminal or ending value.

Changing the Sentry Variable

The final critical element of a `for` loop is some mechanism for changing the value of the sentry variable. At some point the value of `$i` must become `10` or larger or the loop continues forever. In the `basicLoop` program, the part of the `for` structure that makes this happen looks like `$i++`. The notation `$i++` is just like saying *add one to $i* or `$i = $i + 1`. The ++ symbol is called an *increment operator* because it provides an easy way to increment (add 1) to a variable.

Building the Loop

Once you've set up the parts of the `for` statement, the loop itself is easy to use. Place braces (`{}`) around your code and indent all code that's inside the loop. You can have as many lines of code as you wish inside a loop, including branching statements and other loops.

The sentry variable has special behavior inside the loop. It begins with the initial value. Each time the loop repeats, it is changed as specified in the `for` structure, and the interpreter checks the condition to ensure that it's still true. If so, the code in the loop occurs again.

In the case of the `basicArray` program, `$i` begins as `0`. The first time the `print` statement occurs, it prints `0` because that is the current value of `$i`. When the interpreter reaches the right brace that ends the loop, it increments `$i` by 1 (following the `$i++` directive in the `for` structure) and checks the condition (`$i < 10`).

Because `0` is less than `10`, the condition is true and the code inside the loop occurs again. Eventually, the value of `$i` becomes 10, so the condition (`$i < 10`) is no longer true. Program control then reverts to the next line of code after the end of the loop, which ends the program.

Modifying the for Loop

Once you understand `for` loop structure basics, you can modify it in a couple of interesting ways. You can build a loop that counts by fives or that counts backwards.

Counting by Fives

The `countByFive.php` program shown in Figure 4.4 illustrates a program that counts by fives.

The program is very much like the `basicArray` program, but with a couple of twists.

```
<html>

<head>
<title>
```

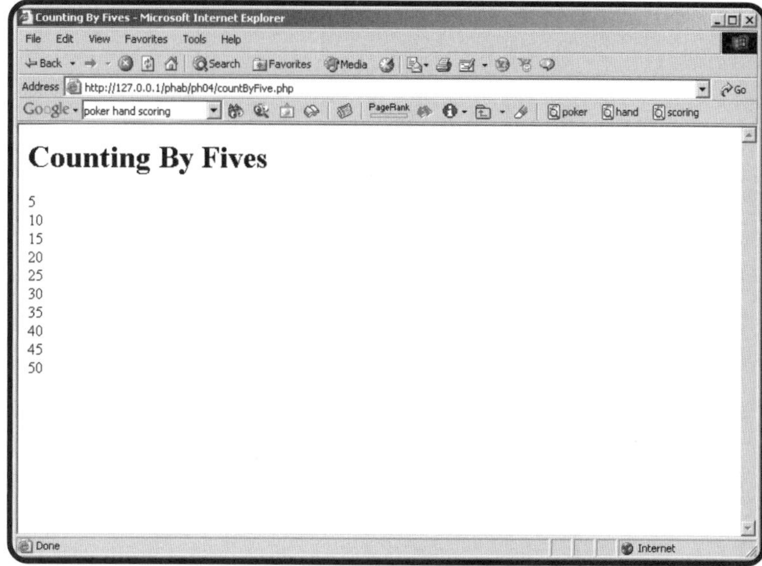

FIGURE 4.4

This program uses a `for` loop to count by five.

```
Counting By Fives
</title>
</head>

<body>

<h1>Counting By Fives</h1>

<?

for ($i = 5; $i <= 50; $i+= 5){
  print "$i <br>\n";
} // end for loop

?>

</body>

</html>
```

The only thing I changed was the various parameters in the `for` statement. Since it seems silly to start counting at `0`, I set the initial value of `$i` to `5`. I decided to stop when `$i` reached `50` (after 10 iterations). Each time through the loop, `$i` is incremented by five.

The += syntax in the following code increments a variable:

```
$i += 5;
```

The above is the same thing as this:

```
$i = $i + 5;
```

Counting Backwards

It is fairly simple to modify a `for` loop so it counts backwards. Figure 4.5 illustrates this feat.

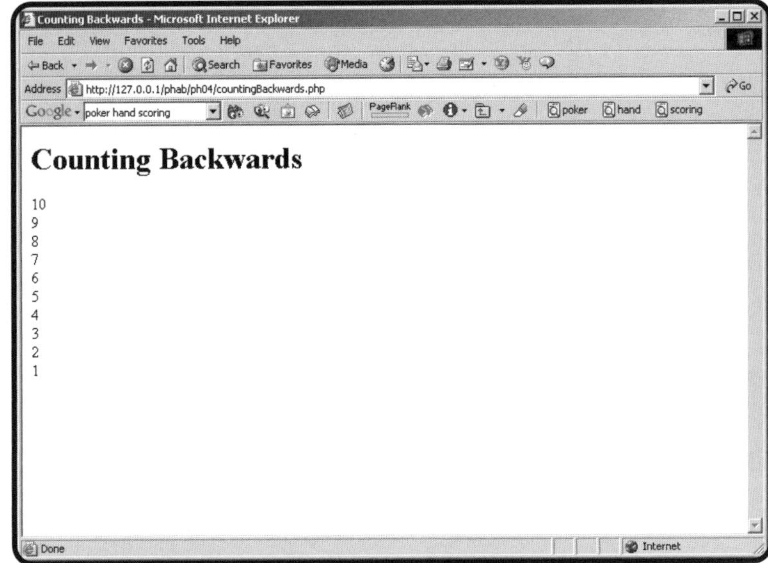

FIGURE 4.5

This program counts backwards from 10 to 1 using a `for` loop.

Once again, the basic structure is just like the basic `for` loop program, but changing the `for` structure parameters alters the program's behavior. The code for this program shows how it is done:

```
<html>

<head>
<title>
Counting Backwards
</title>
</head>

<body>
```

```
<h1>Counting Backwards</h1>

<?

for ($i = 10; $i > 0; $i--){
  print "$i <br>\n";
} // end for loop

?>


</body>
</html>
```

If you understand how `for` loops work, the changes all make sense. I'm counting backwards this time, so `$i` begins with a large value (in this case `10`). The condition for continuing the loop is now `$i > 0`, which means the loop continues as long as `$i` is greater than `0`. The loop ends as soon as `$i` is `0` or less.

Note that rather than adding a value to `$i`, this time I decrement by 1 each time through the loop. If you're counting backwards, be very careful that the sentry variable has a mechanism for getting smaller. Otherwise the loop never ends. Recall that `$i++` adds 1 to `$i`; `$i--` subtracts 1 from `$i`.

Using a while Loop

PHP, like most languages, provides another kind of looping structure even more flexible than the `for` loop. You can use the `while` loop when you know how many times something will happen. Figure 4.6 shows how a `while` loop can work much like a `for` loop.

Repeating Code with a while Loop

The code for the `while.php` program is much like the `for` loop example, but you can see that the `while` loop is a little bit simpler:

```
<html>

<head>
<title>
A simple While Loop
</title>
```

```
</head>

<body>

<h1>A simple while loop</h1>

<?

$i = 1;

while ($i <= 10){
  print "$i <br>\n";
  $i++;
} // end while

?>

</body>
</html>
```

The `while` loop requires only one parameter, which is a condition. The loop continues as long as the condition is evaluated as `TRUE`. As soon as the condition is evaluated as `FALSE`, the loop exits.

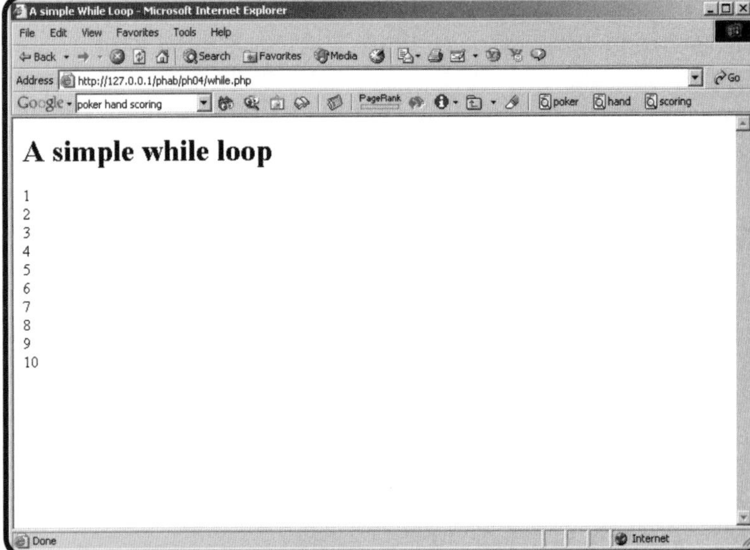

FIGURE 4.6

Although this program's output looks a lot like the basic `for` loop, it uses a different construct to achieve the same result.

This particular program starts by initializing the variable `$i`, then checking to see if it's greater than or equal to `10` in the `while` statement. Inside the loop body, the program prints the current value of `$i` and increments `$i`.

Recognizing Endless Loops

The flexibility of the `while` construct gives it power, but with that power comes potential for problems. `while` loops are easy to build, but a loop that works improperly can cause a lot of trouble. It's possible that the code in the loop will never execute at all. Even worse, you might have some sort of logical error that causes the loop to continue indefinitely. As an example, look at the `badWhile.php` code:

```
<html>

<head>
<title>
A bad While Loop
</title>
</head>

<body>

<h1>A bad while loop</h1>

<?

$i = 1;

while ($i <= 10){
  print "$i <br>\n";
  $j++;
} // end while

?>

</body>
</html>
```

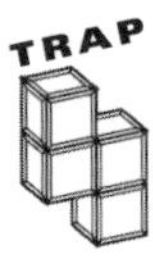

The `badWhile.php` program shows what happens when you have an endless loop in your code. If you run this program, it may temporarily slow down your Web server. Be sure your server is configured to stop a PHP process when the user presses the `stop` button on the browser. (This is a default setting on most PHP installations.)

The `badWhile.php` program has a subtle but deadly error. Look carefully at the source code and see if you can spot it. The code is just like the first `while` program, except instead of incrementing `$i`, I incremented `$j`. The variable `$j` has nothing to do with `$i` and `$i` never changes. The loop keeps going on forever, because it cannot end until `$i` is greater than or equal to `10`, which never happens. This program is an example of the classic *endless loop.* Every programmer alive has written them accidentally, and you will too.

Usually the culprit of an endless loop is a sloppy variable name, spelling, or capitalization. If you use a variable like `$myCounter` as the sentry variable but then increment `$MyCounter`, PHP tracks two entirely different variables. Your program won't work correctly. This is another reason to be consistent on your variable naming and capitalization conventions.

Building a Well-Behaved Loop

Fortunately, you have guidelines for building a loop that behaves as you wish. Even better, you've already learned most of the important ideas, because these fundamental concepts are built into the `for` loop's structure. When you write a `while` loop, you are responsible for these three things:

- Creating a sentry variable
- Building a condition
- Ensuring the loop can exit

I discuss each of these ideas in the following sections.

Creating and Initializing a Sentry Variable

If your loop is based on a variable's value (there are alternatives), make sure you do these three things:

- Identify that variable.
- Ensure that variable has appropriate scope.
- Make sure that variable has a reasonable starting value.

You might also check that value to ensure the loop runs at least one time (at least if that's your intent). Creating a variable is much like the initialization stage of a `for` construct.

Building a Condition to Continue the Loop

Your condition usually compares a variable and a value. Make sure you have a condition that can be met and be broken. The hard part is ensuring that the program gets out of the loop at the correct time. This condition is much like the condition in the `for` loop.

Ensuring the Loop Can Exit

There must be some trigger that changes the sentry variable so the loop can exit. This code must exist inside the code body. Be sure it is possible for the sentry variable to achieve the value necessary to exit the loop by making the condition `false`.

Working with Basic Arrays

Programming is about the combination of control structures (like loops) and data structures (like variables). You know the very powerful looping structures. Now it's time to look at a data structure that works naturally with loops.

Arrays are special variables made to hold lists of information. PHP makes it quite easy to work with arrays. Look at Figure 4.7, whose `basicArray.php` program demonstrates two arrays.

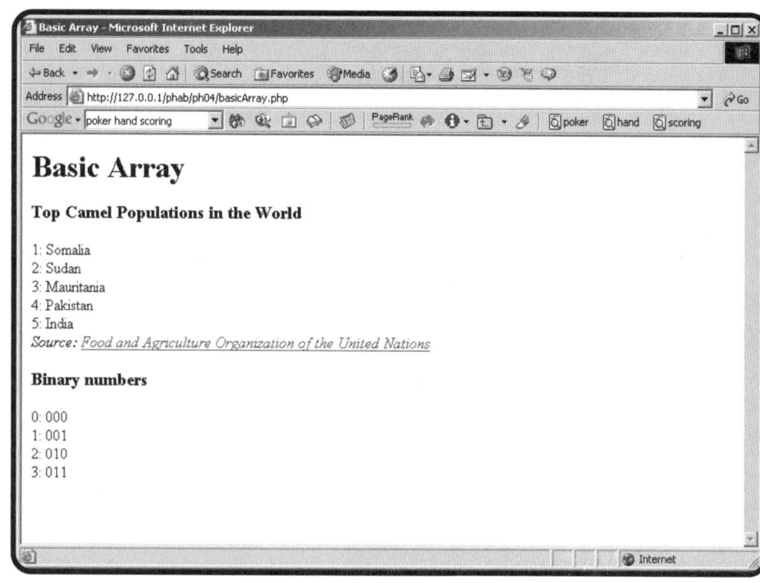

FIGURE 4.7

The information displayed on this page is stored in two array variables.

First look over the entire program, then see how it does its work.

```
<html>
<head>
<title>
Basic Array
</title>
</head>

<body>

<h1>Basic Array</h1>

<?

//simply assign values to array
$camelPop[1] = "Somalia";
$camelPop[2] = "Sudan";
$camelPop[3] = "Mauritania";
$camelPop[4] = "Pakistan";
$camelPop[5] = "India";

//output array values
print "<h3>Top Camel Populations in the World</h3>\n";
for ($i = 1; $i <= 5; $i++){
  print "$i: $camelPop[$i]<br>\n";
} // end for loop

print "<i>Source: <a href = http://www.fao.org/ag/aga/glipha/index.jsp>
Food and Agriculture Organization of the United Nations</a></i>\n";

//use array function to load up array
$binary = array("000", "001", "010", "011");

print "<h3>Binary numbers</h3>\n";
for ($i = 0; $i < count($binary); $i++){
  print "$i: $binary[$i]<br>\n";
} // end for loop

?>

</body>
</html>
```

Generating a Basic Array

Look at the lines that describe `$camelPop`:

```
//simply assign values to array
$camelPop[1] = "Somalia";
$camelPop[2] = "Sudan";
$camelPop[3] = "Mauritania";
$camelPop[4] = "Pakistan";
$camelPop[5] = "India";
```

The `$camelPop` variable is a variable meant to hold the five countries with the largest camel populations in the world. (If this array stuff isn't working for you, at least you've learned something in this chapter!) Since `$camelPop` is going to hold the names of five different countries, it makes sense that this is an *array* (computer geek lingo for list) rather than an ordinary variable.

The only thing different about `$camelPop` and all the other variables you've worked with so far is `$camelPop` can have multiple values. To tell these values apart, use a numeric index in square brackets.

Apparently the boxer George Foreman has several sons also named George. I've often wondered what Mrs. Foreman does when she wants somebody to take out the trash. I suspect she has assigned a number to each George, so there is no ambiguity. This is exactly how arrays work. Each element has the same name, but a different numerical index so you can tell them apart.

Many languages require you to explicitly create array variables, but PHP is very easygoing in this regard. Simply assign a value to a variable with an index in square brackets and you've created an array.

Even though PHP is good natured about letting you create an array variable on-the-fly, you might get a warning about this behavior on those Web servers that have error reporting set to `E_ALL`. If that's the case, you can create an empty array with the `array()` function described in the following sections and then add values to it.

Using a Loop to Examine an Array's Contents

Arrays go naturally with `for` loops. Very often when you have an array variable, you step through all of its values and do something to each one. In this example, I want to print the index and the corresponding country's name. Here's the `for` loop that performs this task:

```
//output array values
print "<h3>Top Camel Populations in the World</h3>\n";
for ($i = 1; $i <= 5; $i++){
  print "$i: $camelPop[$i]<br>\n";
} // end for loop
```

Because I know the array indices will vary between `1` and `5`, I set up my loop so the value of `$i` will go from `1` to `5`. Inside the loop, I simply print the index (`$i`) and the corresponding country (`$camelPop[$i]`). The first time through the loop, `$i` is `1`, so `$camelPop[$i]` is `$camelPop[1]`, which is `Somalia`. Each time through the loop, the value of `$i` is incremented, so eventually every array element is displayed.

The advantage of combining loops and arrays is convenience. If you want to do something with each element of an array, you only have to write the code one time, then put that code inside a loop. This is especially powerful when you start designing programs that work with large amounts of data. If, for example, I want to list the camel population of every country in the UN database rather than simply the top five countries, all I have to do is make a bigger array and modify the `for` loop.

Using the array() Function to Preload an Array

Often you start out knowing exactly which values you want placed in an array. PHP provides a shortcut for loading an array with a set of values.

```
//use array function to load up array
$binary = array("000", "001", "010", "011");
```

In this example, I create an array of the first four binary digits (starting at zero). The `array` keyword can assign a list of values to an array. Note that when you use this technique, the indices of the elements are created for you.

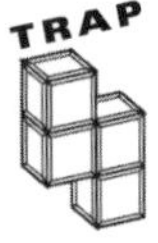

Most computer languages automatically begin counting things with zero rather than one (the way humans tend to count). This can cause confusion. When PHP builds an array for you, the first index is `0` automatically, not `1`.

Detecting the Size of an Array

Arrays are meant to add flexibility to your code. You don't actually need to know how many elements are in an array, because PHP provides a function called `count()`, which can determine how many elements an array has. In the following code, I use the `count()` function to determine the array size:

```
print "<h3>Binary numbers</h3>\n";
for ($i = 0; $i < count($binary); $i++){
  print "$i: $binary[$i]<br>\n";
} // end for loop
```

Note that my loop sentry goes from `0` to `1` less than the number of elements in the array. If you have four elements in an array and the array begins with `0`, the largest index is `3`. This is a standard way of looping through an array.

Since it is so common to step through arrays, PHP provides another kind of loop that makes this even easier. You get a chance to see that looping structure in chapter 5, "Better Arrays and String Handling." For now, understand how an ordinary `for` loop is used with an array.

Improving This Old Man with Arrays and Loops

The `basicArray.php` program shows how to build arrays, but it doesn't illustrate the power of arrays and loops working together. To see how these features can help you, revisit an old friend from chapter 3, "Controlling Your Code with Conditions and Functions." The version of the `This Old Man` program featured in Figure 4.8 looks a lot like it did in chapter 3, but the code is quite a bit more compact.

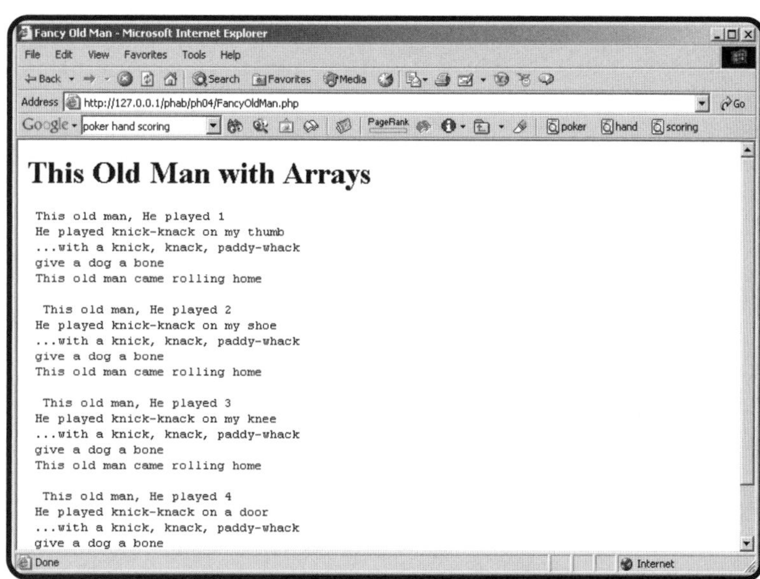

FIGURE 4.8

The `Fancy Old Man` program uses a more compact structure than `This Old Man`.

The improvements in this version are only apparent when you look under the hood:

```
<html>
<head>
<title>
Fancy Old Man
</title>
</head>
<body>
<h1>This Old Man with Arrays</h1>
<pre>
<?
$place = array(
  "",
  "on my thumb",
  "on my shoe",
  "on my knee",
  "on a door");

//print out song
for ($verse = 1; $verse <= 4; $verse++){

print <<<HERE
 This old man, He played $verse
 He played knick-knack $place[$verse]
 ...with a knick, knack, paddy-whack
 give a dog a bone
 This old man came rolling home


HERE;
  } // end for loop

?>
</pre>
</body>
</html>
```

This improved version takes advantage of the fact that the only things that change from verse to verse is the verse number and the place where the old man plays paddy-whack (whatever that means). Organizing the places into an array greatly simplify writing out the song lyrics.

Building the Place Array

I notice that each place is a string value associated with some number. I use the `array()` directive to preload the `$place` array with appropriate values. Zero has no corresponding place, so I simply left the `0` element blank.

```
$place = array(
  "",
  "on my thumb",
  "on my shoe",
  "on my knee",
  "on a door");
```

Like most places in PHP, carriage returns don't matter when you're writing the source code. I put each place on a separate line, just because it looked neater that way.

Writing Out the Lyrics

The song itself is incredibly repetitive. Each verse is identical except for the verse number and place. For each verse, the value of the `$verse` variable is the current verse number. The corresponding place is stored in `$place[$verse]`. A large `print` statement in a `for` loop prints the entire code.

```
//print out song
for ($verse = 1; $verse <= 4; $verse++){

print <<<HERE
 This old man, He played $verse
 He played knick-knack $place[$verse]
 ...with a knick, knack, paddy-whack
 give a dog a bone
 This old man came rolling home



HERE;
  } // end for loop
```

The `Fancy Old Man` program illustrates very nicely the tradeoff associated with using arrays. Creating a program that uses arrays correctly often takes a little more planning than using control structures alone (as in `This Old Man`). However, the extra work up front pays off because the program is easier to modify and extend.

Keeping Persistent Data

Most traditional kinds of programming presume that the user and the program are engaging in a continual dialog. A program begins running, might ask the user some questions, responds to these inputs, and continues interacting with the user until he indicates an interest in leaving the program.

Programs written on a Web server are different. The PHP programs you are writing have an incredibly short life span. When the user makes a request to your PHP program through a Web browser, the server runs the PHP *interpreter* (the program that converts your PHP code into the underlying machine language your server understands). The result of the program is a Web page that is sent back to the user's browser. Once your program sends a page to the user, the PHP program shuts down because its work is done. Web servers do not maintain contact with the browser after sending a page. Each request from the user is seen as an entirely new transaction.

The `Poker Dice` program at the beginning of this chapter appears to interact with the user indefinitely. Actually, the same program is being called repeatedly. The program acts differently in different circumstances. Somehow it needs to keep track of what state it's currently in.

In the Real World

The underlying Web protocol (HTTP) that Web servers use does not keep connections open any longer than necessary. This behavior is referred to as being a *stateless protocol.* Imagine if your program were kept running as long as anybody anywhere on the Web were looking at it. What if a person fired up your program and went to bed? Your Web server would have to maintain a connection to that page all night. Also remember that your program might be called by thousands of people all at the same time.

It can be very hard on your server to have all these concurrent connections open. Having stateless behavior improves your Web server's performance, but that performance comes at a cost. Essentially, your programs have complete amnesia every time they run. You need a mechanism for determining the current state.

Counting with Form Fields

You can store information a couple of ways, including files, XML, and databases. The second half of this book details these important ideas. The easiest approach to achieving data permanence is to hide the data in the user's page. To illustrate, take a look at Figures 4.9 and 4.10.

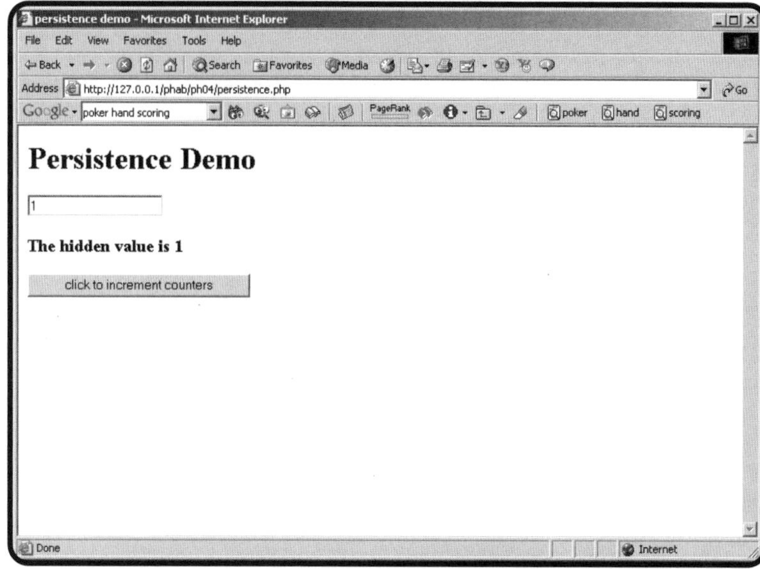

FIGURE 4.9

The program has two counters that read `1` when the program is run the first time.

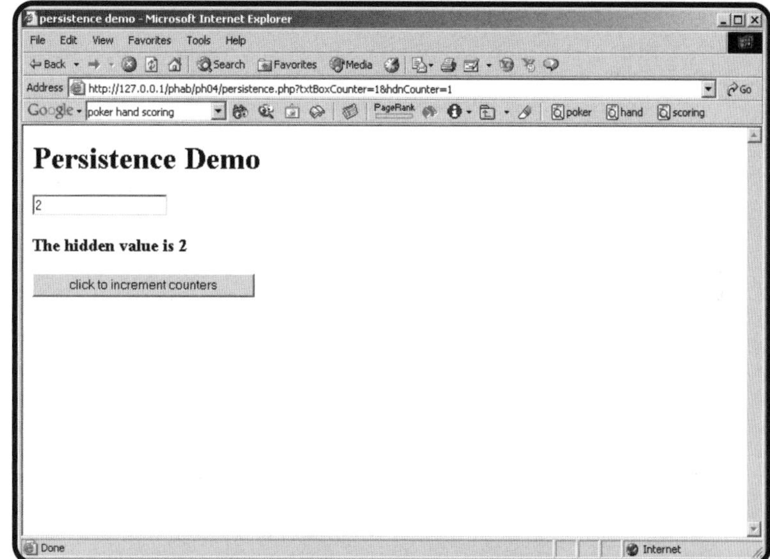

FIGURE 4.10

Both values are incremented after the user clicks the `submit` button.

Each time you click the `Persistence` program's `submit` button, the counters increment by one. The program behavior appears to contradict the basic nature of server-side programs because it seems to remember the previous counter value. In fact, if two users were accessing the `Persistence` program at the same time, each would count correctly. Look at the source code to see how it works:

```
<html>
<head>
<title>
persistence demo
</title>
</head>

<body>

<h1>Persistence Demo</h1>
<form>
<?
//increment the counters
$txtBoxCounter++;
$hdnCounter++;

print <<<HERE

<input type = "text"
       name = "txtBoxCounter"
       value = "$txtBoxCounter">

<input type = "hidden"
       name = "hdnCounter"
       value = "$hdnCounter">
<h3>The hidden value is $hdnCounter</h3>
<input type = "submit"
       value = "click to increment counters">
HERE;

?>

</form>
</body>
</html>
```

Storing Data in the Text Box

The program has two variables: `$txtBoxCounter` and `$hdnCounter`. For now, concentrate on `$txtBoxCounter`, which is related to the text box. When the program begins, it grabs the value of `$txtBoxCounter` (if it exists) and adds one to it. When the program prints the text box, it automatically places the `$txtBoxCounter` value in the text box.

Since the form has no action attribute defined, the program automatically calls itself when the user clicks the `submit` button. This time, `$txtBoxCounter` has a value (`1`). When the program runs again, it increments `$txtBoxCounter` and stores the new value (now `2`) in the text box. Each time the program runs, it stores in the text box the value it needs on the *next* run.

Using a Hidden Field for Persistence

The text box is convenient for this example because you can see it, but using a text box this way in real programs causes serious problems. Text boxes are editable by the user, which means she could insert any kind of information and really mess up your day.

Hidden form fields are the unsung heroes of server-side programming. Look at `$hdnCounter` in the source code. This hidden field also has a counter, but the user never sees it. However, the value of the `$hdnCounter` variable is sent to the PHP program indicated by the form's `action` attribute. That program can do anything with the attribute, including printing it in the HTML code body.

Very often when you want to track information between pages, you store the information in hidden fields on the user's page.

The hidden fields technique shown here works fine for storing small amounts of information, but it is very inefficient and insecure when you are working with more serious forms of data.

Writing the Poker Dice Program

It's time to take another look at the `Poker Dice` program that made its debut at the beginning of this chapter. As usual, this program doesn't do anything you haven't already learned. It is a little more complex than the trivial sample programs I show you in this chapter, but it's surprisingly compact considering how much it does. It won't surprise you that arrays and loops are the secret to this program's success.

Setting Up the HTML

As always, a basic HTML page serves as the foundation for the PHP program. I add a simple style sheet to this page to make tan characters on a green background.

```
<html>
<head>
<title>poker dice</title>
<style type = "text/css">
body {
  background: green;
  color: tan;
}

</style>
</head>

<body>
<center>
<h1>Poker Dice</h1>

<form>

<?
```

Building the Main Code Body

The `Poker Dice` program is long enough to merit functions. I broke it into smaller segments here, but you may want to look at its entirety, which is on the CD that accompanies this book.

The main part of the code sets up the general program flow. Most of the work is done in other functions called from this main area.

```
//check to see if this is first time here
if (empty($cash)){
  $cash = 100;
} // end if

rollDice();

if ($secondRoll == TRUE){
  print "<h2>Second roll</h2>\n";
  $secondRoll = FALSE;
  evaluate();
} else {
```

```
  print "<h2>First roll</h2>\n";
  $secondRoll = TRUE;
} // end if

printStuff();
```

The first order of business: See if this is the first time the user has come to this page. It's important to understand how timing works in this program. The user thinks he is playing the same game for several turns, but the entire program runs again each time he rolls the dice. The program has different behavior based on which form elements (if any) have values. If the user has never been to the page before, the value for the `$cash` variable is `null`. The first `if` statement checks this condition. If the `$cash` variable has not yet been created, the user gets a starting value of $100. (I wish real casinos worked like this.)

The program then calls the `rollDice()` function, which is described momentarily. This function rolls the dice and prints them to the screen.

If you look carefully at the program as it is running, you see it runs in two different modes. Each turn consists of two possible rolls. On the first roll, the user is given the ability to save a roll with a checkbox. No scoring is performed. The second roll has no checkboxes (because the user needs to start with all fresh dice on the next turn). The program tracks the player's score by adding money for various combinations.

The `$secondRoll` variable keeps track of whether the user is on the second roll. I gave it the value `TRUE` when the user is on the second roll and `FALSE` when on the first roll. If `$secondRoll` is `TRUE`, the program calls the `evaluate()` function, which tallies any losses or winnings. Regardless, I inform the user which roll it is and change the value of `$secondRoll` to reflect what should happen the *next* time this program is called (which happens when the user clicks the `submit` button).

Making the rollDice() Function

The job of the `rollDice()` function is, well, to roll the dice. It's a somewhat long function, so I print it for you here and explain it in smaller chunks. Essentially, this function builds an HTML table based on five die rolls. It determines if the user kept any previous dice and rolls a new die only if she did not keep it. If it is the first roll, the program prints a checkbox, which allows the user to select a die to keep.

```
function rollDice(){
  global $die, $secondRoll, $keepIt;
```

```
  print "<table border = 1><td><tr>";

  for ($i = 0; $i < 5; $i++){
    if ($keepIt[$i] == ""){
      $die[$i] = rand(1, 6);
    } else {
      $die[$i] = $keepIt[$i];
    } // end if
    $theFile = "die" . $die[$i] . ".jpg";

    //print out dice images
    print <<<HERE
    <td>
    <img src = "$theFile"
         height = 50
         width = 50><br>

HERE;
    //print out a checkbox on first roll only
    if ($secondRoll == FALSE){
      print <<<HERE
    <input type = "checkbox"
           name = "keepIt[$i]"
           value = $die[$i]>
    </td>

HERE;

    } // end if
  } // end for loop

  //print out submit button and end of table
  print <<<HERE
  </tr></td>
  <tr>
    <td colspan = "5">
    <center>
    <input type = "submit"
           value = "roll again">
    </center>
```

```
      </td>
    </tr>
    </table>

HERE;

} // end rollDice
```

The checkboxes that appear sometimes are special. The general strategy for them is this: If it's the first turn, I print a checkbox under each die. All the checkboxes are called `keepIt` and all have an index. When PHP sees these variables with the same name but different indices, it automatically creates an array.

Recall from chapter 2, "Using Variables and Input," that PHP checkboxes are a little different than some of the other form elements. They only send a value if they are checked. Any checkbox the user does not check is not passed to the program. Any selected checkbox's value is passed to the program.

Rolling the Dice if Necessary

The program uses two arrays to keep track of the dice. The `$die` array stores the current values of all the dice. The `$keepIt` array contains no values unless the user has checked the corresponding checkbox (which only happens on the first roll, because the checkboxes are not printed on the second roll).

```
if ($keepIt[$i] == ""){
      $die[$i] = rand(1, 6);
    } else {
      $die[$i] = $keepIt[$i];
    } // end if
    $theFile = "die" . $die[$i] . ".jpg";
```

The program rolls a new value for each die if the user did not choose to keep it. If the user did choose to keep a die, the corresponding value of the `$keepIt` array is non-null, and this new value is transferred to the appropriate element in the `$die array.`

Printing the Table Contents

Print the image corresponding to each die after the function has determined a value for each (by copying from `$keepIt` or rolling a new value as appropriate).

```
//print out dice images
    print <<<HERE
```

```
    <td>
    <img src = "$theFile"
         height = 50
         width = 50><br>

HERE;
    //print out a checkbox on first roll only
    if ($secondRoll == FALSE){
      print <<<HERE
    <input type = "checkbox"
           name = "keepIt[$i]"
           value = $die[$i]>
    </td>

HERE;

    } // end if
```

If it's the first roll, the function also prints out the `keepIt` checkbox corresponding to this die. Note how the checkbox name corresponds to the die name. (Remember, the value `$i` is translated to a number before the HTML page is printed.) The value of the current die is stored as the value of the `keepIt` checkbox.

It can be hard to see how all this works together. It might help to run the program a couple of times and look carefully at the HTML source that's being generated. To fully understand a PHP program, you can't always look at it on the surface. You may need to see the HTML elements that are hidden from the user.

Printing the End of the Table

After the loop that rolls and prints the dice, it's a simple matter to print the `submit` button and the end of table HTML.

```
//print out submit button and end of table
  print <<<HERE
  </tr></td>
  <tr>
    <td colspan = "5">
    <center>
    <input type = "submit"
           value = "roll again">
    </center>
```

```
    </td>
  </tr>
  </table>

HERE;
```

Because the form specifies no action, PHP defaults to the same page that contains the form. Programs that repeatedly call themselves benefit from this option.

Creating the evaluate() Function

The `evaluate()` function's purpose is to examine the `$die` array and see if the user has achieved patterns worthy of reward. Again, I print the entire function here and show some highlights after.

```
function evaluate(){
  global $die, $cash;
  //set up payoff
  $payoff = 0;

  //subtract some money for this roll
  $cash -= 2;

  //count the dice
  $numVals = array(6);
  for ($theVal = 1; $theVal <= 6; $theVal++){
    for ($dieNum = 0; $dieNum < 5; $dieNum++){
      if ($die[$dieNum] == $theVal){
        $numVals[$theVal]++;
      } // end if
    } // end dieNum for loop
  } // end theVal for loop

  //print out results
  //  for ($i = 1; $i <= 6; $i++){
  //    print "$i:  $numVals[$i]<br>\n";
  //  } // end for loop

  //count how many pairs, threes, fours, fives
  $numPairs = 0;
  $numThrees = 0;
```

```
$numFours = 0;
$numFives = 0;

for ($i = 1; $i <= 6; $i++){
  switch ($numVals[$i]){
    case 2:
      $numPairs++;
      break;
    case 3:
      $numThrees++;
      break;
    case 4:
      $numFours++;
      break;
    case 5:
      $numFives++;
      break;
  } // end switch
} // end for loop

//check for two pairs
if ($numPairs == 2){
  print "You have two pairs!<br>\n";
  $payoff = 1;
} // end if

//check for three of a kind and full house
if ($numThrees == 1){
  if ($numPairs == 1){
    //three of a kind and a pair is a full house
    print "You have a full house!<br>\n";
    $payoff = 5;
  } else {
    print "You have three of a kind!<br>\n";
    $payoff = 2;
  } // end 'pair' if
} // end 'three' if

//check for four of a kind
if ($numFours == 1){
```

```
    print "You have four of a kind!<br>\n";
    $payoff = 5;
  } // end if

  //check for five of a kind
  if ($numFives == 1){
    print "You got five of a kind!<br>\n";
    $payoff = 10;
  } // end if

  //check for flushes
  if (($numVals[1] == 1)
    && ($numVals[2] == 1)
    && ($numVals[3] == 1)
    && ($numVals[4] == 1)
    && ($numVals[5] == 1)){
    print "You have a flush!<br>\n";
    $payoff = 10;
  } // end if

  if (($numVals[2] == 1)
    && ($numVals[3] == 1)
    && ($numVals[4] == 1)
    && ($numVals[5] == 1)
    && ($numVals[6] == 1)){
    print "You have a flush!<br>\n";
    $payoff = 10;

  } // end if
  print "You bet 2<br>\n";
  print "Payoff is $payoff<br>\n";
  $cash += $payoff;

} // end evaluate
```

The `evaluate()` function's general strategy is to subtract $2 for the player's bet each time. (Change this to make the game easier or harder.) I create a new array called `$numVals`, which tracks how many times each possible value appears. Analyzing the `$numVals` array is an easier way to track the various scoring combinations than looking directly at the `$die` array. The rest of the function checks each of the possible scoring combinations and calculates an appropriate payoff.

Counting the Dice Values

When you think about the various scoring combinations in this game, it's important to know how many of each value the user rolled. The user gets points for pairs, three-, four-, and five of a kind, and straights (five values in a row). I made a new array called `$numVals`, which has six elements. `$numVals[1]` contains the number of ones the user rolled. `$numVals[2]` shows how many twos, and so on.

```
//count the dice
  for ($theVal = 1; $theVal <= 6; $theVal++){
    for ($dieNum = 0; $dieNum < 5; $dieNum++){
      if ($die[$dieNum] == $theVal){
        $numVals[$theVal]++;
      } // end if
    } // end dieNum for loop
  } // end theVal for loop

  //print out results
  //  for ($i = 1; $i <= 6; $i++){
  //    print "$i:  $numVals[$i]<br>\n";
  //  } // end for loop
```

To build the `$numVals` array, I stepped through each possible value (1 through 6) with a `for` loop. I used another `for` loop to look at each die and determine if it showed the appropriate value. (In other words, I checked for 1s the first time through the outer loop, then 2s, then 3s, and so on.) If I found the current value, I incremented `$numVals[$theVal]` appropriately.

Notice the lines at the end of this segment that are commented out. Moving on with the scorekeeping code if the `$numVals` array did not work as expected was moot, so I put in a quick loop that tells me how many of each value the program found. This ensures my program works properly before I add functionality.

It's smart to periodically check your work and make sure that things are working as you expected. When I determined things were working correctly, I placed comments in front of each line to temporarily turn the debugging code off. Doing this removes the code, but it remains if something goes wrong and I need to look at the `$numVals` array again.

Counting Pairs, Twos, Threes, Fours, and Fives

The `$numVals` array has most of the information I need, but it's not quite in the right format. The user earns cash for pairs and for three-, four-, and five of a kind.

To check for these conditions, I use some other variables and another loop to look at `$numVals`.

```
//count how many pairs, threes, fours, fives
$numPairs = 0;
$numThrees = 0;
$numFours = 0;
$numFives = 0;

for ($i = 1; $i <= 6; $i++){
  switch ($numVals[$i]){
    case 2:
      $numPairs++;
      break;
    case 3:
      $numThrees++;
      break;
    case 4:
      $numFours++;
      break;
    case 5:
      $numFives++;
      break;
  } // end switch
} // end for loop
```

First I created variables to track pairs, and three-, four-, and five of a kind. I initialized all these variables to `0`. I then stepped through the `$numVals` array to see how many of each value occurred. If, for example, the user rolled 1, 1, 5, 5, 5, `$numVals[1]` equals `2` and `$numVals[5]` equals `3`.

After the `switch` statement executes, `$numPairs` equals `1` and `$numThrees` equals `1`. All the other `$num` variables still contain `0`. Creating these variables makes it easy to determine which scoring situations (if any) have occurred.

Looking for Two Pairs

All the work setting up the scoring variables pays off, because it's now very easy to determine when a scoring condition has occurred. I award the user $1 for two pairs (and nothing for one pair). If the value of `$numPairs` is `2`, the user has gotten two pairs; the `$payoff` variable is given the value `1`.

```
//check for two pairs
if ($numPairs == 2){
  print "You have two pairs!<br>\n";
  $payoff = 1;
} // end if
```

Of course, you're welcome to change the payoffs. As it stands, this game is incredibly generous, but that makes it fun for the user.

Looking for Three of a Kind and a Full House

I combine the checks for three of a kind and full house (which is three of a kind and a pair). The code first checks for three of a kind by looking at `$numThrees`. If the user has three of a kind, it then checks for a pair. If both these conditions are true, it's a full house and the user is rewarded appropriately. If there isn't a pair, the user gets a meager reward for the three of a kind.

```
//check for three of a kind and full house
if ($numThrees == 1){
  if ($numPairs == 1){
    //three of a kind and a pair is a full house
    print "You have a full house!<br>\n";
    $payoff = 5;
  } else {
    print "You have three of a kind!<br>\n";
    $payoff = 2;
  } // end 'pair' if
} // end 'three' if
```

Checking for Four of a Kind and Five of a Kind

Checking for four- and five of a kind is trivial. Looking at the appropriate variables is the only necessity.

```
//check for four of a kind
if ($numFours == 1){
  print "You have four of a kind!<br>\n";
  $payoff = 5;
} // end if

//check for five of a kind
if ($numFives == 1){
```

```
    print "You got five of a kind!<br>\n";
    $payoff = 10;
  } // end if
```

Checking for Straights

Straights are a little trickier, because two are possible. The player could have the values 1-5 or 2-6. To check these situations, I used two compound conditions. A compound condition is made of a number of ordinary conditions combined with special logical operators. Look at the straight-checking code to see an example:

```
  //check for straights
  if (($numVals[1] == 1)
    && ($numVals[2] == 1)
    && ($numVals[3] == 1)
    && ($numVals[4] == 1)
    && ($numVals[5] == 1)){
    print "You have a straight!<br>\n";
    $payoff = 10;
  } // end if

  if (($numVals[2] == 1)
    && ($numVals[3] == 1)
    && ($numVals[4] == 1)
    && ($numVals[5] == 1)
    && ($numVals[6] == 1)){
    print "You have a straight!<br>\n";
    $payoff = 10;
```

Notice how each `if` statement has a condition made of several subconditions joined by the `&&` operator? The `&&` operator is called a *Boolean and* operator. You can read it as *and*. The condition is evaluated to `TRUE` only if all the subconditions are true.

The two conditions are similar to each other, simply checking the two possible straight situations.

Printing the Results

The program's last function prints variable information to the user. The `$cash` value describes the user's current wealth. Two hidden elements store information the program needs on the next run. The `secondRoll` element contains a `TRUE` or FALSE value indicating whether the *next* run should be considered the second roll. The cash element describes how much cash should be attributed to the player on the next turn.

```
function printStuff(){
  global $cash, $secondRoll;

  print "Cash: $cash\n";

  //store variables in hidden fields
  print <<<HERE
  <input type = "hidden"
         name = "secondRoll"
         value = "$secondRoll">

  <input type = "hidden"
         name = "cash"
         value = "$cash">

HERE;
} // end printStuff

?>
</form>
</html>
```

Summary

You are rounding out your basic training as a programmer, adding rudimentary looping behavior to your bag of tricks. Your programs can repeat based on conditions you establish. You know how to build for loops that work forwards, backwards, and by skipping values. You also know how to create while loops. You know the guidelines for creating a well-behaved loop and how to form arrays manually and with the array() directive. Stepping through all elements of an array using a loop is possible, and your program can keep track of persistent variables by storing them in form fields in your output pages. You put all these skills together to build an interesting game. In chapter 5 you extend your ability to work with arrays and loops by building more-powerful arrays and using specialized looping structures.

CHALLENGES

1. Modify the `Poker Dice` game in some way. Add a custom background, change the die images, or modify the payoffs to balance the game to your liking.
2. Write the classic `I'm Thinking of a Number` game. Have the computer randomly generate a number and let the user guess its value. Tell the user if he is too high, too low, or correct. When he guesses correctly, tell how many turns it took. No arrays are necessary for this game, but you must store values in hidden form elements.
3. Write `I'm Thinking of a Number` in reverse. This time the user generates a random number between `1` and `100` and the computer guesses the number. Let the user choose from too high, too low, or correct. Your algorithm should always be able to guess the number in seven turns or fewer.
4. Write a program that deals a random poker hand. Use playing card images from http://waste.org/~oxymoron/cards/ or another source. Your program does not need to score the hand. It simply needs to deal out a hand of five random cards. Use an array to handle the deck.

Better Arrays and String Handling

In this chapter you learn some important skills that improve your work with data. You learn about some more-sophisticated ways to work with arrays and how to manage text information with more flair. Specifically, you learn how to do these things:

- Manage arrays with the `foreach` loop
- Create and use associative arrays
- Extract useful information from some of PHP's built-in arrays
- Build basic two-dimensional arrays
- Build two-dimensional associative arrays
- Break a string into smaller segments
- Search for one string inside another

Introducing the Word Search Program Creator

By the end of this chapter you can create a fun program that generates word search puzzles. The user enters a series of words into a list box, as shown in Figure 5.1.

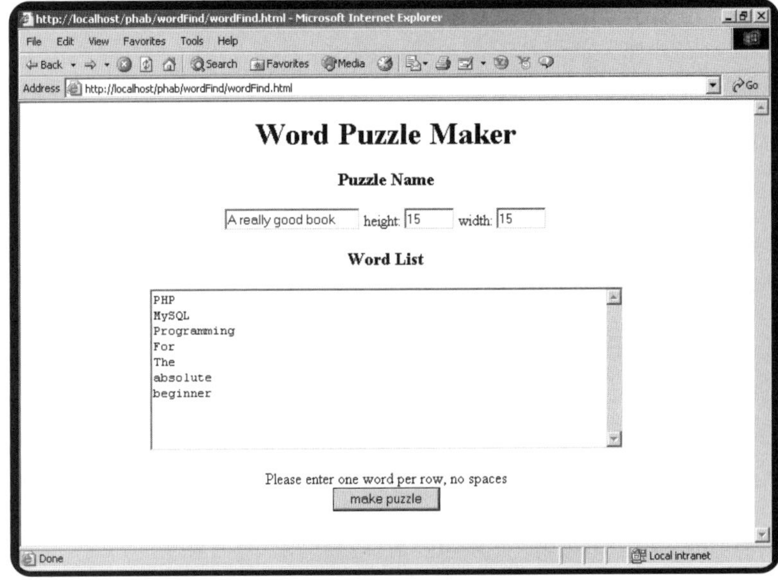

FIGURE 5.1

The user enters a list of words and a size for the finished puzzle.

The program then tries to generate a word search based on the user's word list. (It isn't always possible, but the program can usually generate a puzzle.) One possible solution for the word list shown in Figure 5. 1 is demonstrated in Figure 5.2.

If desired, the program can also generate an answer key based on the puzzle. This capability is shown in Figure 5.3.

The secret to the word find game (and indeed most computer programs) is the way the data is handled. Once I determined a good scheme for working with the data in the program, the actual programming wasn't too tough.

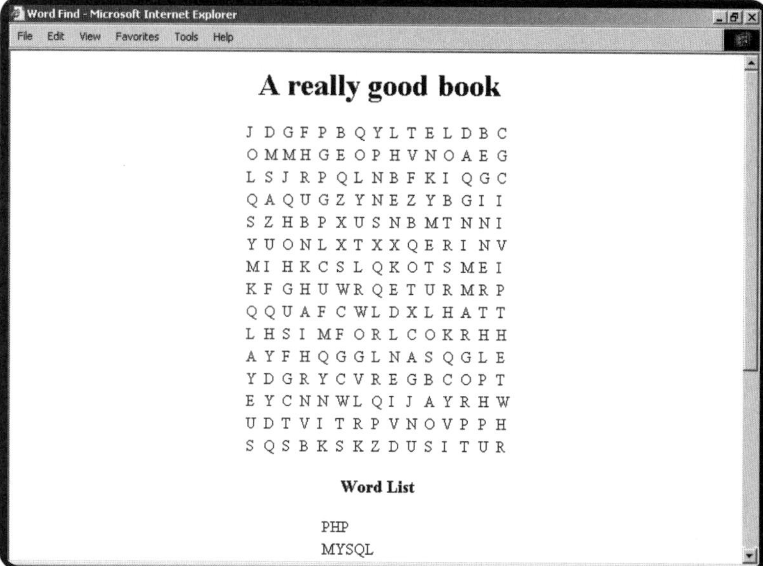

FIGURE 5.2

This puzzle contains all the words in the list.

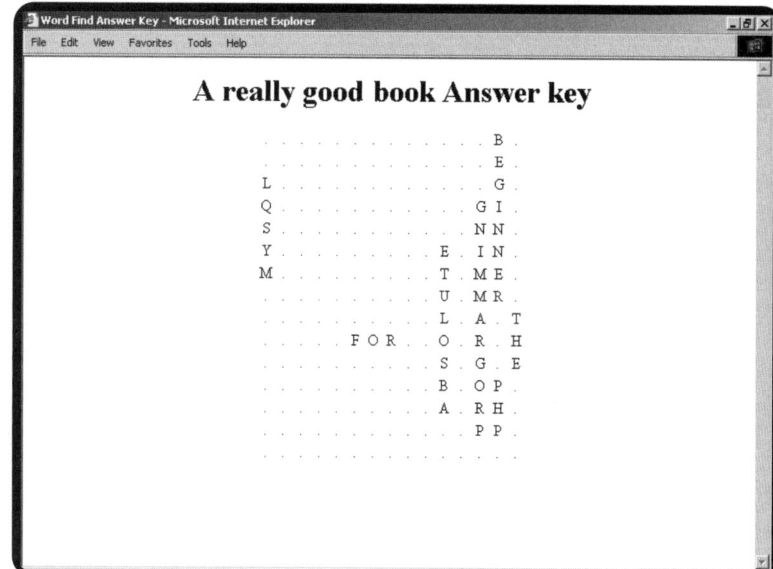

FIGURE 5.3

Here's the answer key for the puzzle.

Using the foreach Loop to Work with an Array

As I mention in chapter 4, "Loops and Arrays," `for` loops and arrays are natural companions. In fact, PHP supplies a special kind of loop called the *foreach* loop that makes it even easier to step through each array element.

Introducing the foreach.php Program

The program shown in Figure 5.4 illustrates how the `foreach` loop works.

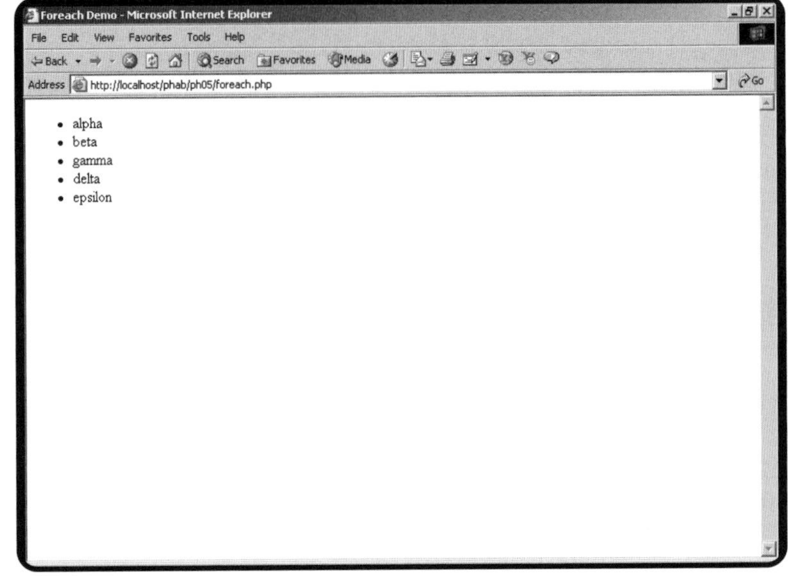

FIGURE 5.4

Although it looks just like normal HTML, this page was created with an array and a `foreach` loop.

The HTML page is generated by surprisingly simple code:

```
<html>
<head>
<title>Foreach Demo</title>
</head>
<body>
<?

$list = array("alpha", "beta", "gamma", "delta", "epsilon");

print "<ul>\n";
foreach ($list as $value){
  print "  <li>$value</li>\n";
} // end foreach
print "</ul>\n";

?>
</body>
</html>
```

All the values in the list are created in the `$list` variable using the `array` function.

The `foreach` loop works a lot like a `for` loop, except it is a bit simpler. The first parameter of the `foreach` construct is an array—in this case, `$list`. The keyword `as` indicates the name of a variable that holds each value in turn. In this case, the `foreach` loop steps through the `$list` array as many times as necessary. Each time through the loop, the function populates the `$value` variable with the current member of the `$list` array. In essence, this `foreach` loop works just like the following traditional `for` loop:

```
foreach ($list as $value){
  print "  <li>$value</li>\n";
} // end foreach
```

Here's your traditional `for` loop:

```
for ($i = 0; $i < length($list); $i++);
  $value = $list[$i];
  print "  <li>$value</li>\n";
} // end for loop
```

The main difference between a `foreach` loop and a `for` loop is the presence of the index variable (`$i` in this example). If you're using a `foreach` loop and need to know the current element's index, use the `key()` function.

The `foreach` loop can be an extremely handy shortcut for stepping through each value of an array. Since this is a common task, knowing how to use the `foreach` loop is an important skill. As you learn some other kinds of arrays, you see how to modify the `foreach` loop to handle these other array styles.

Creating an Associative Array

PHP is known for its extremely flexible arrays. You can easily generate a number of interesting and useful array types in addition to the ordinary arrays you've already made. One of the handiest types is called an associative array.

While it sounds complicated, an *associative array* is much like a normal array. While regular arrays rely on numeric indices, an associative array has a string index. Figure 5.5 shows a page created with two associative arrays.

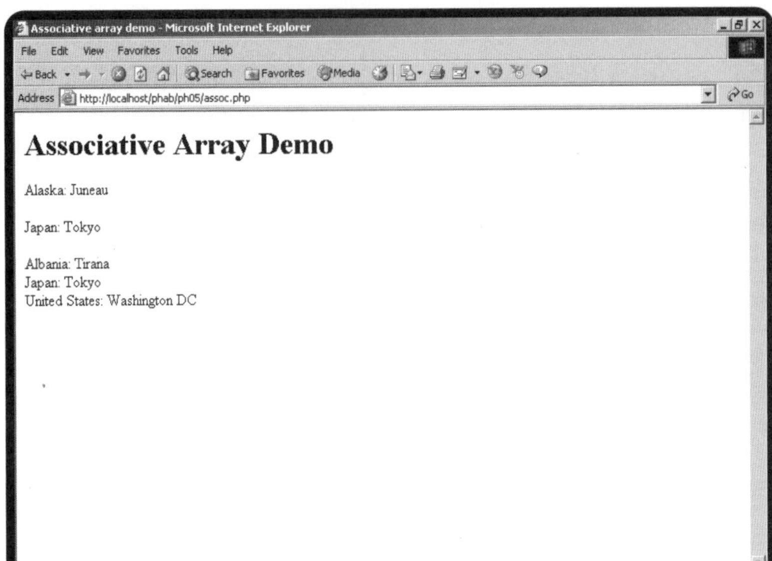

FIGURE 5.5

This page uses associative arrays to relate countries and states to their capital cities.

Examining the assoc.php Program

Imagine that you want to store a list of capital cities. You could certainly store the cities in an array. However, if your main interest is in the relationship between a state and its capital, it could be difficult to maintain the relationship using arrays. In this particular instance, it would be nice if you could use the name of the state as the array index (the element's number, or position, within the array) rather than a number.

Building an Associative Array

Here is the code from `assoc.php`, which generates the array of state capitals:

```
$stateCap["Alaska"] = "Juneau";
$stateCap["Indiana"] = "Indianapolis";
$stateCap["Michigan"] = "Lansing";
```

The associative array is just like a normal array, except the index values are strings. Note that the indices must be inside quotation marks. Once you have created an associative array, it is used much like a normal array.

```
print "Alaska: ";
print $stateCap["Alaska"];
print "<br><br>";
```

IN DIZZY-ARRAY

If all this associative array talk is making you dizzy, don't panic. It's just a new name for something you're very familiar with. Think about the way HTML attributes work. Each tag has a number of attributes that you can use in any order. For example, a standard button might look like this:

```
<input type = "button"
       value = "Save the world.">
```

This button has two attributes. Each attribute is made up of a name/value pair. The keywords `type` and `value` are *names* (or indices, or keys, depending on how you want to think of it) and the terms `button` and `Save the world.` are the *values* associated with those names. Cascading style sheets (CSS) use a different syntax for exactly the same idea. The CSS element indicates a series of modifications to the paragraph tag:

```
p {background-color:red;
   color:yellow;
   font-size:14pt}
```

While the syntax is different, the same pattern applies. The critical part of a CSS definition is a list of name/value pairs.

Associative arrays naturally pop up in one more place. As information comes into your program from an HTML form, it comes in as an associative array. The name of each element becomes an index, and the value of that form element is translated to the value of the array element. Later in this chapter you see how to take advantage of this.

An associative array is simply a data structure used when the name/value relationship is the easiest way to work with some kind of data.

Once again, the array's index is a quoted string. The associative form is terrific for data like this. In essence, it lets you "look up" the capital city if you know the state name.

Building an Associative Array with the array() Function

If you know the values you want in your array, you can use the `array()` function to build an associative array. However, building associative arrays requires a slightly different syntax than the garden variety arrays you encountered in Chapter 4.

I build the `$worldCap` array using the `array()` syntax:

```
$worldCap = array(
  "Albania"=>"Tirana",
  "Japan"=>"Tokyo",
  "United States"=>"Washington DC"
  );
```

The `array()` function requires the data when you are building an ordinary array, but doesn't require specified indices. The function automatically generates each element's index by grabbing the next available integer. In an associative array, you are responsible for providing both the data and the index.

The general format for this assignment uses a special kind of assignment operator. The => operator indicates that an element holds some kind of value. I generally read it as *holds,* so you can say *Japan holds Tokyo.* In other words, `"Japan" => "Tokyo"` indicates that PHP should generate an array element with the index `"Japan"` and store the value `"Tokyo"` in that element. You can access the value of this array just like any other associative array:

```
print "Japan: ";
print $worldCap["Japan"];
print "<br><br>";
```

Using foreach with Associative Arrays

The `foreach` loop is just as useful with associative arrays as it is with vanilla arrays. However, it uses a slightly different syntax. Take a look at this code from the `assoc.php` page:

```
foreach ($worldCap as $country => $capital){
  print "$country: $capital<br>\n";
} // end foreach
```

A `foreach` loop for a regular array uses only one variable because the index can be easily calculated. In an associative array, each element in the array has a unique index and value. The associative form of the `foreach` loop takes this into account by indicating two variables. The first variable holds the index. The second variable refers to the value associated with that index. Inside the loop, you can refer to the current index and value using whatever variable names you designated in the `foreach` structure.

Each time through the loop, you are given a name/value pair. In this example, the name is stored in the variable `$country`, because all the indices in this array are names of countries. Each time through the loop, `$country` has a different value. In each iteration, the value of the `$capital` variable contains the array value corresponding to the current value of `$country`.

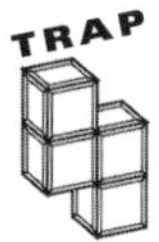

Unlike traditional arrays, you cannot rely on associative arrays to return in any particular order when you use a `foreach` loop to access array elements. If you need elements to show up in a particular order, call them explicitly.

Using Built-In Associative Arrays

Associative arrays are extremely handy because they reflect a kind of information storage very frequently used. In fact, you've been using associative arrays in disguise ever since chapter 2, "Using Variables and Input." Whenever your PHP program receives data from a form, that data is actually stored in a number of associative arrays for you. A variable was automatically created for you by PHP for each form element.

However, you can't always rely on that particular bit of magic. Increasingly, server administrators are turning off this automatic variable creation for security reasons. In fact, the default setup for PHP is now to have this behavior (with the odd name `render_globals`) turned off.

It's handy to know how PHP gets data from the form as a good example of associative arrays. It's also useful because you may need to know how to get form data without the variables being created explicitly for you.

Introducing the formReader.php Program

The `formReader.php` program is actually one of the first PHP programs I ever wrote, and it's one I use frequently. It's very handy, because it can take the input from any HTML form and report the names and values of each of the form elements on the page. To illustrate, Figure 5.6 shows a typical Web page with a form.

When the user clicks the `Submit Query` button, `formReader` responds with some basic diagnostics, as you can see from Figure 5.7.

Reading the $_REQUEST Array

The `formReader.php` program does its work by taking advantage of an associative array built into PHP. Until now, you've simply relied on PHP to create a variable for you based on the input elements of whatever form calls your program. This

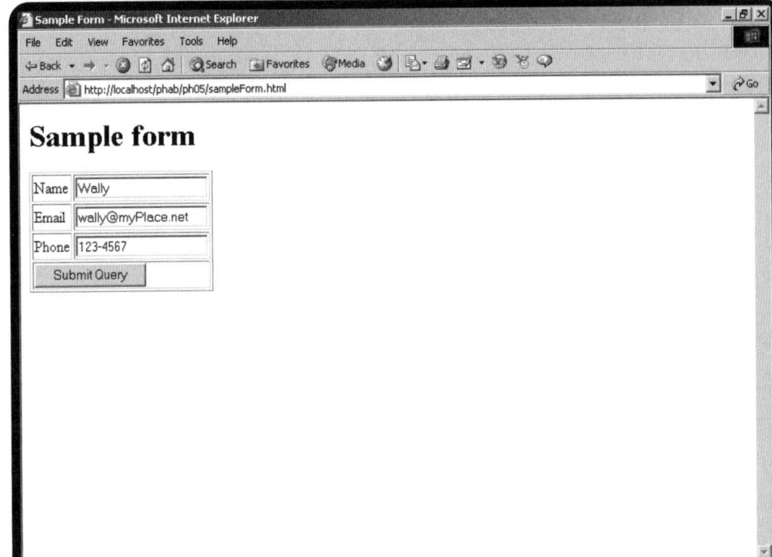

FIGURE 5.6

This form, which has three basic fields, calls the `formReader.php` program.

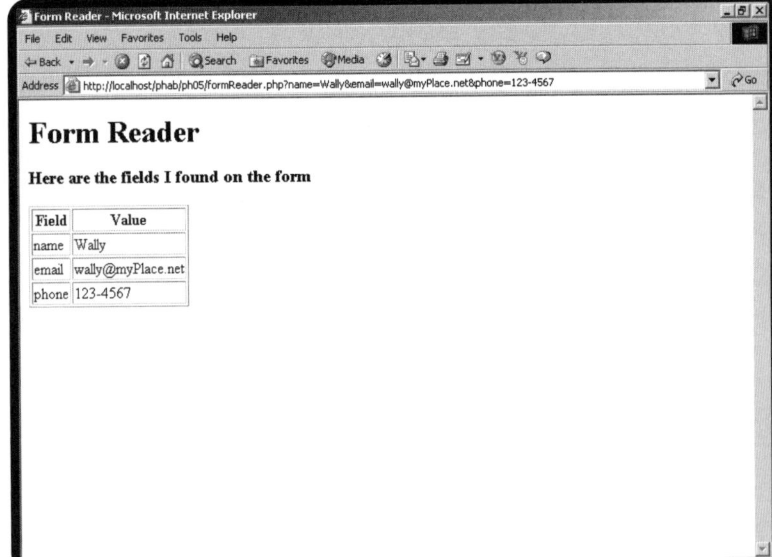

FIGURE 5.7

The `formReader.php` program determines each field and its value.

automatic variable creation is called `register_globals`. While this is an extremely convenient feature, it can be dangerous, so some administrators turn it off. Even when `register_globals` is active, it can be useful to know other ways of accessing the information that comes from the form.

All the fields sent to your program are automatically stored in a special associative array called `$_REQUEST`. Each field name on the original form becomes a key, and the value of that field becomes the value associated with that key. If you have a form with a field called `userName`, you can get the value of the field by calling `$_REQUEST["userName"]`.

The `$_REQUEST` array is also useful because you can use a `foreach` loop to quickly determine the names and values of all form elements known to the program. The `formReader.php` program source code illustrates how this is done:

```
<!doctype html public "-//W3C//DTD HTML 4.0 //EN">
<html>
<head>
        <title>Form Reader</title>
</head>
<body>
<h1>Form Reader</h1>
<h3>Here are the fields I found on the form</h3>
<?
print <<<HERE
<table border = 1>
<tr>
  <th>Field</th>
  <th>Value</th>
</tr>
HERE;

foreach ($_REQUEST as $field => $value){
  print <<<HERE
  <tr>
    <td>$field</td>
    <td>$value</td>
  </tr>
HERE;
} // end foreach
print "</table>\n";

?>

</body>
</html>
```

Note how I stepped through the `$_REQUEST` array. Each time through the `foreach` loop, the current field name is stored in the `$field` variable and the value of that field is stored in `$value`.

I use this script when I'm debugging my programs. If I'm not getting the form elements I expected from a form, I put a `foreach $_REQUEST` loop in at the top of my program to make sure I know exactly what's being sent to the program. Often this type of procedure can help you find misspellings or other bugs.

In the Real World

PHP provides some other variables related to `$_REQUEST`. The `$HTTP_POST_VARS` array holds all the names and values sent through a `POST` request, and `$HTTP_GET_VARS` array holds names and values sent through a `get` request. You can use this feature to make your code more secure. If you create variables only from the `$HTTP_POST_VARS` array, for example, all input sent via the `get` method are ignored. This makes it harder for users to forge data by putting field names in the browser's address bar. Of course, a clever user can still write a form that contains bogus fields, so you always have to be a little suspicious whenever you get any data from the user.

Creating a Multidimensional Array

Arrays are very useful structures for storing various kinds of data into the computer's memory. Normal arrays are much like lists. Associative arrays are like name/value pairs. A third special type, a *multidimensional array*, acts much like table data. For instance, imagine you were trying to write a program to help users determine the distance between major cities. You might start on paper with a table like Table 5.1.

Table 5.1 Distances Between Major Cities

	Indianapolis	New York	Tokyo	London
Indianapolis	0	648	6476	4000
New York	648	0	6760	3470
Tokyo	6476	6760	0	5956
London	4000	3470	5956	0

It's reasonably common to work with this sort of tabular data in a computer program. PHP (and most languages) provides a special type of array to assist in working with this kind of information. The `basicMultiArray` program featured in Figures 5.8 and 5.9 illustrates how a program can encapsulate a table.

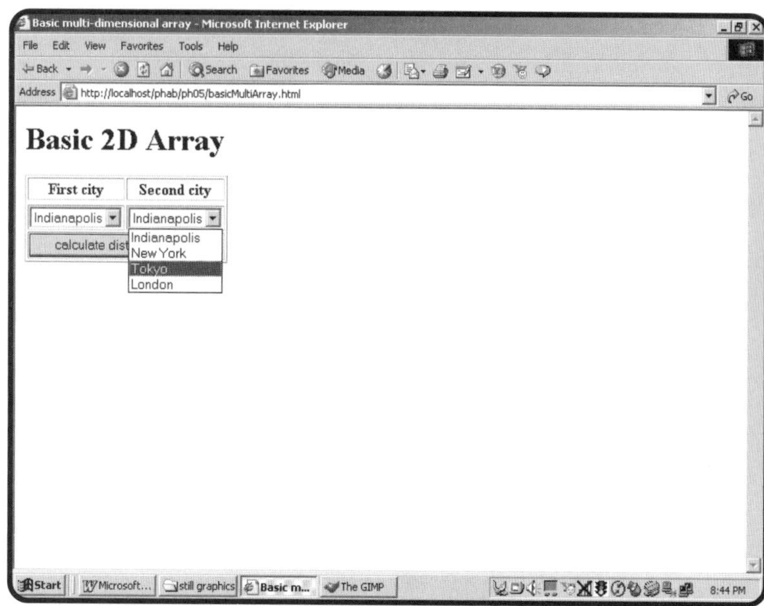

FIGURE 5.8

The user can choose origin and destination cities from select groups.

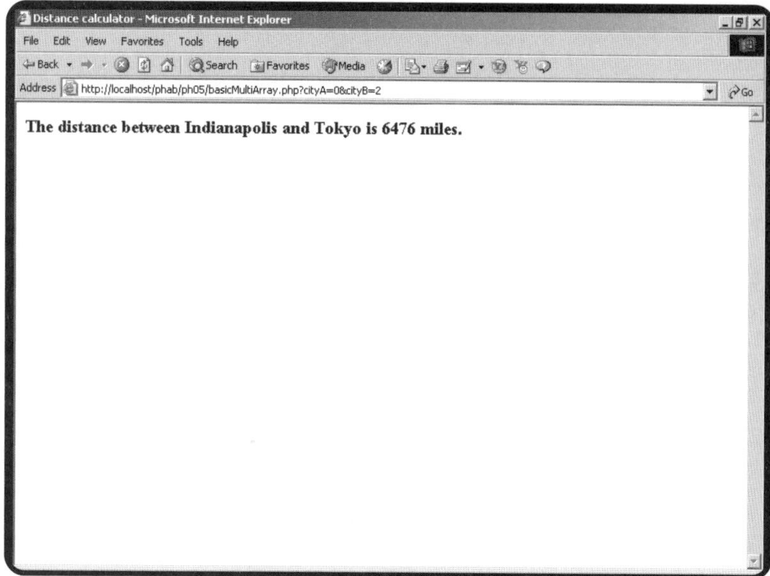

FIGURE 5.9

The program looks up the distance between the cities and returns an appropriate value.

Building the HTML for the Basic Multidimensional Array

Using a two-dimensional array is pretty easy if you plan well. I first wrote out my table on paper. (Actually, I have a write-on, wipe-off board in my office for exactly this kind of situation.) I assigned a numeric value to each city:

Indianapolis = 0

New York = 1

Tokyo = 2

London = 3

This makes it easier to track the cities later on.

The HTML code builds the two select boxes and a `submit` button in a form.

```
<!doctype html public "-//W3C//DTD HTML 4.0 //EN">
<html>
<head>
       <title>Basic multi-dimensional array</title>
</head>
<body>
<h1>Basic 2D Array</h1>

<form action = basicMultiArray.php>
<table border = 1>
<tr>
  <th>First city</th>
  <th>Second city</th>
<tr>

<!-- note each option value is numeric -->

<tr>
  <td>
    <select name = "cityA">
      <option value = 0>Indianapolis</option>
      <option value = 1>New York</option>
      <option value = 2>Tokyo</option>
      <option value = 3>London</option>
     </select>
   </td>
```

```
  <td>
    <select name = "cityB">
      <option value = 0>Indianapolis</option>
      <option value = 1>New York</option>
      <option value = 2>Tokyo</option>
      <option value = 3>London</option>
     </select>
  </td>
</tr>

<tr>
  <td colspan = 2>
    <input type = "submit"
           value = "calculate distance">
  </td>
</tr>
</table>
</body>
</html>
```

Recall that when the user submits this form, it sends two variables. The `cityA` variable contains the value property associated with whatever city the user selected; `cityB` likewise contains the value of the currently selected destination city. I carefully set up the value properties so they coordinate with each city's numeric index. If the user chooses New York as the origin city, the value of `$cityA` is `1`, because I decided that New York would be represented by the value `1`. I'm giving numeric values because the information is all stored in arrays, and normal arrays take numeric indices. (In the next section I show you how to do the same thing with associative arrays.)

Responding to the Distance Query

The PHP code that determines the distance between cities is actually quite simple once the arrays are in place:

```
<!doctype html public "-//W3C//DTD HTML 4.0 //EN">
<html>
<head>
       <title>Distance calculator</title>
</head>
<body>
```

```
<?
$city = array (
  "Indianapolis",
  "New York",
  "Tokyo",
  "London"
  );

$distance = array (
  array (0, 648, 6476, 4000),
  array (648, 0, 6760, 3470),
  array (6476, 6760, 0, 5956),
  array (4000, 3470, 5956, 0)
  );

$result = $distance[$cityA][$cityB];
print "<h3>The distance between ";
print "$city[$cityA] and $city[$cityB]";
print " is $result miles.</h3>";

?>
</body>
</html>
```

Storing City Names in the $city Array

I have two arrays in this program, `$city` and `$distance`. The `$city` array is a completely normal array of string values. It contains a list of city names. I set up the array so the numeric values I assigned to the city would correspond to the index in this array. Remember that array indices usually start with `0`, so `Indianapolis` is `0`, `New York` is `1`, and so on.

The user won't care that `Indianapolis` is city `0`, so the `$city` array assigns names to the various cities. If the user chose city `0` (`Indianapolis`) for the `$cityA` field, I can refer to the name of that city as `$city[$cityA]` because `$cityA` contains the value `0` and `$city[0]` is `Indianapolis`.

Storing Distances in the $distance Array

The distances don't fit into a regular list, because it requires two values to determine a distance. You must know from which city you are coming and going to calculate a distance. These two values correspond to rows and columns in the original table. Look again at the code that generates the `$distance` array:

```
$distance = array (
  array (0, 648, 6476, 4000),
  array (648, 0, 6760, 3470),
  array (6476, 6760, 0, 5956),
  array (4000, 3470, 5956, 0)
  );
```

The `$distance` array is actually an array full of other arrays! Each of the inner arrays corresponds to distance from a certain destination city. For example, since `Indianapolis` is city `0`, the first (zeroth?) inner array refers to the distance between Indy and the other cities. If it helps, you can think of each inner array as a row of a table, and the table as an array of rows.

It might sound complicated to build a two-dimensional array, but it is more natural than you may think. If you compare the original data in Table 5.1 with the code that creates the two-dimensional array, you see that all the numbers are in the right place.

No need to stop at two dimensions. It's possible to build arrays with three, four, or any other number of dimensions. However, it becomes difficult to visualize how the data works with these complex arrays. Generally, one and two dimensions are as complex as ordinary arrays should get. For more complex data types, look toward file-manipulation tools and relational data structures, which you learn throughout the rest of this book.

Getting Data from the $distance Array

Once data is stored in a two-dimensional array, it is reasonably easy to retrieve. To look up information in a table, you need to know the row and column. A two-dimensional array requires two indices—one for the row and one for the column.

To find the distance from `Tokyo` (city number `2`) to `New York` (city number `1`), simply refer to `$distance[2][1]`. The code for the program gets the index values from the form:

```
$result = $distance[$cityA][$cityB];
```

This value is stored in the variable `$result` and then sent to the user.

Making a Two-Dimensional Associative Array

You can also create two-dimensional associative arrays. It takes a little more work to set it up, but can be worth it because the name/value relationship eliminates the need to track numeric identifiers for each element. Another version of the `multiArray` program illustrates how to use associative arrays to generate the same city-distance program.

Since this program looks exactly like the `basicMultiArray` program to the user, I am not showing the screen shots. All of this program's interesting features are in the source code.

Building the HTML for the Associative Array

The HTML page for this program's associative version is much like the indexed version, except for one major difference. See if you can spot the difference in the source code:

```
<!doctype html public "-//W3C//DTD HTML 4.0 //EN">
<html>
<head>
<title>2D Array</title>
</head>
<body>
<h1>2D Array</h1>

<form action = multiArray.php>
<table border = 1>
<tr>
  <th>First city</th>
  <th>Second city</th>
<tr>

<!-- note each option value is a string -->

<tr>
  <td>
    <select name = "cityA">
      <option value = "Indianapolis">Indianapolis</option>
      <option value = "New York">New York</option>
```

```
        <option value = "Tokyo">Tokyo</option>
        <option value = "London">London</option>
      </select>
    </td>

  <td>
    <select name = "cityB">
      <option value = "Indianapolis">Indianapolis</option>
      <option value = "New York">New York</option>
      <option value = "Tokyo">Tokyo</option>
      <option value = "London">London</option>
    </select>
  </td>
</tr>

<tr>
  <td colspan = 2>
    <input type = "submit"
           value = "calculate distance">
  </td>
</tr>
</table>

</body>
</html>
```

The only difference between this HTML page and the last one is the `value` properties of the `select` objects. In this case, the distance array is an associative array, so it does not have numeric indices. Since the indices can be text based, I send the actual city name as the value for `$cityA` and `$cityB`.

Responding to the Query

The code for the associative response is interesting, because it spends a lot of effort to build the fancy associative array. Once the array is created, it's very easy to work with.

```
<!doctype html public "-//W3C//DTD HTML 4.0 //EN">
<html>
<head>
<title>Distance Calculator</title>
```

```
</head>
<body>
<h1>Distance Calculator</h1>

<?
//create arrays
$indy = array (
  "Indianapolis" => 0,
  "New York" => 648,
  "Tokyo" => 6476,
  "London" => 4000
  );
$ny = array (
  "Indianapolis" =>648,
  "New York" => 0,
  "Tokyo" => 6760,
  "London" => 3470
  );
$tokyo = array (
  "Indianapolis" => 6476,
  "New York" => 6760,
  "Tokyo" => 0,
  "London" => 5956
  );
$london = array (
  "Indianapolis" => 4000,
  "New York" => 3470,
  "Tokyo" => 5956,
  "London" => 0
  );

//set up master array
$distance = array (
  "Indianapolis" => $indy,
  "New York" => $ny,
  "Tokyo" => $tokyo,
  "London" => $london
  );
```

```
$result = $distance[$cityA][$cityB];
print "<h3>The distance between $cityA and $cityB is $result miles.</h3>";

?>

</body>
</html>
```

Building the Two-Dimensional Associative Array

The basic approach to building a two-dimensional array is the same whether it's a normal array or uses associative indexing. Essentially, you create each row as an array and then build an array of the existing arrays. In the traditional array, the indices were automatically created. The development of an associative array is a little more complex, because you need to specify the key for each value. As an example, look at the code used to generate the `$indy` array:

```
$indy = array (
  "Indianapolis" => 0,
  "New York" => 648,
  "Tokyo" => 6476,
  "London" => 4000
  );
```

Inside the array, I used city names as indices. The value for each index refers to the distance from the current city (`Indianapolis`) to the particular destination. The distance from Indianapolis to Indianapolis is `0`, and the distance from Indy to New York is `648`, and so on.

I created an associative array for each city and put those associative arrays together in a kind of mega-associative array:

```
//set up master array
$distance = array (
  "Indianapolis" => $indy,
  "New York" => $ny,
  "Tokyo" => $tokyo,
  "London" => $london
  );
```

This new array is also an associative array, but each of its indices refers to an array of distances.

Getting Data from the Two-Dimensional Associative Array

Once the two-dimensional array is constructed, it's extremely easy to use. The city names themselves are used as indices, so there's no need for a separate array to hold city names. The data can be output in two lines of code:

```
$result = $distance[$cityA][$cityB];
print "<h3>The distance between $cityA and $cityB is $result miles.</h3>";
```

You can combine associative and normal arrays. It is possible to have a list of associative arrays and put them together in a normal array, or vice versa. PHP's array-handling capabilities allow for a phenomenal level of control over your data structures.

Manipulating String Values

The `Word Search` program featured at the beginning of this chapter uses arrays to do some of its magic, but arrays alone are insufficient for handling the tasks needed for this program. The `Word Search` program takes advantage of a number of special string manipulation functions to work extensively with text values. PHP has a huge number of string functions that give you an incredible ability to fold, spindle, and mutilate string values.

Demonstrating String Manipulation with the Pig Latin Translator

As a context for describing string manipulation functions, consider the program featured in Figures 5.10 and 5.11. This program allows the user to enter a phrase into a text box and converts the phrase into a bogus form of Latin.

If you're not familiar with pig Latin, it's a silly kid's game. Essentially, you take the first letter of each word, move it to the end of the word, and add *ay.* If the word begins with a vowel, simply end the word with *way.*

The `pigify` program uses a number of string functions to manipulate the text:

```
<!doctype html public "-//W3C//DTD HTML 4.0 //EN">
<html>
<head>
       <title>Pig Latin Generator</title>
</head>
```

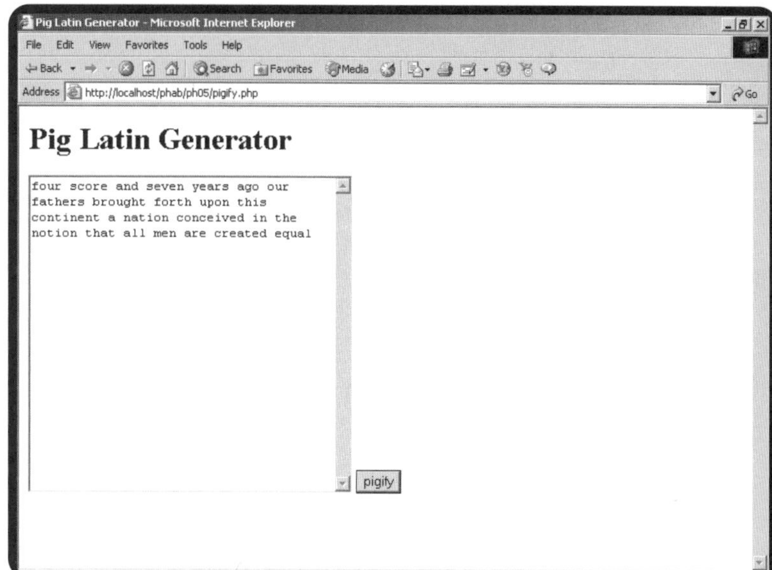

FIGURE 5.10

The pigify program lets the user type some text into a text area.

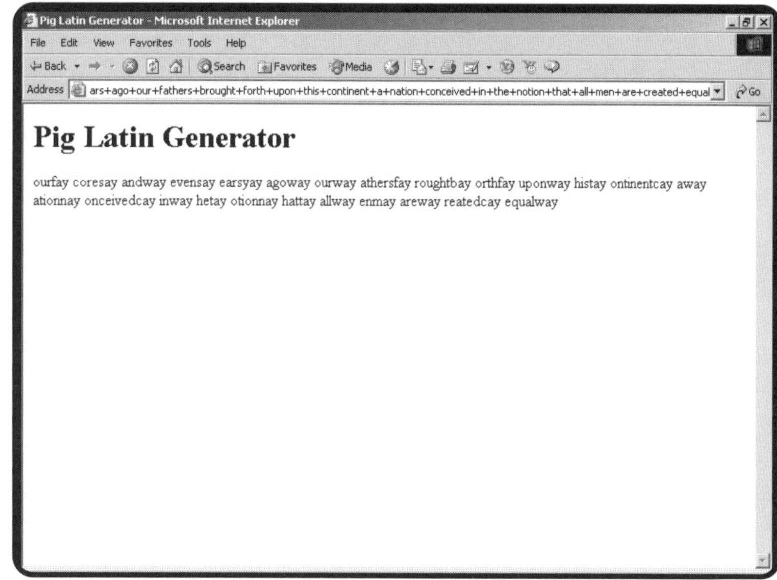

FIGURE 5.11

The program translates immortal prose into incredible silliness.

```
<body>
<h1>Pig Latin Generator</h1>
<?
if ($inputString == NULL){
  print <<<HERE
```

```
  <form>
  <textarea name = "inputString"
            rows = 20
            cols = 40></textarea>
   <input type = "submit"
          value = "pigify">
   </form>

HERE;
} else {
  //there is a value, so we'll deal with it

  //break phrase into array
  $words = split(" ", $inputString);
  foreach ($words as $theWord){
    $theWord = rtrim($theWord);
    $firstLetter = substr($theWord, 0, 1);
    $restOfWord = substr($theWord, 1, strlen($theWord));
    //print "$firstLetter) $restOfWord <br> \n";
    if (strstr("aeiouAEIOU", $firstLetter)){
      //it's a vowel
      $newWord = $theWord . "way";
    } else {
      //it's a consonant
      $newWord = $restOfWord . $firstLetter . "ay";
    } // end if
    $newPhrase = $newPhrase . $newWord . " ";
  } // end foreach
  print $newPhrase;

} // end if

?>


</body>
</html>
```

Building the Form

This program uses a PHP page to create an input form and to respond directly to the input. It begins by looking for the existence of the `$inputString` variable. This variable does not exist the first time the user gets to the page. In this situation, the program builds the appropriate HTML page and awaits user input. The program runs again after the user hits the `submit` button, but this time the `$inputString` variable has a value. The rest of the program uses string manipulation functions to create a pig Latin version of the input string.

Using the split() Function to Break a String into an Array

One of the first tasks for `pigify` is to break the entire string that comes from the user into individual words. PHP provides a couple of interesting functions for this purpose. The `split()` function takes a string and breaks it into an array based on some sort of delimiter, or separator character. The `split()` function takes two arguments. The first argument is a delimiter and the second is a string to break up.

I want each word to be a different element in the array, so I use space (`" "`) as a delimiter. The following line takes the `$inputString` variable and breaks it into an array called `$words`. Each word is a new array element.

```
$words = split(" ", $inputString);
```

Once the `$word` array is constructed, I stepped through it with a `foreach` loop. I stored each word temporarily in `$theWord` inside the array.

Trimming a String with rtrim()

Sometimes when you split a string into an array, each array element still has the split character at the end. In the pig Latin game, there is a space at the end of each word, which can cause some problems later. PHP provides a function called `rtrim()` which automatically removes spaces, tabs, newlines, and other whitespace from the end of a string. I used the `rtrim()` function to clean off any trailing spaces from the `split()` operation and returned the results to `$theWord`.

```
$theWord = rtrim($theWord);
```

In addition to `rtrim()`, PHP has `ltrim()`, which trims excess whitespace from the beginning of a string and `trim()`, which cleans up both ends of a string. Also, there's a variation of the `trim` commands that allows you to specify exactly which characters are removed.

Finding a Substring with substr()

The algorithm's behavior depends on the first character of each word. I need to know all the rest of the word without the first character. The `substr()` function is useful for getting part of a string. It requires three parameters.

- The string you want to get a piece from
- Which character you want to begin with (starting with `0` as usual)
- How many characters you want to extract

I got the first letter of the word with this line:

```
$firstLetter = substr($theWord, 0, 1);
```

It gets one letter from `$theWord` starting at the beginning of the word (position `0`). I stored that value in the `$firstLetter` variable.

It's not much more complicated to get the rest of the word:

```
$restOfWord = substr($theWord, 1, strlen($theWord) -1);
```

Once again, I need to extract values from `$theWord`. This time I begin at character `1` (which humans would refer to as the *second character*). I don't know directly how many characters to get, but I can calculate it. I should grab one less character than the total number of characters in the word. The `strlen()` function is perfect for this operation, because it returns the number of characters in any string. I can calculate the number of letters I need with `strlen($theWord) - 1`. This new decapitated word is stored in the `$restOfWord` variable.

Using strstr() to Search for One String Inside Another

The next task is to determine if the first character of the word is a vowel. You can take a number of approaches to this problem, but perhaps the easiest is a searching function. I created a string with all the vowels (`"aeiouAEIOU"`) and then I searched for the existence of the `$firstLetter` variable in the vowel string.

The `strstr()` function is perfect for this task. It takes two parameters: the string you are looking for (given the adorable name *haystack* in the online documentation) and the string you are searching in (the *needle*).

To search for the value of the `$firstLetter` variable in the string constant `"aeiouAEIOU"`, I used the following line:

```
if (strstr("aeiouAEIOU", $firstLetter)){
```

The `strstr()` function returns the value `FALSE` if the needle was not found in the haystack. If the needle was found, it returns the position of the needle in the haystack parameter. In this case, I'm really concerned only whether `$firstLetter` is found in the list of variables. If so, it's a vowel, which changes the way I modify the word.

Using the Concatenation Operator

Most of the time in PHP you can use string interpolation to combine string values. However, sometimes you need a formal operation to combine strings. The process of combining two strings is called *concatenation*. (I love it when simple ideas have complicated names.) The period (`.`) is PHP's concatenation operator.

If a word in pig Latin begins with a vowel, it should end with the string `"way"`. I used string concatenation to make this work:

```
$newWord = $theWord . "way";
```

When the word begins with a consonant, the formula for creating the new word is slightly more complicated, but is still performed with string concatenation:

```
$newWord = $restOfWord . $firstLetter . "ay";
```

Recent testing has shown that the concatenation method of building strings is dramatically faster than interpolation. If speed is an issue, you might want to use string concatenation rather than string interpolation.

Finishing the Pig Latin Program

Once I created the new word, I added it and a trailing space to the `$newPhrase` variable. When the `foreach` loop has finished executing, `$newPhrase` contains the pig Latin translation of the original phrase.

Translating Between Characters and ASCII Values

Although it isn't necessary in the pig Latin program, the `Word Search` program requires the ability to randomly generate a character. I do this by randomly generating an ASCII value and translating that number to the appropriate character. (ASCII is the code used to store characters as binary numbers in the computer's memory.) The `ord()` function is useful in this situation. The uppercase letters are represented in ASCII by numbers between 65 and 90.

To get a random uppercase letter, I can use the following code:

```
$theNumber = random(65, 90);
$theLetter = ord($theNumber);
```

Returning to the Word Search Creator

The `Word Search` program is stored in three files. First, the user enters a word list and puzzle information into an HTML page. This page calls the main `wordFind.php` program, which analyzes the word list, creates the puzzle, and prints it out. Finally, the user has the opportunity to print an answer key, which is created by a simple PHP program.

Getting the Puzzle Data from the User

The `wordFind.html` page is the user's entry point into the word find system. This page is a standard HTML form with a number of basic elements:

```
<html>
<head>
        <title>Word Puzzle Maker</title>
</head>
<body>
<center>
<h1>Word Puzzle Maker</h1>

<form action = "wordFind.php"
      method = "post">
<h3>Puzzle Name</h3>
<input type = "text"
       name = "name"
       value = "My Word Find">
height: <input type = "text"
               name = "height"
               value = "10"
               size = "5">
width: <input type = "text"
              name = "width"
              value = "10"
              size = "5">
<br><br>
```

```
<h3>Word List</h3>
<textarea rows=10 cols=60 name = "wordList"></textarea>
<br><br>
Please enter one word per row, no spaces
<br>
<input type="submit" value="make puzzle">
</form>
</center>
</body>
</html>
```

The form's `action` property points to the `wordFind.php` program, which is the primary program in the system. I used the `post` method to send data to the program because I expect to send large strings to the program. The `get` method allows only small amounts of data to be sent to the server.

The form features basic text boxes for the puzzle name, height, and width. This data determines how the puzzle is built. The `wordList` text area is expected to house a list of words, which create the puzzle.

Setting Up the Response Page

The bulk of the work in the `wordFind` system happens in the `wordFind.php` page. This program has a small amount of HTML to set the stage, but the vast bulk of this file is made up of PHP code.

```
<html>
<head>
<title>
Word Find
</title>
</head>

<body>

<?
// word Find
// by Andy Harris, 2003
// for PHP/MySQL programming for the Absolute Beginner
// Generates a word search puzzle based on a word list
// entered by user. User can also specify the size of
// the puzzle and print out an answer key if desired
```

Notice the comments at the beginning of the code. Since this program's code is a little more involved than most of the programs you have seen in this book, I decided to comment it more carefully. My comments here basically lay out the plan for this program.

It's a really good idea to add comments to your programs so you can more easily determine what they do. You'll be amazed how little you understand your own code after you've been away from it for a couple of days. Good comments can make it much easier to maintain your code, and make it easier for others to fix and improve your programs later.

Working with the Empty Data Set

For testing purposes, I wrote the `Word Search` PHP page before I worried about the HTML. For that reason, I simply added default values for a word list and for the other main variables that determine the board's layout (height, width, and name). In a production version of the program, I don't expect the PHP code to ever be called without an HTML page, but I left the default values in place so you could see how they work.

```
if ($wordList == NULL){
  //make default puzzle
  $word = array(
    "ANDY",
    "HEATHER",
    "LIZ",
    "MATT",
    "JACOB"
    );
  $boardData = array(
    width => 10,
    height => 10,
    name => "Generic Puzzle"
  );
```

This code builds two arrays, which define the entire program. The `$word` array holds the list of words to hide in the puzzle, and `$boardData` is an associative array holding critical information about how the board is to be created.

Of course, I don't expect to use these values, because this program usually is called from an HTML form, which generates the values. The next section of code fills up these variables if the program is called from the appropriate form.

Building the Program's Main Logic

The main logic for the program begins by retrieving the word list and puzzle parameters from the user's form. Then it tries to convert the list into an array. This type of text analysis is sometimes called *parsing.*

The program then repeatedly tries to build the board until it succeeds. Once the program has successfully created the board, it creates an answer key and adds the random letters with the `addFoils()` function. Finally, the program prints the completed puzzle.

```
} else {
  //get puzzle data from HTML form
  $boardData = array(
    width => $width,
    height => $height,
    name => $name
  );

  //try to get a word list from user input
  if (parseList() == TRUE){
    $legalBoard = FALSE;

    //keep trying to build a board until you get a legal result
    while ($legalBoard == FALSE){
      clearBoard();
      $legalBoard = fillBoard();
    } // end while

    //make the answer key
    $key = $board;
    $keyPuzzle = makeBoard($key);

    //make the final puzzle
    addFoils();
    $puzzle = makeBoard($board);

    //print out the result page
    printPuzzle();

  } // end parsed list if
} // end word list exists if
```

You should be able to tell the general program flow even if you don't understand exactly how things happen. The main section of a well-defined program should give you a bird's eye view of the action. Most of the details are delegated to functions.

Most of the remaining chapter is devoted to explaining how these functions work. Try to make sure you've got the basic gist of the program's flow; then you see how all of it is done.

Parsing the Word List

One important early task involves analyzing the word list that comes from the user. The word list comes as one long string separated by newline (`\n`) characters. The `parseList()` function converts this string into an array of words. It has some other important functions too, including converting each word to uppercase, checking for words that do not fit in the designated puzzle size, and removing unneeded carriage returns.

```
function parseList(){
  //gets word list, creates array of words from it
  //or return false if impossible

  global $word, $wordList, $boardData;

  $itWorked = TRUE;

  //convert word list entirely to upper case
  $wordList = strtoupper($wordList);

  //split word list into array
  $word = split("\n", $wordList);

  foreach ($word as $currentWord){
    //take out trailing newline characters
    $currentWord = rtrim($currentWord);

    //stop if any words are too long to fit in puzzle
    if ((strLen($currentWord) > $boardData["width"]) &&
        (strLen($currentWord) > $boardData["height"])){
      print "$currentWord is too long for puzzle";
      $itWorked = FALSE;
    } // end if

  } // end foreach
  return $itWorked;
} // end parseList
```

The first thing I did was use the `strtoupper()` function to convert the entire word list into uppercase letters. Word search puzzles always seem to use capital letters, so I decided to convert everything to that format.

The long string of characters with newlines is not a useful format here, so I converted the long string into an array called `$word`. The `split()` function works perfectly for this task. I split on the string `"\n"`. This is the newline character, so it should convert each line of the text area into an element of the new `$word` array.

The next task was to analyze each word in the array with a `foreach` loop. When I tested this part of the program, it became clear that sometimes the trailing newline character was still there, so I used the `rtrim()` function to trim off any unnecessary trailing whitespace.

It is impossible to create the puzzle if the user enters a word larger than the height or width of the puzzle board, so I check for this situation by comparing the length of each word to the board's height and width. Note that if the word is too long, I simply set the value of the `$itWorked` variable to `FALSE`.

Earlier in this function, I initialized the value of `$itWorked` to `TRUE`. By the time the function is finished, `$itWorked` still contains the value `TRUE` if all the words were small enough to fit in the puzzle. If any of the words were too large, the value of `$itWorked` is `FALSE` and the program stops.

Clearing the Board

`Word Search` uses a crude but effective technique to generate legal game boards (boards which contain all the words in the list). It creates random boards repeatedly until it finds one that is legal. While this may seem like a wasteful approach, it is much easier to program than many more sophisticated methods and produces remarkably good results for simple problems.

In the Real World

Although this program does use a brute force approach to find a good solution, you see a number of ways the code is optimized to make a good solution more likely. One example of this is the way the program stops if one of the words is too long to fit in the puzzle. This prevents a long processing time while the program tries to fit a word in the puzzle when it cannot be done. A number of other places in the code do some work to steer the algorithm toward good solutions and away from pitfalls. Because of these efforts, you find that the program is actually pretty good at finding word search puzzles unless there are too many words or the game board is too small.

The game board is often re-created several times during one program execution. I needed a function that could initialize the game board or reset it easily. The game board is stored in a two-dimensional array called `$board`. When the board is "empty," each cell contains the period (.) character. I chose this convention because it gives me something visible in each cell and provides a character that represents an empty cell. The `clearBoard()` function sets or resets the `$board` array so that every cell contains a period.

```
function clearBoard(){
  //initialize board with a . in each cell
  global $board, $boardData;

  for ($row = 0; $row < $boardData["height"]; $row++){
    for ($col = 0; $col < $boardData["width"]; $col++){
      $board[$row][$col] = ".";
    } // end col for loop
  } // end row for loop
} // end clearBoard
```

This code is the classic nested `for` loop so common to two-dimensional arrays. Note that I used `for` loops rather than `foreach` loops because I was interested in the loop indices. The outer `for` loop steps through the rows. Inside each row loop, another loop steps through each column. I assigned the value `"."` to the `$board` array at the current `$row` and `$col` locations. Eventually, `"."` is in every cell in the array.

I determined the size of the `for` loops by referring to the `$boardData` associative array. Although I could have done this a number of ways, I chose the associative array for several reasons. The most important is clarity. It's easy for me to see by this structure that I'm working with the height and width related to board data. Another advantage in this context is convenience. Since the height, width, and board name are stored in the `$boardData` array, I could make a global reference to the `$boardData` variable and all its values would come along. It's like having three variables for the price of one.

Filling the Board

Of course, the purpose of clearing the board is to fill it in with the words from the word list. This happens in two stages: filling the board, and adding the words. The `fillBoard()` function controls the entire process of filling up the whole board, but the details of adding each word to the board are relegated to the `addWord()` function (which you see next).

The board is only complete if each word is added correctly. Each word is added only if each of its letters is added without problems. The program calls `fillBoard()` as often as necessary to get a correct solution. Each time `fillBoard()` runs, it may call `addWord()` as many times as necessary until each word is added. The `addWord()` function in turn keeps track of whether it is able to successfully add each character to the board.

The general `fillBoard()` function plan is to generate a random direction for each word and then tell the `addWord()` function to place the specified word in the specified direction on the board.

The looping structure for the `fillBoard()` function is a little unique, because the loop could exit two ways. If any of the words cannot be placed in the requested manner, the puzzle generation stops immediately and the function returns the value `FALSE`. However, if the entire word list is successfully placed on the game board, the function should stop looping, but report the value `TRUE`.

You can achieve this effect a number of ways, but I prefer often to use a special Boolean variable for this purpose. *Boolean variables* are variables meant to contain only the values `TRUE` and `FALSE`. Of course, PHP is pretty easygoing about variable types, but you can make a variable act like a Boolean simply by assigning it only the values `TRUE` or `FALSE`. In the `fillBoard()` function, look at how the `$keepGoing` variable is used. It is initialized to `TRUE`, and the function's main loop keeps running as long as this is the case.

However, the two conditions that can cause the loop to exit—the `addWord()` function failed to place a word correctly, or the entire word list has been exhausted—cause the `$keepGoing` variable to become `FALSE`. When this happens, the loop stops and the function shortly exits.

```
function fillBoard(){
  //fill board with list by calling addWord() for each word
  //or return false if failed

  global $word;
  $direction = array("N", "S", "E", "W");
  $itWorked = TRUE;
  $counter = 0;
  $keepGoing = TRUE;
  while($keepGoing){
    $dir = rand(0, 3);
    $result = addWord($word[$counter], $direction[$dir]);
    if ($result == FALSE){
```

```
      //print "failed to place $word[$counter]";
      $keepGoing = FALSE;
      $itWorked = FALSE;
    } // end if
    $counter++;
    if ($counter >= count($word)){
      $keepGoing = FALSE;
    } // end if
  } // end while
  return $itWorked;

} // end fillBoard
```

The function begins by defining an array for directions. At this point, I decided only to support placing words in the four cardinal directions, although it would be easy enough to add diagonals. (Hey, that sounds like a *dandy* end-of-chapter exercise!) The `$direction` array holds the initials of the four directions I have decided to support at this time. The `$itWorked` variable is a Boolean which reports whether the board has been successfully filled. It is initialized to `TRUE`. If the `addWord()` function fails to place a word, the `$itWorked` value is changed to `FALSE`.

The `$counter` variable counts which word I'm currently trying to place. I increment the value of `$counter` each time through the loop. When `$counter` is larger than the `$word` array, the function has successfully added every word and can exit triumphantly.

To choose a direction, I simply created a random value between `0` and `3` and referred to the associated value of the `$direction` array.

The last line of the function returns the value of `$itWorked`. The `fillBoard()` function is called by the main program until it succeeds. This success or failure is reported to the main program by returning the value of `$itWorked`.

Adding a Word

The `fillBoard()` function handles the global process of adding the word list to the game board, but `addWord()` adds each word to the board. This function expects two parameters: the word and a direction.

The function cleans up the word and renders slightly different service based on which direction the word is placed. It places each letter of the word in an appropriate cell while preventing it from being placed outside the game board's boundary. It also checks to make sure that the cell does not currently house some other letter from another word (unless that letter happens to be the one the function is already trying to place). The function may look long and complex at first, but when you look at it more closely you find it's extremely repetitive.

```
function addWord($theWord, $dir){
  //attempt to add a word to the board or return false if failed
  global $board, $boardData;

  //remove trailing characters if necessary
  $theWord = rtrim($theWord);

  $itWorked = TRUE;

  switch ($dir){
    case "E":
      //col from 0 to board width - word width
      //row from 0 to board height
      $newCol = rand(0, $boardData["width"] - 1 - strlen($theWord));
      $newRow = rand(0, $boardData["height"]-1);

      for ($i = 0; $i < strlen($theWord); $i++){
        //new character same row, initial column + $i
        $boardLetter = $board[$newRow][$newCol + $i];
        $wordLetter = substr($theWord, $i, 1);

        //check for legal values in current space on board
        if (($boardLetter == $wordLetter) ||
            ($boardLetter == ".")){
          $board[$newRow][$newCol + $i] = $wordLetter;
        } else {
          $itWorked = FALSE;
        } // end if
      } // end for loop
      break;

    case "W":
      //col from word width to board width
      //row from 0 to board height
      $newCol = rand(strlen($theWord), $boardData["width"] -1);
      $newRow = rand(0, $boardData["height"]-1);
      //print "west:\tRow: $newRow\tCol: $newCol<br>\n";
```

```
  for ($i = 0; $i < strlen($theWord); $i++){
    //check for a legal move
    $boardLetter = $board[$newRow][$newCol - $i];
    $wordLetter = substr($theWord, $i, 1);
    if (($boardLetter == wordLetter) ||
        ($boardLetter == ".")){
      $board[$newRow][$newCol - $i] = $wordLetter;
    } else {
      $itWorked = FALSE;
    } // end if
  } // end for loop
  break;

case "S":
  //col from 0 to board width
  //row from 0 to board height - word length
  $newCol = rand(0, $boardData["width"] -1);
  $newRow = rand(0, $boardData["height"]-1 - strlen($theWord));
  //print "south:\tRow: $newRow\tCol: $newCol<br>\n";

  for ($i = 0; $i < strlen($theWord); $i++){
    //check for a legal move
    $boardLetter = $board[$newRow + $i][$newCol];
    $wordLetter = substr($theWord, $i, 1);
    if (($boardLetter == $wordLetter) ||
        ($boardLetter == ".")){
      $board[$newRow + $i][$newCol] = $wordLetter;
    } else {
     $itWorked = FALSE;
    } // end if
  } // end for loop
  break;

case "N":
  //col from 0 to board width
  //row from word length to board height
  $newCol = rand(0, $boardData["width"] -1);
  $newRow = rand(strlen($theWord), $boardData["height"]-1);

  for ($i = 0; $i < strlen($theWord); $i++){
```

```
        //check for a legal move
        $boardLetter = $board[$newRow - $i][$newCol];
        $wordLetter = substr($theWord, $i, 1);
        if (($boardLetter == $wordLetter) ||
            ($boardLetter == ".")){
          $board[$newRow - $i][$newCol] = $wordLetter;
        } else {
         $itWorked = FALSE;
        } // end if
      } // end for loop
      break;

  } // end switch
  return $itWorked;
} // end addWord
```

The `addWord()` function's main focus is a `switch` structure based on the word direction. The code inside the `switch` branches are similar in their general approach.

Closely Examining the East Code

It's customary in Western languages to write from left to right, so the code for `E`, which indicates *write towards the East,* is probably the most natural to understand. I explain how that code works and then show you how the other directions differ.

Here's the code fragment that attempts to write a word in the Easterly direction:

```
case "E":
      //col from 0 to board width - word width
      //row from 0 to board height
      $newCol = rand(0,
                $boardData["width"] - 1 - strlen($theWord));
      $newRow = rand(0, $boardData["height"]-1);

      for ($i = 0; $i < strlen($theWord); $i++){
        //new character same row, initial column + $i
        $boardLetter = $board[$newRow][$newCol + $i];
        $wordLetter = substr($theWord, $i, 1);

        //check for legal values in current space on board
        if (($boardLetter == $wordLetter) ||
            ($boardLetter == ".")){
          $board[$newRow][$newCol + $i] = $wordLetter;
```

```
    } else {
      $itWorked = FALSE;
    } // end if
  } // end for loop
  break;
```

Determining Starting Values for the Characters

Essentially, the code steps through the word one letter at a time, placing each letter in the next cell to the right. I could have chosen any random cell and checked to see when the code got outside the board range, but this would have involved some complicated and clunky code.

A more elegant solution is to carefully determine what the range of appropriate starting cells are and choose cells within that range. For example, if I'm placing the word `elephant` (with eight letters) from left to right in a puzzle with a width of 10, zero and one are the only legal columns. (Remember, computers usually start counting at zero.) If I place `elephant` in the same puzzle but from right to left, the last two columns (eight and nine) are the only legal options. Once I recognized this fact, I had to figure out how to encode this idea so it could work with any size words in any size puzzle.

> **IN THE REAL WORLD**
>
> **By far the most critical part of this code is the comments at the beginning. Even though I'm a reasonably experienced programmer, it's easy to get confused when I start solving problems of any reasonable complexity. Just to remind myself, I placed these comments to explain exactly what the parameters of this chunk of code are.**
>
> **I referred to these comments many times while I was writing and debugging the code. If I hadn't given myself clear guidance on what I was trying to do, I would have gotten so lost I probably wouldn't have been able to write the program.**

I need a random value for the row and column to figure out where to place each word. However, that random value must be within an appropriate range based on the word length and board width. By trial and error and some sketches on a white board, I determined that `$boardData["width"] - 1` is the largest column in the game board and that `strlen($theWord)` is the length of the current word in characters.

If I subtract the word length from the board width, I get the largest legal starting value for a left-to-right placement. That's how I got this slightly scary formula:

```
$boardData["width"] - 1 - strlen($theWord)
```

The smallest legal starting value for this kind of placement is 0, because column zero always works when you're going right-to-left and the word is the same size or smaller than the puzzle (which has been established). Row number doesn't matter in an Eastward placement, because any row in the puzzle is legal—all letters are placed on the same row.

Once I know the word's largest and smallest legal starting places, I can randomly generate that starting point knowing that the entire word can be placed there legally as long as it doesn't overlap any other.

I used a `for` loop to pull one character at a time using the `substr()` function. The for loop counter (`$i`) is used to determine the starting character of the substring, which is always one character long. Each character is placed at the same row as the starting character, but at a column offset by the position in the word. Revisit the elephant example: If the starting position chosen is column one, the character `E` is placed in column one, because `E` is at the 0th position in the word `elephant`, and 1 + 0 = 1. When the counter (`$i`) gets to the letter `L`, it has the value `1`, so it is placed in column two, and so on.

If the formula for choosing the starting place and the plan for placing subsequent letters in place work correctly, you cannot add a letter outside the puzzle board. However, another bad thing could happen if a character from a previously placed word is in a cell that the current word wants. The code checks the current cell on the game board to see its current status. If the cell contains the value `"."`, it is empty and the new character can be freely placed there. If the cell contains the value that the current word wants to place in the cell, the program can likewise continue without interruption. However, if the cell contains any other character, the loop must exit and the program must reset the board and try again. Do this by setting the `$itWorked` value to `FALSE`.

Printing in the Other Directions

Once you understand how to print words when the direction is East, you see that the other directions are similar. However, I need to figure out each direction's appropriate starting values and what cell to place each letter in. Table 5.2 summarizes these values.

A little explanation of Table 5.2 is in order. Within the table, I identified the minimum and maximum column for each direction, as well as the minimum and maximum row. This was easiest to figure out by writing some examples on graph paper. The placement of each letter is based on the starting row and column, with `i` standing for the position of the current letter within the word. In direction `W`, I put the letter at position `2` of my word into the randomly chosen starting row, but at the starting column minus `2`. This prints the letters from right to left. Work out the other examples on graph paper so you can see how they work.

In the Real World

This is exactly where computer programming becomes mystical for most people. Up to now you've probably been following, but this business of placing the characters has a lot of math in it, and you didn't get to see me struggle with it. It might look to you as if I just knew what the right formulas were. I didn't. I had to think about it carefully *without* the computer turned on. I got out a white board (my favorite programming tool) and some graph paper and tried to figure out what I meant mathematically when I said *write the characters from bottom to top.*

This is hard, but you can do it. The main thing to remember? Turn off the computer. Get some paper and figure out what it is you're trying to tell the computer to do. Then you can start writing code. You may get it wrong (at least I did). But if you've written down your strategy, you can compare what you expected to happen with what did happen, and likely solve even this kind of somewhat mathematical problem.

Making a Puzzle Board

By the time the `fillBoard()` function has finished calling `addWord()` to add all the words, the answer key is complete. Each word is in place and any cell that does not contain one of the words still has a period. The main program copies the current `$board` variable over to the `$key` array. The answer key is now ready to be formatted into a form the user can use.

Table 5.2 Summary of Placement Data

	E	W	S	N
min Col	0	word width	0	0
max Col	board width – 1 – word width	board width – 1	board width – 1	board width – 1
min Row	0	0	0	word width
max Row	board height – 1	board height – 1	board height – 1 – word width	board height – 1
letter col	start + i	start – i	start	start
letter row	start	start	start + i	start – i

However, rather than writing one function to print the answer key and another to print the finished puzzle, I wrote one function that takes the array as a parameter and creates a long string of HTML code placing that puzzle in a table.

```
function makeBoard($theBoard){
  //given a board array, return an HTML table based on the array
  global $boardData;
  $puzzle = "";
  $puzzle .= "<table border = 0>\n";
  for ($row = 0; $row < $boardData["height"]; $row++){
    $puzzle .= "<tr>\n";
    for ($col = 0; $col < $boardData["width"]; $col++){
      $puzzle .= "  <td width = 15>{$theBoard[$row][$col]}</td>\n";
    } // end col for loop
    $puzzle .= "</tr>\n";
  } // end row for loop
  $puzzle .= "</table>\n";
  return $puzzle;
} // end printBoard;
```

Most of the function deals with creating an HTML table, which is stored in the variable `$puzzle`. Each puzzle row begins by building an HTML `<tr>` tag and creates a `<td></td>` pair for each table element.

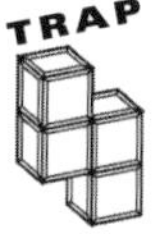

Sometimes PHP has trouble correctly interpolating two-dimensional arrays. If you find an array is not being correctly interpolated, try two things:

- **Surround the array reference in braces as I did in the code in** `makeBoard()`
- **Forego interpolation and use concatenation instead. For example, you could have built each cell with the following code:**

```
$puzzle .= "<td> width = 15>" . $theBoard[$row][$col] . "</td>\n";
```

Adding the Foil Letters

The puzzle itself can be easily derived from the answer key. Once the words in the list are in place, all it takes to generate a puzzle is replacing the periods with some other random letters. I call these other characters *foil letters* because it is their job to foil the user. This is actually quite easy compared to the process of adding the words.

```
function addFoils(){
  //add random dummy characters to board
  global $board, $boardData;
```

```
  for ($row = 0; $row < $boardData["height"]; $row++){
    for ($col = 0; $col < $boardData["width"]; $col++){
      if ($board[$row][$col] == "."){
        $newLetter = rand(65, 90);
        $board[$row][$col] = chr($newLetter);
      } // end if
    } // end col for loop
  } // end row for loop
} // end addFoils
```

The function uses the standard pair of nested loops to cycle through each cell in the array. For each cell that contains a period, the function generates a random number between `65` and `90`. These numbers correspond to the ASCII numeric codes for the capital letters. I used the `chr()` function to retrieve the letter that corresponds to that number and stored the new random letter in the array.

Printing the Puzzle

The last step in the main program is to print results to the user. So far, all the work has been done behind the scenes. Now it is necessary to produce an HTML page with the results. The `printPuzzle()` function performs this duty. The `printBoard()` function has already formatted the actual puzzle and answer key tables as HTML. The puzzle HTML is stored in the `$puzzle` variable, and the answer key is stored in `$keyPuzzle`.

```
function printPuzzle(){
  //print out page to user with puzzle on it

  global $puzzle, $word, $keyPuzzle, $boardData;
  //print puzzle itself

  print <<<HERE
  <center>
  <h1>{$boardData["name"]}</h1>
  $puzzle
  <h3>Word List</h3>
  <table border = 0>

HERE;

  //print word list
  foreach ($word as $theWord){
```

```
    print "<tr><td>$theWord</td></tr>\n";
  } // end foreach
  print "</table>\n";
  $puzzleName = $boardData["name"];

  //print form for requesting answer key.
  //send answer key to that form (sneaky!)
  print <<<HERE
  <br><br><br><br><br><br><br><br>
  <form action = "wordFindKey.php"
        method = "post">
  <input type = "hidden"
         name = "key"
         value = "$keyPuzzle">
  <input type = "hidden"
         name = "puzzleName"
         value = "$puzzleName">

  <input type = "submit"
         value = "show answer key">
  </form>
  </center>

HERE;
?>
</body>
</html>
} // end printPuzzle
```

This function mainly deals with printing standard HTML from variables that have been created during the program's run. The name of the puzzle is stored in `$boardData["name"]`. The puzzle itself is simply the value of the `$puzzle` variable. I printed the word list by a `foreach` loop creating a list from the `$word` array.

The trickiest part of the code is working with the answer key. It is easy enough to print the answer key directly on the same HTML page. In fact, this is exactly what I did as I was testing the program. However, the puzzle won't be much fun if the answer is right there, so I allowed the user to press a button to get the answer key. The key is related only to the currently generated puzzle. If the same word list were sent to the `Word Search` program again, it would likely produce a different puzzle with a different answer.

The secret is to store the current answer key in a hidden form element and pass this element to another program. I created a form with two hidden fields. I stored the name of the puzzle in a field called `puzzleName` and the entire HTML of the answer key in a field called `key`. When the user presses the `submit` key, it calls `wordFindKey`.

IN THE REAL WORLD

Passing the answer key to another program is a kind of dirty trick. It works for a couple of reasons. First, since the `key` field is hidden and the form sends data through the `post` method, the user is unlikely to know that the answer to the puzzle is literally under his nose. Since I expect this program mainly to be used by teachers who would print the puzzle anyway, this is fine. Even without the secrecy concerns, it is necessary to pass the key data by `post` because it is longer than the 256 characters allowed by the `get` method.

Sending the HTML-formatted answer key to the next program made the second program quite simple, but there is another advantage to this approach: It is difficult to send entire arrays through form variables. However, by creating the HTML table, all the array data was reduced to one string value, which can be passed to another program through a form.

Printing the Answer Key

The `wordFindKey` program is very simplistic, because all the work of generating the answer key was done by the `Word Search` program. `wordFindKey` has only to retrieve the puzzle name and answer key from form variables and print them out. Since the key has even been formatted as a table, the `wordFindKey` program needn't do any heavy lifting.

```
<!doctype html public "-//W3C//DTD HTML 4.0 //EN">
<html>
<head>
<title>Word Find Answer Key</title>
</head>
<body>

<?
//answer key for word find
//called from wordFind.php
```

```
print <<<HERE
<center>
<h1>$puzzleName Answer key</h1>
$key
</center>

HERE;
?>
</body>
</html>
```

Summary

In this chapter you see how important it is to put together data in meaningful ways. You look at a number of more powerful arrays and tools to manipulate them. You learn how to use the `foreach` loop to look at each element of an array in turn. You can use string indices to generate associative arrays and make two-dimensional arrays using both numeric and string indices. You learn how to do several kinds of string-manipulation tricks, including searching for one string inside another, extracting substrings, and splitting a string into an array. You put all these skills together in an interesting and detailed application. You should be proud of your efforts.

CHALLENGES

1. **Add the ability to use diagonals in your puzzles. (Hint: You need only combine the formulas I established. You don't need any new ones.)**
2. **Create a game of Battle Ship for two players on the same computer. The game prints a grid. (Preset the fleet locations to make it easier.) Let the user choose a location on the grid via a checkbox. Report the result of his firing back and then give the screen to the second user.**
3. **Write a version of `Conway's Life`. This program simulates cellular life on a grid with three simple rules.**
   a. **Each cell with exactly three neighbors becomes or remains alive.**
   b. **Each cell currently alive with exactly two neighbors remains alive.**
   c. **All other cells die off.**
4. **Randomly generate the first cell and let the user press a button to generate the next generation.**

Working with Files

As your experience in programming grows, the relative importance of data becomes increasingly apparent. You began your understanding of data with simple variables, but learned how simple and more complex arrays can make your programs more flexible and more powerful. However, data stored in the computer's memory is transient, especially in the server environment. It is often necessary to store information in a form that is more permanent than the constructs you have learned so far. PHP provides a number of powerful functions for working with text files. With these skills, you create extremely useful programs. Specifically, you learn how to:

- Open files for read, write, and append access
- Use file handles to manipulate text files
- Write data to a text file
- Read data from a text file
- Open an entire file into an array
- Modify text data on-the-fly
- Get information about all the files in a particular directory
- Get a subset of files based on filenames

Previewing the Quiz Machine

This chapter's main program is a fun and powerful tool that you can use in many different ways. It is not simply one program, but a system of programs that work together to let you automatically create, administer, and grade multiple-choice quizzes.

> **IN THE REAL WORLD**
>
> **It is reasonably easy to build an HTML page that presents a quiz and a PHP program to grade only that quiz. However, if you want several quizzes, it might be worth the investment in time and energy to build a system that can automate the creation and administration of quizzes. The real power of programming comes into play not just when you solve one immediate problem, but when you can produce a solution that can be applied to an entire range of related problems. The quiz machine is an example of exactly such a system. It takes a little more effort to build, but the effort really pays off when you have a system to reuse.**

Entering the Quiz Machine System

Figure 6.1 shows the system's main page. The user needs a password to take a test and an administrator password to edit a test. In this case, I entered the administrative password (it's `absolute`—like in *Absolute Beginner's Guide*) into the appropriate password box, and I'm going to edit the Monty Python quiz.

I refer to the quiz machine as a *system* rather than a program because it uses a number of programs intended to work together.

Editing a Quiz

The screen shown in Figure 6.2 appears when the user has the correct password. You can see the requested quiz in a special format on the screen.

The quiz administrator can edit the quiz. Each quiz has a name, instructor e-mail address, and password. Each question is stored in a single line with the question, four possible answers, and the correct answer separated by colon (:) characters.

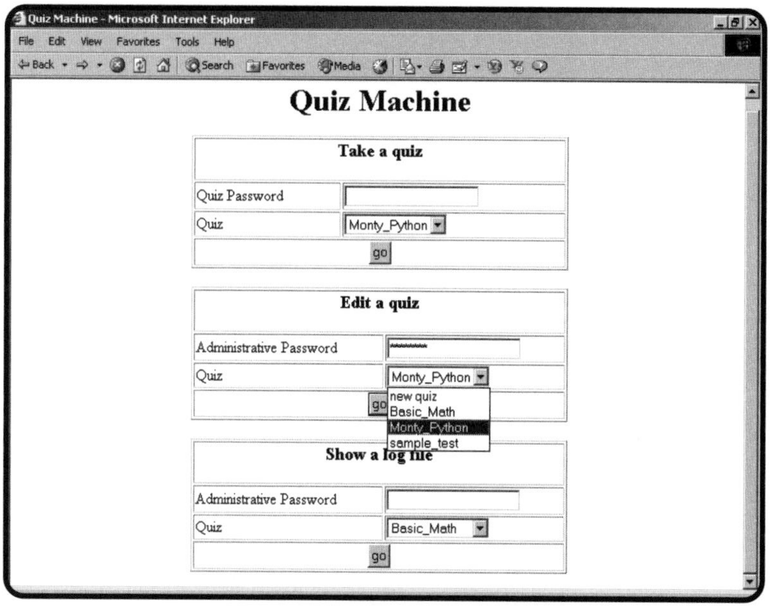

FIGURE 6.1

The user is an administrator preparing to edit a quiz.

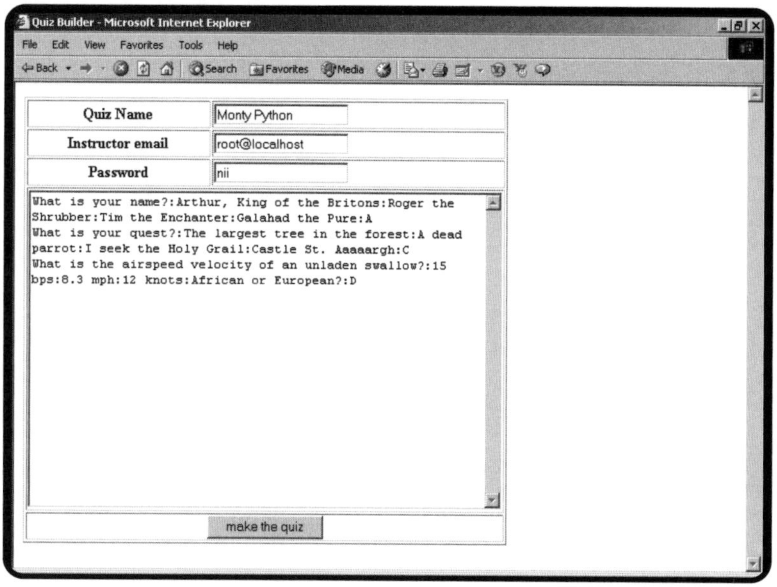

FIGURE 6.2

The user has chosen to edit the Monty Python quiz.

Taking a Quiz

Users with knowledge of the appropriate password can take any of the quizzes known to the system. If a user chooses to take the Monty Python quiz, the screen shown in Figure 6.3 appears.

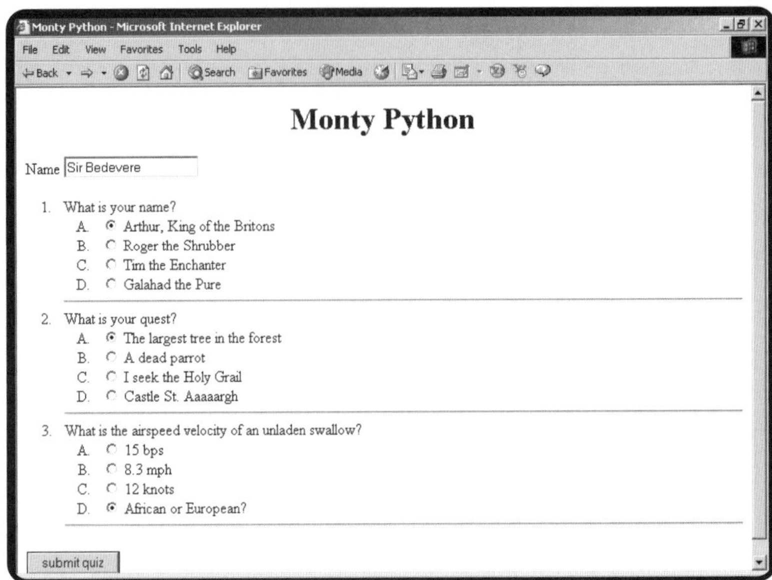

FIGURE 6.3

The user is taking the Monty Python quiz. If you want to become a serious programmer, you should probably rent this movie. It's part of the culture.

Seeing the Results

When the user takes a quiz, the user's responses are sent to a program that grades the quiz and provides immediate feedback, as shown in Figure 6.4.

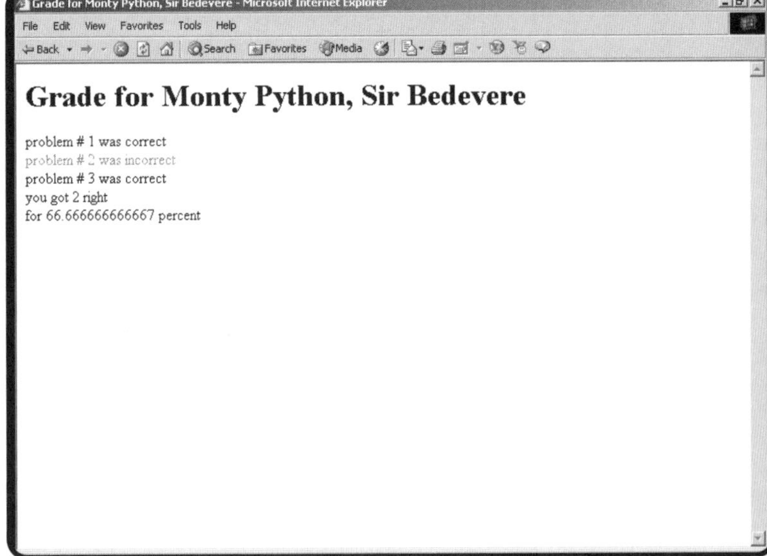

FIGURE 6.4

The grading program provides immediate feedback and stores the information in a file so the administrator can see it later.

Viewing the Quiz Log

The system keeps a log file for each quiz so the administrator can see each person's score. Figure 6.5 shows how people have done on the Monty Python quiz.

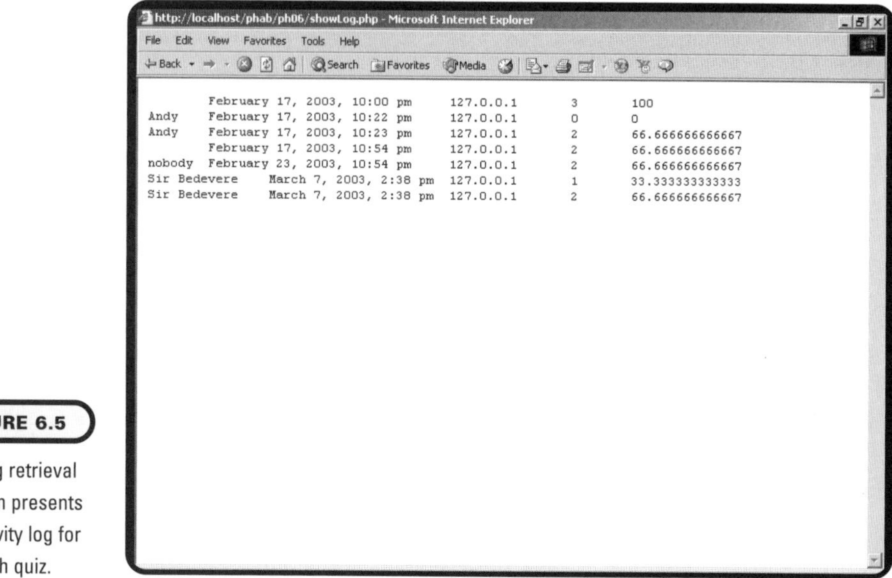

FIGURE 6.5

The log retrieval program presents an activity log for each quiz.

Although the resulting log looks very simplistic, it is generated in a format that can easily be imported into most gradebook programs and spreadsheets. This is very handy if you use the quiz in a classroom setting.

Saving a File to the File System

Your PHP programs can access the server's file system to store and retrieve information. Your programs can create new files, add data to files, and read information from the files. You start by writing a program that creates a file and adds data to it.

Introducing the saveSonnet.php Program

The `saveSonnet.php` program shown in the following code opens a file on the server and writes one of Shakespeare's sonnets to that file on the server.

Normally I show you a screen shot of every program, but that isn't useful since this particular program doesn't display anything on the screen. The next couple of programs read this file and display it onscreen. You see what they look like when the time comes.

```
<head>
<title>SaveSonnet</title>
</head>
<body>
<?

$sonnet76 = <<<HERE
Sonnet # 76, William Shakespeare

Why is my verse so barren of new pride,
So far from variation or quick change?
Why with the time do I not glance aside
To new-found methods, and to compounds strange?
Why write I still all one, ever the same,
And keep invention in a noted weed,
That every word doth almost tell my name,
Showing their birth, and where they did proceed?
O! know sweet love I always write of you,
And you and love are still my argument;
So all my best is dressing old words new,
Spending again what is already spent:
For as the sun is daily new and old,
So is my love still telling what is told.

HERE;

$fp = fopen("sonnet76.txt", "w");
fputs($fp, $sonnet76);
fclose($fp);

?>
</body>
</html>
```

Most of the code stores the contents of Shakespeare's 76th sonnet to a variable called `$sonnet76`. The remaining three lines save the data in the variable to a text file.

Opening a File with fopen()

The `fopen()` command opens a file. Note that you can create files on the Web server only—you cannot directly create a file on the client machine, because you do not have access to that machine's file system. (If you did, any server-side program would be able to create viruses with extreme ease.) However, as a server-side programmer, you already have the ability to create files on the server. The programs you are writing are files. Your programs can write files as if they are you.

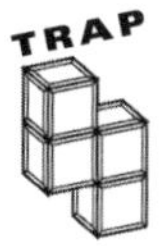

The ownership of files created by your PHP programs can be a little more complicated, depending on your operating system, server, and PHP configurations. Generally, any file that your program creates is owned by a special user called `PHP` or by the account you were in when you wrote the program. This makes a big difference in an operating system like UNIX, where file ownership is a major part of the security mechanism. The best way to discover how this works is to write a program that creates a file and then look at that file's properties.

The filename is the first parameter of the `fopen()` function. This filename can include directory information or it can be a relative reference starting from the current file's location.

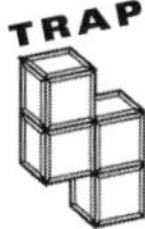

Always test your programs, especially if they use a relative reference for a filename. It's possible that your current directory is not the default directory. Also, the filename is based on the actual file server system, rather than the file's URL.

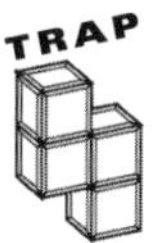

Some servers are set up to require a full filename for `fopen()` and included files. If you have trouble opening a file, use the complete filename for the file rather than a relative reference to that file. On Windows systems, this should begin with the drive name (eg c:\apache\htdocs\myFile.txt) in Unix and Linux, use the pwd command to find the complete path of the file (eg /home/aharris/htdocs/myFile.txt).

You can create a file anywhere on the server to which you have access. Your files can be in the parts of your directory system open to the Web server (usually subdirectories of `public_html` or `htdocs`). Sometimes, though, you might not want your files to be directly accessible to users by typing a URL. You can control access to these files as follows:

- Place them outside the public HTML space.
- Set permissions so they can be read by you (and programs you create) but not by anyone else.

Creating a File Handle

When you create a file with the `fopen()` command, the function returns an integer called a *file handle* (sometimes also called a *file pointer*). This special number refers to the file in subsequent commands. You aren't usually concerned about this handle's actual value, but need to store it in a variable (I usually use `$fp`) so your other file-access commands know which file to work with.

Examining File Access Modifiers

The final parameter in the fopen() command is an access modifier. PHP supports a number of access modifiers, which determine how your program interacts with the file. Files are usually opened for these modes: reading, writing, or appending. Read mode opens a file for input, so your program can read information from the file. You cannot write data to a file that is opened in read mode. Write mode allows you to open a file for output access. If the file does not exist, PHP automatically creates it for you. Append mode allows you to write to a file without destroying the current contents. When you write to a file in append mode, all new data is added to the end of the file.

You can use a file for random access, which allows a file to be open simultaneously for input and output, but such files are often not needed in PHP. The relational database techniques provide the same capability with more flexibility and a lot less work. However, the other forms of file access (read, write, and output) are extremely useful, because they provide easy access to the file information.

Table 6.1 File Access Modifiers

Modifier	Type	Description
"r"	Read-only	Program can read from the file
"w"	Write	Writes to the file, overwriting it if it already exists
"a"	Append	Writes to the end of the file
"r+" "w+"	Read and write	Random access. Read or write to a specified part of the file

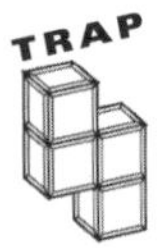

Be very careful about opening a file in write mode. If you open an already existing file for write access, PHP creates a new file and overwrites and destroys the old file's contents.

In the Real World

The "r+" and "w+" modifiers are used for another form of file access, called *random access,* which allows simultaneous reading and writing to the same file. While this is a very useful tool, I won't spend a lot of time on it in this book. The sequential-access methods in this chapter are fine for simple file storage problems; the XML and relational database functions in the remainder of this book aren't any more difficult than the random access model and provide far more power.

Writing to a File

The saveSonnet program opens the sonnet76.txt file for write access. If there were already a file in the current directory, it is destroyed. The $fp variable stores the file pointer for the text file. Once this is done, you can use the fputs() function to actually write data to the file.

You might be noticing a trend here. Most of the file access functions begin with the letter f: fopen(), fclose(), fputs(), fgets(), feof(). This convention is inherited from the C language. It can help you remember that a particular function works with files. Of course, every statement in PHP that begins with f isn't necessarily a file function (foreach is a good example), but most function names in PHP that begin with f are file-handling commands.

The fputs() function requires two parameters. The first is a file pointer, which tells PHP where to write the data. The second parameter is the text to write out to the file.

Closing a File

The fclose() function tells the system that your program is done working with the file and should close it.

Drive systems are much slower than computer memory and take a long time to spool up to speed. For that reason, when a program encounters an fputs() command, it doesn't always immediately save the data to a file on the disk. Instead, it adds the data to a special buffer and writes the data only when a sufficient amount is on the buffer or the program encounters an fclose() command. This is why it's important to close your files. If the program ends without encountering an fclose() statement, PHP is supposed to automatically close the file for you, but what's supposed to happen and what actually happens are often two very different things.

Loading a File from the Drive System

You can retrieve information from the file system. If you open a file with the "r" access modifier, you can read information from the file.

Introducing the loadSonnet.php Program

The loadSonnet.php program, shown in Figure 6.6 loads the sonnet saved by saveSonnet.php and displays it as befits the work of the Bard.

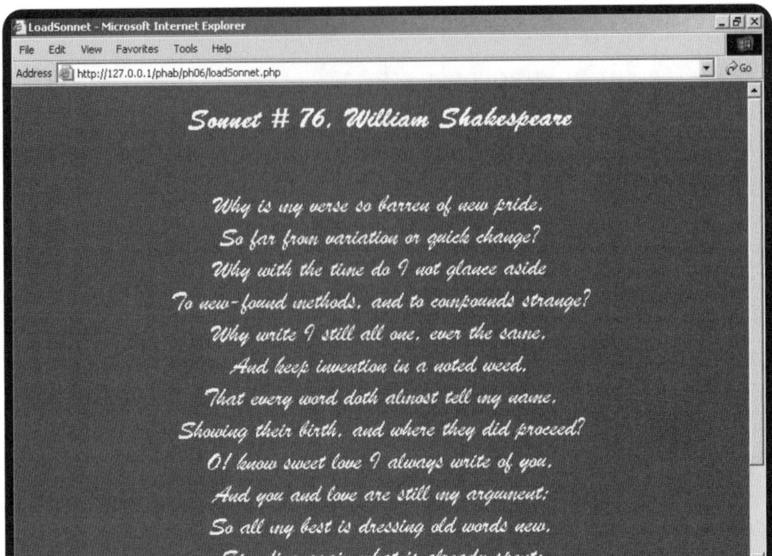

FIGURE 6.6

The file has been loaded from the drive system and prettied up a bit with some cascading style sheets (CSS) tricks.

The code for the `loadSonnet` program follows:

```
<html>
<head>
<title>LoadSonnet</title>
<style type = "text/css">
body{
  background-color:darkred;
  color:white;
  font-family:'Brush Script MT', script;
  font-size:20pt
}
</style>

</head>
<body>
<?
$fp = fopen("sonnet76.txt", "r");

//first line is title
$line = fgets($fp);
print "<center><h1>$line</h1></center>\n";

print "<center>\n";
```

```
//print rest of sonnet
while (!feof($fp)){
  $line = fgets($fp);
  print "$line <br>\n";
} // end while

print "</center>\n";

fclose($fp);

?>

</body>
</html>
```

Beautifying Output with CSS

CSS styles are the best way to improve text appearance. By setting up a simple style sheet, I very quickly improve the sonnet's appearance without changing the text. Notice especially how I indicated multiple fonts in case my preferred font was not installed on the user's system.

Using the "r" Access Modifier

To read from a file, you must get a file pointer by opening that file for `"r"` access. If the file does not exist, you get the result `FALSE` rather than a file pointer.

You can open files anywhere on the Internet for read access. If you supply a URL as a filename you can read the URL as if it were a local file. However, you cannot open URL files for output.

I opened `sonnet76.txt` with the `fopen()` command using the `"r"` access modifier and again copied the resulting integer to the `$fp` file pointer variable.

Checking for the End of the File with feof()

When you are reading data from a file, your program doesn't generally know the file length. The `fgets()` command, which gets data from a file, reads one line of the file at a time. Since you can't be sure how many lines are in a file until you read it, PHP provides a special function called `feof()`, which stands for file end of file (apparently named by the Department of Redundancy Department).

This function returns the value FALSE if any more lines of data are left in the file. It returns TRUE when the program is at the end of the data file. Most of the time when you read file data, you use a while loop that continues as long as feof() is not true. The easiest way to set up this loop is with a statement like this:

```
while (!feof($fp)){
```

The feof() function requires a file pointer as its sole parameter.

Reading Data from the File with fgets()

The fgets() function gets one line of data from the file, returns that value as a string, and moves a special pointer to the next line of the file. Usually this function is called inside a loop that continues until feof() is TRUE.

Reading a File into an Array

It is often useful to work with a file by loading it into an array in memory. Frequently you find yourself doing some operation on each array line. PHP provides a couple of features that simplify this type of operation. The cartoonifier.php program demonstrates one way of manipulating an entire file without using a file pointer.

Introducing the cartoonifier.php Program

The cartoonifier.php program illustrated in Figure 6.7 is a truly serious and weighty use of advanced server technology.

This program loads the entire sonnet into an array, steps through each line, and converts it to a unique cartoon dialect by performing a search and replace operation.

```
<html>
<head>
<title>Cartoonify</title>
</head>
<body>
<?
$fileName = "sonnet76.txt";

$sonnet = file($fileName);
$output = "";
```

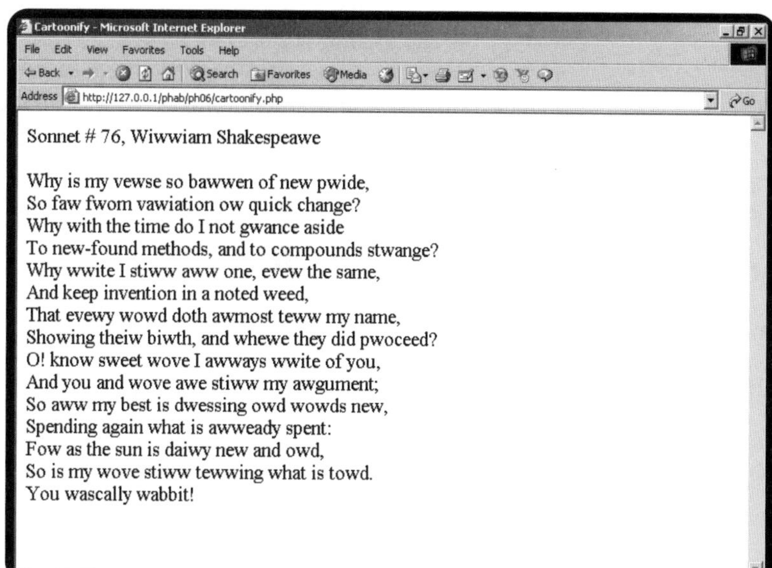

FIGURE 6.7

The `cartoonifier.php` program shows what would happen if Shakespeare were a cartoon character.

```
foreach ($sonnet as $currentLine){
  $currentLine = str_replace("r", "w", $currentLine);
  $currentLine = str_replace("l", "w", $currentLine);
  $output .= rtrim($currentLine) . "<br>\n";
} // end foreach
  $output .= "You wascally wabbit!<br>\n";

print $output;

?>
</body>
</html>
```

Loading the File into an Array with file()

Some shortcut file-handling tricks do not require you to create a file pointer. You might recall the `readFile()` command from chapter 1, "Exploring the PHP Environment." That file simply reads a file and echoes it to the output. The `file()` command is similar, because it does not require a file pointer. It opens a file for input and returns an array, with each file line occupying one array element. This can make file work easy, because you can use a `foreach` loop to step through each line and perform modifications.

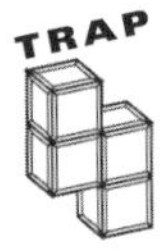

Reading a file into an array is attractive because it's easy; you can quickly work with the file once it's in memory. The problem comes when working with very large files. The computer's memory is finite and large files can cause problems. For larger data files, try a one-line-at-a-time approach using the `fgets()` function inside a loop.

Using str_replace() to Modify File Contents

Inside the `foreach` loop, it's a simple matter to convert all occurrences of `"r"` and `"l"` to the letter `"w"` with the `str_replace()` function. The resulting string is added to the `$output` variable, which is ultimately printed to the screen.

IN THE REAL WORLD

This particular application is silly and pointless, but the ability to replace all occurrences of one string with another in a text file is useful in a variety of circumstances. For example, you could replace every occurrence of the left brace (<) character in an HTML document with the `<` sequence. This results in a source code listing that's directly viewable on the browser. You might use such technology for form letters, taking information in a text template and replacing it with values pulled from the user or another file.

Working with Directory Information

When you are working with file systems, you often need to work with the directory structure that contains the files. PHP contains several commands that assist in directory manipulation.

Introducing the imageIndex.php Program

The `imageIndex.php` program featured in Figure 6.8 is a simple utility that generates an index of all `jpg` and `gif` image files in a particular directory.

Anytime the user clicks a thumbnail, a full version of the image is displayed. The techniques that display the images can be used to get selected file sets from any directory. The `imageIndex.php` program automatically generates a thumbnail page based on all the image files in a particular directory.

```
<html>
<head>
<title>imageIndex</title>
</head>
```

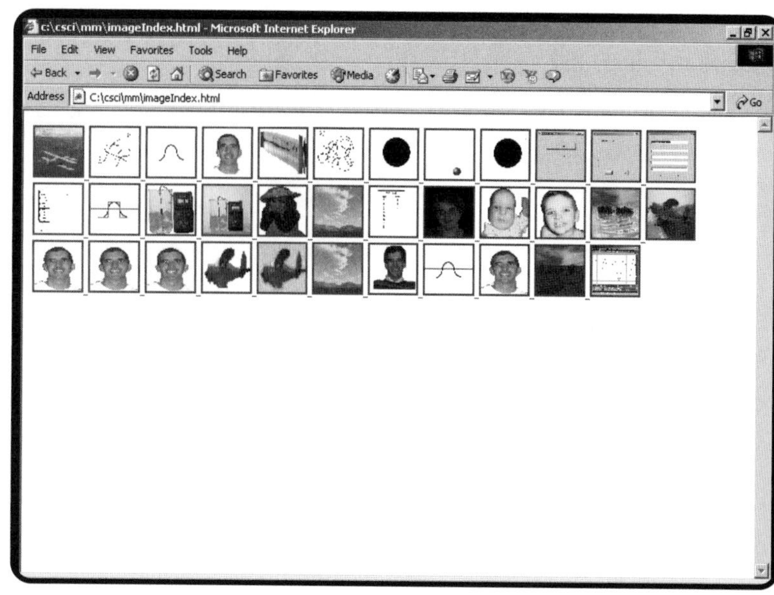

FIGURE 6.8

imageIndex.php automatically created this HTML file.

```
<body>

<?
// image index
// generates an index file containing all images in a particular directory

//point to whatever directory you wish to index.
//index will be written to this directory as imageIndex.html
$dirName = "C:\csci\mm";
$dp = opendir($dirName);
chdir($dirName);

//add all files in directory to $theFiles array
while ($currentFile !== false){
  $currentFile = readDir($dp);
  $theFiles[] = $currentFile;
} // end while

//extract gif and jpg images
$imageFiles = preg_grep("/jpg$|gif$/", $theFiles);

$output = "";
foreach ($imageFiles as $currentFile){
  $output .= <<<HERE
<a href = $currentFile>
```

```
    <img src = "$currentFile"
         height = 50
         width = 50>
  </a>

  HERE;

  } // end foreach

  //save the index to the local file system
  $fp = fopen("imageIndex.html", "w");
  fputs ($fp, $output);
  fclose($fp);
  //readFile("imageIndex.html");
  print "<a href = $dirName/imageIndex.html>image index</a>\n";

   ?>

  </body>
  </html>
```

Creating a Directory Handle with openDir()

Of course, directory operations focus on a particular directory. It's smart to store a directory name in a variable for easy changing, as directory conventions change when you migrate your programs to different systems. In the `imageIndex` program, I stored the target directory in a variable called `$dirName`. You can store the directory as a relative reference (in which case it is located in reference to the current program's directory) or absolute (in the current file system).

Getting a List of Files with readdir()

The `readdir()` function reads a file from a valid directory pointer. Each time you call the `readdir()` function, it returns the name of the next file it finds, until no files are left. When the function has run out of files, it returns the value `FALSE`.

I find it useful to store all the directory files in an array, so I usually loop like this:

```
while ($currentFile !== FALSE){
  $currentFile = readDir($dp);
  $theFiles[] = $currentFile;
} // end while
```

This loop keeps going until the `$currentFile` variable is `FALSE`, which happens when no files are left in the directory. Each time through the loop, it uses the `readdir()` function to load a new value into `$currentFile`, then adds the value of `$currentFile` to the `$theFiles` array. When I assign a value to an array without specifying the index, the item is simply placed at the next available index value. Loading an array in PHP is easy this way.

The special `!==` operator is a little different than the comparison operators you have seen before. Here it prevents a very specific type of error. It's possible that the user might have a file actually called `"false"` in the directory. If that's the case, the more normal condition `$currentFile != false` would give a strange result, because PHP could confuse a file named `"false"` with the actual literal value `false`. The `!==` operator specifies a comparison between actual objects rather than values, and it works correctly in this particular odd circumstance.

Selecting Particular Files with preg_grep()

Once all the files from a particular directory are stored in an array, you often want to work with a subset of those files. In this particular case, I'm interested in graphic files, which end with the characters `gif` or `jpg`.

The oddly named `preg_grep()` function is perfect. It borrows some clever ideas from UNIX shells and the Perl programming language. `grep` is the name of a UNIX command that filters files according to a pattern. `preg` indicates that this form of `grep` uses Perl-style regular expressions. Regardless of the funny name, the function is very handy. If you look back at the code in `imageIndex.php`, you see this line:

```
$imageFiles = preg_grep("/jpg$|gif$/", $theFiles);
```

This code selects all the files that end with `jpg` or `gif` and copies them to another array called `$imageFiles`.

Using Basic Regular Expressions

While it's possible to use string-manipulation functions to determine which files to copy to the new array, you might want to work with string data in a more detailed way. In this particular situation, I want all the files with `gif` *or* `jpg` in them. Comparing for two possible values with normal string manipulations isn't easy. Also, I didn't want *any* filename containing these two values, but only those filenames that *end* with `gif` or `jpg`. Regular expressions are a special convention often used to handle exactly this kind of situation, and much more.

Table 6.2 summarizes the main regular expression elements.

TABLE 6.2 SUMMARY OF BASIC REGULAR EXPRESSION OPERATORS

Operator	Description	Sample Pattern	Matches	Doesn't match
.	any character but newline	.	e	\n
^	beginning of string	^a	apple	banana
$	end of string	a$	banana	apple
[*characters*]	any characters in braces	[abcABC]	a	d
[*char range*]	describe range of characters	[a-zA-z]	r	9
\d	any digit	\d\d\d-\d\d\d\d	123-4567	the-thing
\b	word boundary	\bthe\b	the	theater
+	one or more occurrences of preceding character	\d+	1234	text
*	zero or more occurrences of preceding character	[a-zA-z]\d*		
{*digit*}	repeat preceding character that many times	\d{3}-\d{4}	123-4567	999-99-9999
|	or operator	apple|banana	apple, banana	peach
(*pattern segment*)	store results in pattern memory returned with numeric code	(^.).*/1$	gig, blab (any word that starts and ends with same letter)	any other word

Note that square braces can contain either characters or a range of characters as indicated in the examples.

To illustrate, I explain how the `"/jpg$|gif$/"` expression works. The expression `"/jpg$|gif$/"` matches on any string that ends with `jpg` or `gif`.

- Slashes usually mark the beginning and end of regular expressions. The first and last characters of the expression are these slashes.

- The pipe (|) character indicates *or*, so I'm looking for jpg or gif.
- The dollar sign ($) indicates the end of a string in the context of regular expressions, so jpg$ only matches on the value jpg if it's at the end of a string.

Regular expressions are extremely powerful if a bit cryptic. PHP supports a number of special functions that use regular expressions in addition to preg_grep. Look in the online Help under "Regular Expression Functions—Perl compatible" for a list of these functions as well as details on how regular expressions work in PHP. If you find regular expressions baffling, you can usually find a string-manipulation function (or two) that does the same general job.

Storing the Output

Once the $imageFiles array is completed, the program uses the data to build an HTML index of all images and stores that data to a file. Since it's been a bit since you've seen that code, I reproduce a piece of it here:

```
foreach ($imageFiles as $currentFile){
  $output .= <<<HERE
<a href = $currentFile>
  <img src = "$currentFile"
       height = 50
       width = 50>
</a>

HERE;

} // end foreach

//save the index to the local file system
$fp = fopen("imageIndex.html", "w");
fputs ($fp, $output);
fclose($fp);

print "<a href = $dirName/imageIndex.html>image index</a>\n";
```

I use a foreach loop to step through each $imageFiles array element. I add the HTML to generate a thumbnail version of each image to a variable called $output. Finally, I open a file called imageIndex.html in the current directory for writing, put the value of $output to the file, and closed the file handle. Finally, I add a link to the file.

You might be tempted to use a `readFile()` command to immediately view the contents of the file. I was. This may not work correctly, because the Web browser assumes the `imageList.php` directory is the current directory. Inside the program, I changed to another directory within the local file system, but the Web browser has no way of knowing that. The HTML was full of broken links when I did a `readFile()`, because all the relative links in the HTML page pointed towards files in another directory. When I add a link to the page instead, the Web browser itself can find all the images, because it's sent to the correct directory.

Working with Formatted Text

Text files are easy to work with, but they are extremely unstructured. Sometimes you might want to impose a bit of formatting on a text file to work with data. You learn some more formal data management skills in the next couple of chapters, but with a few simple tricks you can do quite a lot with plain text files.

Introducing the mailMerge.php Program

To illustrate how to use text files for basic data storage, I created a simple mail-merge program. The results are shown in Figure 6.9.

You can see that the same letter was used repeatedly, each time with a different name and e-mail address. The name and e-mail information was pulled from a file.

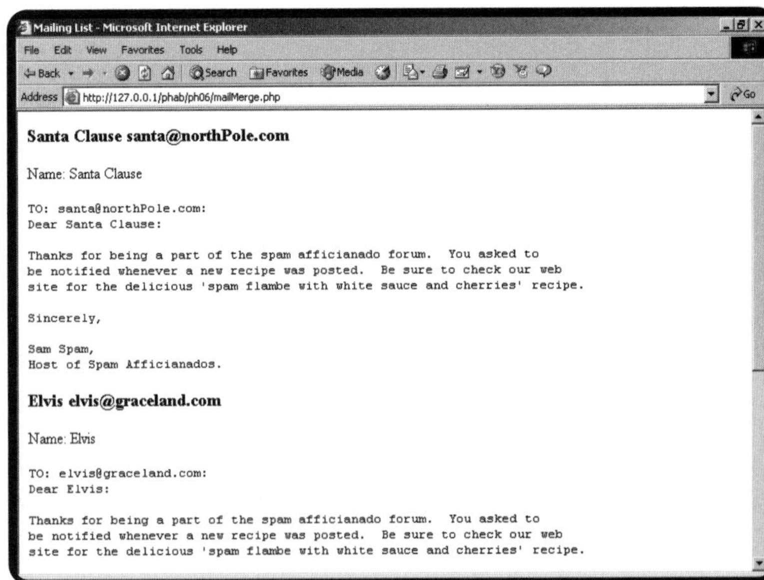

FIGURE 6.9

The program creates several form letters from a list of names and e-mail addresses.

Determining a Data Format

The data file (shown in Figure 6.10) for this program is simply a file created in Notepad. Each line consists of a name and an e-mail address, separated by a tab character.

This particular format (one line per record, tab-separated fields) is called a *tab-delimited file.* Because you can easily create a tab-delimited file in a text editor, spreadsheet, or any other kind of program, such files are popular. It's also quite easy to use another character as a separator. Spreadsheet programs often save in a comma-delimited format (*CSV* for *comma-separated values*) but string data does not work well in this format because it might already have embedded commas.

FIGURE 6.10

The data file for this program was created in Notepad.

Examining the mailMerge.php Code

The basic strategy for the `mailMerge.php` program is very simple. Take a look at the code and you might be surprised:

```
<html>
<head>
<title>Mailing List</title>
</head>
<body>
<form>
```

```
<?
//Simple Mail merge
//presumes tab-delimited file called maillist.dat

$theData = file("maillist.dat");

foreach($theData as $line){
  $line = rtrim($line);
  print "<h3>$line</h3>";
  list($name, $email) = split("\t", $line);
  print "Name: $name";

  $message = <<<HERE
TO: $email:
Dear $name:

Thanks for being a part of the spam afficionado forum. You asked to
be notified whenever a new recipe was posted. Be sure to check our Web
site for the delicious 'spam flambe with white sauce and cherries' recipe.

Sincerely,

Sam Spam,
Host of Spam Afficionados.

HERE;

  print "<pre>$message</pre>";

} // end foreach

?>
</body>
</html>
```

Loading Data with the file() Command

The first step is loading the data into the form. Instead of using the file pointer technique, I use a special shortcut. The `file()` command takes a filename and automatically loads that file into an array. Each line of the file becomes an element of the array. This is especially useful when your text file contains data, because each line in my data file represents one individual's data.

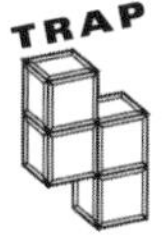

The `file()` command is so easy you might be tempted to use it all the time. The command loads the entire file into memory, so you should only use it for relatively small files. When you use the `fgets()` technique, you only need one line from the file in memory at a time, so the `fgets()` method can be effectively used on any size file without affecting performance. Using `file()` on a very large file can be extremely slow.

Splitting a Line into an Array and to Scalar Values

You might recall the `split()` function from chapter 5, "Better Arrays and String Handling." This function separates string elements based on some delimiter. I use the `split()` function inside a `foreach` loop to break each line into its constituent values.

However, I really don't want an array in this situation. Instead, I want the first value on the line to be read into the `$name` variable, and the second value stored in `$email`. The `list()` function allows you to take an array and distribute its contents into *scalar* (non-array) variables. In this particular situation, I never stored the results of the `split()` function in an array at all, but immediately listed the contents into the appropriate scalar variables. Once the data is in the variables, you can easily interpolate it into a mail-merge message.

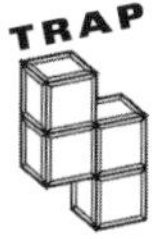

The next obvious step for this program is to automatically send each message as an e-mail. PHP provides a function called `mail()`, which makes it quite easy to add this functionality. However, the function is dependent on how the server is set up and doesn't work with equal reliability on every server.

Also, there are good and not-so-good reasons to send e-mail through a program. It's completely legitimate to send e-mails to people when they request it or to have a program send you e-mails when certain things happen. For example, my own more secure version of the tester program sends an e-mail when conditions indicate potential cheating. A program that sends unsolicited e-mail to people is rude and causes bad feelings about your site.

Creating the QuizMachine.php Program

The quiz tool from the beginning of this chapter is an entire system of programs designed to work together—in this case, five different programs. Each quiz is stored in two separate files, which the programs automatically generate. Figure 6.11 illustrates how the various programs fit together.

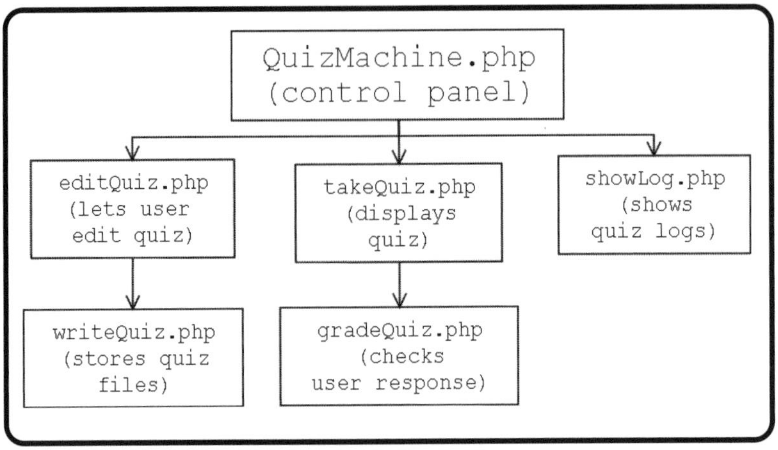

FIGURE 6.11

This diagram illustrates a user's movement through the `Quiz Machine` system.

The `QuizMachine.php` program is the entry point to the system for both the test administrator and the quiz taker. The program essentially consists of three forms that allow access to the other parts of the program. To ensure a minimal level of security, all other programs in the system require password access.

The `QuizMachine.php` program primarily serves as a gateway to the other parts of the system. If the user has administrative access (determined by a password), he can select an exam and call the `editQuiz.php` page. This page loads the quiz's actual master file (if it already exists) or sets up a prototype quiz and places the quiz data in a Web page as a simple editor. The `editQuiz` program calls the `writeQuiz.php` program, which takes the results of the `editQuiz` form and writes it to a master test file and an HTML page.

If the user wants to take a quiz, the system moves to the `takeQuiz.php` page, which checks the user's password and presents the quiz if authorized. When the user indicates he is finished, the `gradeQuiz.php` program grades the quiz and stores the result in a text file.

Finally, the administrator can examine the log files resulting from any of the quizzes by indicating a quiz from the `quizMachine` page. The `showLog.php` program displays the appropriate log file.

Building the QuizMachine.php Control Page

The heart of the quiz system is the `QuizMachine.php` page. The user directly enters this page only. All the other parts are called from this page or from one of the pages it calls. This page acts as a control panel. It consists of three parts, which correspond to the three primary jobs this system can do: writing or editing quizzes, taking quizzes, and analyzing quiz results. In each of these cases, the user has a particular quiz in mind, so the control panel automatically provides a list of appropriate files in each segment. Also, each of these tasks requires a password.

The main part of the QuizMachine.php program simply sets up the opening HTML and calls a series of functions, which do all the real work:

```
<html>
<head>
<title>Quiz Machine</title>
</head>
<body>
<center>
<h1>Quiz Machine</h1>

<?

getFiles();
showTest();
showEdit();
showLog();
```

The program calls getFiles() first. This function examines a directory and gets a list of the files in that directory. This list of filenames is used in the other functions. The next three functions generate HTML forms. Each form contains a select list that is dynamically generated from the file list. The button corresponding to each form submits the form to the appropriate PHP page.

Make another version of this main page for the people who will take your test. On the new page, you don't even show the administrative options. It's very easy to make such a page. Simply copy the QuizMachine.php **program to another file and remove the calls to the** showEdit() **and** showLog() **functions.**

Getting the File List

Since most of the code in the QuizMachine program works with a list of files, the getFiles() function shown below is charged with that important task.

```
function getFiles(){
  //get list of all files for use in other routines

  global $dirPtr, $theFiles;
```

```
  chdir(".");
  $dirPtr = openDir(".");
  $currentFile = readDir($dirPtr);
  while ($currentFile !== false){
    $theFiles[] = $currentFile;
    $currentFile = readDir($dirPtr);
  } // end while

} // end getFiles
```

The first thing this function does is change the file system so it points at the current directory, then the program sets up a pointer variable to that directory.

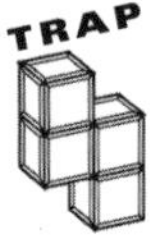

The directory that holds the PHP programs is open for anybody to see. You might not want your test files to be so conspicuous. To simplify this example, I kept all the test files in the same directory as the program itself, but you can keep the data files in a different directory. You might store all the data files in a part of your directory that is unavailable to the Web (away from your `public_html` structure, for instance) so that people can't see the answer key by browsing to it. If you do this, change each directory reference throughout the system.

I then created an array called `theFiles`, which holds every filename in the directory. The `theFiles` variable is global, so it is shared with the program and other functions that declare a reference to it.

Showing the Take a Test List

Most of your users don't create or edit quizzes. Instead, they take them. To take a test, the user must choose a test and enter the password associated with it. To simplify choosing a test, the `showTest()` function grabs all the HTML files in the `quiz` directory and places them in a select list. The password goes in an ordinary `password` field. The code in `showTest()` creates a form that calls the `takeQuiz.php` program when it is submitted:

```
function showTest(){
  //print a list of tests for user to take

  global $theFiles;
  print <<<HERE
<form action = "takeQuiz.php"
      method = "post">
```

```
<table border = 1
       width = 400>
<tr>
  <td colspan = 2><center>
    <h3>Take a quiz</h3>
  </td>
</tr>

<tr>
  <td>Quiz Password</td>
  <td>
    <input type = "password"
           name = "password">
  </td>
</tr>

<tr>
  <td>Quiz</td>
  <td>
    <select name = "takeFile">

HERE;

  //select only quiz html files
  $testFiles = preg_grep("/html$/", $theFiles);

  foreach ($testFiles as $myFile){
    $fileBase = substr($myFile, 0, strlen($myFile) - 5);
    print "    <option value = $fileBase>$fileBase</option>\n";
  } // end foreach

  print <<<HERE
    </select>
  </td>
</tr>

<tr>
  <td colspan = 2><center>
    <input type = "submit"
           value = "go">
```

```
  </center></td>
</tr>
</table>

</form>

HERE;

} // end showTest
```

Although the code is long, almost all of it is pure HTML. The PHP part selects HTML files and places them in the select group. This code fragment uses the `preg_grep()` to select filenames ending in `HTML` and creates an `option` tag for that file.

Note that I stripped out the `.html` part of the filename because I won't need it. It would complicate some of the code coming up in the `takeQuiz` program.

Showing the Edit List

The `showEdit()` function works a lot like `showTest()`, listing the system's master files. Although it is often exactly the same as the list of tests, it won't always be the same; some master files may not have been made into HTML files.

```
function showEdit(){
  // let user select a master file to edit

  global $theFiles;
  //get only quiz master files
  $testFiles = preg_grep("/mas$/", $theFiles);

  //edit a quiz
  print <<<HERE
<form action = "editQuiz.php"
      method = "post">
<table border = 1
       width = 400>
<tr>
  <td colspan = 2><center>
    <h3>Edit a quiz</h3>
  </center></td>
</tr>
```

```
<tr>
  <td>Administrative Password</td>
  <td>
    <input type = "password"
           name = "password"
           value = "">
  </td>
</tr>

<tr>
  <td>Quiz</td>
  <td>
    <select name = "editFile">
      <option value = "new">new quiz</option>

HERE;
  foreach ($testFiles as $myFile){
    $fileBase = substr($myFile, 0, strlen($myFile) - 4);
    print "  <option value = $myFile>$fileBase</option>\n";
  } // end foreach

  print <<<HERE
    </select>
  </td>
</tr>

<tr>
  <td colspan = 2><center>
    <input type = "submit"
           value = "go">
  </center></td>
</tr>
</table>
</form>

HERE;

} // end showEdit
```

The showEdit() function is just like showQuiz() but the form points to the editQuiz.php program and the file list is based on those files ending in mas.

There's one other subtle but important difference: Look at the code for the select element and see a new quiz option. If the user chooses this option, the editQuiz() function won't try to load a quiz file into memory, but sets up for a new quiz instead.

Showing the Log List

The last segment is meant for the quiz administrator. It allows the user with administrator access to view the log of any system quiz. This log shows who has taken the test, where and when she took it, and her score. When the user clicks the submit button associated with this part of the page, the showLog.php program takes over.

```
function showLog(){

  //let user choose from a list of log files
  global $theFiles;

  print <<<HERE

<form action = "showLog.php"
      method = "post">
<table border = 1
       width = 400>
<tr>
  <td colspan = 2><center>
    <h3>Show a log file</h3>
  </td>
</tr>

<tr>
  <td>Administrative Password</td>
  <td>
    <input type = "password"
           name = "password"
           value = "">
  </td>
</tr>
```

```
<tr>
  <td>Quiz</td>
  <td>
    <select name = "logFile">

HERE;

  //select only log files
  $logFiles = preg_grep("/log$/", $theFiles);
  foreach ($logFiles as $myFile){
    $fileBase = substr($myFile, 0, strlen($myFile) - 4);
    print "       <option value = $myFile>$fileBase</option>\n";
  } // end foreach

  print <<<HERE
    </select>
  </td>
</tr>

<tr>
  <td colspan = 2><center>
    <input type = "submit"
           value = "go">
  </td>
</tr>
</table>
</form>

HERE;
} // end showLog

?>

</center>
</body>
</html>
```

I decided that all log files would end with `.log`, so the program can easily get a list of log files to place in the select group.

Editing a Test

For simplicity's sake I decided on a very simple test format. The first three lines of the test file contain the test's name, the instructor's e-mail address, and the test's password. The test data itself follows. Each problem takes up one line (although it can wrap freely—a line is defined by a carriage return character). The problem has a question followed by four possible answers and the correct answer. A colon separates each element.

> **IN THE REAL WORLD**
>
> **You think question formatting has too many rules? I agree. This is a limitation of the sequential-file access technique that's storing the data. In chapters 8-12, you learn ways that aren't quite so picky. However, this is a relatively easy way to store your data, so I wrote the program to assist the process as much as is practical. You generally want to write your program so the user never has to know the underlying data structure.**

The `editQuiz.php` program assists the user in creating and editing quizzes. It's a simple program, because the real work happens after the user edits and presses the `submit` button.

Getting Existing Test Data

The first chore of the `editQuiz` program is determining which quiz the user is requesting. Remember that the value `new` indicates that the user wants to build a new test; that value is treated specially. Any other value is the foundation of a test filename, so I open the appropriate master file and load its values into the appropriate form elements:

```
<html>
<head>
<title>Quiz Builder</title>
</head>
<body>
<?

if ($password != "absolute"){
  print <<<HERE

<font color = "red" size = +3>
```

```
Invalid Password!
</font>

HERE;
} else {
  //check to see if user has chosen a form to edit
  if ($editFile == "new"){
    //if it's a new file, put in some dummy values
    $quizName = "sample test";
    $quizEmail = "root@localhost";
    $quizData = "q:a:b:c:d:correct";
    $quizPwd = "php";
  } else {
    //open up the file and get the data from it
    $fp = fopen($editFile, "r");
    $quizName = fgets($fp);
    $quizEmail = fgets($fp);
    $quizPwd = fgets($fp);
    while (!feof($fp)){
      $quizData .= fgets($fp);
    } // end while
    fclose($fp);
} // end 'new form' if
```

I decided to code the value `absolute` (from the name of this book series) as an administrative password. Each test has its own password and the administrative functions (like editing a quiz) have their own passwords. If the `password` field has any other value besides my chosen password, the program indicates a problem and refuses to move forward.

An administrative password keeps casual snoops out of your system, but it's nowhere near bullet-proof security. This system is not appropriate for situations where you must absolutely secure the tests.

Once you know the user is authorized to edit tests, determine if it's a new or existing quiz. If the quiz is new, I simply add sample data to the variables, which are used for the upcoming form. If the user wants to see an existing test, I open the file for read access and grab the first three lines, which correspond to the `$quizName`, `$quizEmail`, and `$quizPwd` fields. A `foreach` loop loads the rest of the file into the `$quizData` variable.

You might wonder why the quiz needs a `password` field if it took a password to get to this form. The quiz system has multiple levels of security. Anybody can get to the `quizBuilder.php` page. However, to move to one of the other pages, the user must have the right kind of password. Only an administrator should go to the `editPage` and `showLog` programs, so these programs require special administrative password access. Each quiz also has an associated password. The quiz master file stores the password so you can associate a different password for each quiz. In this way, the users authorized to take one test won't take other tests (and confuse your log files).

Printing the Form

Once the variables are loaded with appropriate values, it's a simple matter to print an HTML form and let the user edit the quiz. The form is almost all pure HTML with the quiz variables interpolated into the appropriate places:

```
print <<<HERE

<form action = "writeQuiz.php"
      method = "post">

<table border = 1>
<tr>
  <th>Quiz Name</th>
  <td>
    <input type = "text"
           name = "quizName"
           value = "$quizName">
  </td>
</tr>

<tr>
  <th>Instructor email</th>
  <td>
    <input type = "text"
           name = "quizEmail"
           value = "$quizEmail">
  </td>
</tr>
```

```
<tr>
  <th>Password</th>
  <td>
    <input type = "text"
           name = "quizPwd"
           value = "$quizPwd">

<tr>
  <td rowspan = 1
      colspan = 2>
    <textarea name = "quizData"
              rows = 20
              cols = 60>
$quizData</textarea>
  </td>
</tr>

<tr>
  <td colspan = 2><center>
    <input type = "submit"
           value = "make the quiz">
  </center></td>
</tr>

</table>
</form>
HERE;
} // end if

?>
</body>
</html>
```

Writing the Test

The administrator has finished editing a quiz file. Now what? That quiz file must be stored to the file system and an HTML page generated for the quiz. The `writeQuiz.php` program performs these duties.

Setting Up the Main Logic

Creating two files is your first job. The quiz name can be the filename's foundation, but many file systems choke at spaces within filenames. I use the `str_replace()` function to replace all spaces in `$quizName` to underscore characters (_). Then I create a filename ending in `.mas` for the master file and another filename ending in `.html` for the actual quiz.

To create the HTML file, I open it for write output. Then I use the `buildHTML()` function (described shortly) to build the HTML code, write that code to the HTML file, and close the file. The master file is built pretty much the same way, except it calls the `buildMas()` function to create the appropriate text for the file.

```
<html>
<head>
<title>Write Quiz</title>
</head>
<body>
<?
//given a quiz file from editQuiz,
//generates a master file and an HTML file for the quiz

//open the output file
$fileBase = str_replace(" ", "_", $quizName);
$htmlFile = $fileBase . ".html";
$masFile = $fileBase . ".mas";

$htfp = fopen($htmlFile, "w");
$htData = buildHTML();
fputs($htfp, $htData);
fclose($htfp);

$msfp = fopen($masFile, "w");
$msData = buildMas();
fputs($msfp, $msData);
fclose($msfp);

//preview the actual master file
print <<<HERE
<pre>
$msData
</pre>

HERE;
```

To make sure things are going well, I add a check to the end of the page that prints out the master file's actual contents. This program's output lets the administrator see that the test is working correctly. The administrator can take the test and submit it to the grading program from this page. If there is a problem, it's convenient to have the actual contents of the .mas file visible on the page. Of course, the final HTML page does not contain this data, because it holds the answers.

Building the Master File

The master file routine is very straightforward:

```
function buildMas(){
  //builds the master file
  global $quizName, $quizEmail, $quizPwd, $quizData;
  $msData = $quizName . "\n";
  $msData .= $quizEmail . "\n";
  $msData .= $quizPwd . "\n";
  $msData .=  $quizData;
  return $msData;
} // end buildMas
```

The critical part is remembering the file structure rules, so any program that reads this file doesn't get confused. The elements come in this order:

- Quiz name
- A newline character
- The `$quizEmail` variable
- The `$quizPwd` variable
- All `$quizData` (usually several lines)

Note that the function doesn't actually store the data to the file, but returns it to the main program. This allows me to write the data to both the file and to the page.

Building the HTML File

The function that creates the HTML is a little more involved, but is manageable. The basic strategy is this: Build an HTML form containing all the questions. For each line of the master file, build a radio group. Place the question and all the possible answers in a set of nested `<ol>` elements. At the end of the page, there should be one `submit` button. When the user clicks the `submit` button, the system calls the `gradeQuiz.php` page, which evaluates the user's responses.

```
function buildHTML(){
  global $quizName, $quizData;
  $htData = <<<HERE
<html>
<head>
<title>$quizName</title>
</head>
<body>

HERE;

  //get the quiz data
  $problems = split("\n", $quizData);
  $htData .= <<<HERE
<center>
<h1>$quizName</h1>
</center>

<form action = "gradeQuiz.php"
      method = "post">

Name
<input type = "text"
       name = "student">

<ol>

HERE;
  $questionNumber = 1;

  foreach ($problems as $currentProblem){
      list($question, $answerA, $answerB, $answerC, $answerD, $correct) =
      split (":", $currentProblem);
      $htData .= <<<HERE
<li>
  $question
  <ol type = "A">
    <li>
      <input type = "radio"
             name = "quest[$questionNumber]"
```

```
              value = "A">
        $answerA
      </li>

      <li>
        <input type = "radio"
               name = "quest[$questionNumber]"
               value = "B">
        $answerB
      </li>

      <li>
        <input type = "radio"
               name = "quest[$questionNumber]"
               value = "C">
        $answerC
      </li>

      <li>
        <input type = "radio"
               name = "quest[$questionNumber]"
               value = "D">
        $answerD
      </li>

    </ol>

</li>

HERE;
    $questionNumber++;

  } // end foreach
  $htData .= <<<HERE
</ol>

<input type = "hidden"
       name = "quizName"
       value = "$quizName">

<input type = "submit"
       value = "submit quiz">
```

```
</form>

HERE;

  print $htData;
  return $htData;
} // end buildHTML

?>
</body>
</html>
```

Most of the critical information this function needs is stored in `$quizData`. Each line of `$quizData` stores one question, so I use a `split()` function to break `$quizData` into an array called `$problems`. A `foreach` loop steps through each problem. Each problem contains a list of values, which is separated into a series of scalar variables with the combination of `split()` and `list()`.

Within the `foreach` loop, I also add the HTML code necessary to print the current question's information. Take a careful look at the code for the radio buttons. Recall from your HTML experience or Appendix A that radio buttons that operate as a group should all have the same name. I did this by calling them all `quest[$questionNumber]`. The `$questionNumber` variable contains the current question number, and this value is interpolated before the HTML code is written. Question number 1 has four different radio buttons called `quest[1]`. The `gradeQuiz` program sees this as an array called `$quest`.

At the end of the HTML, I add the quiz name (as a hidden field) and the `submit` button.

Taking a Quiz

The point of all this work is to have a set of quizzes your users can take, so it's good to have a program to present the quizzes. Actually, since the quizzes are saved as HTML pages, you could simply provide a link to a quiz and be done with it, but I wanted a little more security. I wanted the ability to store my quiz files outside the normal `public_html` file space and to have basic password protection so people don't take a quiz until I know it's ready. (I don't release the password until I'm ready for people to take the quiz.) Also, I can easily turn "off" a quiz by simply changing its password.

The `takeQuiz` page's only real job is to check the user's password against the indicated test's password and allow access to the quiz if appropriate.

```
<?
//takeQuiz.php
//given a quiz file, prints out that quiz

//get the password from the file
$masterFile = $takeFile . ".mas";
$fp = fopen($masterFile, "r");
//the password is the third line, so get the first two lines, but ignore them
$dummy = fgets($fp);
$dummy = fgets($fp);
$magicWord = fgets($fp);
$magicWord = rtrim($magicWord);
fclose($fp);

if ($password == $magicWord){
  $htmlFile = $takeFile . ".html";
  //print out the page if the user got the password right
  readFile($htmlFile);
} else {
  print <<<HERE
  <font color = "red"
        size = +3>
Incorrect Password.<br>
You must have a password in order to take this quiz
</font>

HERE;
} // end if
?>
```

The password associated with a test is stored in the test file, so once I know which test the user wants to take, I can open that file and extract the password. The password is stored in the file's third line. The only way to get to it with a sequential access file is to load the first two lines into a dummy variable and then load the password into a variable called `$magicWord`. If the user indicates a password that matches `$magicWord`, I use the `readFile()` function to send the contents of the quiz HTML page to the browser. If not, I send a message indicating the password was incorrect.

This is a dandy place to set up a little more security. I keep a log file of every access in a production version of this system, so I know if somebody has been trying to get at my system 1,000 times from the same machine within a second (a sure sign of some kind of automated attack) or other mischief. I can also check to see that later on when a page has been submitted, it comes from the same computer that requested the file in the first place. I can also check the request and submission times to reject quizzes that have been out longer than my time limit.

Grading the Quiz

One advantage of this kind of system is the potential for instantaneous feedback for the user. As soon as the user clicks the `submit` button, the `gradeQuiz.php` program automatically grades the quiz and stores a results log for the administrator.

Opening the Files

The `gradeQuiz` program, like all the programs in this system, relies on files to do all its important work. In this case, the program uses the master file to get the answer key for the quiz and writes to a log file.

```
<?
print <<<HERE
<html>
<head>
<title>Grade for $quizName, $student</title>
</head>
<body>

</body>
<h1>Grade for $quizName, $student</h1>
HERE;

//open up the correct master file for reading
$fileBase = str_replace(" ", "_", $quizName);
$masFile = $fileBase . ".mas";
$msfp = fopen($masFile, "r");

$logFile = $fileBase . ".log";
```

```
//the first three lines are name, instructor's email, and password
$quizName = fgets($msfp);
$quizEmail = fgets($msfp);
$quizPwd = fgets($msfp);
```

The master file is opened with read access. The first three lines are unimportant, but I must read them to get to the quiz data.

Creating an Answer Key

I start by generating an answer key from the master file, stepping through each question in the file and extracting all the normal variables from it (although I'm interested only in the `$correct` variable). I then store the `$correct` value in an array called `$key`. At the end of this loop, the `$key` array holds the correct answer for each quiz question.

```
//step through the questions building an answer key
$numCorrect = 0;
$questionNumber = 1;
while (!feof($msfp)){
  $currentProblem = fgets($msfp);

  list($question, $answerA, $answerB, $answerC, $answerD, $correct) =
  split (":", $currentProblem);
  $key[$questionNumber] = $correct;
  $questionNumber++;
} // end while
fclose($msfp);
```

Checking the User's Response

The user's responses come from the HTML form as an array called `$quest`. The correct answers are in an array called `$key`. To grade the test, I step through both arrays at the same time, comparing the user's response with the correct response. Each time these values are the same, the user has gotten an answer correct. The user was incorrect when the values are different or there was a problem with the test itself; don't discount that as a possibility. Unfortunately, you can't do much about that, because the test author is responsible for making sure the test is correct. Still, you might be able to improve the situation somewhat by providing a better editor that ensures the test is in the right format and each question has an answer registered with it.

```
//Check each answer from user
for ($questionNumber = 1; $questionNumber <= count($quest);
      $questionNumber++){
  $guess = $quest[$questionNumber];
  $correct = $key[$questionNumber];
  $correct = rtrim($correct);
  if ($guess == $correct){
    //user got it right
    $numCorrect++;
    print "problem # $questionNumber was correct<br>\n";
  } else {
    print "<font color = red>problem # $questionNumber was
    incorrect</font><br>\n";
  } // end if
} // end for
```

I give a certain amount of feedback, telling whether the question was correct, but I decide not to display the right answer. You might give the user more or less information, depending on how you're using the quiz program.

Reporting the Results to Screen and Log File

After checking each answer, the program reports the results to the user as a raw score and a percentage. The program also opens a log file for append access and adds the current data to it. Append access is just like write access, but rather than overwriting an existing file, it adds any new data to the end of it.

```
print "you got $numCorrect right<br>\n";
$percentage = ($numCorrect /count($quest)) * 100;
print "for $percentage percent<br>\n";

$today = date ("F j, Y, g:i a");
//print "Date: $today<br>\n";
$location = getenv("REMOTE_ADDR");
//print "Location: $location<br>\n";

//add results to log file
$lgfp = fopen($logFile, "a");
$logLine = $student . "\t";
$logLine .= $today . "\t";
$logLine .= $location . "\t";
$logLine .= $numCorrect . "\t";
```

```
$logLine .= $percentage . "\n";

fputs($lgfp, $logLine);
fclose($lgfp);

?>

</html>
```

I add a few more elements to the log file that might be useful to a test administrator. Of course, I add the student's name and current date. I also added a location variable, which uses the `$REMOTE_ADDR` environment variable to indicate which machine the user was on when she submitted the exam. This can be useful because it can alert you to certain kinds of hacking. (A person taking the same quiz several times on the same machine but with a different name, for example.) The `gradeQuiz` program adds the number correct and the percentage to the log file as well, then closes the file.

Notice that the data in the log file is delimited with tab characters. This is done so an analysis program could easily work with the file using the `split` command. Also, most spreadsheet programs can read a tab-delimited file, so the log file is easily imported into a spreadsheet for further analysis.

Look at the PHP online Help for the `date` functions to see all the ways you can display the current date.

You can really improve the logging functionality if you want to do some in-depth test analysis. For example, store each user's response to each question in the quiz. This gives you a database of performance on every question, so you could easily determine which questions are causing difficulty.

Viewing the Log

The `showLog.php` program is actually very similar to the `takeQuiz` program. It checks the password to ensure the user has administrator access, then opens the log using the `file()` function. It prints the file results inside a `<pre></pre>` pair, so the tab characters are preserved.

```
<?
//showLog.php
//shows a log file
```

```
//requires admin password

if ($password == "absolute"){
  $lines = file($logFile);
  print "<pre>\n";
  foreach ($lines as $theLine){
    print $theLine;
  } // end foreach
  print "</pre>\n";

} else {
  print <<<HERE
<font color = "red"
      size = +2>
You must have the appropriate password to view this log
</font>

HERE;
} // end if

?>
```

Improve this program by writing the data into an HTML table. However, not all spreadsheets can easily work with HTML table data, so I prefer the tab format. It isn't difficult to add data analysis to the log viewer, including mean scores, standard deviation, and suggested curve values.

Summary

This chapter explores the use of sequential files as a data storage and retrieval mechanism. You learned how to open files in read, write, and append modes and you know how file pointers refer to a file. You wrote data to a file and loaded data from a file with appropriate functions. You learned how to load an entire file into an array. You can examine a directory and determine which files are in the directory. You learned how to use basic regular expressions in the `preg_greq()` function to display a subset of files in the directory. Finally, you put all this together in a multi-program system that allows multiple levels of access to an interesting data set. You should be proud.

CHALLENGES

1. **Improve the quiz program in one of the ways I suggested throughout the chapter: Add the ability to e-mail test results, put in some test scores analysis, improve the quiz editing page, or try something of your own.**
2. **A couple of values in this system should be global among each of the PHP programs. The `root` directory of the files and the administrative password are obvious candidates. Write a program that stores these values in an `.ini` file and modify the quiz programs to get these values from that file when needed.**
3. **Create a source code viewer. Given a filename, the program should read in the file and convert each instance of `<` into `<`. Save this new file to another name. This allows you to show your source code to others.**
4. **Create a simple guest book. Let the user enter information into a form, and add her comment to the bottom of the page when she clicks the `submit` button. You can use one or two files for this.**

Chapter 7

Writing Programs with Objects

Object-oriented programming (sometimes abbreviated as *OOP*) is an important development in programming languages. Some languages such as Java are entirely object oriented and require an intimate understanding of the object-oriented paradigm. PHP, in keeping with its easygoing nature, supports a form of object-oriented programming, but does not require it. In this chapter you learn what objects are and how to build them in PHP. Specifically, you learn how to:

- Use a custom class to build enhanced Web pages
- Design a basic class of your own
- Build an instance of a class
- Leverage inheritance, encapsulation, and polymorphism
- Create properties and methods in your classes

Introducing the SuperHTML Object

Back when I used to program in Perl (before PHP existed), I really liked a feature called cgi.pm. This was a module that simplified server-based programming. One of my favorite things about the module was the way it allowed you to quickly build Web pages with function calls. Once I understood how to use cgi.pm, I was creating Web pages with unbelievable speed and ease. PHP doesn't have this feature built in, so I decided to make a similar object myself using the object-oriented paradigm. Throughout this chapter you see the object being used, then you'll learn how to build it and modify it for your own purposes.

As you look at the `SuperHTML` object, you should think of it at two levels:

- First, ignore the inner workings of the object and learn how to use it. There's a lot to this class, and it has a lot of potential to improve your PHP programming.
- Second, examine how it was built. This comes after you've played with the object for a while. There's no doubt you'll have some ideas on how to improve it. Once you understand how objects work in PHP, you'll be able to build even more powerful objects on your own.

Building a Simple Document with SuperHTML

The `SuperHTML` object is a special type of entity that allows you to automatically create and modify a Web page. It can be tricky to understand what an object is, so I'll start by just showing you how it works. Take a look at Figure 7.1 to see a simple HTML page.

What makes this document interesting is the way it was built. The source code for `BasicSuper.php` is different from any other code you've seen so far.

```
<?
include "SuperHTMLDef.php";
$s = new SuperHTML("Basic Super Page");
$s->buildTop();
$s->buildBottom();
print $s->getPage();
?>
```

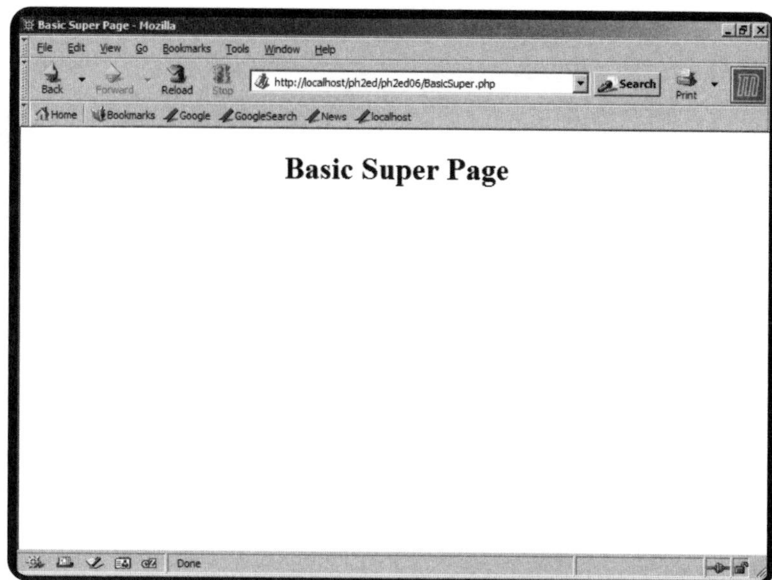

FIGURE 7.1

The basic SuperHTML page looks like a normal HTML page to the user.

Including a File

The first thing this code does is import another file. The `include` statement retrieves data from another file and interprets it as HTML code. In this case, I'm including a file called `SuperHTMLDef.php`. That file contains the definition for the `SuperHTML` object.

One of the joys of OOP is using an object without understanding exactly how it works. Rest assured you'll see the code in the file soon enough. For now be sure you understand how to access code in another program.

If you are having trouble with the `include` command, check the value of `open_basedir` in php.ini. (The easiest way to do this is to run a program with the `phpInfo()` command in it.) The `open_basedir` variable is set to null by default, which means PHP can load files from anywhere in the server's file system, but your administrator may have this access limited. You may need to reset this value on the server or bribe your server administrator to get this value changed. They (administrators, not servers) generally respond well to Twinkies.

Creating an Instance of the SuperHTML Object

The next line creates a new variable called `$s`:

```
$s = new SuperHTML("Basic Super Page");
```

This variable contains an object. Objects are complex variable types that can contain both variables and code. The `SuperHTML` object is a custom object I invented that describes a fancy kind of Web page. Since it's an *object*, it has certain characteristics, called *properties*, and it has certain behaviors, called *methods*. By invoking the object's methods, you can do some really neat things without a lot of work. Most of the properties are hidden in this particular example, but they're still there. Notice that when I created `$s`, I indicated a name for the page: Basic Super Page. That name will be used to form the title of the page as well as a caption.

No doubt you recall my advice to use descriptive names for things. You might be composing an angry e-mail to me now about the variable called `$s`: That's clearly not a descriptive name. However, I'm following a convention that's reasonably common among object-oriented programmers. When I have one particular object that I'm going to use a lot, I give it a one-character name to keep the typing simple. If that bothers you, the global search and replace feature of your favorite text editor is a reasonable option.

Building the Web Page

The Web page shown in Figure 7.1 has all the normal accoutrements, like `<head>` and `<body>` tags, a `<title>`, and even a headline in `<h1>` format. However, you can see that the code doesn't directly include any of these elements. Instead, it has two lines of PHP that both invoke the `$s` object.

```
$s->buildTop();
$s->buildBottom();
```

Both `buildTop()` and `buildBottom()` are considered methods, which are simply functions associated with a particular object type. In effect, because `$s` is a `SuperHTML` object, it knows how to build the top and bottom of the Web page. The `buildTop()` method generates the following HTML code automatically:

```
<!doctype html public "-//W3C//DTD HTML 4.0 //EN">
<html>
<head>
<title>Basic Super Page</title>
</head>
<body>
<center>
<h1>Basic Super Page</h1>
</center>
```

It's not that amazing that the function can generate all that HTML code; the code is fairly predictable. What's neat is the way the `SuperHTML` object knew what its title and headline should be. The phrase `Basic Super Page` is the string that initializes the `SuperHTML` object. The `buildBottom()` method is even easier than `buildTop()`, because it simply adds some boilerplate page-ending code:

```
</body>
</html>
```

Writing Out the Page

The `buildTop()` and `buildBottom()` directives feel a lot like function calls, because they are very similar to the functions you've already created and used many times. However, these functions are designed to work within the context of a particular object. A function attached to an object is referred to as a method of the object. A `cow` object might have `moo()` and `giveMilk()` methods.

The syntax for referring to methods in PHP is with the arrow syntax (->). There isn't one key to indicate this operator. It is the combination of the dash and the greater-than symbol.

Note that neither `buildTop()` nor `buildBottom()` actually write any code to the screen. Instead, they prepare the page as a long string property inside the object. `SuperHTML` has a method called `getPage()` that returns the actual HTML code for the page. The programmer can then save the code to a file, print it out, or whatever. In this case, the following line simply prints out the results of the `getPage()` method:

```
print $s->getPage();
```

Working with the Title Property

It's possible to designate a title when you create a `SuperHTML` object, but what if you want to change the title later? Objects can store code in methods, and they can also store data in properties. A property is like a variable attached to a particular object. The `SuperHTML` object has a title property. The `cow` object might have a `breed` property and an `age` property. The Properties.php page featured in Figure 7.2 illustrates this feature.

The `Property.php` program begins exactly like the Basic Super page you saw earlier. I even created the `$s` variable with the same initial value (`Basic Super Page`).

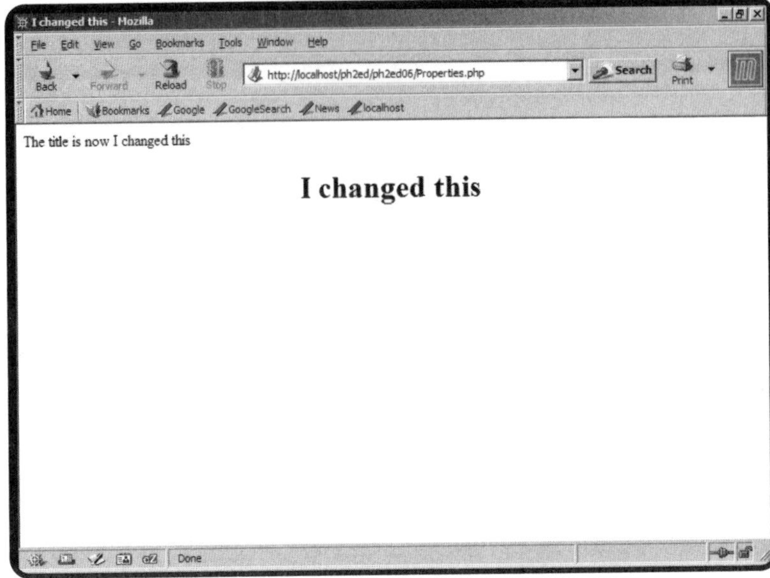

FIGURE 7.2

I created this page with one title and then changed the title.

When I created the `SuperHTML` object, the title property was automatically set to `Basic Super Page`. It's possible to directly change the title, like this:

```
$s ->title = "new title";
```

As you see when you look at the `SuperHTML` code itself, this approach can cause some problems. It's generally better to use special methods to get information to and from properties. Take a look at the following code for Property.php and you'll see a better way to change a property value.

```
<?
include "SuperHTMLDef.php";
$s = new SuperHTML("Basic Super Page");
$s->setTitle("I changed this");
$s->buildTop();
print "The title is now " . $s->getTitle();
$s->buildBottom();
print $s->getPage();
?>
```

The `$s->setTitle()` method allows me to add a new value to a property. The `$s->getTitle()` method gets a value from a property. These special methods are usually called *access methods* because they allow access to properties. I'll explain more about access methods later in this chapter when you start building your own object.

> **IN THE REAL WORLD**
>
> If you've programmed in languages like Visual Basic, C#, or Java, you might argue that you have directly accessed properties without using these access methods. The truth is, access methods in these languages are usually behind the scenes. When you assign a value to an object property, the appropriate access method is automatically implemented.

Adding Text and Tags with SuperHTML

The SuperHTML object makes it easy to build a basic HTML framework, but you always need other kinds of tags. SuperHTML has some general methods for adding various kinds of tags and text to a document. Figure 7.3 illustrates a page using these features.

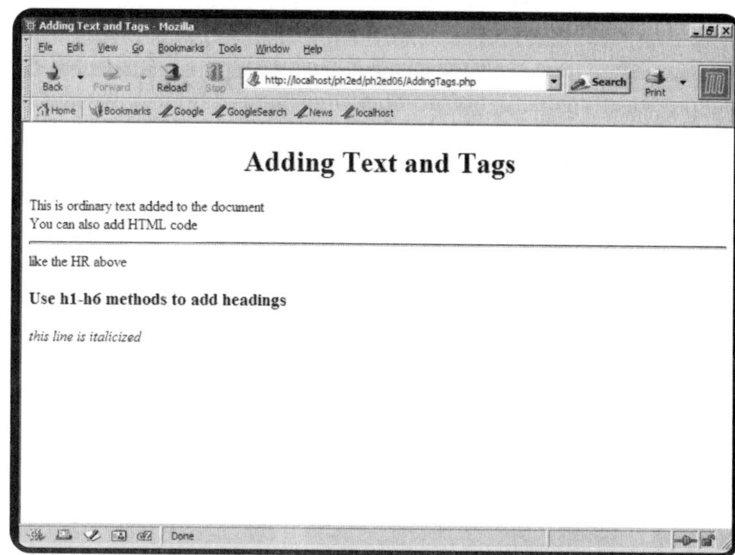

FIGURE 7.3

This page includes some text and HTML tags.

One of the primary features of SuperHTML is the way it separates the creation of a Web page from its display. You want to be able to easily generate a page and then display it onscreen, write it to a file, or do whatever else you want with it. For that reason, you won't simply print things out. Instead, you'll keep adding stuff to the SuperHTML object and then print the whole thing out when you're done.

That means you need some mechanism for adding things to the page. The SuperHTML object contains more than 25 methods for adding various kinds of objects to the document. (Don't panic. Most of them are really very simple.) Two methods in particular are extremely useful. Look at the code for AddText.php and see what I mean.

```
<?
include "SuperHTMLDef.php";
$s = new SuperHTML("Adding Text and Tags");
$s->buildTop();

$s->addText("This is ordinary text added to the document");
$s->addText("<div>You can also add HTML code <hr> like the HR above</div>");

$s->h3("Use h1-h6 methods to add headings");
$s->tag("i", "this line is italicized");

$s->buildBottom();
print $s->getPage();
?>
```

The `addText()` method expects a string as its only parameter. It then adds that text to the document in memory. As you can see, the text can even contain HTML data. You can also pass multi-line strings or text with interpolated variables.

The `addText()` method is really the only method you need in order to build the page in memory. However, the point of the `SuperHTML` object is to make page development faster and easier. I actually use the `addText()` method when I need to add actual text to a page or when I need a tag I haven't yet implemented in `SuperHTML`.

Look at the following line:

```
$s->h3("Use h1-h6 methods to add headings");
```

This code accepts a string as a parameter, then surrounds the text with `<h3></h3>` tags and writes it to the document in memory. Of course, there are similar methods for h1 through h6. You could expect similar methods for all the basic HTML tags.

I didn't create shortcuts for all the HTML tags, for two reasons. One reason is once you see the mechanism for creating a new tag method, you can modify `SuperHTML` very easily to have methods for all your favorite tags. The other reason I didn't make shortcuts for all the tags is the very special method described in the following line:

```
$s->tag("i", "this line is italicized");
```

The `tag()` method is a workhorse. It expects two parameters. The first is the tag you wish to implement (without the angle braces). In this case I want to italicize, so I'm implementing the `i` tag. The second parameter is the text you want sent to the document. After this function is completed, the document has the following text added to the end:

```
<i>this line is italicized</i>
```

If you look at the HTML source code for AddText.php, you see that's exactly what happened.

The great thing about the `tag()` method is its flexibility. It can surround any text with any tag.

Creating Lists the SuperHTML Way

Even if you only use the `addText()` and `tag()` methods, you can create some really nice, flexible Web pages. However, this object's real power comes with some specialized methods that solve specific display problems. When you think about it, a lot of PHP constructs have natural companions in the HTML world. For example, if you have an array of data in PHP, you frequently want to display it in some form of HTML list. Figure 7.4 demonstrates a page with a number of lists, all automatically generated from arrays.

You've probably already written code to generate an HTML list from an array. Although it's not difficult, it can be tedious. It'd be great if you could just hand off that functionality and not worry about it when you've got other problems to solve. The `SuperHTML` object has exactly that capability. The code `list.php` illustrates a number of ways to do this.

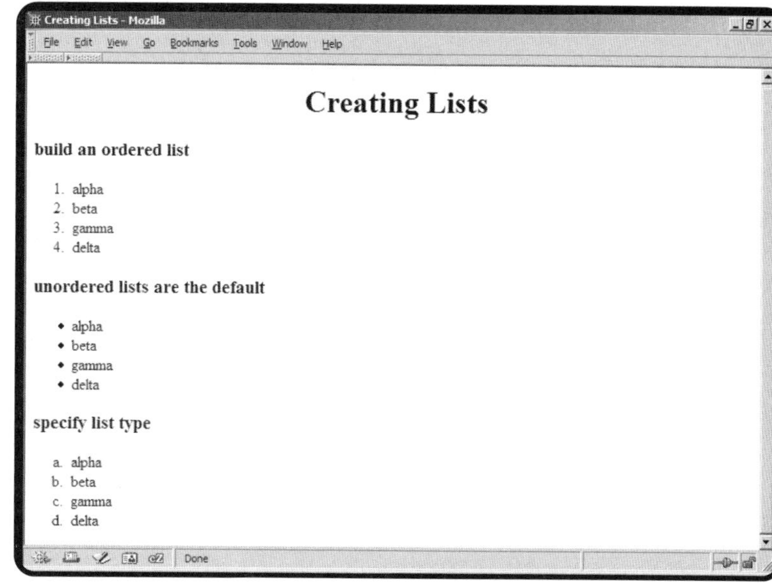

FIGURE 7.4

These HTML lists were created automatically from arrays.

```
<?
include "SuperHTMLDef.php";
$s = new SuperHTML("Creating Lists");
$s->buildTop();

$myArray =array( "alpha", "beta", "gamma", "delta");

$s->h3("build an ordered list");
$s->buildList($myArray, "ol");

$s->h3("unordered lists are the default");
$s->buildList(array("alpha", "beta", "gamma", "delta"));

$s->h3("specify list type");
$s->buildList($myArray, "ol type = 'a'");

$s->buildBottom();
print $s->getPage();
?>
```

Building a Basic List

I started the `list.php` code by creating an array called (cleverly enough) `$myArray`. The `buildList()` method requires two parameters, an array, and a list type. Then I invoke the function:

```
$s->buildList($myArray, "ol");
```

The `SuperHTML` object responds by adding the following code to its internal representation of the page:

```
<ol>
 <li>alpha</li>
 <li>beta</li>
 <li>gamma</li>
 <li>delta</li>
</ol>
```

As you can see, each array item is enclosed in `<li></li>` tags, and the entire array is encased in an `<ol></ol>` set with appropriate indentation. You'll be much more willing to use arrays when you have an easy tool like this to display them.

Building an Ad Hoc List

Of course you don't always want an ordered list. The next call to the `buildList()` method is different from the first version in two ways:

```
$s->buildList(array("alpha", "beta", "gamma", "delta"));
```

- First, I built this one on-the-fly rather than using a predefined array. This is useful when you want to build a list quickly but don't already have an array. Just put the list values in an ad hoc array before sending the array to the `buildList()` method.
- Second, this call is different because of the lack of a list type. If I don't indicate what type of list I want, `SuperHTML` is smart enough to guess and put a legal value in for me. This behavior is a good example of a principle called *polymorphism*, where an object can act differently in different situations. (Of course the formal definition is a little more profound than that, but this is good enough for now.) You can probably guess that the default list type is unordered.

Building More-Specialized Lists

The `buildList()` method has one more trick up its sleeve. If you look back at the third list on the HTML output, it is written with a specific list type (`<ol type = 'a'> </ol>`). I included the list attributes in the list type parameter, like this:

```
$s->buildList($myArray, "ol type = 'a'");
```

You can specify the list type complete with attributes for more flexible lists.

Making Tables with SuperHTML

All the `SuperHTML` features you've seen up to now are pretty handy, but the main thing I wanted was easy work with tables. You'll frequently find yourself outputting data in tables, and it can be confusing to switch from PHP to HTML syntax (especially when you add SQL to the mix, because then you're thinking in three very different languages at once). I wanted some features that easily let you build HTML tables from PHP data structures. Figure 7.5 shows a program with this capability.

The basic plan for building tables with `SuperHTML` is similar to the approach for making lists. However, tables are based on data structures more complex than lists, as you can see when you peruse the code.

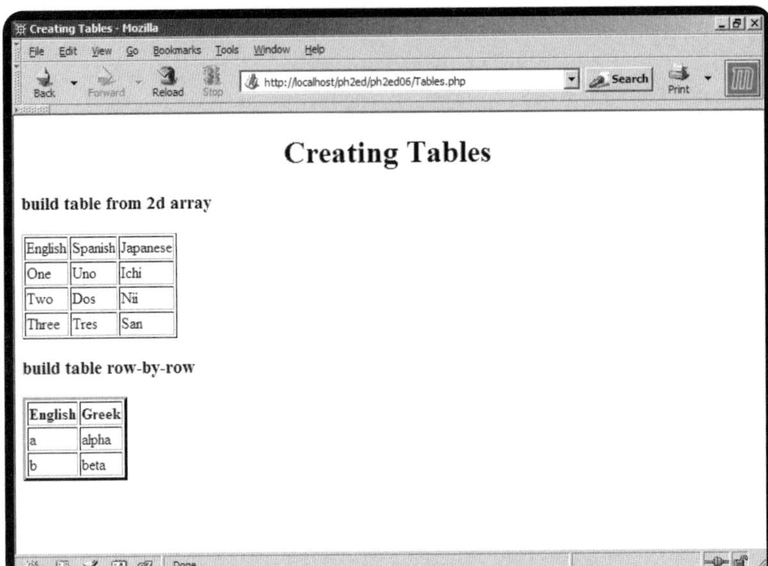

FIGURE 7.5

These tables were made automatically by the `SuperHTML` object.

```
<?
include "SuperHTMLDef.php";
$s = new SuperHTML("Creating Tables");
$s->buildTop();

$s->h3("build table from 2d array");
$myArray = array(
  array("English", "Spanish", "Japanese"),
  array("One", "Uno", "Ichi"),
  array("Two", "Dos", "Nii"),
  array("Three", "Tres", "San")
);
$s->buildTable($myArray);

$s->h3("build table row-by-row");
$s->startTable(3);
$s->tRow(array("English", "Greek"), "th");
$s->tRow(array("a", "alpha"));
$s->tRow(array("b", "beta"));
$s->endTable();

$s->buildBottom();
print $s->getPage();
?>
```

Creating a Basic Table

Early in this chapter I mentioned that PHP arrays and HTML lists are natural companions. Each row of an HTML table can be seen as a PHP array, and a table can be seen as an array of rows. An array of arrays is a *two-dimension array*. It shouldn't surprise you that building a table from a two-dimension array is easy. After I created an array called `$myArray`, turning it into a table with one line of code was trivial:

```
$s->buildTable($myArray);
```

Creating a More-Complex Table

The `buildTable()` method is really easy, but it isn't flexible enough for all needs. Frequently (especially in database applications) I want to build the top of the table, a header row, a series of rows in a loop, and then close off the table. I decided to add a more powerful suite of table-creation methods. These make it possible to make more-sophisticated tables, like the second one on `Table.php`.

The following code builds a table line-by-line:

```
$s->startTable(3);
$s->tRow(array("English", "Greek"), "th");
$s->tRow(array("a", "alpha"));
$s->tRow(array("b", "beta"));
$s->endTable();
```

The `startTable()` method creates the code that begins the table definition. The parameter indicates the table's border width. If you don't indicate a border width, it defaults to 1. (Gosh, polymorphism is wonderful!) It won't surprise you that the end of the table is indicated by the `endTable()` method.

The cool part of this approach is the `tRow()` method, which makes up the table body. This method can accept one or two parameters. The first parameter is an array of values that populates the row. Of course this can be an array variable or created on-the-fly (as in this example). The second `tRow()` parameter is cell type. The default type is `td`, but you can specify `th` if you want a header row. (I explain in the form.php program coming up next how to make a column of headers.) Call the `tRow()` method once for each table row. In an actual program, this frequently happens inside some sort of loop.

Creating Super Forms

The `SuperHTML` object is useful, but if it is really going to be helpful it must easily build form elements such as textboxes and submit buttons. Most of these objects are reasonably easy to build, but I've always found dropdown menus (HTML select objects) tedious to program. The `SuperHTML` object has a powerful, flexible, and easy approach to building various form elements. The page featured in Figure 7.6 was produced using some special object features.

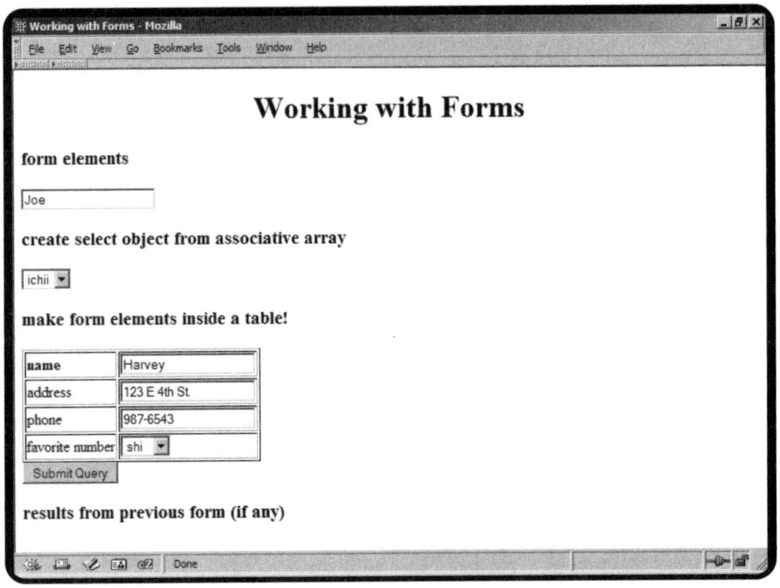

FIGURE 7.6

Forms are no problem for `SuperHTML`.

The form program code looks a little more involved than some other examples, but it's not any more difficult than anything you've already seen. First I give you the code in full, and then I break it apart and show you the features.

```
<?
include "SuperHTMLDef.php";
$s = new SuperHTML("Working with Forms");
$s->buildTop();

$s->h3("form elements");

$s->addText("<form> \n");
$s->textbox("userName", "Joe");

$s->h3("create select object from associative array");
```

```
$numArray = array(
  "1"=>"ichii",
  "2"=>"nii",
  "3"=>"san",
  "4"=>"shi"
);

$s->select("options", $numArray);

$s->h3("make form elements inside a table!");

$myArray = array(
  array($s->gTag("b","name"), $s->gTextbox("name")),
  array($s->gAddText("address"), $s->gTextbox("address")),
  array($s->gAddText("phone"), $s->gTextbox("phone")),
  array($s->gAddText("favorite number"), $s->gSelect("number", $numArray))
);

$s->buildTable($myArray);
$s->submit();

$s->addText("</form> \n");

$s->h3("results from previous form (if any)");
$s->formResults();

$s->buildBottom();
print $s->getPage();
?>
```

Building a Simple Form and Adding a Text Box

The following code snippet builds the most basic `SuperHTML` form:

```
$s->addText("<form>");
$s->textbox("userName", "Joe");
$s->submit();
$s->addText("</form>");
```

I used the `addText()` method to provide the basic form tags and then created a textbox and submit button using the `SuperHTML` object's special methods.

You might be surprised that I don't have special methods to begin and end the form. They would be easy, but I felt they wouldn't simplify things much, so I just used the `addText()` method to add form tags. (Of course you are free to add these methods yourself if you wish. The `SuperHTML` project is designed as a framework only, and I'm eager to see people add new functionality to it.)

The `textbox()` method can take one or two parameters. The first parameter is the name of the resulting `<input>` element. The second (optional) parameter is the element's default value. If you do not specify a value, it is left blank.

Of course, the submit button resolves to almost the same kind of HTML code, and it works very much like the textbox. However, if you leave off the `submit` method's second parameter, your HTML code will show the typical `Submit Query` caption.

Building Drop-Down Menus

There are a number of times you'll want the user to choose input from a limited number of options. Often, the value you want to send to the next program isn't exactly what the user sees. The appropriate HTML device for this situation is the `<select>` element with a bunch of `<option>` objects inside. If you try to map the select and option combination to a PHP structure, the most obvious comparison is an associative array as you used in chapter 5, "Better Arrays and String Handling." Take a look at the following code fragment to see how this works.

```
$numArray = array(
  "1"=>"ichii",
  "2"=>"nii",
  "3"=>"san",
  "4"=>"shi"
);

$s->select("options", $numArray);
```

I created an associative array using numbers as indices and the Japanese names for the numerals as the values.

Once I had created the array, it was easy to create a select object with the cleverly named `select()` method. The two parameters are the name of the resulting `select` object and the array. This code produces the following HTML:

```
<select name = "options" >
  <option value = "1">ichii</option>
  <option value = "2">nii</option>
```

```
  <option value = "3">san</option>
  <option value = "4">shi</option>
</select>
```

Building Form Elements Inside a Table

It's important to have professional-looking documents. Most programmers place all form elements inside a table. The `SuperHTML` object makes this relatively easy to do, using the `buildTable()` method described previously in this chapter. However, there's one new twist. Take a look at the code and see if you can spot it.

```
$myArray = array(
  array($s->gTag("b","name"), $s->gTextbox("name")),
  array("address", $s->gTextbox("address")),
  array("phone", $s->gTextbox("phone")),
  array("favorite number", $s->gSelect("number", $numArray))
);

$s->buildTable($myArray);
```

The `$myArray` variable is a big array that controls the eventual table. Each row consists of two columns. The first column is a label specifying the type of data being collected; the second column is some sort of form element.

Here's the twist: Although the methods used inside the array look familiar, every single one is new! Recall that all the methods for building a page in `SuperHTML` work by adding content directly to some variable in memory. This is done to make the program more flexible, so it can be used both to print a result and save it to a file.

When I'm building the array, I don't want to actually add anything to the HTML document. Instead, I want to receive the results of the function so I can add it to my array. I then add the entire array to the page using the `buildTable()` method. Most `SuperHTML` methods have a `get` variant, preceded with `g`. For example, recall that `$s->tag("b","name")` produces the code `<b>name</b>` and immediately adds that code to the internal HTML document. The `g` variant of the same command (following) produces exactly the same code but *does not add it* to the internal representation:

```
$s->gTag("b", "name");
```

Instead, it returns the value so you can do whatever you want with it. In this case, I simply want to add the code to my table as a pseudo-heading. (In fact I could do any kind of HTML here, including Cascading Style Sheets magic to get exactly the look I want.)

All other elements in the table are either plain text (the other labels) or other calls to `get` versions of methods in the `SuperHTML` object. After describing all the information in a two-dimension array, it's very easy to add it to the internal document using the `buildTable()` method.

Although it may seem tedious to build a two-dimension array, consider the complexity of the output that is produced by this function:

```
<table border = 1>
<tr>
  <td><b>
name
</b>
</td>
  <td><input type = "text"
       name = "name"
       value = "" />
</td>
</tr>
<tr>
  <td>address</td>
  <td><input type = "text"
       name = "address"
       value = "" />
</td>
</tr>
<tr>
  <td>phone</td>
  <td><input type = "text"
       name = "phone"
       value = "" />
</td>
</tr>
<tr>
  <td>favorite number</td>
  <td><select name = "number" >
  <option value = "1">ichii</option>
  <option value = "2">nii</option>
  <option value = "3">san</option>
  <option value = "4">shi</option> </select>
</td>
```

```
</tr>
</table>
```

I think the version written with SuperHTML is quite a bit easier to understand and maintain. I like that most of the details are hidden away in the object definition.

Viewing Form Results

Usually when I build a PHP page that responds to a form, I begin by retrieving the names and values of all the fields that come from the form. This is useful because often I make mistakes in my field names or forget exactly what I'm expecting the form to send. It would be nice to have a really easy way to do this. Of course, SuperHTML has this feature built in. If you fill in the form elements in Forms.php and click the submit button, you get another version of Forms.php, but this one also includes form data, as shown in Figure 7.7.

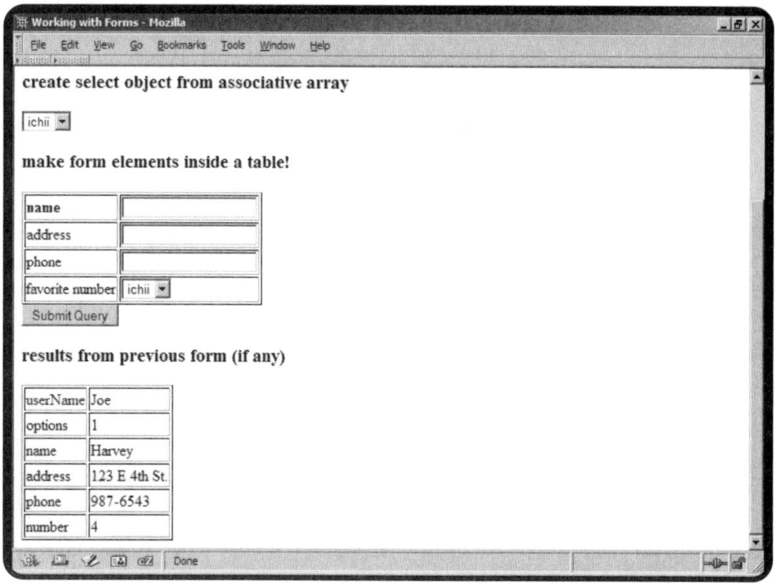

FIGURE 7.7

After submitting Forms.php, the second call to Forms.php returns a table of field names and values.

The code that produces these results is quite simple:

```
$s->formResults();
```

If there was no previous form, formResults() returns an empty string. If the page has been called from a form, the resulting code looks something like this:

```
<table border = "1">
<tr>
  <td>userName</td>
```

```
    <td>Joe</td>
  </tr>
  <tr>
    <td>options</td>
    <td>1</td>
  </tr>
  <tr>
    <td>name</td>
    <td>Jonathon</td>
  </tr>
  <tr>
    <td>address</td>
    <td>123 W 4th St</td>
  </tr>
  <tr>
    <td>phone</td>
    <td>999-9999</td>
  </tr>
  <tr>
    <td>number</td>
    <td>3</td>
  </tr>
</table>
</body>
</html>
```

Understanding OOP

The `SuperHTML` project uses many OOP features to do its work. Before digging into the innards of `SuperHTML` itself, it makes sense to think more about what objects are and how to create them in PHP.

Objects Overview

As you've seen, objects have *properties*, which are characteristics of the object, and *methods*, which are things the object can do.

In addition to supporting properties and methods, a properly designed object should reflect certain values of the object-oriented paradigm.

Many discussions of OOP indicate that objects also have *events.* An event is some sort of stimulus the object can respond to. Events are indeed important in OOP, but they are not often used in PHP programming, because events are meant to capture things that happen in real time. PHP programs rarely involve real-time interaction with the user, so events are not as critical in PHP objects as they are in other languages.

Encapsulation

An object can be seen as some data (the properties) and some code (the methods) for working with that data. Alternatively, you could see an object as a series of methods and the data that supports these methods. Regardless, you can use an object without knowing exactly how it is constructed. This principle of encapsulation is well supported by PHP. You take advantage of *encapsulation* when you build ordinary functions. Objects take the notion of encapsulation one step further by grouping together code and data.

Inheritance

Inheritance is the idea that an object can be inherited from another object. Imagine if you had to build a police car. You could build a factory that begins with sheet metal and other raw materials, or you could start with a more typical car and simply add the features that make it a police car. Inheritance involves taking an existing type of object and adding new features to create a new object type. PHP supports at least one kind of inheritance, as you see later in this chapter.

Polymorphism

You've encountered polymorphism in the `SuperHTML` description. *Polymorphism* involves an object's ability to act somewhat differently under different circumstances. Specifically, it is often used to handle unexpected or missing data. PHP supports some types of polymorphism, but to be honest this is more a factor of the permissive and loose variable typing of PHP than any particular object-oriented design consideration.

Creating a Basic Object

One of the easiest ways to understand something is to look at an example. Begin by looking at the basic critter in Figure 7.8.

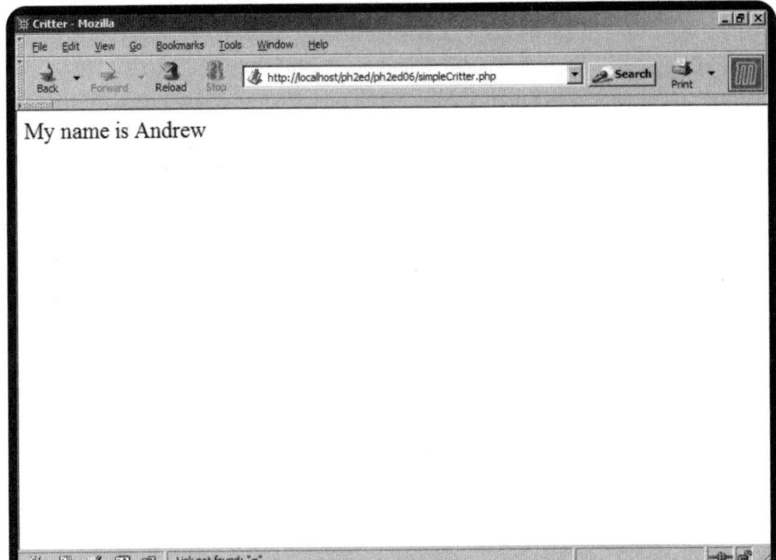

FIGURE 7.8

The Critter is a simplistic animal, but it is a simple example of object-oriented design.

Of course you won't see anything special if you look at the HTML output or the `Critter.html` HTML source code. The interesting work was done in the `php` code:

```
<!doctype html public "-//W3C//DTD HTML 4.0 //EN">
<html>
<head>
<title>Critter</title>
</head>
<body>
<?
// BASIC OOP DEMO

//define the critter class
class Critter{
  var $name;
} // end Critter class

//make an instance of the critter
$theCritter = new Critter();

//assign a value to the name property
$theCritter->name = "Andrew";
```

```
//return the value of the name property
print "My name is ";
print $theCritter->name;

?>
</body>
</html>
```

Defining the SimpleCritter Class

The `SimpleCritter` program works in classic object-oriented style. First it defines what a critter is and then it creates an instance of that design. Consider this part of the code:

```
//define the critter class
class Critter{
  var $name;
} // end Critter class
```

The `class` keyword indicates that I am defining a class. A *class* is a design or template for something. A recipe is a good example of a class. You wouldn't actually eat the index card with the cookie recipe on it, but you use that recipe to create cookies, which you can eat. The recipe is the class and cookies are instances of that class. (Great. Now I'm hungry.)

When I defined the `Critter` class, I was defining what a critter would be like (the recipe), but I haven't made one yet (the cookie). My `Critter` class is extremely simple. Right now it only has one property, which is the variable `$name`. Class definitions get a lot more complicated, but this is a good start.

Note the use of the `var` keyword to specify an instance variable. You don't have to use the `var` keyword when you create ordinary variables in PHP (and almost nobody does). The `var` keyword is necessary in a class definition, or the variable will not be interpreted correctly.

Creating an Instance of the Critter Class

Once you've defined a class, you want to have an instance or two of that class. One of the great things about objects is how easily you can make multiple instances of some class. However, for this example you just make one instance. The code that creates an instance looks like this:

```
$theCritter = new Critter();
```

I created a new variable called `$theCritter` and used the `new` keyword to indicate I wanted to instantiate some sort of object. Of course, I made an instance of the `Critter` class.

It's traditional to begin class names with uppercase letters and instances (like most other variables) in lowercase letters. I follow that convention through this book, so `$theCritter` is an instance and `Critter` is a class. In PHP, it's also easy to see that `Critter` isn't a variable because it doesn't begin with a dollar sign.

Working with an Object's Properties

Once you have an instance of an object, you can manipulate the properties of that instance. The `$theCritter` variable is an instance of the `Critter` class, so I can assign a value to the `name` property of `$theCritter`.

```
//assign a value to the name property
$theCritter->name = "Andrew";
```

Notice a couple of things about this:

- You can attach values to *instances* of a class, not to the class itself.
- Look carefully at the syntax for assigning a value to the `name` property. The variable you are dealing with is `$theCritter`. The `name` property is kind of like a subvariable of `$theCritter`. Use the `instance->property` syntax to refer to an object's property.

It's actually considered dangerous to directly access a property as I'm doing in this example. However, I do it here for the sake of clarity. As soon as I show you how to create a method, you'll build access methods. That way you don't have to directly access properties.

Retrieving Properties from a Class

The basic syntax for retrieving a property value from a class is much like adding a property.

```
//return the value of the name property
print "My name is ";
print $theCritter->name;
```

Again, note the syntax: `$theCritter` is the variable and `name` is its property.

Adding Methods to a Class

To make a class really interesting, it needs to have some sort of behavior as well as data. This is where methods come in. I'll improve on the simple `Critter` class so it has methods with which to manipulate the `name` property. Here's the new code, found in `methods.php`:

```
<!doctype html public "-//W3C//DTD HTML 4.0 //EN">
<html>
<head>
<title>Critter</title>
</head>
<body>
<?
// Adding methods

//define the critter class
class Critter{

  var $name;

  function __construct($handle = "anonymous"){
    $this->name = $handle;
  } // end constructor

  function setName($newName){
    $this->name = $newName;
  } // end setName

  function getName(){
    return $this->name;
  } // end getName

} // end Critter class

//make an instance of the critter
$theCritter = new Critter();

//print original name
print "Initial name: " . $theCritter->getName() . "<br>\n";
```

```
print "Changing name...<br>\n";
$theCritter->setName("Melville");
print "New name: " . $theCritter->getName() . "<br>\n";

?>
</body>
</html>
```

This code produces the output indicated in Figure 7.9.

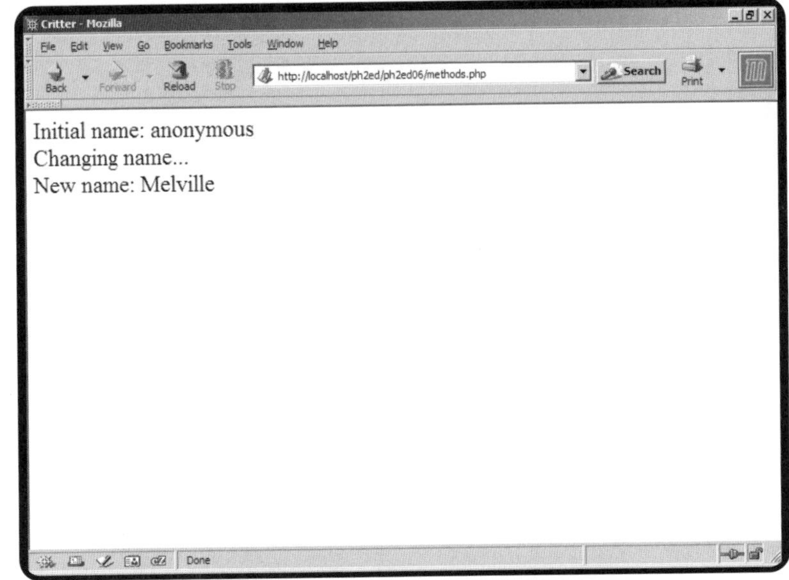

FIGURE 7.9

This `Critter` can change his name on-the-fly.

The basic technique for creating methods is to build a function within the context of a class definition. That function then becomes a method of the class.

Building a Constructor

The first function defined in most classes is called the *constructor*. Constructors are special methods used to build an object. Any code you want to occur when the object first appears should go in the constructor. Most often you use the constructor to initialize your properties, so I do that for the `Critter` class:

```
function __construct($handle = "anonymous"){
  $this->name = $handle;
} // end constructor
```

To specify that a function is a class constructor, it should be called `__construct`. (That's `construct` preceded by two underscores.)

The __construct name for constructors was added in PHP 5.0. If you have an earlier version of PHP, the constructor will have the same name as the class, but is still a function defined within the class.

The constructor is often used to initialize properties—in this case the `name` property. Notice that the constructor accepts a parameter. If you want to make a parameter optional in any PHP function, assign a default value to the parameter, as I have done here. This is a sneaky way that PHP achieves polymorphism.

Creating a Property Setter

The `setName()` method is an example of a property access method that allows you to change a property through a method. The code for `setName()` is pretty clean:

```
function setName($newName){
  $this->name = $newName;
} // end setName
```

Setter methods usually begin with `set` and they always accept a parameter. The parameter is the value the user wants to change. Inside the method, I modify the actual instance variable associated with the name property. Access methods are useful because I can do a number of things to test the information before I make any property changes. For example, if I decided that all my critter names should be fewer than five characters, I could modify `setName()` to enforce that rule. The *this* keyword is used to refer to the current object. Use *this* to indicate an object inside one of its methods.

```
function setName($newName){
  if(strlen($newName) > 5){
    $newName = substr($newName, 0, 5);
  } // end if

  $this->name = $newName;
} // end setName
```

This is a trivial example, but access methods can do a lot to prevent certain kinds of problems. For example, if your program is expecting numeric input and gets a string instead, your access method can quietly (or not-so-quietly, if you wish) change the value to something legal without the program crashing. Use of access methods can be a splendid way to add polymorphism to your classes. If you are using a class that has access methods, you should always use them rather than directly modifying a property. If you directly modify a property, you are circumventing the safety net provided by the access method.

Building a Getter Method to Retrieve Property Values

It's also good to have methods that return property values. These methods are called `getter` methods, and they are usually very straightforward, such as this one:

```
function getName(){
  return $this->name;
} // end getName
```

The `getName()` method simply returns the value of the appropriate property. This is useful because you might have different ways of returning the same value. Sometimes you might have a getter for a property that doesn't actually exist! For example, if you were creating a `circle` class, it might have `setRadius()`, `getRadius()`, `getArea()`, and `getCircumference()` methods. The user should be able to read and write the circle's radius and should be able to read the circumference and area. These values aren't actually stored in the class, because they are derived from the radius. The programmer using the class doesn't have to know or care about this, but simply knows that some properties are read/write and some are read only.

Using Access Methods to Manipulate Properties

With getter and setter methods in place, it's easy to manipulate an object's properties.

```
//make an instance of the critter
$theCritter = new Critter();

//print original name
print "Initial name: " . $theCritter->getName() . "<br>\n";

print "Changing name...<br>\n";
$theCritter->setName("Melville");
print "New name: " . $theCritter->getName() . "<br>\n";
```

Anytime I want to change the name, I invoke the `setName()` method. To retrieve the name, I use the `getName()` method.

Note that the terms *get* and *set* make sense in the context of the programmer *using* the class, not the programmer *designing* the class. The target audience for most objects is programmers rather than the general public. You're writing code to make a programmer's job easier.

Inheriting from a Parent Class

You've seen encapsulation and polymorphism. The third pillar of OOP is a concept called *inheritance*.

Inheritance is used to build on previous work and add new features to it. It is used to build common functionality and at the same time allow variation. In writing a game using Critters, for example, I define all the characteristics common to everything in the base Critter class and then add a bunch of subclasses for the various types. These subclasses incorporate additions or deviations from the basic behavior. Think again of the police car I mentioned earlier in this chapter. The car is a base class while a police car is an extension of the base class.

I'll take the Critter definition and put it in its own file, like this:

```
<?
// Critter definition

//define the critter class
class Critter{

  var $name;

  function __construct($handle = "anonymous"){
    $this->setname($handle);
  } // end constructor

  function setName($newName){
    $this->name = $newName;
  } // end setName

  function getName(){
    return $this->name;
  } // end getName

} // end Critter class

?>
```

Notice there's no HTML and no code that uses the class. This file simply contains the definition for the class inside the normal php tags. Once I've got the class definition safely stored in a file, I can reuse it easily. I made one minor but useful change in the Critter class definition: Notice that the constructor no longer sets the name property directly, but uses the setName method instead. This is useful in a moment.

The Inherit.php program adds some new features to the basic Critter class:

```
<!doctype html public "-//W3C//DTD HTML 4.0 //EN">
<html>
<head>
<title>Glitter Critter</title>
</head>
<body>
<?

// Incorporating Inheritance

//pull up the Critter class
include "critter.php";

//create new Glitter Critter based on Critter

class GlitterCritter extends Critter{

  //add one method
  function glow(){
    print $this->name . " gently shimmers...<br> \n";
  } // end glow

  //override the setName method
  function setName($newName){
    $this->name = "Glittery " . $newName;
  } // end setName

} // end GC class def

//make an instance of the new critter
$theCritter = new GlitterCritter("Gloria");

//GC has no constructor, so it 'borrows' from its parent

print "Critter name: " . $theCritter->getName() . "<br>\n";
```

```
//invoke new glow method
$theCritter->glow();

?>
</body>
</html>
```

The program begins by including the previously designed `Critter` class. I could now make instances of that class, but I have something sneakier in mind. I want to make a new type of `Critter` that knows how to glow. I'll call it the `GlitterCritter`. (I also wrote prototypes for the `HitterCritter`, `BitterCritter`, and `SpitterCritter`, but I decided not to include them in the book.)

I defined the `GlitterCritter` just like any other class, except for the `extends` keyword:

```
class GlitterCritter extends Critter{
```

Unless I indicate otherwise, the `GlitterCritter` will act just like an ordinary `Critter`. It automatically inherits all properties, methods, and even the constructor from the parent class. I added two methods to the class. One brand new method is called `glow()`. The original `Critter` class doesn't have a `glow()` method. The other method is called `setName()`. The original `Critter` class has a `setName()` method as well.

When you run the program, you see a page like Figure 7.10.

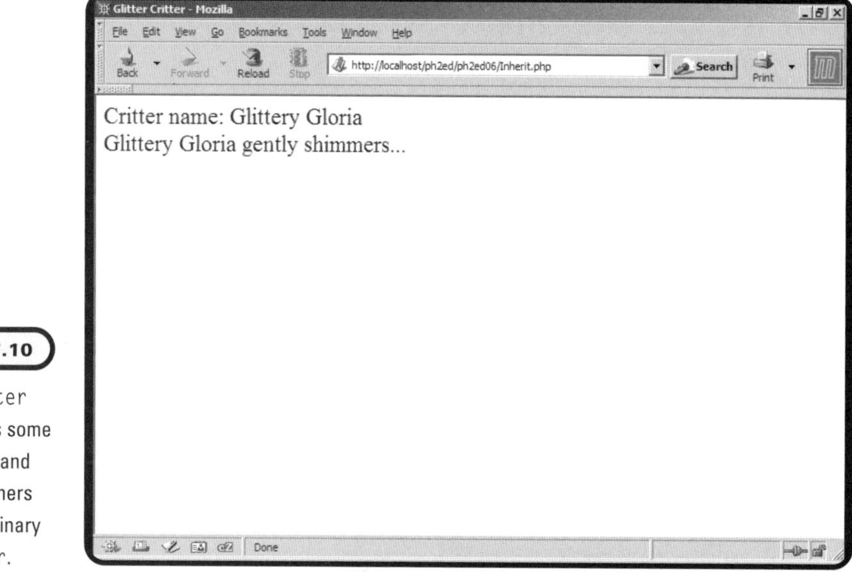

FIGURE 7.10

The `Glitter Critter` has some new tricks and borrows others from the ordinary `Critter`.

Since GlitterCritter is based on Critter and I'm making an instance of GlitterCritter, the default behavior of $theCritter is just like an ordinary Critter. GlitterCritter doesn't have a constructor, so it uses the constructor from Critter. When I added the glow() method, the GlitterCritter was able to do something its parent could not. When I created a new method that had the same name as a method in the parent class, the new method overrode the original method, changing the behavior. Note that I didn't change the constructor at all, but since the constructor calls the addName() method, GlitterCritter names all begin with Glittery.

IN THE REAL WORLD

Entire books have been written about OOP. This chapter means to whet your appetite for the power and flexibility this programming style offers. I encourage you to read more about OOP and to investigate languages that support the paradigm more completely than does PHP.

Building the SuperHTML Class

Now that you understand something about object-oriented methodology, you can look at the innards of the SuperHTML. Although the class has a lot of code, everything is made up of very simple code elements. The object-oriented nature of the class is what gives it its real power. As you look through the code, I give suggestions on areas you could improve the code or ways to extend the class.

Setting Up the File

The class file is meant to be included in other programs, so I stripped it of all unnecessary HTML and PHP code. The only thing in the file is the class definition.

```
<?

//SuperHTML Class Def
class SuperHTML{

  //properties
  var $title;
  var $thePage;
```

You might be surprised that the entire SuperHTML class has only two properties. It could have a lot more, but I didn't need them to get the basic functionality I wanted. The title property holds the page title, which appears as both the title and a level-one headline. The thePage property is special, because it is a string variable that contains all the code for the resulting HTML output.

Creating the Constructor

You might expect a complex object to have an involved constructor, but it isn't necessarily so.

```
function __construct($tTitle = "Super HTML"){
  //constructor
  $this->SetTitle($tTitle);
} // end constructor
```

The constructor copies a temporary title value over to the `title` property using the currently undefined `setTitle()` method.

Manipulating Properties

You would expect to find access methods for the properties, and `SuperHTML` has a few. There is a `setTitle()`, a `getTitle()`, and a `getPage()` method. However, there's no explicit `setPage()` method because I intend for the programmer to build the page incrementally through all the other methods.

```
function getTitle(){
  return $this->title;
} // end getTitle

function setTitle($tTitle){
  $this->title = $tTitle;
} // end setTitle

function getPage(){
  return $this->thePage;
} // end getPage
```

Each of these methods is simplistic. You could improve them by checking for possible illegal values or adding default values.

Adding Text

The `SuperHTML` program doesn't print anything. All it ever does is create a big string (`thePage`) and allow a programmer to retrieve that page.

The `addText()` function adds to the end of `$thePage` whatever input is fed it, along with a trailing newline character. Like most of the functions in the class, a `g` version returns the value with a newline but doesn't write anything to `$thePage`.

The gAddText() method isn't necessary, but I included it for completeness.

```
function addText($content){
  //given any text (including HTML markup)
  //adds the text to the page
  $this->thePage .= $content;
  $this->thePage .= "\n";
} // end addText

function gAddText($content){
  //given any text (including HTML markup)
  //returns the text
  $temp= $content;
  $temp .= "\n";
  return $temp;
} // end addText
```

Building the Top of the Page

The top of almost every Web page I make is nearly identical, so I wanted a function to automatically build that stuff for me. The buildTop() method takes a multi-line string of all my favorite page-beginning code and adds it to the page using the addText() method.

```
  function buildTop(){
    $temp = <<<HERE
<!doctype html public "-//W3C//DTD HTML 4.0 //EN">
<html>
<head>
<title>$this->title</title>
</head>
<body>
<center>
<h1>$this->title</h1>
</center>
HERE;
    $this->addText($temp);
  } // end buildTop;
```

If you want a different beginning code (a particular CSS style, for example), you can override my buildTop() with one that includes your own code.

Creating the Bottom of the Page

The bottom of the page is very easy. I just built some standard page-ending HTML and added it to thePage.

```
  function buildBottom(){
    //builds the bottom of a generic web page
    $temp = <<<HERE
</body>
</html>
HERE;
    $this->addText($temp);
  } // end buildBottom;
```

Adding Headers and Generic Tags

The tag() method is very useful, because it allows you to surround any text with any HTML tag (or even an XML tag) you wish. The gTag function is similar, but doesn't store anything to $thePage. To simplify my coding, I wrote gTag() first. This method creates a temporary variable containing the tag name and contents, nicely formatted. (One of the things I didn't like about cgi.pm is how horrible the resulting HTML code looked. I want code produced by my programs to look as good as code produced directly by me.)

The tag() method calls gTag() and adds the results with addText(). If I make a change to the gTag() function, I won't have to remember to make the same change in tag(). It's good to avoid rewriting code when you can.

```
  //general tag functions

  function gTag($tagName, $contents){
    //given any tag, surrounds contents with tag
    //improve so tag can have attributes
    //returns tag but does not add it to page
    $temp = "<$tagName>\n";
    $temp .= "   " . $contents . "\n";
    $temp .= "</$tagName>\n";
    return $temp;
  } // end tag

  function tag($tagName, $contents){
    //given any tag, surrounds contents with tag
```

```
    //improve so tag can have attributes
    $temp = $this->gTag($tagName, $contents);
    $this->addText($temp);
  } // end tag

  //header functions
  function h1($stuff){
    $this->tag("h1", $stuff);
  } // end h1

  function h2($stuff){
    $this->tag("h2", $stuff);
  } // end h2

  function h3($stuff){
    $this->tag("h3", $stuff);
  } // end h3

  function h4($stuff){
    $this->tag("h4", $stuff);
  } // end h4

  function h5($stuff){
    $this->tag("h5", $stuff);
  } // end h5

  function h6($stuff){
    $this->tag("h6", $stuff);
  } // end h6
```

The `h1()` through `h6()` methods are all wrappers around the `tag()` method that simply provide shortcuts for these very common HTML tags. Of course you could add shortcuts for all your other favorite tags.

Creating Lists from Arrays

I like the list methods because they really clean up my code. The `buildList()` methods require two parameters. The first is an array, which contains all the elements in the eventual list. The second parameter is the list type, without the angle braces. The list type defaults to `ul`, but it could also be `ol` or `dl`.

The method uses a `foreach()` loop to step through each element in the array and then adds an `<li></li>` pair around the element. As usual, the function's `g` version returns this value to the programmer, and the other version adds it to `$thePage`.

```
function gBuildList($theArray, $type = "ul"){
  //given an array of values, builds a list based on that array
  $temp= "<$type> \n";
  foreach ($theArray as $value){
    $temp .= " <li>$value</li> \n";
  } // end foreach
  $temp .= "</$type> \n";
  return $temp;
} // end gBuildList

function buildList($theArray, $type = "ul"){
  $temp = $this->gBuildList($theArray, $type);
  $this->addText($temp);
} // end buildList
```

Creating Tables from 2-Dimension Arrays

The `buildTable()` methods work much like the `buildList()` methods. The `gBuildTable()` code begins by printing the table header. It then creates a `foreach` loop to handle the rows. Inside the loop it adds the `<tr>` tag and then opens a second loop to handle the data array representing each of the row's cells. This data is encased in `<td></td>` tags and added to the temporary variable. At the end of the cell loop it is the end of a table row, so the `</tr>` tag is added to the temporary variable. By the time both loops are finished, the function has provided an HTML table with decent formatting.

```
function gBuildTable($theArray){
  //given a 2D array, builds an HTML table based on that array
  $table = "<table border = 1> \n";
  foreach ($theArray as $row){
    $table .= "<tr> \n";
    foreach ($row as $cell){
      $table .= "  <td>$cell</td> \n";
    } // end foreach
    $table .= "</tr> \n";
  } // end foreach
```

```
    $table .= "</table> \n";

    return $table;
  } // end gBuildTable

  function buildTable($theArray){
    $temp = $this->gBuildTable($theArray);
    $this->addText($temp);
  } // end buildTable
```

You might improve this code to allow variables including a table caption, border size, style sheet, and whether the first row or column should be treated as table headers.

Creating Tables One Row at a Time

The other set of table functions allows you to build a table one row at a time. The `startTable()` method begins the table. The `$tRow()` method builds a table row from an array and accepts a `rowType` parameter. `EndTable()` builds the end-of-table code.

```
  function startTable($border = "1"){
    $this->thePage .= "<table border = \"$border\">\n";
  } // end startTable

  function tRow ($rowData, $rowType = "td"){
    //expects an array in rowdata, prints a row of th values
    $this->thePage .= "<tr> \n";
    foreach ($rowData as $cell){
      $this->thePage .= "  <$rowType>$cell</$rowType> \n";
    } // end foreach
    $this->thePage .= "</tr> \n";
  } // end thRow

  function endTable(){
    $this->thePage .= "</table> \n";
  } // end endTable
```

To be honest, I find the 2D array approach in `buildTable()` a lot more flexible and powerful than this technique, but I kept it in so you could see an alternative.

Building Basic Form Objects

The basic form-element methods involve no fancy programming. I added the text that should be printed and allowed appropriate parameters so the user could customize the form objects as needed.

```
  function gTextbox($name, $value = ""){
    // returns but does not print
    // an input type = text element
    // used if you want to place form elements in a table
    $temp .= <<<HERE
<input type = "text"
       name = "$name"
       value = "$value" />

HERE;
    return $temp;
  } // end textBox

  function textbox($name, $value = ""){
    $this->addText($this->gTextbox($name, $value));
  } // end textBox

  function gSubmit($value = "Submit Query"){
    // returns but does not print
    // an input type = submit element
    // used if you want to place form elements in a table
    $temp .= <<<HERE
<input type = "submit"
       value = "$value" />

HERE;
    return $temp;
  } // end submit

  function submit($value = "Submit Query"){
    $this->addText($this->gSubmit($value));
  } // end submit
```

You might want to add some similar functions for creating passwords, hidden fields, and text areas.

Building Select Objects

The select object is derived from an associative array. It expects a name for the entire structure and an associative array. For each element in the associative array, the index is translated to the value property of an `option` object. Also, the value of the array element becomes the text visible to the user.

```
function gSelect($name, $listVals){
  //given an associative array,
  //prints an HTML select object
  //Each element has the appropriate
  //value and displays the associated name
  $temp = "";
  $temp .= "<select name = \"$name\" >\n";
  foreach ($listVals as $val => $desc){
    $temp .= "  <option value = \"$val\">$desc</option> \n";
  } // end foreach
  $temp .= "</select> \n";
  return $temp;

} // end gSelect

function select($name, $listVals){
  $this->addText($this->gSelect($name, $listVals));
} // end buildSelect
```

Responding to Form Input

One more `SuperHTML` object method quickly produces a name/value pair for each element in the `$_REQUEST` array. In effect, this returns any form variables and their associated values.

```
function formResults(){
  //returns the names and values of all form elements
  //in an HTML table
  $this->startTable();
  foreach ($_REQUEST as $name => $value){
    $this->tRow(array($name,$value));
  } // end foreach
  $this->endTable();
} // end formResults
```

```
} // end class def

?>
```

Summary

This chapter introduced to the basic concepts of object-oriented programming. You saw that objects incorporate properties and methods. You learned how objects implement inheritance, polymorphism, and encapsulation. You experimented with the `SuperHTML` class and learned how to expand it when creating your own useful and powerful object classes.

CHALLENGES

1. **Rewrite one of your earlier programs using the `SuperHTML` object.**
2. **Add support for more HTML tags in the `SuperHTML` class.**
3. **Create an extension of `SuperHTML` that has a custom header reflecting the way you begin your Web pages.**
4. **Add support for checkboxes and radio buttons.**
5. **Improve the `buildTable()` method so it automatically makes the first row or column a parameter-based header.**
6. **Rewrite an earlier program with custom objects.**

XML and Content Management Systems

The Web has been changing since its inception. Two particular advances are especially important for PHP programmers to understand. The first is the concept of a *content management system* (*CMS*). This is a type of application that simplifies the creation and manipulation of complex Web sites. XML is a data management technique often used in CMS applications as well as other kinds of programming. PHP is an ideal language for implementing XML and CMS solutions. In this chapter you explore these exciting topics. You also do these things:

- Explore some common CMSs in popular use
- Build a basic CMS system using only one PHP program
- Examine XML as a data storage scheme
- Implement the `simpleXML` Application Programming Interface (API) for working with XML
- Create a more sophisticated CMS using XML

Introducing XCMS

You examine three different forms of CMS here. First, you look at a powerful CMS system called PHPNuke. Then you build a basic CMS using ordinary PHP. Finally you learn how to incorporate the power of XML to build the foundation of a powerful and flexible CMS engine.

You begin by installing and modifying an existing system to create a custom, high-end Web site like the one featured in Figure 8.1.

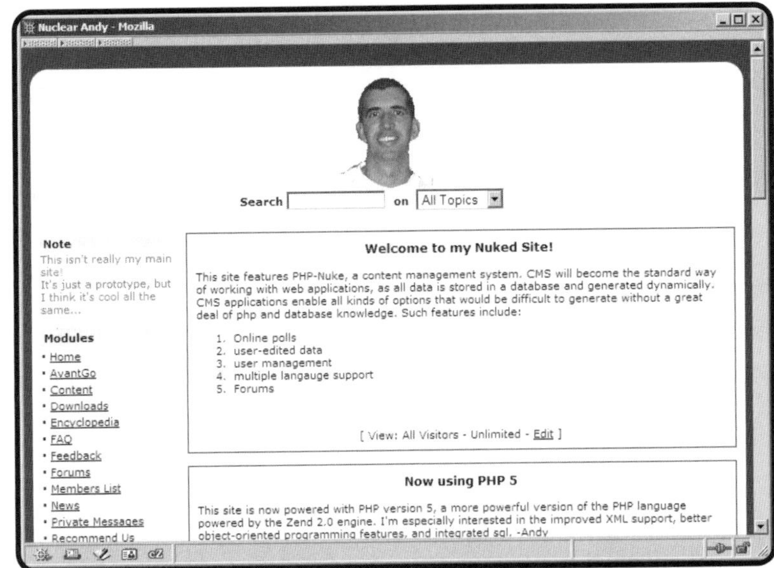

FIGURE 8.1

You can develop this fancy page with a minimum of PHP programming.

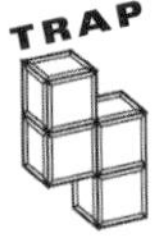

TRAP **Because PHP-Nuke requires a functioning MySQL server, I did not include this particular example on the CD. PHP-Nuke is on this book's CD, however, so use it to build sites just like this one.**

A CMS site can be extremely powerful, but you may not want all of the features of a high-end package like PHP-Nuke. On the other hand, you may wish to "roll your own" CMS. This type of program is very easy to build once you understand the basic concepts. By the end of the chapter you can build a site much like the one displayed in Figure 8.2.

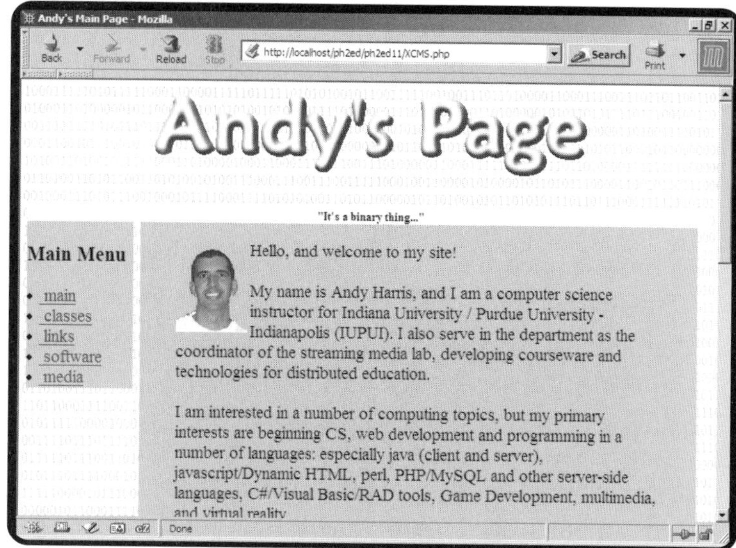

FIGURE 8.2

This CMS is much simpler but still profoundly powerful.

You also learn how to build an even more powerful CMS using a cool technology called XML. I won't give you a screenshot of that program though, because to the user it looks just like the simple CMS described in Figure 8.2.

Understanding Content Management Systems

When the Web began, it was conceived as a web of interconnected documents. The ability to link any document to any other was powerful. However, as developers began utilizing the Web, the freeform nature of the Internet sometimes caused headaches. In particular, it became somewhat challenging to manage a large system of related pages, to customize content for individual users, and to maintain consistency in a Web site that might contain hundreds or thousands of documents. Also, the nature of the Web began to change. Instead of simply being a repository of *documents*, the Web has become a series of interconnected *applications*. Much of the Web's content is no longer stored in HTML pages, but is created dynamically by programs such as PHP.

CMS has become a popular solution for creating a dynamic Web site that connects many HTML pages and serves them up in a flexible, efficient manner. (Flexibility in this context means the site owner has a lot of options for determining the layout and content of the page.) A number of very popular free and commercial CMSs are based on PHP. CMSs frequently include such features like these:

- **User management.** Users can log into the system. A CMS often has multiple user-access levels so some can add content and others can view content.

- **Separation of content into blocks.** Content can be grouped into semantic blocks based on its meaning. For example, rather than having arbitrary Web pages as the basic unit, you can organize news stories, Web links, and other elements into HTML pages.
- **Isolation of layout from content.** A CMS usually separates the system content from the layout. This is done for a number of reasons:
  - The appearance of the entire site should be uniform, even if many people contribute content.
  - Content developers shouldn't have to worry about formatting or how to write HTML code.
  - The layout should be adaptable to handle new designs or technologies.
- **User-contributed content.** Many CMSs include the ability to support online forums and message boards. In addition, you can often grant write access so users can add content to your site. For example, if you're running a site for a church, you might allow the children's pastor to directly add content to appropriate parts. You could control access, so people cannot access parts they should not change. You can even allow public access through message forums or automated content management based on individual user preferences.

Working with PHP-Nuke

PHP-Nuke is one of the most popular open-source CMSs. It uses PHP and MySQL to dynamically generate a Web portal (portal is another term for a customized system meant to be run as the starting place of a Web site). When you get used to PHP-Nuke you notice how many sites run this system or a variant of it. Figure 8.3 illustrates a version of my Web site using PHP-Nuke.

PHP-Nuke is an extremely capable CMS system. It supports all the features listed earlier, plus many more. If I log in as the administrator, I get a different display, giving me the opportunity to modify all kinds of options in the site, as shown in Figure 8.4.

Any user with appropriate access (determined by the administrator) can alter content by adding news items, surveys, links, and other elements. Additionally, authorized users can change the site's overall appearance by choosing a new theme, which could include new colors, fonts, icons, and layout. Figure 8.5 demonstrates the main page using a different theme.

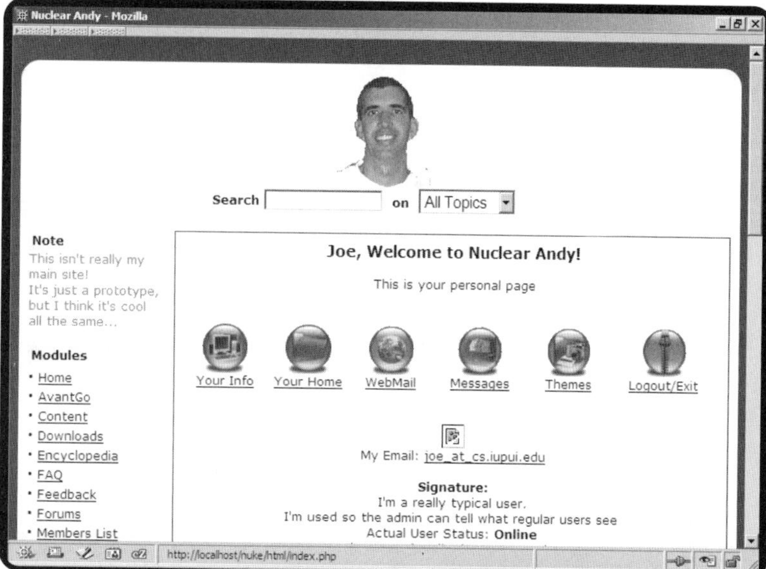

FIGURE 8.3

I built this professional-looking Web page without writing a single line of PHP code. Thanks, PHP-Nuke.

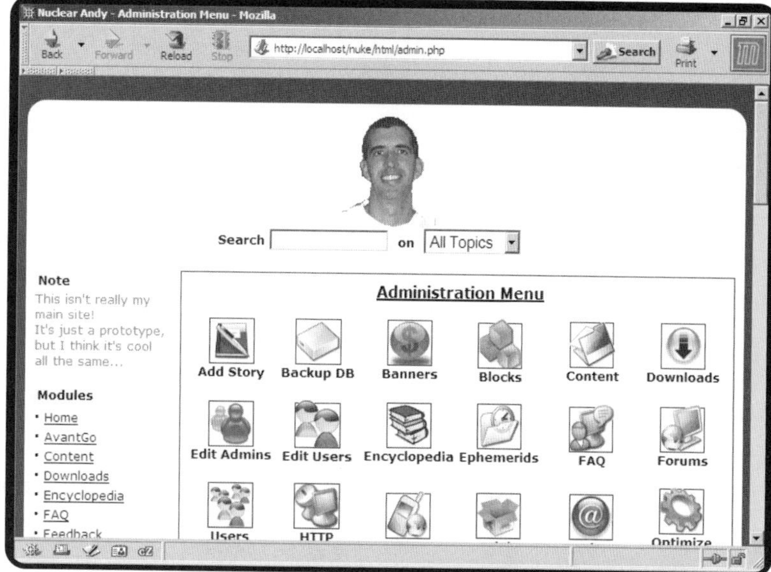

FIGURE 8.4

The administrator can change much of the system's functionality without any programming.

Of course, the real fun comes when you create your own themes or add new modules. Modifying PHP-Nuke is surprisingly simple once you understand the file structure. First things first: Install the system.

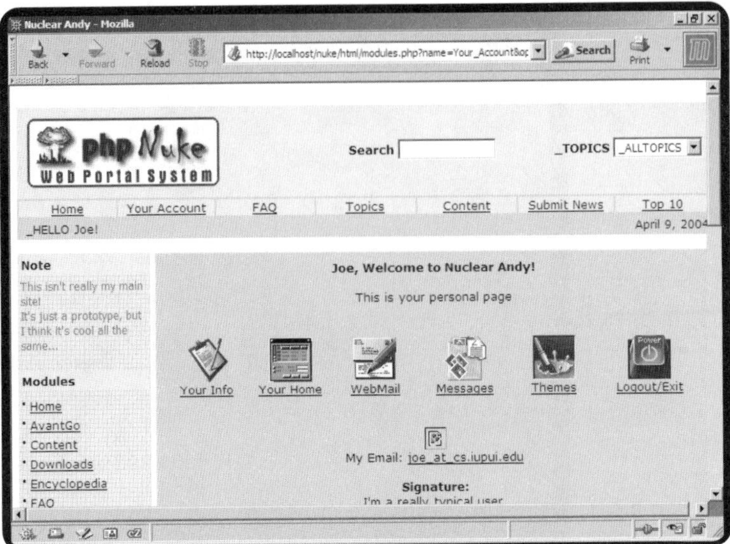

FIGURE 8.5

The content is the same, but this new theme uses different colors and graphics.

Installing PHP-Nuke

A copy of PHP-Nuke is included on the CD that accompanies this book. You might also go directly to the PHP-Nuke Web page (http://phpnuke.org) and ensure you have the latest version of the software. PHP-Nuke is written entirely in PHP and MySQL, so it doesn't matter which operating system you use.

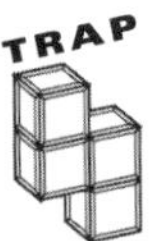

Be sure to install the files in a subdirectory of your Web server's document root (usually `htdocs`).

PHP-Nuke relies heavily on a series of MySQL tables. (My installation has 92 tables devoted to PHP-Nuke.) Fortunately, you don't have to install these tables by hand. All the necessary code is in an MySQL script called `nuke.sql` and is included with PHP-Nuke. Use the MySQL console or phpMyAdmin to run the SQL script. You learn more about how to use these tools in chapter 9, "Using MySQL to Create Databases." For now, you can simply follow the instructions in the readme file that accompanies PHP-Nuke.

You might have to edit the SQL script to change the username, add your own password, or create data tables according to some other scheme. As usual, work with a copy just in case something goes wrong.

Read the installation instructions that come with PHP-Nuke; they explain how to set up and test your system.

Customizing PHP-Nuke

PHP-Nuke installs with a large number of themes and a huge number of options. Play around with your site quite a bit to get everything working the way you want. You'll still probably make a few changes. As a minimum, you might want to replace some stock images or buttons with custom images. The easiest way to do this is to modify an existing theme:

1. Log in as the administrator by going to the `admin.php` page in your system.
2. Find the preferences option on this site.
3. Browse through the themes until you find one you want to use as your starting point.
4. Go to your file manager and find the appropriate theme's folder.
5. In the default installation, look at your PHP-Nuke subdirectory; find the themes under `html/themes/`.

   Each theme has its own subdirectory.
6. Duplicate the directory of the theme you want to work with and rename the folder to make the new theme.
7. Go to the theme folder and open `theme.php`.
8. Search and replace any references to the old theme name with your new theme.

Now you can edit any of the HTML files or images in the theme directory to customize your theme. For example, the `blocks.html` page controls how a section of the menu on the left side of the screen looks. If you load `blocks.html` by itself, it might look like Figure 8.6.

If you look at the code for `block.html`, it might look like this:

```
<table border="0" cellpadding="3" cellspacing="0"     bgcolor="#FFFF00"
   width="100%"><tr><td align="left">
<font class="block-title"><b>$title</b></font>
</td></tr></table>
<table border="0" cellpadding="0" cellspacing="0" bgcolor="#ffffff"
   width="140">
<tr valign="top"><td bgcolor="#ffffff">
$content
</td></tr></table>
<br>
```

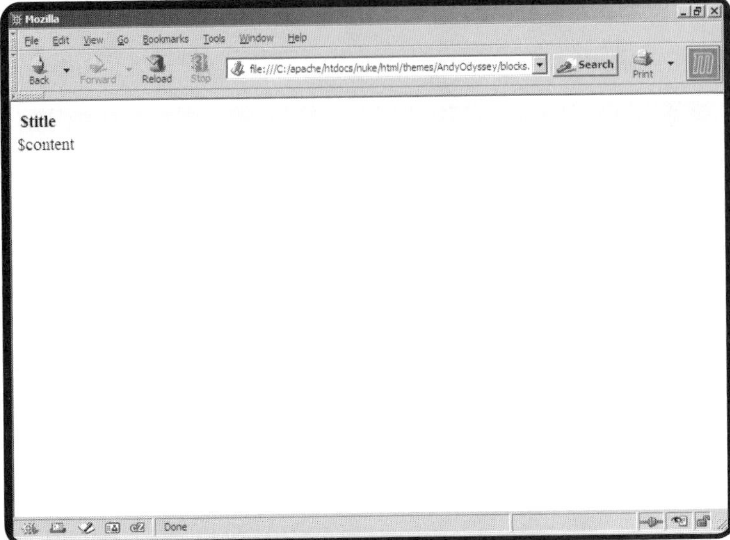

FIGURE 8.6

This is the standard look of `block.html` in the *Odyssey* theme.

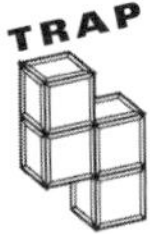

Your code might vary from what you see here, because each theme has a different code fragment for each type of element. The actual details don't matter as much as the general concept.

The notable thing about the code fragment is the lack of any actual content. This is the CMS system hallmark. Rather than displaying any actual values, the code fragments in a theme describe how to display a certain type of text. Notice the placeholders `$title` and `$content`. These are, of course, PHP variables that the actual title and content elements will replace.

You can modify any of the HTML theme pages as long as you don't change the name of any of those pages. Likewise, you can replace all of the graphics with your own, but don't use different names, because the system cannot find them otherwise. Begin with simple changes like color changes and new graphics; get more sophisticated as you begin to understand the file structure.

Introducing simpleCMS

PHP-Nuke is incredibly powerful, but it's overkill for many personal Web sites. It was originally designed to be used as a news site, so it's heavily oriented toward news delivery and online forums. The incredible power of the PHP-Nuke system (and others like it) can also make them very intimidating for new programmers. (Also, I don't love the coding style used to present the resulting pages. PHP-Nuke relies heavily on HTML tables as a formatting tool rather than the positionable CSS elements I prefer.)

I wanted to create a lightweight content management system that provided many of the core features a more complex system provides, but be easier to build and maintain. I actually created two related CMSs, which I describe in the rest of this chapter.

The `simpleCMS` system is easy to use and modify and adds tremendous flexibility to your Web system. You don't need to learn a single new command in PHP or HTML, but you do need to rethink what a Web page is.

Viewing Pages from a User's Perspective

A CMS system is designed to be changed, so although I can show an example of a site using the system, the actual possibilities are much larger than a particular figure will show. Still, Figure 8.7 illustrates how my Web page looks using `simpleCMS`.

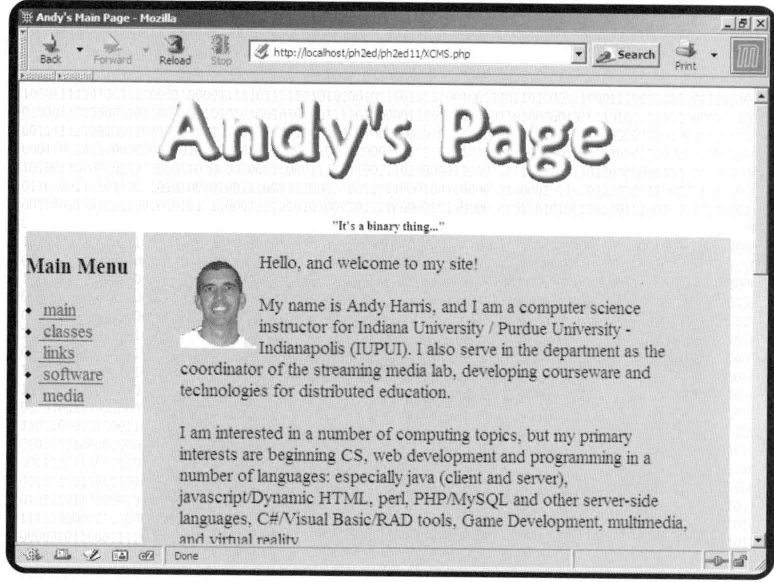

FIGURE 8.7

My main page, `simpleCMS`-style.

This page has a couple of interesting features. It follows a fairly standard design, with three primary segments of the page. A standard banner goes across the top of the page. This banner remains the same even when other parts of the page change. A list of links, which acts as a menu, occupies the left side. You can use multiple menus to support a complex Web hierarchy. The page's main section contains dynamic content. This part of the page will change frequently. When it changes, however, the other parts of the page will not. The HTML code for the page is combined from three different HTML pages and one CSS style. One (surprisingly simple) PHP script controls all the action.

Couldn't I Get the Same Effect with Frames?

HTML frames were originally designed to allow the same sort of functionality, but frames have proven to be extremely frustrating both for users and developers. It's reasonably easy to create a frame-based Web site, but much harder to build such a site that behaves well. If you've traversed the Web for any time, you've bumped into those frames within frames that eventually eat your entire screen away. The Back button acts unpredictably inside a frame context, and it's difficult to maintain a consistent style across multiple frames. While `simpleCMS` looks like a frameset, it's actually all one HTML file generated from a number of smaller files.

Examining the PHP Code

Look at the source code for `simpleCMS`, which is extraordinarily simple:

```
<!DOCTYPE HTML PUBLIC "-//W3C//DTD HTML 3.2 Final//EN">

<?
  //Simple CMS
  //Extremely Simple CMS system
  //Andy Harris for PHP/MySQL Abs. Beg 2nd Ed.

  if (empty($menu)){
    $menu = "menu.html";
  } // end if

  if (empty($content)){
    $content = "default.html";
  } // end if

  include ("menuLeft.css");
  include ("top.html");

  print "<span class = \"menuPanel\"> \n";
  include ($menu);
  print "</span> \n";

  print "<span class = \"item\"> \n";
  include ($content);
```

```
    print "</span> \n";

?>


</body>
</html>
```

The code expects two parameters. These parameters are both URLs for HTML files that are displayed by the system. A default value is supplied if either parameter is blank. The core of the program is a series of `include` statements, which loads and displays a file.

The `simpleCMS` system relies heavily on CSS features including positionable elements and style classes. If you're rusty on these techniques, look through appendix A, "Reviewing HTML and Cascading Style Sheets."

- The first `include` loads a CSS style sheet.
- The next `include` loads a page called `Top.html`. This page (if it exists) appears as a banner across the top of the screen. It is shown for every page in the system.
- The other `include` statements load and display the requested files inside special CSS span elements. If the CSS defines a span class called `menuPanel`, the `$menu` page contents are shown according to that style.
- Likewise, the `$content` variable displays according to an `item` style, if one is defined.

By creating these elements as positionable style sheet elements, it's possible to control where you place objects in addition to any other display specifics.

Recall that the `div` and `span` tags are special HTML tags that are extremely useful for CSS applications. If you need a refresher on these tags or on CSS, refer to appendix A on the CD-ROM.

Viewing the CSS

In a CMS, it's critical that content and layout remain separate. I'm using CSS as my primary layout management tool. At a minimum, I need to define styles for the menu and content area, because the PHP code is placing text in these elements. You can add any other CSS elements you want.

Here's the basic CSS I used:

```
<!--
     this style places a menu on the left and an item section in
     the center. Intended for use with CMS demos for
     PHP/MySql for the Abs. Beg, Andy Harris
-->

<style type = "text/css">
body {
  background-image: url("binaryBG.gif")
}

h1 {
  color: #0000FF;
  font-family: "Comic Sans MS";
  text-align: center
}

span.menuPanel {
  position: absolute;
  left: 1%;
  width: 15%;
  background-color: #CCCCFF
}

span.item {
  position: absolute;
  left: 17%;
  width: 80%;
  background-color: #CCCCFF
}
```

I defined the background style for all pages created by this system. I also built two `span` tag subclasses. You may recall that `span` is useful for CSS because it doesn't carry any formatting baggage. The `span.menuPanel` class is defined as a positionable element near the left border that stretches 15 percent of the browser width. The element's top and height are not defined. This means the element is placed immediately below whatever HTML tag was previously displayed, but all span contents are formatted to fit within the 15-percent limit. I intend for this section of the Web page to be filled with a list of links to serve as a menu.

(Of course, the menu can be much more sophisticated, but it's good to start slowly. In the next section you look at the sneaky (but not difficult) way the menu HTML is coded.)

I kept the code very simple, but of course you can (and should) improve it however you wish. Add background graphics, borders, or improved text. Put the menu across the right or top.

It's important that I used percentage measurements in this element, because I don't know the user's screen resolution. By indicating position and width in percentages, I have a style that works well regardless of the browser size.

In the Real World

What about browsers that don't support CSS? Some would argue that a table-based approach to layout (as PHP-Nuke and many other CMS tools use) would work across more browsers than this CSS-centric approach. While it's true some older browsers support tables but not CSS, tables have their own problems as page layout tools.

Tables were never really designed for that purpose, so to get a layout exactly like you want, you often have to build a Byzantine complex of tables nested within tables, with all sorts of odd `colspan` tricks and invisible borders.

The positionable CSS elements were invented partially to provide a simpler, more uniform solution to page layout headaches. The browsers that don't support CSS still display everything encoded in a CSS-augmented page. The CSS won't take effect, but all the other HTML code will work and the user can use the page.

The `item` class is the other important CSS element in this code sample. It's another specialized span dedicated to placing the Web page's main content. The `item` class works well with the `menuPanel` class. It is placed a little to the right of the menu panel and takes up most of the remaining screen space. Once again, the actual style is quite simplistic and you probably want to spruce it up.

Inspecting the Menu System

The real key to the `simpleCMS` is the way it's used. Each page that the user sees is a combination of three different HTML pages: a banner, menu, and content page. The `simpleCMS.php` program puts these three elements together according to a specific style sheet. For this example, presume that the CSS style and banner remain the same for every system-displayed page. (This is usually the behavior you want.)

You never directly link to any of the pages in your system. Instead, you link to the simpleCMS.php program and pass the content file (and menu file, if you wish) you want displayed. Recall that simpleCMS requires two parameters. Most PHP programs get their parameters from HTML forms, but you may remember from chapter 2, "Using Variables and Input," that parameters can be sent through the URL via the GET protocol. You can make any page display as an element of your CMS by calling it as a parameter.

To clarify, take a look at the menu.html code:

```
<h3>Main Menu</h3>
<ul>
  <li><a href = "simpleCMS.php?content=default.html">
      main</a>
  </li>
  <li><a href = "simpleCMS.php?content=classes.html">
      classes</a>
  </li>
  <li><a href = "simpleCMS.php?content=links.html">
      links</a>
  </li>
  <li><a href = "simpleCMS.php?content= software.html">
      software</a>
  </li>
  <li><a href = "simpleCMS.php?content=wallyindex.html">
      media</a>
  </li>
</ul>
```

Notice the trick? The first link refers to a page called default.html. Rather than directly linking to default.html, I linked to simpleCMS and passed the value default.html as the content parameter. When simpleCMS runs, it places the default banner (top.html) and the default menu (menu.html), but places the contents of default.html in the new page's item area. I didn't send a menu parameter, but I could have, and it would have placed some other page in the menu area.

In short, you can place any page in the menu area by assigning its URL to the menu parameter; you can assign any page to the item area by assigning its value to the content parameter. Any page you want displayed using the CMS must be called through a link to the CMS program, which pastes together all the other pages. You can place any HTML into any of the segments, but your menu usually goes in the menu area and is usually written only with links running back through the CMS.

You can create a reasonably sophisticated multilevel CMS with only this very basic program by experimenting with different menus, CSS styles, and banners.

You might wonder why I didn't show you the source code for the CMS top and content areas. There's nothing at all unusual about these pages, so I didn't think it was necessary. Generally, you write the top to be banner-like (very simple, designed to cover the entire width of the page, but just a short height). The pages you want to display in a CMS don't need header areas, titles, or page-level CSS definitions, because many are ignored in this multipage document. The CMS dictates these meanings for the entire composite page.

Improving the CMS with XML

Although the `simpleCMS` presented earlier is extremely powerful, it is limited to only two parameters. It would be great if you could control even more information on every pass through the CMS. It also would be nice to determine the page title, CSS style, top area, menu page, and body on every pass through the system. However, the `GET` method approach used in `simpleCMS` quickly becomes cumbersome when you're sending more than one or two parameters.

The `GET` method allows limited amounts of data to be passed. The URLS get tedious when you have that much information to send. Most CMSs use an alternative method of storing the information about intended page values. A lot of CMSs (like PHP-Nuke) use the full power of relational databases. This is a wonderful way to go, but it can be somewhat involved for a basic demonstration. There is a more-powerful alternative than basic parameter passing, although it's not quite as intimidating as a relational data structure.

Introducing XML

eXtensible Markup Language, or XML, has become a major topic of conversation in the software industry in the last few years. It isn't just a language, but a flexible and sensible alternative for manipulating data. It's really a language for describing languages.

XML feels a lot like HTML (because they're related) but it's quite a bit more flexible. In a nutshell, XML allows you to use HTML-style syntax to describe anything.

For example, if you want to talk about pets, you could use the following code:

```
<?xml version="1.0" encoding="utf-8" ?>
<pets>
  <cat>
    <name>Lucy</name>
    <color>tabby</color>
    <breed>shorthair</breed>
  </cat>

  <dog name = "Muchacha"
       color = "brown"
       breed = "mutt" />
</pets>
```

As you look at this fragment of (entirely fictional) XML code, you see an unmistakable resemblance to HTML. XML uses many conventions that are familiar to HTML developers, including nested and closing tags and attributes. The most significant difference is the tags themselves. HTML tags are specifically about Web page markup, but XML tags can describe anything. As long as you have (or can write) a program to interpret the XML code, you can use HTML-like code to describe the information.

Working with XML

XML has a number of data-management tool advantages. XML files can be stored and manipulated as string data and ordinary text files. This makes it easy to duplicate data and move it around the Internet. XML data is somewhat self-documenting. You can look at XML data in a text editor and have a good idea what it means. This would be impossible if the data were stored in a database table or proprietary format. Most languages have features that allow you to easily extract data from an XML document even if you don't know exactly how the document is formatted.

Understanding XML Rules

XML is very similar to HTML, but it is not quite as forgiving on syntax. Remember these rules when creating an XML document:

- **XML is case sensitive.** Most tags use lowercase or camelCase (just like PHP). `<pet>` and `<PET>` are two different tags.

- **All attributes must be encased in quotation marks.** In HTML, quotation marks are always optional. In XML, almost all attribute values should be quoted. For example, `<dog name = muchacha>` is not legal in XML. The appropriate expression is `<dog name = "muchacha">`.
- **All tags require an ending tag.** HTML is pretty forgiving about whether you include ending tags. XML is much more strict. Every tag must have an ending tag or indicate with a trailing slash that it doesn't have an end. In the earlier example, `<cat>` has an ending `</cat>` tag. I defined `dog` to encase all its data in attributes rather than subtags, so it doesn't have an explicit ending tag. Notice how the `dog` tag ends with a slash (/>) to indicate it has no end tag.

Examining main.xml

The second CMS system in this chapter uses XML files to store page information. To see why this could be useful, take a look at the XML file that describes my main page in the new XML-based content management system (XCMS):

```
<?xml version="1.0" encoding="utf-8"?>
<cpage>
  <title>Andy's main Page</title>
  <css>menuLeft.css</css>
  <top>top.html</top>
  <menu>menuX.html</menu>
  <content>http://www.cs.iupui.edu/~aharris/default</content>
</cpage>
```

The entire document is stored in a `<cpage></cpage>` element. `cpage` represents a CMS page. Inside the page are five parameters. Each page has a title as well as URLs to a CSS style, top page, menu page, and content page. The XML succinctly describes all the data necessary to build a page in my CMS. I build such an XML page for every page I want displayed in my system. It is actually pretty easy because most of the pages are the same except for the content.

It would be even easier in a real-world application, because I would probably build an editor to create the XML pages automatically. That way the user would never have to know he was building XML. Sounds like another great end-of-chapter project!

Simplifying the Menu Pages

The menu page isn't as complicated when all the data is stored in the XML pages. Each call to the system requires only one parameter: the name of the XML file containing all the layout instructions. Here's the menu page after changing it to work with the XML files:

```
<h3>Main Menu</h3>
<!--  menu page modified for XML version of CMS -->

<ul>
  <li><a href = "XCMS.php?theXML=main.xml">
      main</a>
  </li>
  <li><a href = "XCMS.php?theXML=classes.xml">
      classes</a>
  </li>
  <li><a href = "XCMS.php?theXML=links.xml">
      links</a>
  </li>
  <li><a href = "XCMS.php?theXML=software.xml">
      software</a>
  </li>
  <li><a href = "XCMS.php?theXML=media.xml">
      media</a>
  </li>
</ul>
```

This menu calls the XML version of the CMS code (`XCMS.php`) and sends to it the XML filename that describes each page to be created. Of course, you must examine how the XML data is manipulated in that program. Start, though, with a simpler program that looks at XML data.

Introducing XML Parsers

A program that reads and interprets XML data is usually called an *XML parser*. PHP 5 actually ships with three different XML parsers. I focus on the one that's easiest to use. It's called the `simpleXML` API and comes standard with PHP 5. An API is an application programming interface—an extension that adds functionality to a language.

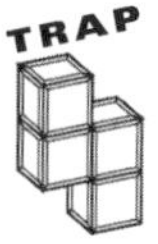

If you're using another version of PHP, you can either try loading the `simpleXML` API as an add-on or work with another XML parser. The DOM (Document Object Model) parser, if it's enabled, works much like `simpleXML`. Older versions of PHP include a parser based on SAX (Simple API for XML). This is also relatively easy to use, but uses a completely different model for file manipulation. Still, with careful reading of the online help, you can figure it out: The concepts remain the same. If you can use `simpleXML`, it's a great place to start, because it's a very easy entry into the world of XML programming.

Working with Simple XML

The `simpleXML` model is well named, because it's remarkably simple to use once you understand how it sees data. XML data can be thought of as a hierarchy tree (much like the directory structure on your hard drive). Each element (except the root) has exactly one parent, and each element has the capacity to have a number of children. The `simpleXML` model treats the entire XML document as a special object called an *XML node*. Table 8.1 illustrates the main methods of the `simplexml_element` object.

Table 8.1 Methods of the simpleXML Object

Method	Returns
`->asXML()`	An XML string containing the contents of the node
`->attributes()`	An associative array of the node's attributes
`->children()`	An array of `simplexml_element` nodes
`->xpath()`	An array of `simplexml_elements` addressed by the path

These various elements manipulate an XML file to maneuver the various file elements.

Working with the simpleXML API

Take a look at the `XMLDemo` program featured in Figure 8.8, which illustrates the `simpleXML` API.

The HTML output isn't remarkable, but the source code that generates the page is interesting in a number of ways.

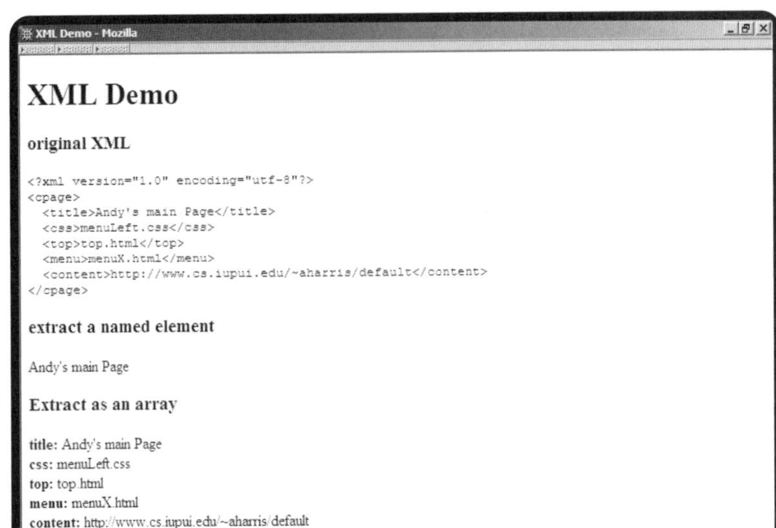

FIGURE 8.8

This program analyzes an XML data file from my content management system.

```
<!doctype html public "-//W3C//DTD HTML 4.0 //EN">
<html>
<head>
<title>XML Demo</title>
</head>
<body>

<h1>XML Demo</h1>

<?
//load up main.xml and examine it

$xml = simplexml_load_file("main.xml");

print "<h3>original XML</h3> \n";

$xmlText = $xml->asXML();
$xmlText = htmlentities($xmlText);
print "<pre>$xmlText</pre> \n";

print "<h3>extract a named element</h3> \n";
print $xml->title;
print "<br />";
```

```
print "<h3>Extract as an array</h3> \n";
foreach ($xml->children() as $name => $value){
  print "<b>$name:</b>   $value<br /> \n";
} // end foreach

?>
</body>
</html>
```

Creating a simpleXML Object

The first significant line of code uses the `simplexml_load_file()` command to load an XML document into memory. This command loads a document and creates an instance of the `simpleXML` object. All your other work with `simpleXML` involves using the `simpleXML` object's methods.

You can also create an XML object from a string using `simplexml_load_string()`. This might be useful if you want to build an XML file from within your code.

The XML object is stored in the aptly named `$xml` variable. I can then extract data easily from XML.

Viewing the XML Code

It might be useful to look at the actual XML code as you explore the code, so I reproduced it on the page. `simpleXML` does not keep the data in its plain text format, but converts it into a special data structure so it is easier to use. If you do want to see it as text-based XML, you can use the `asXML()` method to produce the XML code used to show part of the document. Note that you can use `asXML()` on the entire XML object or on specific subsets of it. This can be handy when you need to debug XML code. XML code does not display well in an HTML page, so I used PHP's built-in `htmlentities()` function to convert all HTML/XML characters to their appropriate HTML entity tags, then displayed the entire XML document inside a `<pre></pre>` set.

Accessing XML Nodes Directly

If you know the names of various tags in your document, you can access elements directly. For example, the following line pulls the `title` element from the main page:

```
print $xml->title;
```

Note that the top-level tag set in my document (`<cpage></cpage>`) is automatically copied over to the `$xml` variable. Since `title` is a `cpage` subtag, the value of title is returned.

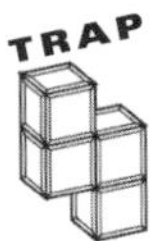

The node of an XML element can be seen as a string or an object. This can cause confusion, because PHP won't always treat a value extracted from XML exactly like you expect.

The `title` element is actually not a string variable, but another `simpleXML` object. You can use all the `simpleXML` methods on this object just as you do the main one. In this case, I simply wanted to print the text associated with `title`. `simpleXML` usually (but not always) correctly converts `simpleXML` elements to strings. In some cases (particularly when you want to use the results of a `simpleXML` query as part of an assignment or condition) you may need to force PHP to treat the element as string data.

For example, the following condition does not work as expected:

```
if ($xml->title == "main"){
```

It won't work because `main` is a string value and `$xml->title` is an object. They may appear to human readers to have the same value, but since they have different internal representations, PHP won't always recognize them as the same thing without minor coercion. You can use a technique called *type casting* to resolve this problem.

```
if ((string)$xml->title == "main"){
```

This version of the code forces the value from `$xml->title` into a string representation so it can be compared correctly.

Using a foreach Loop on a Node

Much of the time you work with XML through various looping structures. Since XML code consists of name-value structures, it won't surprise you to find associative arrays especially helpful. The following code steps through a simple XML file and extracts the name and value of every tag evident from the top layer.

```
print "<h3>Extract as an array</h3> \n";
foreach ($xml->children() as $name => $value){
  print "<b>$name:</b>   $value<br /> \n";
} // end foreach
```

The reference to `$xml->children()` is a call to the `$xml` `simpleXML` object's `children()` method. This method returns an array of all the nodes belonging to `$xml`. Each of the elements in the array is a new `simpleXML` object with all the same methods as `$xml`. Since the `children()` method returns an array of values, I can use the `foreach` loop to conveniently step through each element of the array. Using the `foreach` loop's associative variant (described in chapter 5, "Better Arrays and String Handling") allows access to the document's name/value pairs.

Each time through the loop, the current tag is stored in `$name` and its associated value is stored in `$value`. This allows me to rapidly print all the data in the XML element according to whatever format I wish.

Manipulating More-Complex XML with the simpleXML API

The features demonstrated in the `XMLdemo` are enough for working with the extremely simple XML variant used in the XCMS system, but you will want to work with more-complex XML files with multiple tags. As an example, consider the following code, which could be used in an XML-enabled form of the quiz program featured in chapter 6, "Working with Files."

```
<?xml version="1.0" encoding="utf-8"?>
<test>
  <problem type="mc">
    <question>What is your name?</question>
    <answerA>Roger the Shrubber</answerA>
    <answerB>Galahad the pure</answerB>
    <answerC>Arthur, King of the Britons</answerC>
    <answerD>Brave Sir Robin</answerD>
    <correct>C</correct>
  </problem>
  <problem type="mc">
    <question>What is your quest?</question>
    <answerA>I seek the holy grail</answerA>
    <answerB>I'm looking for a swallow</answerB>
    <answerC>I'm pining for the Fjords</answerC>
    <answerD>I want to be a lumberjack!</answerD>
    <correct>A</correct>
  </problem>
  <problem type="mc">
    <question>What is your favorite color?</question>
    <answerA>Red</answerA>
    <answerB>Green</answerB>
    <answerC>Orange</answerC>
    <answerD>Yellow. No, Blue!</answerD>
    <correct>D</correct>
```

```
  </problem>
  <problem type="mc">
    <question>What is your command?</question>
    <answerA>I'm not to leave the room until you come and get him</answerA>
    <answerB>I'm going with you</answerB>
    <answerC>I'm not to let him enter the room</answerC>
    <answerD>It seems daft to be guarding a guard!</answerD>
    <correct>A</correct>
  </problem>
</test>
```

This code is a little more typical of most XML data because it has multiple levels of encoding. The entire document can be seen as an array of problem nodes, and each problem node can be viewed as a set of answers and the correct answer. The `simpleXML` API can handle these more-complex documents with ease, as shown in Figure 8.9.

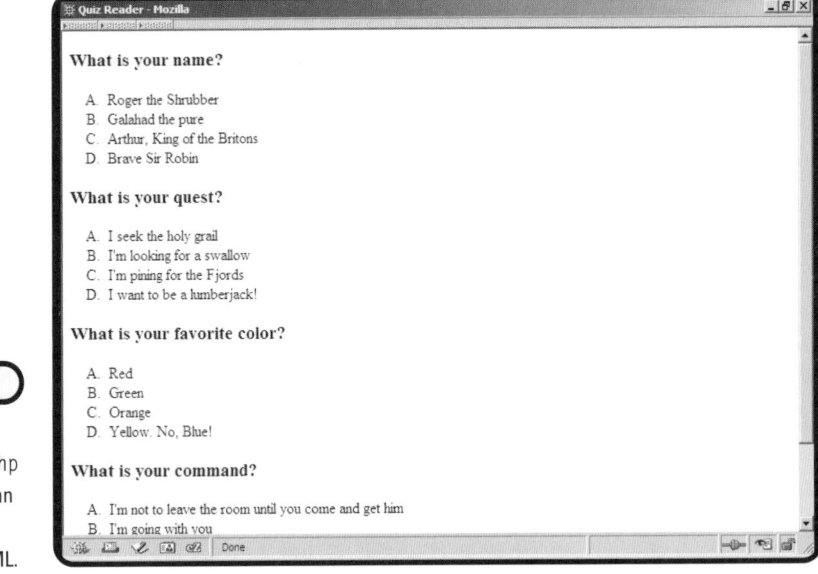

FIGURE 8.9

The `quizreader.php` program reads an XML file and formats it in HTML.

When the XML code is a little more complex, you may need to carefully examine the raw XML code to best interpret it. Once I recognized that the document is essentially an array of problems, the XML interpretation became relatively easy:

```
<!doctype html public "-//W3C//DTD HTML 4.0 //EN">
<html>
<head>
```

```
<title>Quiz Reader</title>
</head>
<body>
<?
//quiz reader
//demonstrates working with more complex XML files

//load up a quiz file
$xml = simplexml_load_file("python.xml");

//step through quiz as associative array
foreach ($xml->children() as $problem){

  //print each question as an ordered list.
  print <<<HERE
  <h3>$problem->question</h3>
  <ol type = "A">
    <li>$problem->answerA</li>
    <li>$problem->answerB</li>
    <li>$problem->answerC</li>
    <li>$problem->answerD</li>
  </ol>
HERE;
} // end foreach

//directly accessing a node:

print $xml->problem[0]->question;

?>
</body>
</html>
```

This procedure can be done in a number of steps:

1. Load the quiz as XML data.
2. Use a `foreach` loop to examine each element of the xml's `children()` array as an individual problem. In this example, the `$problem` variable doesn't contain simple string data, but another node with its own elements.
3. Inside the loop, use tag references to indicate the elements of the problem you wish to display. (Note that I chose not to display each question's answer, but I could have if I wished.)

If you want to display a particular element's value, do so using array-style syntax. This line refers to problem number 0:

```
print $xml->problem[0]->question;
```

It then looks for a subelement of a problem called `question` and displays that value. If you are working with an extremely complicated XML document, you can use structures like this to map directly to a particular element. Essentially, the `simpleXML` system lets you think of an XML document as a set of nested arrays. This allows you access to a potentially complex document in whatever detail you wish.

In the Real World

You might want to use XML data in these main instances:

- **You want a better organizational scheme for your information but don't want to deal with a formal database system. In this case you can create your own XML language and build programs that work with the data. This is the use of XML described in this chapter.**
- **You have XML data formatted in a predefined XML structure that you want to manipulate. There are XML standards published for describing everything from virtual reality scenes and molecular models to multimedia slideshows. You can use the features of `simpleXML` (or one of PHP's other XML parsers) to manipulate this existing data and create your own program for interpreting it. Of course, HTML is rapidly becoming a subset of XML (in fact, the XHTML standard is simply HTML following stricter XML standards), so you can use XML tricks to load and manage an HTML file. This might be useful for extracting a Web page's links or examining a Web page's images.**
- **You need a stand-in for relational data. Most database management systems allow you import and export data in XML format. XML can be a terrific way to send complex data, such as database query results or complete data tables, to remote programs. Often programmers write client-side code in a language such as JavaScript or Flash and use a server-side program to send query results to the client as XML data.**

Returning to XCMS

With all this XML knowledge, you're ready to refit the CMS introduced earlier in this chapter with an XML structure. My basic plan for the XCMS is to allow more parameters for each page. The original CMS (without XML) allows two parameters. The parameters are added directly to URLs with the get method. This quickly becomes unwieldy. By switching to an XML format, I can place all the parameters necessary for displaying a page into an XML document, then have my CMS program extract that data from the document.

Extracting Data from the XML File

The XCMS program relies on repeated calls to the same program to generate the page data. The XCMS program is much like `simpleCMS` except—rather than pulling parameters directly from the URL—XCMS takes an XML filename as its single parameter and extracts all the necessary information from that file.

```
<?

//XCMS
//XML-Based Simple CMS system
//Andy Harris for PHP/MySQL Abs. Beg 2nd Ed.
// NOTE:  Requires simpleXML extensions in PHP 5.0!

//get an XML file or load a default
if (empty($theXML)){
  $theXML = "main.xml";
} // end if

//Open up XML file
$xml = simplexml_load_file($theXML);

if ( !$xml){
  print ("there was a problem opening the XML");

} else {

  include ($xml->css);
  include($xml->top);

  print "<span class = \"menuPanel\"> \n";
  include ($xml->menu);
  print "</span> \n";

  print "<span class = \"item\"> \n";
  include ($xml->content);
  print "</span> \n";

} // end if

?>
```

The first step is determining if an XML file has been sent through the `$theXML` parameter. If not, a default value of `main.xml` is defined. This, of course, presumes that a copy of `main.xml` is available and properly formatted. If the program is called with some other XML file as its parameter, that file is interpreted again.

I then attempt to open the XML file. If the `simplexml_load_file` command is unsuccessful, it returns the value `FALSE`. The program reports this failure if it occurs. If it does not fail, the program creates a page based on the parameters indicated in this file. I expect a page with five parameters (`top`, `css`, `title`, `menu`, and `content`), but I could easily modify the program to accept as many parameters as you wish. I ignored the `title` parameter in this particular program version because I have the page title already stored in `top.html`.

The program includes all the files indicated in the XML code, incorporating them in CSS styles when appropriate.

Summary

Content management systems can help automate your Web site's creation. CMS tools allow you to build powerful multipart Web documents, combining pages with a single style and layout. You learned how to install and customize the popular PHP-Nuke CMS. You also learned how to build a very basic CMS of your own using `GET` parameters to customize your page. You learned about XML and how to use the `simpleXML` tools to parse any XML files you encounter. Finally, you learned how to combine your newfound XML skills with CMS to build an XML-aware CMS.

CHALLENGES

1. **Install and configure PHP-Nuke or another CMS on your system.**
2. **Create a custom theme by analyzing and modifying an existing theme.**
3. **Modify `simpleCMS` with your own layout, images, and banner files.**
4. **Create an editor that allows the user to build XML pages for XCMS.**
5. **Write an XCMS module that allows authorized users to add new content (a news or guest book, for example).**

Using MySQL to Create Databases

When you begin programming in PHP, you start with very simple variables. Soon you learned how to do more interesting things with arrays and associative arrays. You added the power of files to gain tremendous new skills. Now you learn how relational databases can be used to manage data. In this chapter you discover how to build a basic database and how to hook it up to your PHP programs. Specifically, you learn:

- How to start the MySQL executable
- How to build basic databases
- The essential data definition SQL statements
- How to return a basic SQL query
- How to use phpMyAdmin to manage your databases

Introducing the Adventure Generator Program

Databases are a serious tool but they can be fun, too. The program shown in Figures 9.1 through 9.4 shows how a database can be used to fuel an adventure game generator. The adventure generator is a system that allows users to create and play simple multiple-choice adventures. This style of game consists of several nodes. Each node describes some sort of decision. In each case, the user can choose from up to three options. The user's choice leads to a new decision. If the user makes a sequence of correct choices, he wins the game.

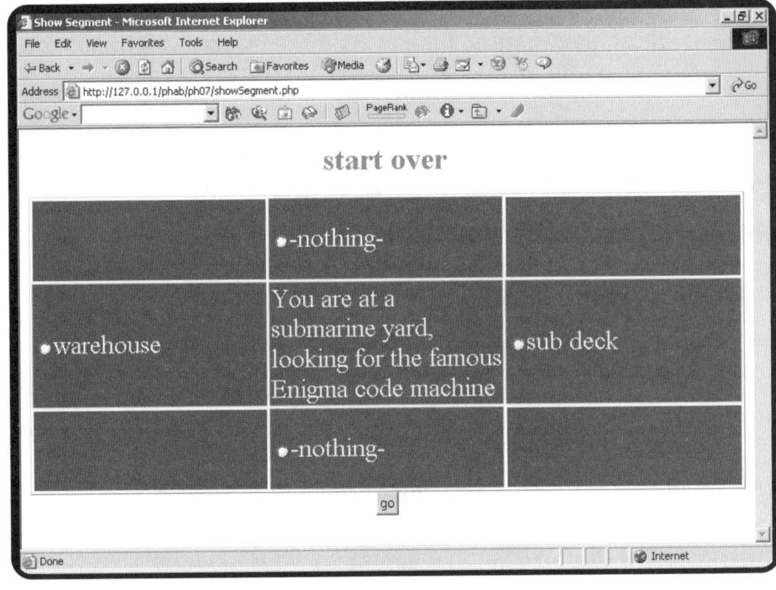

FIGURE 9.1

The user can choose an option. I'm hopping onto that sub...

This program is interesting as a game, but the really exciting part is how the user can modify this game. A user can use the same system to create and modify adventures. Figure 9.3 shows the data behind the Enigma game. Note that you can edit any node by clicking the appropriate button from this screen.

If the user chooses to edit a segment, the page shown in Figure 9.4 appears.

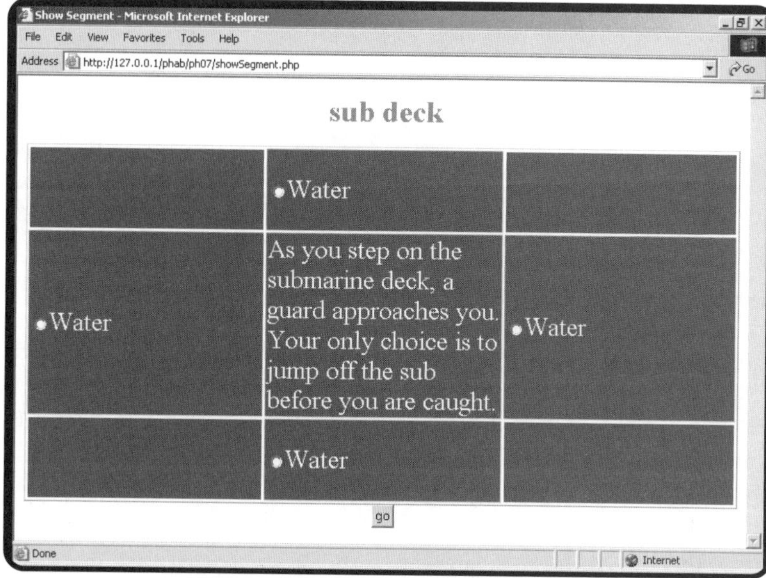

FIGURE 9.2

Maybe the warehouse would have been a better choice after all.

List Segments - Microsoft Internet Explorer

File Edit View Favorites Tools Help

Address http://127.0.0.1/phab/ph07/listSegments.php

id	1
name	start over
description	You are at a submarine yard, looking for the famous Enigma code machine
north	0
east	3
south	0
west	2
	Edit this room go

id	2
name	sub deck
description	As you step on the submarine deck, a guard approaches you. Your only choice is to jump off the sub before you are caught.
north	15
east	15
south	15
west	15
	Edit this room go

FIGURE 9.3

This page provides information about each segment in the game, including links to directly edit each segment.

As you can see, the data structure is the most important element of this game. You already know some ways to work with data, but this chapter introduces the notion of *relational database management systems* (RDBMS). An RDBMS is a system that helps programmers work with data. The adventure generator program uses a database to store and manipulate all the data.

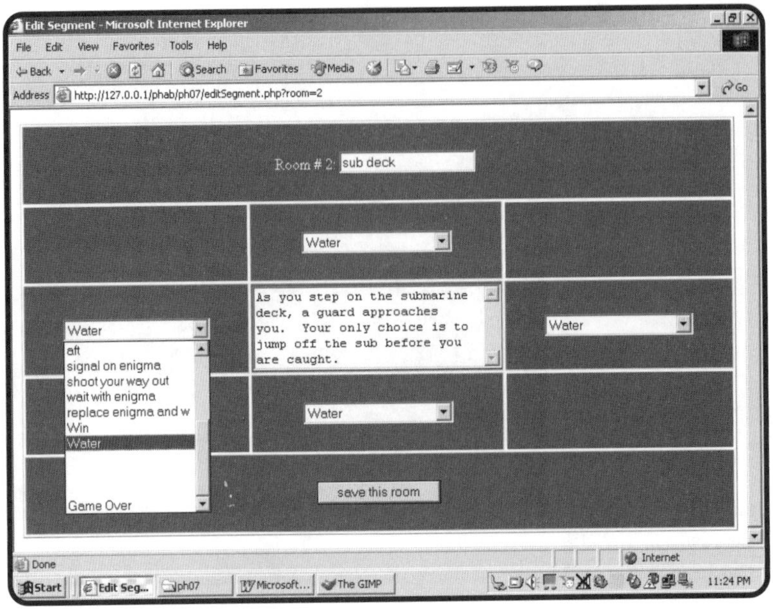

FIGURE 9.4

From this screen it is possible to change everything about a node. All the nodes that have been created so far are available as new locations.

Using a Database Management System

Data is such an important part of modern programming that entire programming languages are devoted to manipulating databases. The primary standard for database languages is *Structured Query Language* (SQL). SQL is a standardized language for creating databases, storing information in databases, and retrieving information from databases. Special applications and programming environments specialize in interpreting SQL data and acting on it.

Often a programmer begins by creating a data structure in SQL, and then writes a program in some other language (such as PHP) to allow access to that data. The PHP program can then formulate data requests or updates, which are passed on to the SQL interpreter. This approach has a couple of advantages:

- Once you learn SQL, you can apply it easily to a new programming language.
- You can easily add multiple interfaces to an existing data set because many programming languages have ways to access an SQL interpreter.

Many relational database management systems are available, but the MySQL environment is especially well suited to working with PHP.

The basic concepts of SQL remain the same no matter what type of database you are working on. Most of the SQL commands described in this chapter work without modification in Microsoft Access, Microsoft SQL Server, and Oracle, as well as a number of other RDBMS packages.

I begin this chapter by explaining how to create a simple database in MySQL. You can work with this package a number of ways, but start by writing a script that builds a database in a text file. I use the SQL language, which is different in syntax and style from PHP. I show you how to use some visual tools to help work with databases and how to use the SQLite data library built into PHP 5. In chapter 10, "Connecting to Databases within PHP," I show you how to contact and manipulate your MySQL database from within PHP.

Working with MySQL

There are a number of RDBMS packages available. These programs vary in power, flexibility, and price. However, they all work in essentially the same way. Most examples in this book use the `MySQL` database.

- It is a very powerful program in its own right. It handles a large subset of the functionality of the most expensive and powerful database packages.
- It uses a standard form of the well-known SQL data language.
- It is released under an open-source license.
- It works on many operating systems and with many languages.
- It works very quickly and works well even with large data sets.
- PHP ships with a number of functions designed to support MySQL databases.

Installing MySQL

If PHP is already on your Web server, chances are that MySQL is there as well. Many installation packages install both MySQL and PHP on your system. If you do not control the Web server directly, you might need to convince your server administrator to install MySQL. A version of the MySQL binary is available on the CD that accompanies this book.

Earlier versions of PHP had built-in MySQL support. The beta version of PHP 5 that I used for this book requires some minor configuration before it will use the MySQL functions. Run the `phpInfo()` **command you learned in chapter 1, "Exploring the PHP Environment," to see how your server is configured. If** `phpInfo()` **does not indicate support for MySQL, modify your PHP.INI file. Add or uncomment the following line in the** `Dynamic Extensions` **section of PHP.INI to enable MySQL support if it is not currently turned on:**

```
extension=php_mysql.dll
```

If you cannot get MySQL running on your server, use the new SQLite extensions built into PHP 5. Appendix B (on this book's CD) describes how to use SQLite, which is another database program installed as the default. The two packages have some differences, but the main ideas remain the same. If you end up using SQLite, read this chapter to get the main ideas and then read appendix B to see how SQLite is different from MySQL. I included SQLite versions of every database in the book on the CD for your reference.

Using the MySQL Executable

MySQL is actually a number of programs. It has a server component that is always running, as well as a number of utility programs. The `MySQL` command line console shown in Figure 9.5 is a basic program run from the command line. It isn't a very pretty program, but it provides powerful access to the database engine.

```
command prompt - mysql
Microsoft Windows 2000 [Version 5.00.2195]
(C) Copyright 1985-2000 Microsoft Corp.

C:\WINNT>cd ..

C:\>cd mysql

C:\mysql>cd bin

C:\mysql\bin>mysql
Welcome to the MySQL monitor.  Commands end with ; or \g.
Your MySQL connection id is 13 to server version: 3.23.52-nt

Type 'help;' or '\h' for help. Type '\c' to clear the buffer.

mysql> _
```

FIGURE 9.5

The MySQL program connects to a database.

You can use MySQL a number of ways, but the basic procedure involves connecting to a MySQL server, choosing a database, and then using the SQL language to control the database by creating tables, viewing data, and so on.

You must run mysql.exe from the command line. In Windows, choose "run" from the Start menu, then type in "cmd" and press the Enter key. At this text window, move to the appropriate window with the cd command (e.g., cd \apache\mysql\bin) and finally type "mysql" to begin the console.

The MySQL.exe console shipped with MySQL is the most basic way to work with the `MySQL` database. Although it won't win any user interface awards, the program offers low-level access to the database. This interface is important to learn, however, because it is very much like the way your programs will interface with the database system.

If you're running your own Web server, you must run the MySQL server before you can run the client. Under Windows, run the WinMySQLAdmin tool to start the MySQL server. This automatically starts the MySQL server and sets up your system so that MySQL is run as a service when your computer is booted (much like Apache). Turn off the MySQL server in the Control Panel's Services section or with the MySQL tool menu that appears in the system tray.

Creating a Database

Databases are described by a very specific organization scheme. To illustrate database concepts, I create and view a simple phone list. The phone list's basic structure is in Table 9.1.

TABLE 9.1 PHONE LIST SUMMARY

id	firstName	lastName	e-mail	phone
0	Andy	Harris	aharris@cs.iupui.edu	123-4567
1	Joe	Slow	jslow@myPlace.net	987-6543

The phone list shows a very typical data table. Database people like to give special names to the parts of the database.

- Each row of the table is called a *record*. Records describe discrete (individually defined) entities.
- The list of records is called a *table*.
- Each record in a table has the same elements, which are called *fields* or *columns*.

Every record in the table has the same field definitions, but records can have different values in the fields. The fields in a table are defined in specific ways. Because of the way database tables are stored in files, the computer must always know how much room to allocate for each field. Therefore, each field's size and type is important. This particular database is defined with five fields. The `id` field is an integer. All the other fields contain string (text) data.

Creating a Table

Of course, to use a database system, you need to learn how to build a table.

RDBMS programs use a language called SQL to create and manipulate databases. SQL is pretty easy to understand, compared to full-blown programming languages. You can usually guess what's going on even without a lot of knowledge. As an example, look at the following SQL code:

```
USE chapter9;

CREATE TABLE phoneList (
  id INT PRIMARY KEY,
  firstName VARCHAR(15),
  lastName VARCHAR (15),
  email VARCHAR(20),
  phone VARCHAR(15)
);

DESCRIBE phoneList;
```

This code is an SQL script. It's like a PHP program in that it is a set of instructions for the computer. However, the PHP interpreter doesn't directly interact with the SQL language. Instead, these commands are sent to another program. As a PHP programmer, you will write code that sends commands to a database language. Just as your PHP code often writes code in HTML format for the browser to interpret, you'll write SQL code for the MySQL interpreter to use.

When this code is sent to an SQL-compliant database program (such as MySQL), it creates the database structure shown in Table 9.1.

Using a Database

You may have several database projects working in the same relational database system. In my case, each chapter has its own database. Sometimes your system administrator will assign a database to you. In any case, you will probably need to invoke that database with the `USE` command.

SQL Advantages

Databases have been an important part of programming since the beginning, but the process of working with data has evolved. The advent of a common language that can be used in many applications was a very important step. SQL is a *fourth-generation* language. In general, these languages are designed to solve a particular type of problem. Some fourth-generation languages (like SQL) aren't full-blown programming languages, because they don't support data structures like branches and loops.

Still, these languages can serve a purpose. SQL is handy because it's widely supported. The SQL commands you learn in this chapter apply to most modern database programs with little to no modification. You can take the script in MySQL and send the same code to an Oracle or MS SQL Server database (two other very common choices), and all three data programs build the same database. If you upgrade to a more powerful data package, you can use your existing scripts to manipulate the data. If you're working with SQLite, your SQL commands will be almost identical to the commands used in MySQL.

Programming in traditional languages is perhaps the most powerful reason to have a scripting language with which to control databases. You can write a program in any language (like PHP, for example) that generates SQL code. You can then use that code to manipulate the database. This allows you to have complete flexibility, and lets your program act as the database interface.

SQL syntax is not exactly like that of PHP. SQL has a different culture, and it makes sense to respect the way SQL code has historically been written. SQL is generally not case-sensitive, but most SQL coders put all SQL commands in all uppercase letters. Also, you usually end each line with a semicolon when a bunch of SQL commands are placed in a file (as this code is).

If you don't already have a database to `USE`, you can make one with the `CREATE` command. For example, use these commands to create a database called `myStuff`:

```
CREATE DATABASE myStuff;
USE myStuff;
```

Creating a Table

To create a table, you must indicate the table name as well as each field. For each field, list what type of data is held in the field, and (for text data) the field's characters length. As an example, the following code creates the `phoneList` table:

```
CREATE TABLE phoneList (
  id INT PRIMARY KEY,
  firstName VARCHAR(15),
  lastName VARCHAR (15),
  email VARCHAR(20),
  phone VARCHAR(15)
);
```

You can think of fields as being much like variables, but while PHP is easy-going about what type of data is in a variable, SQL is very picky about the type of data in fields. In order to create an efficient database, MySQL needs to know exactly how many bytes of memory to set aside for every single field in the database. It does this primarily by requiring the database designer to specify the type and size of every field in each table. Table 9.2 lists a few of the primary data types supported by MySQL.

TABLE 9.2 COMMON DATA TYPES IN MYSQL

Data Type	Description
`INT`	Standard integer +/– 2 billion (roughly)
`BIGINT`	Big integer +/– 9 x 10 ^18th
`FLOAT`	Floating-point decimal number 38 digits
`DOUBLE`	Double-precision floating-point 308 digits
`CHAR(n)`	Text with *n* digits; if actual value is less than *n*, field is padded with trailing spaces
`VARCHAR(n)`	Text with *n* digits; trailing spaces are automatically culled
`DATE`	Date in YYYY-MM-DD format
`TIME`	Time in HH:MM:SS format
`YEAR`	Year in YYYY format

While the data types listed in Table 9.2 are by far the most commonly used, MySQL supports many others. Look in the online Help that ships with MySQL if you need a more specific data type. Other databases have a very similar list of data types.

You might notice that it is unnecessary to specify the length of numeric types (although you can determine a maximum size for numeric types as well as the number of digits you want stored in float and double fields). The storage requirements for numeric fields are based on the field type itself.

Working with String Data in MySQL

Text values are usually stored in `VARCHAR` fields. These fields must include the number of characters allocated for the field. Both `CHAR` and `VARCHAR` fields have fixed lengths. The primary difference between them is what happens when the field contains a value shorter than the specified length.

Assume you declared a `CHAR` field to have a length of `10` with the following SQL segment:

```
firstName VARCHAR(10);
```

Later you store the value `'Andy'` into the field. The field actually contains `'Andy      '`. (That is, `Andy` followed by six spaces.) `CHAR` fields pad any remaining characters with spaces. The `VARCHAR` field type removes any padded spaces. The `VARCHAR` field type is the one you use most often to store string data.

> **DETERMINING THE LENGTH OF A VARCHAR FIELD**
>
> **Data design is both a science and an art. Determining the appropriate length for your text fields is one of the oldest problems in data.**
>
> **If you don't allocate enough room for your text data, you can cause a lot of problems for your users. I once taught a course called CLT SD WEB PRG because the database that held the course names didn't have enough room for the actual course name (Client-Side Web Programming). My students renamed it the Buy a Vowel course.**
>
> **However, you can't make every text field a thousand characters long, either, because it would waste system resources. If you have a field that will usually contain only five characters and you allocate one hundred characters, the drive still requires room for the extra 95 characters. If your database has thousands of entries, this can be a substantial cost in drive space. In a distributed environment, you have to wait for those unnecessary spaces to come across limited bandwidth.**
>
> **It takes experimentation and practice to determine the appropriate width for your string fields. Test your application with real users so you can be sure you've made the right decision.**

Finishing the CREATE TABLE Statement

Once you understand field data types, the `CREATE TABLE` syntax makes a lot of sense. Only a few more details to understand:

- Use a pair of parentheses to indicate the field list once you specify `CREATE TABLE`.

- Name each field and follow it with its type (and length, if it's a `CHAR` or `VARCHAR`).
- Separate the fields with commas.
- Put each field on its own line and indent the field definitions. You don't have to, but I prefer to, because these practices make the code much easier to read and debug.

Creating a Primary Key

You might be curious about the very first field in the phone list database. Just to refresh your memory, the line that defines that field looks like this:

```
id INT PRIMARY KEY,
```

Most database tables have some sort of field that holds a numeric value. This special field is called the *primary key.*

You can enter the code presented so far directly into the MySQL program. You can see the code and its results in Figure 9.6.

In the Real World

A simple database could theoretically go without a primary key, but such fields are so important to more sophisticated databases that you might as well start putting them in. It's traditional to put a primary key in every table.

In chapter 11, "Data Normalization," you learn more about the relational data model. In that discussion you learn how keys build powerful databases and more about creating proper primary keys. In fact, the adventure program you've already seen heavily relies on a key field even though there's only one table in the database.

Using the DESCRIBE Command to Check a Table's Structure

Checking the structure of a table can be helpful, especially if somebody else created it or you don't remember exactly its field types or sizes. The `DESCRIBE` command lets you view a table structure.

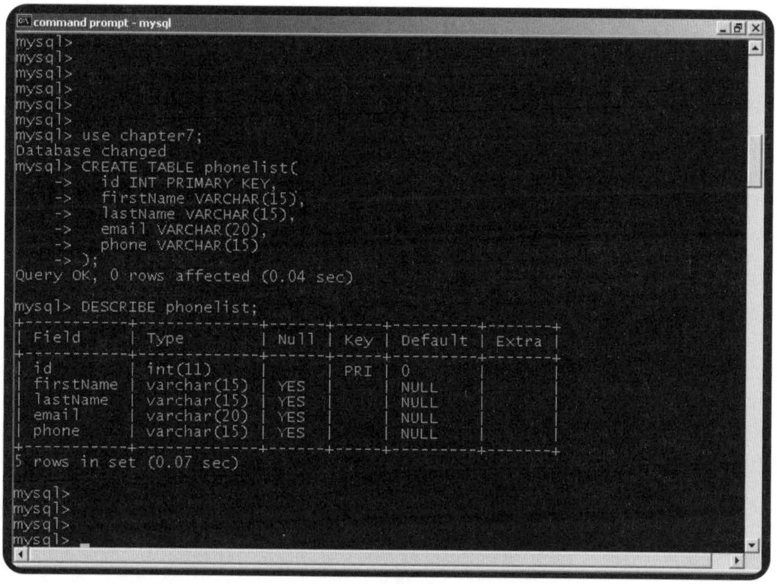

```
mysql>
mysql>
mysql>
mysql>
mysql>
mysql>
mysql> use chapter7;
Database changed
mysql> CREATE TABLE phonelist(
    ->   id INT PRIMARY KEY,
    ->   firstName VARCHAR(15),
    ->   lastName VARCHAR(15),
    ->   email VARCHAR(20),
    ->   phone VARCHAR(15)
    -> );
Query OK, 0 rows affected (0.04 sec)

mysql> DESCRIBE phonelist;
+-----------+-------------+------+-----+---------+-------+
| Field     | Type        | Null | Key | Default | Extra |
+-----------+-------------+------+-----+---------+-------+
| id        | int(11)     |      | PRI | 0       |       |
| firstName | varchar(15) | YES  |     | NULL    |       |
| lastName  | varchar(15) | YES  |     | NULL    |       |
| email     | varchar(20) | YES  |     | NULL    |       |
| phone     | varchar(15) | YES  |     | NULL    |       |
+-----------+-------------+------+-----+---------+-------+
5 rows in set (0.07 sec)

mysql>
mysql>
mysql>
mysql>
```

FIGURE 9.6

This is the MySQL command-line tool after I created the `phoneList` table.

Inserting Values

Once you've created a table, you can begin adding data to it. The `INSERT` command is the primary tool for adding records.

```
INSERT INTO phoneList
VALUES (
  0, 'Andy', 'Harris', 'aharris@cs.iupui.edu', '123-4567'
);
```

The `INSERT` statement allows you to add a record into a database. The values must be listed in exactly the same order the fields were defined. Each value is separated by a comma, and all `VARCHAR` and `CHAR` values must be enclosed in single quotation marks.

If you have a large amount of data to load, you can use the `LOAD DATA` command. This command accepts a tab-delimited text file with one row per record and fields separated by tabs. It then loads that entire file into the database. This is often the fastest way to load a database with test data. The following line loads data from a file called `addresses.txt` into the `phoneList` table:

```
LOAD DATA LOCAL INFILE "addresses.txt" INTO TABLE phoneList;
```

Figure 9.7 shows the MySQL tool after I have added one record to the table.

IN THE REAL WORLD

As you are building a database, populate the database with test values. Don't use actual data at this point, because your database will not work correctly until you've messed with it for some time. However, your test values should be reflective of the kinds of data your database will house. This helps you spot certain problems like fields that are too small or missing.

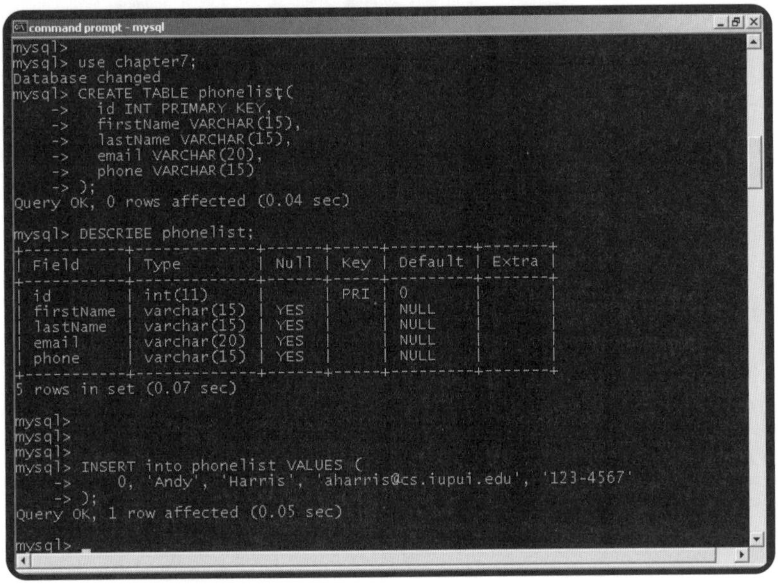

```
mysql>
mysql> use chapter7;
Database changed
mysql> CREATE TABLE phonelist(
    ->   id INT PRIMARY KEY,
    ->   firstName VARCHAR(15),
    ->   lastName VARCHAR(15),
    ->   email VARCHAR(20),
    ->   phone VARCHAR(15)
    -> );
Query OK, 0 rows affected (0.04 sec)

mysql> DESCRIBE phonelist;
+-----------+-------------+------+-----+---------+-------+
| Field     | Type        | Null | Key | Default | Extra |
+-----------+-------------+------+-----+---------+-------+
| id        | int(11)     |      | PRI | 0       |       |
| firstName | varchar(15) | YES  |     | NULL    |       |
| lastName  | varchar(15) | YES  |     | NULL    |       |
| email     | varchar(20) | YES  |     | NULL    |       |
| phone     | varchar(15) | YES  |     | NULL    |       |
+-----------+-------------+------+-----+---------+-------+
5 rows in set (0.07 sec)

mysql>
mysql>
mysql>
mysql> INSERT into phonelist VALUES (
    ->   0, 'Andy', 'Harris', 'aharris@cs.iupui.edu', '123-4567'
    -> );
Query OK, 1 row affected (0.05 sec)

mysql> _
```

FIGURE 9.7

MySQL tells you the operation succeeded, but you don't get a lot more information.

Selecting Results

Of course, you want to see the results of all your table-building activities. If you want to see the data in a table, you can use the `SELECT` command. This is perhaps the most powerful command in SQL, but its basic use is quite simple. Use this command to see all of the data in the `phoneList` table:

```
SELECT * FROM phoneList
```

This command grabs all fields of all records of the `phoneList` database and displays them in table format.

Figure 9.8 shows what happens after I add a `SELECT` statement to get the results.

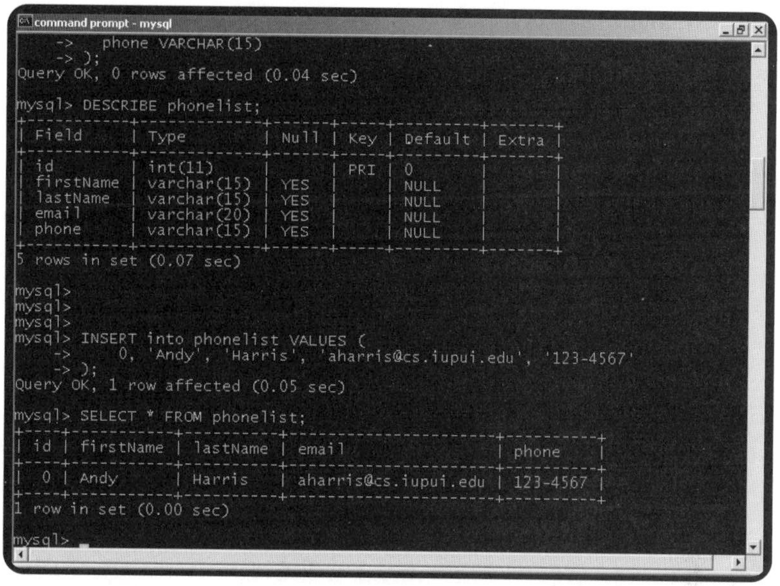

```
command prompt - mysql
    ->   phone VARCHAR(15)
    -> );
Query OK, 0 rows affected (0.04 sec)

mysql> DESCRIBE phonelist;
+-----------+-------------+------+-----+---------+-------+
| Field     | Type        | Null | Key | Default | Extra |
+-----------+-------------+------+-----+---------+-------+
| id        | int(11)     |      | PRI | 0       |       |
| firstName | varchar(15) | YES  |     | NULL    |       |
| lastName  | varchar(15) | YES  |     | NULL    |       |
| email     | varchar(20) | YES  |     | NULL    |       |
| phone     | varchar(15) | YES  |     | NULL    |       |
+-----------+-------------+------+-----+---------+-------+
5 rows in set (0.07 sec)

mysql>
mysql>
mysql>
mysql> INSERT into phonelist VALUES (
    ->     0, 'Andy', 'Harris', 'aharris@cs.iupui.edu', '123-4567'
    -> );
Query OK, 1 row affected (0.05 sec)

mysql> SELECT * FROM phonelist;
+----+-----------+----------+----------------------+----------+
| id | firstName | lastName | email                | phone    |
+----+-----------+----------+----------------------+----------+
|  0 | Andy      | Harris   | aharris@cs.iupui.edu | 123-4567 |
+----+-----------+----------+----------------------+----------+
1 row in set (0.00 sec)

mysql> _
```

FIGURE 9.8

The result of the SELECT statement is a table, just like the original plan.

Writing a Script to Build a Table

It is very important to understand how to create tables by hand in SQL, because your programs have to do this same work. However, it's very tedious to write your SQL code in the MySQL window directly. When you create real data applications, you often have to build and rebuild your data tables several times before you are satisfied with them, and this would be awkward in the command-line interface. Also, as you are writing programs that work with your database, you will likely make mistakes that corrupt the original data.

It's good to have a script ready for easily rebuilding the database with test data. Most programmers create a script of SQL commands with a text editor (use the same editor in which you write your PHP code) and use the SOURCE command to load that code. Here is an SQL script for creating the phoneList database:

```
## build phone list
## for mySQL

USE chapter9;
DROP TABLE IF EXISTS phoneList;

CREATE TABLE phoneList (
  id INT PRIMARY KEY,
  firstName VARCHAR(15),
  lastName VARCHAR (15),
```

```
  email VARCHAR(20),
  phone VARCHAR(15)
);

INSERT INTO phoneList
VALUES (
  0, 'Andy', 'Harris', 'aharris@cs.iupui.edu', '123-4567'
);

SELECT * FROM phoneList;
```

This code isn't exactly like what I used in the interactive session, because the new code shows a few more features that are especially handy when you create SQL code in a script.

Creating Comments in SQL

SQL is actually a language. Although it isn't technically a programming language, it has many of the same features. Like PHP and other languages, SQL supports several types of comment characters. The # sign is often used to signify a comment in SQL. Comments are especially important when you save a group of SQL commands in a file for later reuse. These comments can help you remember what type of database you were trying to build. It's critical to put basic comments in your scripts.

Dropping a Table

It may seem strange to talk about deleting a table from a database before you've built one, but often (as in this case) a database is created using a script. Before you create a new table, you should check to see if it already exists. If it does exist, delete it with the `DROP` command. The following command does exactly that:

```
DROP TABLE IF EXISTS phoneList;
```

If the `phoneList` table currently exists, it is deleted to avoid confusion.

Running a Script with SOURCE

You can create an SQL script with any text editor. It is common to save SQL scripts with the `.sql` extension. Inside MySQL, you can use the `SOURCE` command to load and execute a script file. Figure 9.9 shows MySQL after I run the `buildPhonelist.sql` script.

```
mysql>
mysql>
mysql>
mysql> INSERT into phonelist VALUES (
    ->     0, 'Andy', 'Harris', 'aharris@cs.iupui.edu', '123-4567'
    -> );
Query OK, 1 row affected (0.05 sec)

mysql> SELECT * FROM phonelist;
+----+-----------+----------+----------------------+----------+
| id | firstName | lastName | email                | phone    |
+----+-----------+----------+----------------------+----------+
|  0 | Andy      | Harris   | aharris@cs.iupui.edu | 123-4567 |
+----+-----------+----------+----------------------+----------+
1 row in set (0.00 sec)

mysql> SOURCE buildPhoneList.sql;
Database changed
Query OK, 0 rows affected (0.00 sec)

Query OK, 0 rows affected (0.00 sec)

Query OK, 1 row affected (0.00 sec)

+----+-----------+----------+----------------------+----------+
| id | firstName | lastName | email                | phone    |
+----+-----------+----------+----------------------+----------+
|  0 | Andy      | Harris   | aharris@cs.iupui.edu | 123-4567 |
+----+-----------+----------+----------------------+----------+
1 row in set (0.00 sec)

mysql> _
```

FIGURE 9.9

The SOURCE command allows you to read in SQL instructions from a file.

In Windows I often drag a file from a directory view into a command-line program like MySQL. Windows copies the entire filename over, but it includes double quotation marks, which causes problems for the MySQL interpreter. If you drag a filename into MySQL, edit out the quotation marks.

Working with a Database via phpMyAdmin

It's critical to understand the SQL language, but sometimes you may want an alternative way to build and view your databases. The command line is functional, but it can be tedious to use. If you are running a Web server, you can use an excellent front end called phpMyAdmin. This freeware program makes it much easier to create, modify, and manipulate databases.

In the Real World

The phpMyAdmin interface is so cool that you'll be tempted to use it all the time. That's fine, but be sure you understand the underlying SQL code—your PHP programs have to work with plain-text SQL commands. It's fine to use a front-end tool while building and manipulating your data, but your users won't use this program. Your application is the user's interface to your database, so you must be able to do all commands in plain text from within PHP. I use phpMyAdmin, but I also make sure I always look at the code it produces so I can write it myself.

phpMyAdmin basically adds the visual editing tools of a program like Microsoft Access to the MySQL environment. It also adds some wonderful tools for adding records, viewing your data structure, exporting data to useful formats, and experimenting with data structures. The program is written in PHP, so install it to your server's HTML document path (usually `htdocs` if you're using the Apache server).

Some of the more advanced phpMyAdmin features—including the ability to automate relationships and create PDF diagrams of your data structures—require table installation and some other special configuration. If your server administrator has not enabled these features, consult an excellent tutorial at http://www.garvinhicking.de/tops/texte/mimetutorial.

Connecting to a Server

MySQL is a client/server application. The MySQL server usually runs on the Web server where your PHP programs reside. You can connect a MySQL client such as phpMyAdmin to any MySQL server. Figure 9.10 shows a connection to the local MySQL connection.

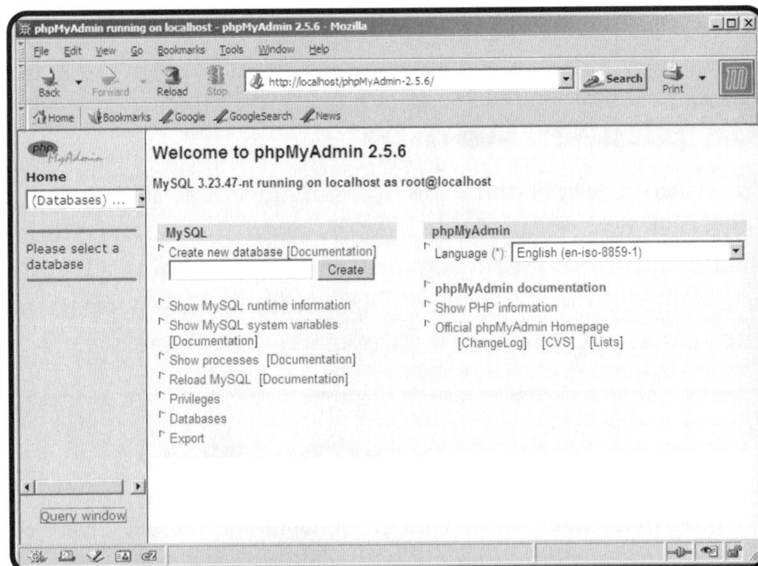

FIGURE 9.10

The main phpMyAdmin screen lets you choose a database in the left frame or perform administrative tasks in the main frame.

It's important to recognize that you can connect to any data server you have permission to use. This data server doesn't need to be on the same physical machine you are using. This is useful if you want to use phpMyAdmin to view data on a remote Web server you are maintaining, for example. However, many remote Web servers are not configured to accept this kind of access, so you should know how to work with the plain MySQL console.

The first time you run phpMyAdmin, it will probably ask for some login information. This data is stored so you don't have to remember it every time. However, if you want to change your login or experiment with some other phpMyAdmin features, edit the `config.inc.php` **file installed in the main phpMyAdmin folder.**

Creating and Modifying a Table

phpMyAdmin provides visual tools to help you create and modify your tables. The phone list is way too mundane for my tastes, so I'll build a new table to illustrate phpMyAdmin features. This new table contains a number of randomly generated super heroes. Select a table from the left frame and use the Create New Table section of the resulting page to build a new table. Figure 9.11 shows the dialog box used to create a table or alter its structure.

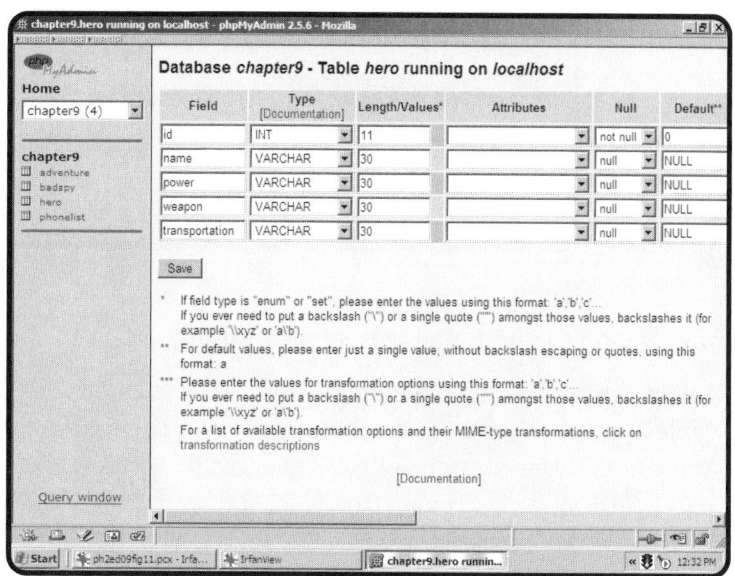

FIGURE 9.11

It's easy to create a table and modify its structure with phpMyAdmin.

With phpMyAdmin you can choose variable types from a drop-down list; many field properties are available as checkboxes. It's critical that you choose a variable type (and a field length in case of character fields). When you finish creating or modifying the table, the proper SQL code is generated and executed for you.

Check this site out sometime when you're bored: http://home.hiwaay.net/~lkseitz/comics/herogen/. Special thanks to Lee Seitz and his hysterical Super-Hero generator.

Editing Table Data

You can use phpMyAdmin to browse your table in a format much like a spreadsheet. Figure 9.12 illustrates this capability.

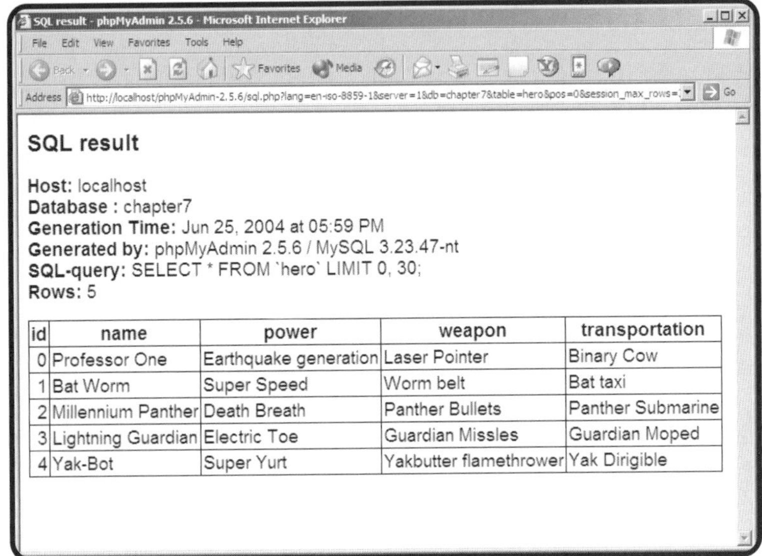

id	name	power	weapon	transportation
0	Professor One	Earthquake generation	Laser Pointer	Binary Cow
1	Bat Worm	Super Speed	Worm belt	Bat taxi
2	Millennium Panther	Death Breath	Panther Bullets	Panther Submarine
3	Lightning Guardian	Electric Toe	Guardian Missles	Guardian Moped
4	Yak-Bot	Super Yurt	Yakbutter flamethrower	Yak Dirigible

FIGURE 9.12

Use the Browse tab to view table data.

Follow these steps to edit a table in phpMyAdmin:

1. Select the table from the table list on the left side of the SQL screen. The table appears in a spreadsheet-like format in the main part of the screen. You can edit the contents of the table in this window.
2. Edit or delete a record by clicking the appropriate icon displayed near the record.
3. Add a row by clicking the corresponding link near the bottom of the table.
4. Leave the cell you edited or press the Enter key. Any changes you make on the table data are automatically converted into the appropriate SQL code.

Exporting a Table

Some of phpMyAdmin's most interesting features involve exporting table information. You can generate a number of data formats. The Export tab looks like the page in Figure 9.13.

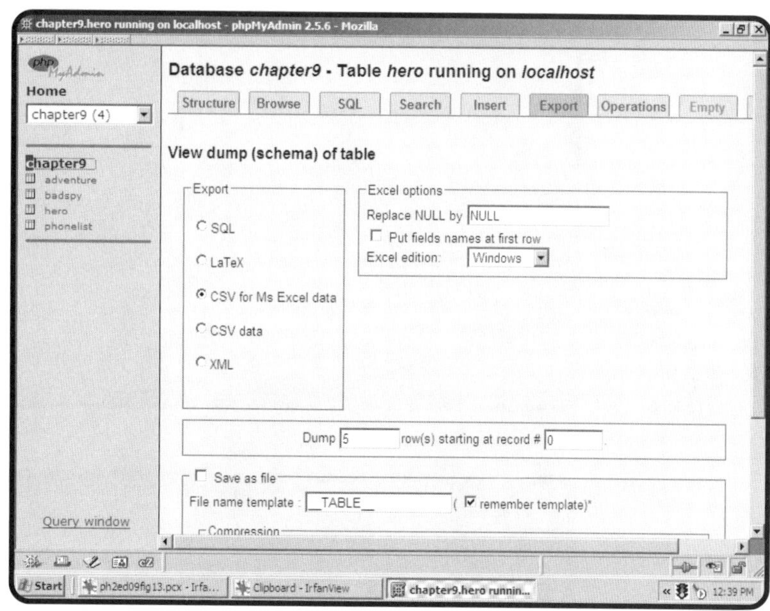

FIGURE 9.13

The Export Result Set dialog box allows you to save table data in a number of formats.

You might prefer to have your results saved in some sort of delimited format such as those discussed in chapter 6, "Working with Files." You can easily generate such a format by choosing the Comma-Separated Value (CSV) option and selecting your delimiters. This is a good choice in these situations:

- You want your data to be readable by a spreadsheet.
- You are writing a program that can handle such a format but cannot directly access databases.

The Excel CSV format configures the data so an Excel spreadsheet can read it easily. The ordinary CSV format allows you to modify your output with a number of options. Figure 9.14 illustrates the CSV version of the `hero` data set.

Once you've created your data file, either save it using the appropriate link or copy and paste it to a spreadsheet. Most spreadsheet programs can read various forms of CSV data with minimal configuration. Figure 9.15 demonstrates the file as seen by Microsoft Excel.

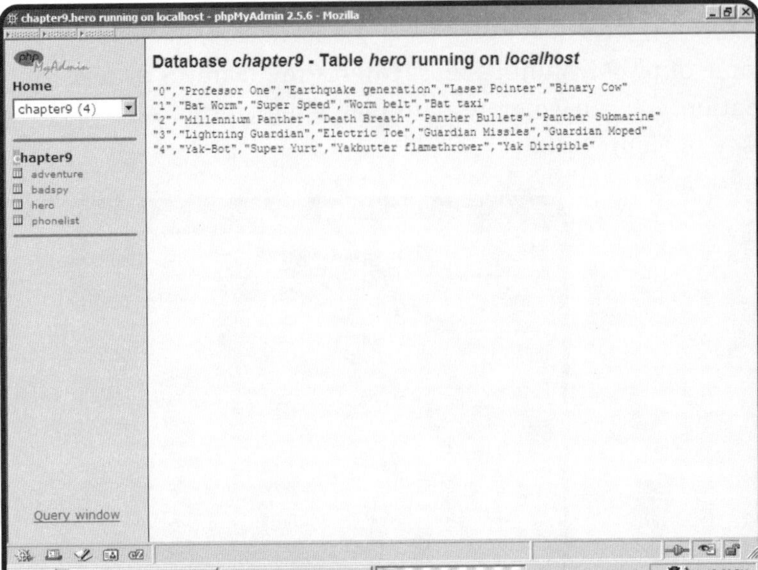

FIGURE 9.14

You can print CSV summaries of your data results.

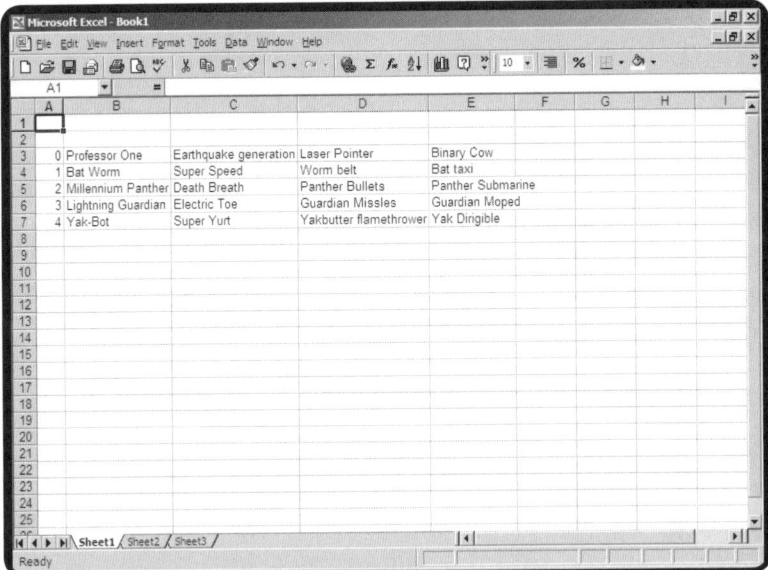

FIGURE 9.15

I set up the data as a tab delimited file and read it into Excel.

You can also set up an XML file to hold the data. As you recall from chapter 8, “XML and Content Management Systems,” XML is much like HTML and describes the information in a self-documenting form, as you can see in Figure 9.16.

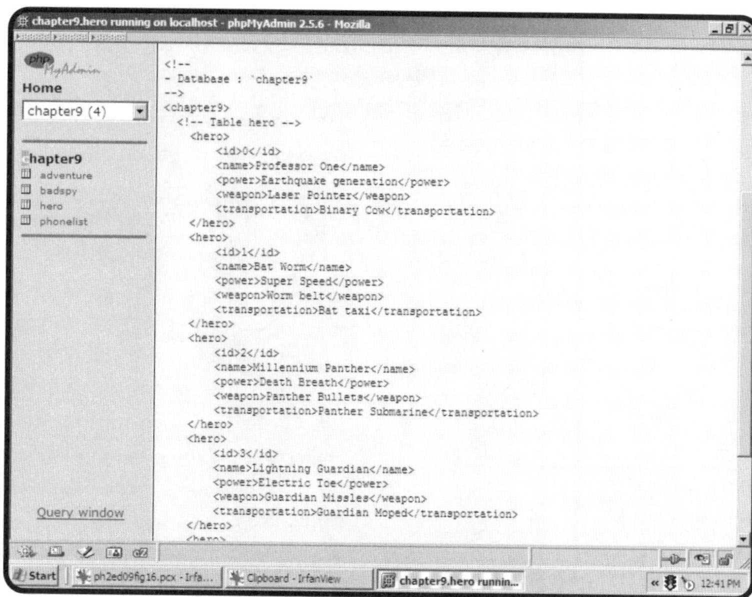

FIGURE 9.16

The XML form of the data generates HTML-like tags to describe the fields.

You might use the XML feature to store a database as an XML file and then have a program read that file using XML techniques. This is a good way to work with a database even when the program can't directly deal with the database server.

One last very useful export option: the SQL format. You can use this tool to automatically generate an SQL script for creating and populating a table. The SQL formatting utility is useful if you use the visual tools for creating and editing a table, but then want to re-create the table through a script. The dialog box shown in Figure 9.17 illustrates this tool's various options.

You can specify whether the resulting script generates the table structure alone or adds the data. You can also specify whether the resulting script contains code to select a database, drop the specified table if it already exists, and the filename of the resulting script. Figure 9.18 shows the code that might result from an SQL export of the `hero` table.

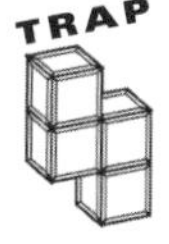

The ability to automatically generate SQL scripts is incredibly powerful. It can be a great timesaver and you can learn a lot by examining the scripts written with such a feature. However, you are still the programmer and are responsible for code in your projects—even if you didn't write it directly. You must understand what the generated code does. Most of the code so far is stuff I've already described, but you may have to look up advanced features. As I've said: Know how to do this stuff by hand.

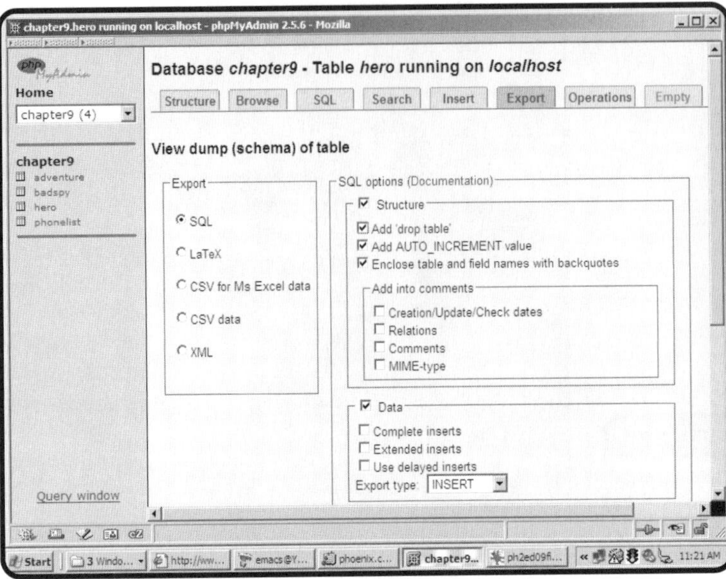

FIGURE 9.17

From this screen you can generate code that manufactures replicas of any database created or viewed with phpMyAdmin.

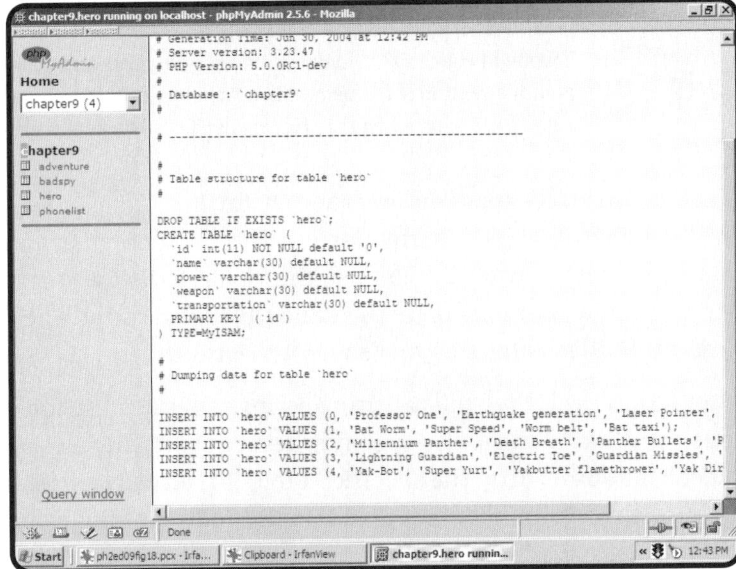

FIGURE 9.18

This code can be run on any MySQL server to make a copy of the `hero` database.

Creating More-Powerful Queries

So far, the tables you've created haven't been any more powerful than HTML tables and they're a lot more trouble. The excitement of databases comes when you use the information to solve problems. Ironically, the most important part of database work isn't usually *getting* the data, but *filtering* the data in order to solve some sort of problem.

You might want to get a listing of all heroes in your database whose last name begins with an E, or perhaps somebody parked a Yak Dirigible in your parking space and need to know who the driver is. You may also want your list sorted by special power or list only vehicles. All these (admittedly contrived) examples involve grabbing a subset of the original data. The SELECT statement is the SQL workhorse.

1. Click the SQL tab to get a query screen in phpMyAdmin.
2. Type in a query.
3. Click the Go button to see the query results.

You've seen the simplest form of this command getting all the data in a table, like this:

```
SELECT * FROM hero;
```

Figure 9.19 shows this form of the SELECT statement operating on the hero table.

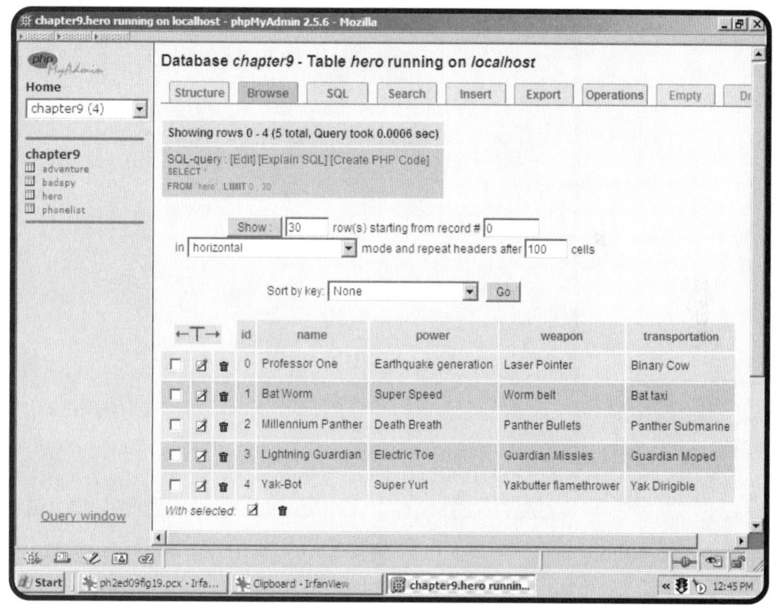

FIGURE 9.19

The SELECT query is in the top section and the results are shown underneath.

phpMyAdmin is a wonderful tool for experimenting with SELECT statements because you can write the actual SQL by hand and see immediate results in a very clean format. If you don't want to (or cannot) use phpMyAdmin, do the same experiments directly in MySQL. It will work, but the results are formatted as text and not always as easy to see.

The `SELECT` statement is extremely powerful because it can grab a subset of data that can return only the requested fields and records. This process of asking questions of the database is commonly called a *query*. Note that phpMyAdmin sometimes adds elements to the query (notably the `limit` information). This increases the query's efficiency, but doesn't substantially change the query.

Limiting Columns

You might not want all of the fields in a table. For example, you might just want a list of the name and weapon of everyone on your list. You can specify this by using the following `SELECT` statement, which is illustrated in Figure 9.20:

```
SELECT name, weapon
FROM hero;
```

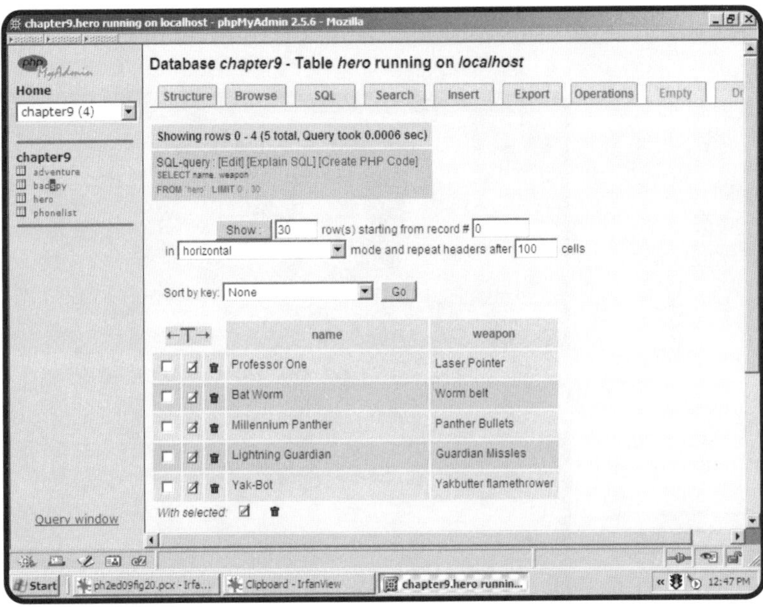

FIGURE 9.20

This query returns only the names and weapons.

This may seem like a silly capability for such a simple database as the hero list. However, but you often run into extremely complicated tables with many fields and need to filter only a few fields. For example, I use a database to track student advisees. Each student's information contains lots of data, but I might just want a list of names and e-mail addresses. The ability to isolate the fields I need is one way to get useful information from a database.

The results of a query look a lot like a new table. You can think of a query result as a temporary table.

Limiting Rows with the WHERE Clause

In addition to limiting the columns returned in a query, you may be interested in limiting the number of rows. For example, you might run across an evil villain who can only be defeated by a laser pointer. The query shown in Figure 9.21 illustrates a query that solves exactly this dilemma.

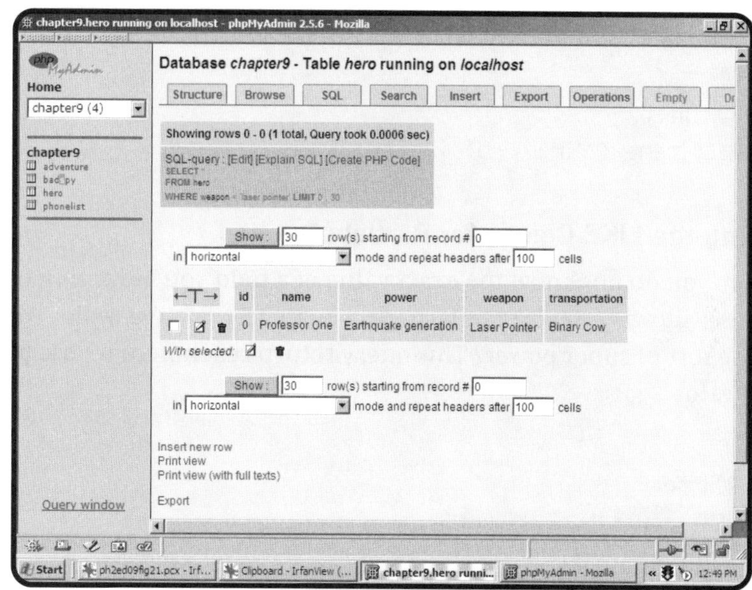

FIGURE 9.21

If you know how to set up the query, you can get very specific results. In this case, the query selects only those heroes with a laser pointer.

This code returns only the rows matching a specific condition:

```
SELECT *
  FROM hero
  WHERE weapon = 'Laser Pointer';
```

Adding a Condition with a WHERE Clause

A `WHERE` statement in a query specifies which row(s) you want to see. This clause allows you to specify a condition. The database manager checks every record in the table. If the condition is `TRUE` for that record, it is included in the result set. The conditions in a `WHERE` clause are similar to those in PHP code, but they are not *exactly* the same. Use these symbols in SQL:

- For equality use the single equal sign (=).
- Encase text elements in single quotation marks (').
- Use <, >, and <= or >= and != conditions to limit your search.

Comparison operators are easy to understand for numeric data, such as integers and real numbers. It's not quite so obvious how a language will treat text comparisons. SQL has developed some standard rules, but each implementation might be somewhat different. SQL generally works in a case-insensitive way, so `Yak-Bot` would match `yak-bot` or `yAK-bOT`. Also, the `<` and `>` operators refer to alphabetic order, so the following selects all the records where the hero's name starts with `A`, `B`, or `C`.

```
SELECT *
  FROM hero
  WHERE name < 'D';
```

Using the LIKE Clause for Partial Matches

Often you do not know the exact value of a field you are trying to match. The `LIKE` clause allows you to specify partial matches. For example, which heroes have some sort of super power? This query returns each hero whose power begins with the value `Super`:

```
SELECT *
  FROM hero
  WHERE power LIKE 'Super%';
```

The percent sign (`%`) can be a wild card, which indicates any character, any number of times. You can use a variation of the `LIKE` clause to find information about all heroes with a transportation scheme that starts with the letter B:

```
SELECT name, transportation
  FROM hero
  WHERE transportation LIKE 'B%';
```

You can also use the underscore character (_) to specify one character.

The simple wildcard character support in SQL is sufficient for many purposes. If you like regular expressions, you can use the `REGEXP` clause to specify whether a field matches a regular expression. This is a very powerful tool, but it is an extension to the SQL standard. It works fine in MySQL, but it is not supported in all SQL databases.

Generating Multiple Conditions

You can combine conditions with `AND`, `OR`, and `NOT` keywords for more-complex expressions. For example, the following code selects those heroes whose transportation starts with B and who have a power with `super` in its name.

```
SELECT *
  FROM hero
  WHERE transportation LIKE 'B%'
    AND power LIKE '%super%';
```

Creating compound expressions is very useful as you build more-complex databases with multiple tables.

Sorting Results with the ORDER BY Clause

One more nifty `SELECT` statement feature is the ability to sort results by any field. Figures 9.22 and 9.23 illustrate how the `ORDER BY` clause can determine how tables are sorted.

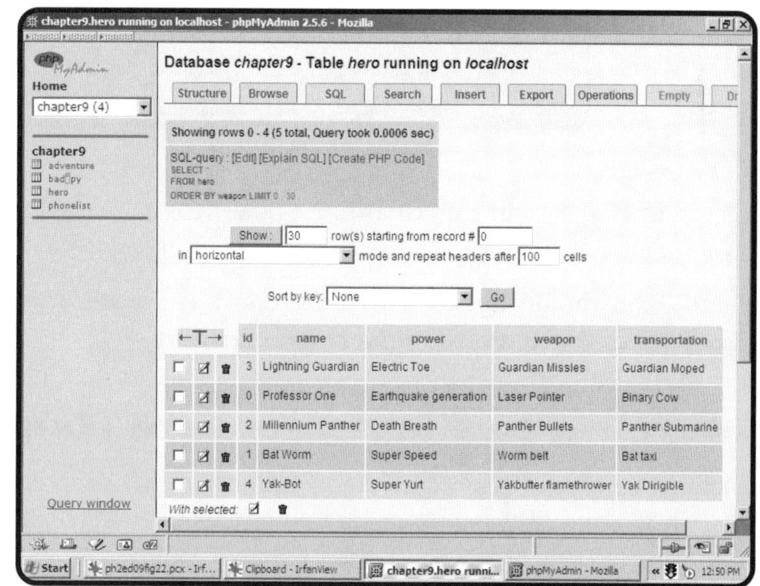

FIGURE 9.22

This query shows the entire database sorted by the weapon name.

The `ORDER BY` clause allows you to determine how the data is sorted. You can specify any field you wish as the sorting field. As you can see in Figure 9.23, the `DESC` clause specifies that data should be sorted in descending order.

Changing Data with the UPDATE Statement

You can use SQL to modify the data in a database. The key to this behavior is the `UPDATE` statement. An example helps it make sense:

```
UPDATE hero
  SET power = 'Super Electric Toe'
  WHERE name = 'Lightning Guardian';
```

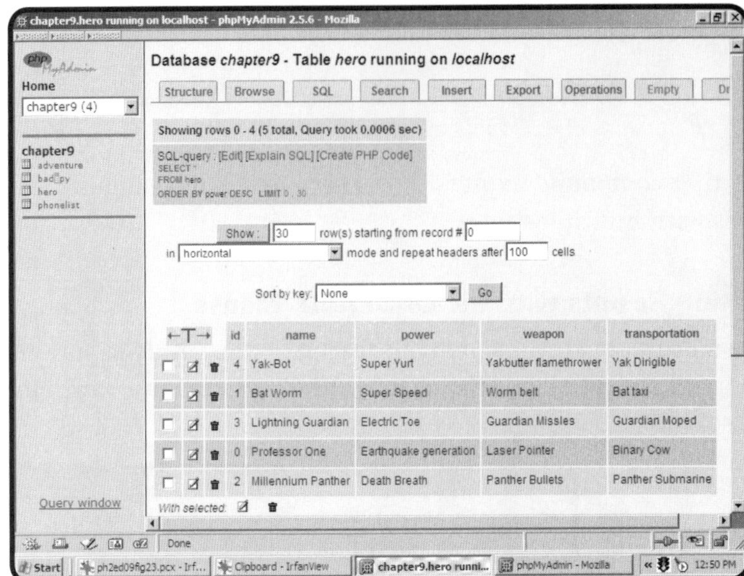

FIGURE 9.23

This query sorts by the power in descending (reverse alphabetical) order.

This code upgrades Lightning Guardian's power to the Super Electric Toe (which is presumably a lot better than the ordinary Electric Toe).

Generally, you should update only one record at a time. You can use a `WHERE` clause to select which record in the table is updated.

Returning to the Adventure Game

The adventure game featured at the beginning of this chapter uses a combination of MySQL and PHP code. You learn more about the PHP part in chapter 10, "Connecting to Databases within PHP." For now you have enough information to start building the data structure that forms the core of the game.

Designing the Data Structure

The adventure game is entirely about data and has an incredibly repetitive structure. The same code operates over and over, but on different parts of the database. I started the program by sketching out the primary play screen and thinking about what data elements I needed for each screen. I ended up building a table like Table 9.3.

You can see that I simplified the game so that each choice boils down to seven elements. Each *node* (or decision point) consists of an `id` (or room number), a room `name`, and a `description` of the current circumstances. Each node also has

Table 9.3 Data Structure of Enigma Adventure

id	name	description	north	east	south	west
0	-nothing-	You cannot go that way!	1	0	0	0
1	start over	You are at a submarine yard, looking for the famous Enigma code machine	0	3	0	2
2	sub deck	As you step on the submarine deck, a guard approaches you. Your only choice is to jump off the sub before you are caught.	15	15	15	15
3	warehouse	You wait inside the warehouse. You see a doorway to the east and a box to the south.	0	4	5	0
4	doorway	You walked right into a group of guards. It does not look good...	0	19	0	15
5	box	You crawl inside the box and wait. Suddenly, you feel the box being picked up and carried across the wharf!	6	0	0	7
6	wait	..You wait until the box settles in a dark space. You can move forward or aft...	8	0	9	0
7	jump out	You decide to jump out of the box, but you are cornered at the end of the wharf.	15	19	15	15
8	forward	As you move forward, two rough sailors grab you and hurl you out of the conning tower.	15	15	15	15
9	aft	In a darkened room, you see the Enigma device. How will you get it out of the sub?	13	11	10	12
10	signal on Enigma	You use the Enigma device to send a signal. Allied forces recognize your signal and surround the ship when it surfaces.	14	0	0	0
11	shoot your way out	A gunfight on a submerged sub is a bad idea...	19	0	0	0
12	wait with Enigma	You wait, but the sailors discover that Enigma is missing and scour the sub for it. You are discovered and cast out in the torpedo tube.	15	0	0	0

Table 9.3 Data Structure of Enigma Adventure (continued)

id	name	description	north	east	south	west
13	replace Enigma and wait	You put the Enigma back in place and wait patiently, but you never get another chance. You are discovered when the sub pulls in to harbor.	19	0	0	0
14	Win	Congratulations! You have captured the device and shortened the war!	1	0	0	0
15	Water	You are in the water. The sub moves away. It looks bad...	19	0	0	0
16			0	0	0	0
17			0	0	0	0
18			0	0	0	0
19	Game Over	The game is over. You lose.	1	0	0	0

pointers that describe what happens when the user chooses to go in various directions from that node. For example, if the user is in the warehouse (node 3) and chooses to go east, he goes to node 4, which represents the doorway. Going south from node 3 takes the user to node 5, which is the box. The data structure represents all the places the user can go in this game. I chose to think of winning and losing as nodes, so everything in the game can be encapsulated in the table.

It's critical to understand that creating the table on paper is the first step. Once you've decided what kind of data your program needs, you can think about how to put that data together. Choosing a database gives me an incredible amount of control and makes it pretty easy to work with the data. Perhaps the most amazing thing is that this program can handle an entirely different game simply by changing the database. I don't have to change a single line of code to make the game entirely different. All I have to do is point to a different database or change the database.

Once I decided on the data structure, I built an SQL script to create the first draft of the database. That script is shown here:

```
## build Adventure SQL File
## for MySQL
## Andy Harris
```

```
DROP TABLE IF EXISTS adventure;

CREATE TABLE ADVENTURE (
  id int PRIMARY KEY,
  name varchar(20),
  description varchar(200),
  north int,
  east int,
  south int,
  west int
);

INSERT INTO adventure values(
  0, 'lost', 'You cannot go that way!',
  1, 0, 0, 0
);

INSERT INTO adventure values(
  1, 'start', 'You are at a submarine yard, looking for the famous Enigma
code machine',
  0, 3, 0, 2
);

INSERT INTO adventure values(
  2, 'sub deck', 'As you step on the submarine deck, a guard approaches
you.  Your only choice is to jump off the sub before you are caught.',
  15, 15, 15, 15
);

INSERT INTO adventure values(
  3, 'warehouse', 'You wait inside the warehouse. You see a doorway to the
east and a box to the south.',
  0, 4, 5, 0
);

INSERT INTO adventure values(
  4, 'doorway', 'You walked right into a group of guards. It does not look
good...', 0, 19, 0, 15
);
```

```
INSERT INTO adventure values(
  5, 'box', 'You crawl inside the box and wait. Suddenly, you feel the box
being picked up and carried across the wharf!', 6, 0, 0, 7
);

INSERT INTO adventure values(
  6, 'wait', '..You wait until the box settles in a dark space. You can
move forward or aft...', 8, 0, 9, 0
);

INSERT INTO adventure values(
  7, 'jump out', 'You decide to jump out of the box, but you are cornered
at the end of the wharf.', 15, 19, 15, 15
);

INSERT INTO adventure values(
  8, 'forward', 'As you move forward, two rough sailors grab you and hurl
you out of the conning tower.', 15, 15, 15, 15
);

INSERT INTO adventure values(
  9, 'aft', 'In a darkened room, you see the Enigma device. How will you
get it out of the sub?', 13, 11, 10, 12
);

INSERT INTO adventure values(
  10, 'signal on Enigma', 'You use the Enigma device to send a signal.
Allied forces recognize your signal and surround the ship when it
surfaces', 14, 0, 0, 0
);

INSERT INTO adventure values(
  11, 'shoot your way out', 'A gunfight on a submerged sub is a bad
idea...', 19, 0, 0, 0
);

INSERT INTO adventure values(
  12, 'wait with Enigma', 'You wait, but the sailors discover that Enigma
is missing and scour the sub for it. You are discovered and cast out in
the torpedo tube.', 15, 0, 0, 0
);
```

```
INSERT INTO adventure values(
  13, 'replace Enigma and wait','You put the Enigma back in place and wait
patiently, but you never get another chance. You are discovered when the
sub pulls in to harbor.', 19, 0, 0, 0
);

INSERT INTO adventure values(
  14, 'Win', 'Congratulations! You have captured the device and shortened
the war!', 1, 0, 0, 0
);

INSERT INTO adventure values(
  15, 'Water', 'You are in the water. The sub moves away. It looks
bad...', 19, 0, 0, 0
);

INSERT INTO adventure values(
  16,'','', 0, 0, 0, 0
);

INSERT INTO adventure values(
  17,'','', 0, 0, 0, 0
);

INSERT INTO adventure values(
  18,'','', 0, 0, 0, 0
);

INSERT INTO adventure values(
  19, 'Game Over' ,'The game is over. You lose.', 1, 0, 0, 0
);

SELECT id, name, north, east, south, west FROM adventure;
SELECT id, description FROM adventure;
```

I wrote this code by hand, but I could have designed it with phpMyAdmin just as easily. Note that I created the table, inserted values, and wrote a couple of `SELECT` statements to check the values. I like to have a script for creating a database even if I built it in a tool like phpMyAdmin, because I managed to mess up this database several times as I was writing the code for this chapter. It is very handy to have a script that instantly rebuilds the database without any tears.

Summary

Although you didn't write any PHP in this chapter, you did learn how to create a basic data structure using the SQL language. You learned how to work with the MySQL console to create and use databases and how to return data from your database using the `SELECT` statement. You know how to modify the `SELECT` statement to get more-specific results. You know how phpMyAdmin can simplify the creation and manipulation of MySQL databases. You built a data structure for an adventure game.

CHALLENGES

1. **Design a database. Start with something simple like a phone list.**
2. **Create your database in SQL.**
3. **Write a batch program to create and populate your database.**
4. **Use phpMyAdmin to manipulate your database and view its results in other formats.**
5. **Read appendix B to see how SQLite is like (and unlike) MySQL. Make a basic table using SQLite.**

CHAPTER 10

Connecting to Databases within PHP

After all this talk of databases, you might be eager to connect a database to your PHP programs. PHP is well known for its seamless database integration, especially with MySQL. It's actually quite easy to connect to a MySQL database from within PHP. Once you've established the connection, you can send SQL commands to the database and receive the results as data you can use in your PHP program.

By the end of this chapter you will have built the adventure game featured at the beginning of chapter 9, "Using MySQL to Create Databases." As you see, the programming isn't very hard if the data is designed well. Specifically, you learn how to:

- Get a connection to a MySQL database from within PHP.
- Use a particular database.
- Send a query to the database.
- Parse the query results.
- Check for data errors.
- Build HTML output from data results.

Connecting to the Hero Database

To show how database connection works, I build a simple PHP program that returns all the values in the Hero database you created in chapter 9. Figure 10.1 illustrates the Show Hero PHP program.

I decided to go back to this simpler database rather than the more complex adventure game. When you're learning new concepts, it's best to work with the simplest environment at first and then move to more complex situations. The adventure database has a lot of information in it, and the way the records point to each other is complicated. With a simpler database I was sure I understood the basics of data connection before working with a production database that is bound to have complexities of its own.

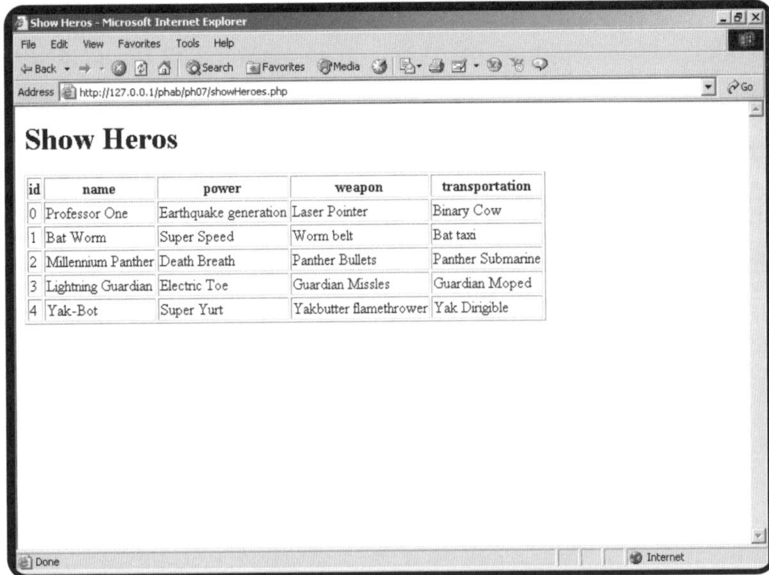

id	name	power	weapon	transportation
0	Professor One	Earthquake generation	Laser Pointer	Binary Cow
1	Bat Worm	Super Speed	Worm belt	Bat taxi
2	Millennium Panther	Death Breath	Panther Bullets	Panther Submarine
3	Lightning Guardian	Electric Toe	Guardian Missles	Guardian Moped
4	Yak-Bot	Super Yurt	Yakbutter flamethrower	Yak Dirigible

FIGURE 10.1

This HTML table is generated by a PHP program reading the database.

This is the code that generates this page:

```
<body>
<h1>Show Heros</h1>
```

```
<?
//make the database connection
$conn  = mysql_connect("localhost", "", "");
mysql_select_db("chapter7", $conn);

//create a query
$sql = "SELECT * FROM hero";
$result = mysql_query($sql, $conn);

print "<table border = 1>\n";

//get field names
print "<tr>\n";
while ($field = mysql_fetch_field($result)){
  print "  <th>$field->name</th>\n";
} // end while
print "</tr>\n\n";

//get row data as an associative array
while ($row = mysql_fetch_assoc($result)){
  print "<tr>\n";
  //look at each field
  foreach ($row as $col=>$val){
    print "  <td>$val</td>\n";
  } // end foreach
  print "</tr>\n\n";
}// end while

print "</table>\n";
?>
</body>
</html>
```

Glance over the code and you see it's mostly familiar except for a few new functions that begin with mysql_. These functions allow access to MySQL databases. If you look through the PHP documentation you see very similar functions for several other types of databases, including Oracle, Informix, mSQL, and ODBC. You'll find the process for connecting to and using other databases is pretty much the same no matter which database you're using.

This chapter details the process of connecting to an MySQL database. If you're using SQLite instead, please see appendix B on the CD for how to modify this chapter's code to work with that alternate database. The concepts remain exactly the same, but some details change.

Getting a Connection

The first job is to get a connection between your PHP program and your MySQL server. You can connect to any server you have permission to use. The `mysql_connect` function arranges the communication link between MySQL and PHP. Here's the `connect` statement from the `showHero` program:

```
$conn  = mysql_connect("localhost", "", "");
```

The `mysql_connect()` function requires three parameters:

- **Server name.** The server name is the name or URL of the MySQL server you wish to connect to. (This is `localhost` if your PHP and MySQL servers reside on the same machine, which is frequently the case.)
- **Username.** The username in MySQL. Most database packages have user accounts.
- **Password.** The password associated with the MySQL user, identified by username.

You will probably have to change the username and password fields if you are running this code on a server somewhere. I used default values that work fine on an isolated test server, but you must change to your username and password if you try this code on a production server.

You can use the same username and password you use to log into MySQL, and your program will have all the same access you do. Of course, you may want more-restricted access for your programs. Create a special account, which has only the appropriate permissions, for program users.

The `mysql_connect()` function returns an integer referring to the database connection. You can think of this identifier much like the file pointers you learned in chapter 6, "Working with Files." The data connection should be stored in a variable—I usually use something like `$conn`—because many of the other database functions need to access the connection.

In the Real World

Database security is an important and challenging issue. You can do a few easy things to protect your data from most hackers. The first thing is to obscure your username and password information whenever you publish your code. I removed my username and password from the code shown here. In a practice environment you can leave these values blank, but ensure you don't have wide-open code that allows access to your data. If you need to post your code (for example, in a class situation), be sure to change the password to something besides your real password.

Choosing a Database

A data connection can have a number of databases connected to it. The `mysql_set_db()` function lets you choose a database. The `mysql_set_db()` function works just like the `USE` command inside SQL. The `mysql_set_db()` function requires the database name and a data connection. This function returns the value `FALSE` if it is unable to connect to the specified database.

Creating a Query

Creating a query is very easy. The relevant code from `showHero.php` is reproduced here:

```
//create a query
$sql = "SELECT * FROM hero";
$result = mysql_query($sql, $conn);
```

Begin by placing SQL code inside a variable.

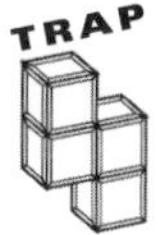

SQL commands entered into the SQL console or phpMyAdmin require a semicolon. When your PHP program sends a command to the DBMS, the semicolon is added automatically, so you should *not* end your SQL commands with semicolons. Of course, you assign these commands within a line of PHP code, which has its own semicolon. (Sheesh!)

The `mysql_query()` function allows you to pass an SQL command through a connection to a database. You can send any SQL command to the database with `mysql_query()`, including table creation statements, updates, and queries. The database returns a special element called a *result set.* If the SQL command was a query, the result variable holds a pointer to the data, which is taken apart in the next step. If it's a *data definition command* (the commands used to create and modify tables) the result object usually contains the string related to the operation's success or failure.

Getting Field Names

I am printing the data in an HTML table. I could create the table headings by hand, because I know what all the fields are, but it's better to get the field information directly from the query. You won't always know which fields are being returned by a particular query. The next chunk of code manages this task:

```
print "<table border = 1>\n";

//get field names
print "<tr>\n";
while ($field = mysql_fetch_field($result)){
  print "  <th>$field->name</th>\n";
} // end while
print "</tr>\n\n";
```

The `mysql_fetch_field()` function expects a query result as its one parameter. It then fetches the next field and stores it in the `$field` variable. If no fields are left in the result, the function returns the value `FALSE`. This allows the field function to also be used as a conditional statement.

The `$field` variable is actually an object. You built a custom object in chapter 7, "Writing Programs with Objects." The `$field` object in this case is much like an associative array. It has a number of properties (which can be thought of as field attributes). The field object has a number of attributes, listed in Table 10.1.

TABLE 10.1 COMMONLY USED FIELD OBJECT PROPERTIES

Property	Attribute
`max_length`	Field length; especially important in VARCHAR fields
`Name`	The field name
`primary_key`	TRUE if the field is a primary key
`Table`	Name of table this field belongs to
`Type`	This field's datatype

By far the most common use of the field object is determining the names of all the fields in a query. The other attributes can be useful in certain situations. You can see the complete list of attributes in MySQL Help that shipped with your copy of MySQL or online at http://www.mysql.com.

You use object-oriented syntax to refer to an object's properties. Notice that I printed `$field->name` to the HTML table. This syntax simply refers to the `name` property of the `field` object. For now it's reasonably accurate to think of it as a fancy associative array.

Parsing the Result Set

The rest of the code examines the result set. Refresh your memory:

```
//get row data as an associative array
while ($row = mysql_fetch_assoc($result)){
  print "<tr>\n";
  //look at each field
  foreach ($row as $col=>$val){
    print "  <td>$val</td>\n";
  } // end foreach
  print "</tr>\n\n";
}// end while
```

The `mysql_fetch_assoc()` function fetches the next row from a result set. It requires a result pointer as its parameter, and it returns an associative array.

A number of related functions are available for pulling a row from a result set. `mysql_fetch_object()` **stores a row as an object, much like the** `mysql_fetch_fields()` **function does. The** `mysql_fetch_array()` **function fetches an array that can be treated as a normal array, an associative array, or both. I tend to use** `mysql_fetch_assoc()` **because I think it's the most straightforward approach for those unfamiliar with object-oriented syntax. Of course, you should feel free to investigate these other functions and use them if they make more sense to you.**

If no rows are left in the result set, `mysql_fetch_assoc()` returns the value `FALSE`. The `mysql_fetch_assoc() function` call is often used as a condition in a `while` loop (as I did here to fetch each row in a result set). Each row represents a row of the eventual HTML table, so I print the HTML code to start a new row inside the `while` loop.

Once you've gotten a row, it's stored as an associative array. You can manipulate this array using a standard `foreach` loop. I assigned each element to `$col` and `$val` variables. I actually don't need `$col` in this case, but it can be handy to have. Inside the `foreach` loop I placed code to print the current field in a table cell.

Returning to the Adventure Game Program

At the end of chapter 9 you create a database for the adventure game. Now that you know how to connect a PHP program to a MySQL database, you're ready to begin writing the game itself.

Connecting to the Adventure Database

Once I built the database, the first PHP program I wrote was the simplest possible connection to the database. I wanted to ensure I got all the data correctly. Here's the code for that program:

```
<html>
<head>
<title>Show Adventure</title>
</head>
<body>

<?
$conn  = mysql_connect("localhost", "", "");
mysql_select_db("chapter7", $conn);
$sql = "SELECT * FROM adventure";
$result = mysql_query($sql);
while ($row = mysql_fetch_assoc($result)){

  foreach($row as $key=>$value){
    print "$key: $value<br>\n";
  } // end foreach
  print "<hr>\n";

} // end while

?>
</body>
</html>
```

This simple program established the connection and ensured that everything was stored as I expected. Whenever I write a data program, I usually write something like this that quickly steps through my data to ensure everything is working correctly. There's no point in moving on until you know you have the basic connection.

I did not give you a screenshot of this program because it isn't very pretty, but I did include it on the CD-ROM so you can run it yourself. The point here is to start small and then turn your basic program into something more sophisticated one step at a time.

Displaying One Segment

The actual gameplay consists of repeated calls to the `showSegment.php` program. This program takes a segment ID as its one input and then uses that data to build a page based on that database's record. The only surprise is how simple the code is for this program.

```
<html>
<head>
<title>Show Segment</title>
<style type = "text/css">
body {
  color:red
}
td {
  color: white;
  background-color: blue;
  width: 20%;
  height: 3em;
  font-size: 20pt
}
</style>
</head>
<body>
<?
if (empty($room)){
  $room = 1;
} // end if

//connect to database
$conn  = mysql_connect("localhost", "", "");
```

```
$select = mysql_select_db("chapter7", $conn);
$sql = "SELECT * FROM adventure WHERE id = '$room'";
$result = mysql_query($sql);
$mainRow = mysql_fetch_assoc($result);

$theText = $mainRow["description"];
$northButton = buildButton("north");
$eastButton = buildButton("east");
$westButton = buildButton("west");
$southButton = buildButton("south");
$roomName = $mainRow["name"];

print <<<HERE
<center><h1>$roomName</h1></center>
<form method = "post">
<table border = 1>
<tr>
  <td></td>
  <td>$northButton</td>
  <td></td>
</tr>

<tr>
  <td>$eastButton</td>
  <td>$theText</td>
  <td>$westButton</td>
</tr>

<tr>
  <td></td>
  <td>$southButton</td>
  <td></td>
</tr>

</table>
<center>
<input type = "submit"
       value = "go">
</center>
</form>
```

```
HERE;

function buildButton($dir){
  //builds a button for the specified direction
  global $mainRow, $conn;
  $newID = $mainRow[$dir];
  //print "newID is $newID";
  $query = "SELECT name FROM adventure WHERE id = $newID";
  $result = mysql_query($query, $conn);
  $row = mysql_fetch_assoc($result);
  $roomName = $row["name"];

  $buttonText = <<< HERE
  <input type = "radio"
         name = "room"
         value = "$newID">$roomName

HERE;

  return $buttonText;

} // end build button
?>
</body>
</html>
```

Creating a CSS Style

I began the HTML with a cascading style sheet (CSS) style. My program is visually unappealing, but placing a CSS style here is the answer to my visual design disability. All I need to do is get somebody with an actual sense of style to clean up my CSS and I have a good-looking page.

Making the Data Connection

As usual, the program begins with some housekeeping. If the user hasn't specifically chosen a segment number, the program places him in room number one, which is designated as the starting room. If the user doesn't specify a value, the default action is a program crash, because it won't know in what room to place the user. I added a default so if this happens, the program assumes it's a new adventure and starts at the beginning.

```
if (empty($room)){
  $room = 1;
} // end if

//connect to database
$conn   = mysql_connect("localhost", "", "");
$select = mysql_select_db("chapter7", $conn);
$sql = "SELECT * FROM adventure WHERE id = '$room'";
$result = mysql_query($sql);
$mainRow = mysql_fetch_assoc($result);
$theText = $mainRow["description"];
```

I then make an ordinary connection to the database and choose the record pertaining to the current room number. That query is stored in the `$mainRow` variable as an associative array.

Generating Variables for the Code

Most of the program writes the HTML for the current record to the screen. To make things simple, I create some variables for anything that might be tricky.

```
$theText = $mainRow["description"];
$roomName = $mainRow["name"];
$northButton = buildButton("north");
$eastButton = buildButton("east");
$westButton = buildButton("west");
$southButton = buildButton("south");
```

I stored the description field of the current row into a variable named `$theText`. I made a similar variable for the room name.

> **IN THE REAL WORLD**
>
> **It isn't strictly necessary to store the description field in a variable, but I interpolate this value into HTML code. I've found that interpolating associative array values can be a little tricky. In general, I like to copy an associative value to some temporary variable if I'm going to interpolate it. It's just a lot easier that way.**

The button variables are a little different. I decided to create an HTML option button to represent each of the places the user could go. I use a custom function called `buildButton()` to make each button.

Writing the buildButton() Function

The procedure for building the buttons was repetitive enough to warrant a function. Each button is a radio button corresponding to a direction. The radio button will have a value that comes from the corresponding direction value from the current record. If the `north` field of the current record is 12 (meaning if the user goes North load the data in record 12), the radio button's value should be 12.

The trickier thing is getting the appropriate label. The next room's ID is all that's stored in the current record. If you want to display the room's name, you must make another query to the database. That's exactly what the `buildButton()` function does:

```
function buildButton($dir){
  //builds a button for the specified direction
  global $mainRow, $conn;
  $newID = $mainRow[$dir];
  //print "newID is $newID";
  $query = "SELECT name FROM adventure WHERE id = $newID";
  $result = mysql_query($query, $conn);
  $row = mysql_fetch_assoc($result);
  $roomName = $row["name"];

  $buttonText = <<< HERE
  <input type = "radio"
         name = "room"
         value = "$newID">$roomName

HERE;

  return $buttonText;

} // end build button
```

The function follows these steps:

1. Borrows the `$mainRow` array (which holds the value of the main record this page is about) and the data connection in `$conn`.
2. Pulls the ID for this button from the `$mainRow` array and stores it in a local variable. The `buildButton()` function requires a direction name sent as a parameter. This direction should be the field name for one of the direction fields.

3. Repeats the query creation process, building a query that requests only the row associated with the new ID.
4. Pulls the room name from that array. Once that's done, it's easy to build the radio button text. The radio button is called `room`, so the next time this program is called, the `$room` variable corresponds to the user-selected radio button.

Finishing the HTML

All that's left is adding a Submit button to the form and closing the form and HTML. The amazing thing is, that's all you need. This code alone is enough to let the user play this game. It takes some effort to set up the data structure, but then all you do is provide a link to the first record (by calling `showSegment.php` without any parameters). The program will keep calling itself.

Viewing and Selecting Records

I suppose you could stop there, because the game is working, but the really great thing about this structure is how flexible it is. It doesn't take much more work to create an editor that lets you add and modify records.

This actually requires a couple of PHP programs. The first, shown in Figure 10.2, prints out a summary of the entire game and allows the user to edit any node.

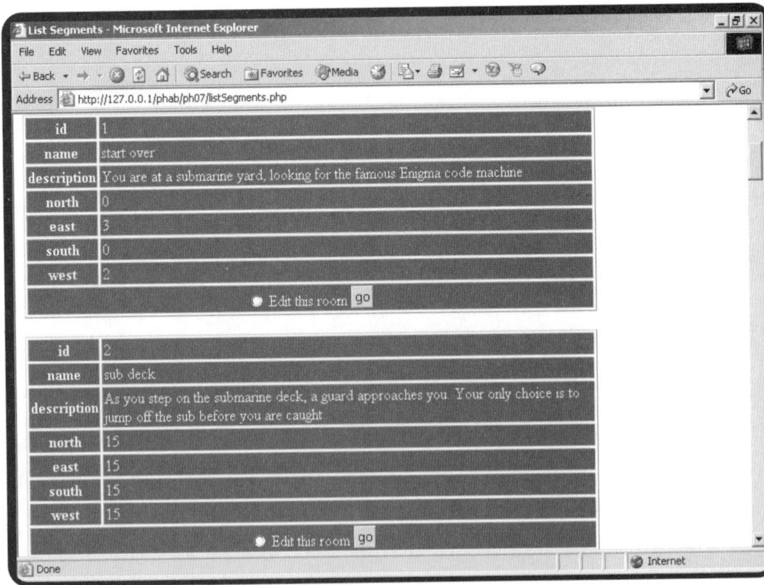

FIGURE 10.2

The `listSegments.php` program lists all the data and allows the user to choose a record for editing.

The code for the `listSegments.php` program is actually quite similar to the `showAdventure.php` program you saw before. It's simply cleaned up a bit to put the data in tables and has a form to call an editor when the user selects a record to modify.

```
<html>
<head>
<title>List Segments</title>
<style type = "text/css">
body {
  color:red
}
td, th {
  color: white;
  background-color: blue;
}
</style>
</head>
<body>

<?
$conn  = mysql_connect("localhost", "", "");
$select = mysql_select_db("chapter7", $conn);
$sql = "SELECT * FROM adventure";
$result = mysql_query($sql);
print <<<HERE
<form action = "editSegment.php"
      method = "post">

HERE;

while ($row = mysql_fetch_assoc($result)){
  print "<table border = 1 width = 80%>\n";

  foreach($row as $key=>$value){
    //print "$key: $value<br>\n";
    $roomNum = $row["id"];
    print <<<HERE
  <tr>
    <th width = 10%>$key</th>
    <td>$value</td>
  </tr>
```

```
HERE;

  } // end foreach
  print <<<HERE
  <tr>
    <td colspan = 2><center>
      <input type = "radio"
             name = "room"
             value = "$roomNum">
      Edit this room
      <input type = "submit"
             value = "go">
    </center></td>
  </tr>
</table><br>

HERE;

} // end while

?>
<center>
<input type = "submit"
       value = "edit indicated room">
</center>
</form>
</body>
</html>
```

The entire program is contained in a form, which calls `editSegment.php` when activated. The program opens a data connection and pulls all elements from the database. It builds an HTML table for each record. Each table contains a radio button called `room`, with the value of the current room number. Each table also has a copy of the Submit button so the user doesn't have to scroll all the way to the bottom of the page to submit the form.

Editing the Record

When the user has chosen a record from `listSegments.php`, the `editSegment.php` program (shown in Figure 10.3) swings into action.

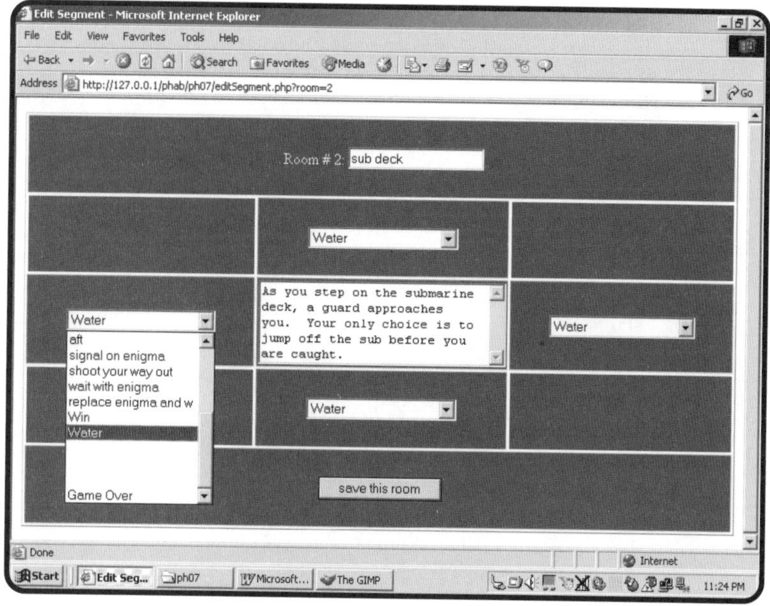

FIGURE 10.3

The editSegment.php program displays data from a requested record and lets the user manipulate that data.

It's important to understand that the editSegment program *doesn't* actually change the record in the database. Instead, it pulls up a form containing the requested record's current values and allows the user to determine the new values. The editSegment page is another form. When the user submits this form, control is passed to one more program, which actually modifies the database. The code for editSegment is very similar to the code that displays a segment in play mode. The primary difference is that all the record data goes into editable fields.

Take a careful look at how the game developer can select a room to go into for each position. A drop-down menu shows all the existing room names. This device allows the game developer to work directly with room names even though the database will be much more concerned with room numbers.

```
<html>
<head>
<title>Edit Segment</title>
<style type = "text/css">
body {
  color:red
}
td {
  color: white;
  background-color: blue;
```

```
  width: 20%;
  height: 5em;
  text-align: center;
}
</style>
</head>
<body>
<?
if (empty($room)){
  $room = 0;
} // end if

//connect to database
$conn  = mysql_connect("localhost", "", "");
$select = mysql_select_db("chapter7", $conn);

$sql = "SELECT * FROM adventure WHERE id = '$room'";
$result = mysql_query($sql);
$mainRow = mysql_fetch_assoc($result);
$theText = $mainRow["description"];
$roomName = $mainRow["name"];
$northList = makeList("north", $mainRow["north"]);
$westList = makeList("west", $mainRow["west"]);
$eastList = makeList("east", $mainRow["east"]);
$southList = makeList("south", $mainRow["south"]);
$roomNum = $mainRow["id"];

print <<<HERE

<form action = "saveRoom.php"
      method = "post">
<table border = 1>
<tr>
  <td colspan = 3>
    Room # $roomNum:
    <input type = "text"
           name = "name"
           value = "$roomName">
    <input type = "hidden"
           name = "id"
```

```
            value = "$roomNum">
    </td>
  </tr>

  <tr>
    <td></td>
    <td>$northList</td>
    <td></td>
  </tr>

  <tr>
    <td>$westList</td>
    <td>
      <textarea rows = 5 cols = 30 name = "description">$theText</textarea>
    </td>
    <td>$eastList</td>
  </tr>

  <tr>
    <td></td>
    <td>$southList</td>
    <td></td>
  </tr>

  <tr>
    <td colspan = 3>
      <input type = "submit"
             value = "save this room">
    </td>

</table>



</form>

HERE;

function makeList($dir, $current){
  //make a list of all the places in the system
```

```
  global $conn;
  $listCode = "<select name = $dir>\n";
  $sql = "SELECT id, name FROM adventure";
  $result = mysql_query($sql);
  $rowNum = 0;
  while ($row = mysql_fetch_assoc($result)){
    $id = $row["id"];
    $placeName = $row["name"];
    $listCode .= "  <option value = $id\n";

    //select this option if it's the one indicated
    if ($rowNum == $current){
      $listCode .= "           selected\n";
    } // end if

    $listCode .= ">$placeName</option>\n";
    $rowNum++;
  } // end while
  return $listCode;
} // end makeList

?>

</body>
</html>
```

Generating Variables

After the standard database connection, the code creates a number of variables. Some of these variables (`$theText`, `$roomName`, and `$roomNum`) are simplifications of the associative array. Another set of variables are the result of the `makeList()` function. This function's job is to return an HTML list box containing the room names of every segment in the database. The list box is set up so that whatever room number is associated with the indicated field is the default.

Printing the HTML Code

The central part of the program consists of a large print statement that develops the HTML code. The code in this case is a large table enclosed in a form. Every field in the record has a form element associated with it. When the user submits this form, it should have all the data necessary to update a record in the database.

The one element the user should not be able to directly edit is the room number. This is stored in a hidden field. The directional room numbers are encoded in the list boxes. All other data is in appropriately named text boxes.

Creating the List Boxes

The list boxes require a little bit of thought to construct.

The `makeList()` function expects two parameters. The `$dir` parameter holds the direction field name of the current list box. The `$current` parameter holds information about which room is currently selected for this particular field of the current record. The data connection handler `$conn` is the only global variable. The variable `$listCode` holds the actual HTML code of the list box returned to the main program.

The function makes a query to the database to request all the room names. Each name is added to the list box code at the appropriate time with the corresponding numeric value. Whenever the record number corresponds to the current value of the record, HTML code specifies that this should be the selected item in the list box.

Committing Changes to the Database

One more program is necessary. The `editSegment.php` program allows the user to edit the data. When finished he submits the form, which calls the `saveRoom.php` program. I won't repeat the screen shot for this program, because the visuals are unimportant. However, this program actually updates the database with whatever values the user has chosen.

```
<head>
<title>SaveRoom.php</title>
</head>
<body>

<?
//Once a room has been edited by editSegment, this program
//updates the database accordingly.

//connect to database
$conn  = mysql_connect("localhost", "", "");
$select = mysql_select_db("chapter7", $conn);
```

```
$sql = <<<HERE
UPDATE adventure
SET
  name = '$name',
  description = '$description',
  north = $north,
  east = $east,
  south = $south,
  west = $west
WHERE
  id = $id

HERE;

//print $sql;
$result = mysql_query($sql);
if ($result){
  print "<h3>$name room updated successfully</h3>\n";
  print "<a href = \"listSegments.php\">view the rooms</a>\n";
} else {
  print "<h3>There was a problem with the database</h3>\n";
} // end if

?>
</body>
</html>
```

This program begins with standard data connections. It then constructs an `UPDATE SQL` statement. The statement is quite simple, because all the work is done in the previous program. I then simply applied the query to the database and checked the result. An `UPDATE` statement won't return a recordset like a `SELECT` statement. Instead, it will return the value `FALSE` if it was unable to process the command. If the update request was successful, I let the user know and provide a link to the `listSegments` program. If there was a problem, I provide some (not very helpful) feedback to the user.

Summary

In this chapter you begin using external programs to manage data. You learn how MySQL can interpret basic SQL statements for defining and manipulating data.

You create a database directly in the MySQL console, and you also learn how to build and manipulate databases with SQLyog. You combine these skills to create an interesting and expandable game.

CHALLENGES

1. **Add a** `new room` **command to the adventure generator. Hint: Think about how I created a new test in the quiz machine program from chapter 6.**
2. **Write PHP programs to view, add, and edit records in the phone list.**
3. **Write a program that asks a user's name and searches the database for that user.**
4. **Create a front end for another simple database.**

Data Normalization

In chapters 9 and 10 you learn how to create a basic database and connect it to a PHP program. PHP and MySQL are wonderful for working with basic databases. However, most real-world problems involve data that is too complex to fit in one table. Database designers have developed some standard techniques for handling complex data that reduce redundancy, improve efficiency, and provide flexibility. In this chapter you learn how to use the relational model to build complex databases involving multiple entities. Specifically, you learn:

- How the relational model works.
- How to build use-case models for predicting data usage.
- How to construct entity-relationship diagrams to model your data.
- How to build multi-table databases.
- How joins are used to connect tables.
- How to build a link table to model many-to-many relationships.
- How to optimize your table design for later programming.

Introducing the spy Database

In this chapter you build a database to manage your international spy ring. (You *do* have an international spy ring, don't you?) Saving the world is a complicated task, so you'll need a database to keep track of all your agents. Secret agents are assigned to various operations around the globe, and certain agents have certain skills. The examples in this chapter will take you through the construction of such a database. You'll see how to construct the database in MySQL. In chapter 12, "Building a Three-Tiered Data Application" you use this database to make a really powerful spymaster application in PHP.

The spy database reflects a few facts about my spy organization (called the Pantheon of Humanitarian Performance, or PHP).

- Each agent has a code name.
- Each agent can have any number of skills.
- More than one agent can have the same skill.
- Each agent is assigned to one operation at a time.
- More than one agent can be assigned to one operation.
- A spy's location is determined by the operation.
- Each operation has only one location.

This list of rules helps explain some characteristics of the data. In database parlance, they are called *business rules.* I need to design the database so these rules are enforced.

In the Real World

I set up this particular set of rules in a somewhat arbitrary way because they help make my database as simple as possible while still illustrating most of the main problems encountered in data design. Usually you don't get to make up business rules. Instead, you learn them by talking to those who use the data every day.

The badSpy Database

As you learned in chapter 9, “Using MySQL to Create Databases,” it isn’t difficult to build a data table, especially if you have a tool like phpMyAdmin. Figure 11.1 illustrates the schema of my first pass at the `spy` database.

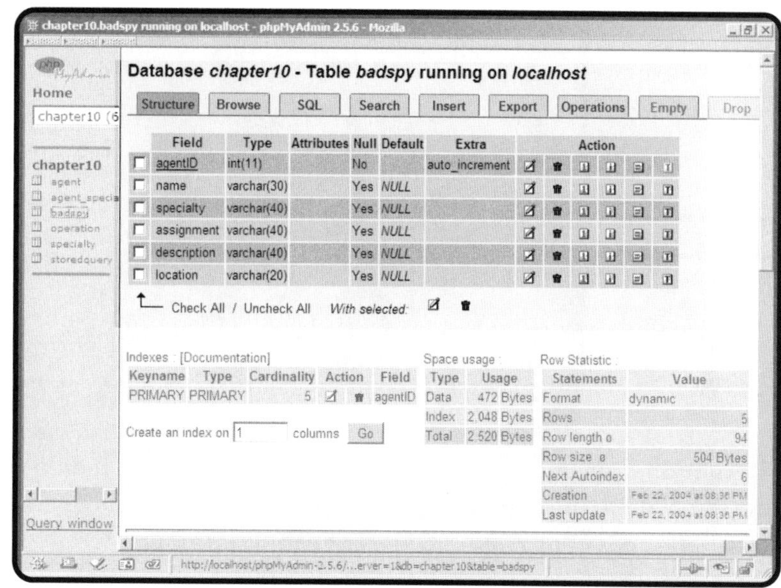

FIGURE 11.1

The `badSpy` database schema looks reasonable enough.

At first glance, the `badSpy` database design seems like it ought to work, but problems crop up as soon as you begin adding data to the table. Figure 11.2 shows the results of the `badSpy` data after I started entering information about some of my field agents.

Inconsistent Data Problems

Gold Elbow’s record indicates that Operation Dancing Elephant is about infiltrating a suspicious zoo. Falcon’s record indicates that the same operation is about infiltrating a suspicious circus. For the purpose of this example, I’m expecting that an assignment has only one description, so one of these descriptions is wrong. There’s no way to know whether it’s a zoo or a circus by looking at the data in the table, so both records are suspect. Likewise, it’s hard to tell if Operation Enduring Angst takes place in Lower Volta or Lower Votla, because the two records that describe this mission have different spellings.

The circus/zoo inconsistency and the Volta/Votla problem share a common cause. In both cases the data-entry person (probably a low-ranking civil servant, because

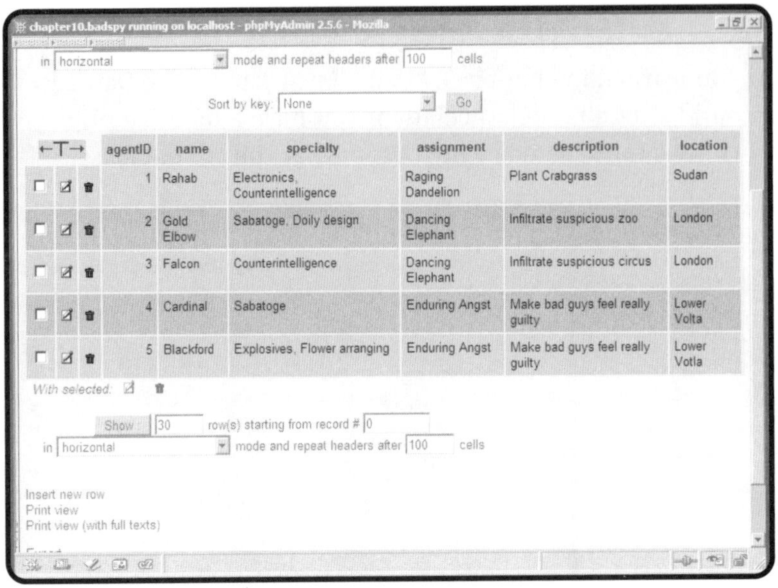

agentID	name	specialty	assignment	description	location
1	Rahab	Electronics, Counterintelligence	Raging Dandelion	Plant Crabgrass	Sudan
2	Gold Elbow	Sabatoge, Doily design	Dancing Elephant	Infiltrate suspicious zoo	London
3	Falcon	Counterintelligence	Dancing Elephant	Infiltrate suspicious circus	London
4	Cardinal	Sabatoge	Enduring Angst	Make bad guys feel really guilty	Lower Volta
5	Blackford	Explosives, Flower arranging	Enduring Angst	Make bad guys feel really guilty	Lower Votla

FIGURE 11.2

The badSpy database after I added a few agents.

international spy masters are *far* too busy to do their own data entry) had to type the same data into the database multiple times. This kind of inconsistency causes all kinds of problems. Different people choose different abbreviations. You may see multiple spellings of the same term. Some people simply do not enter data if it's too difficult. When this happens, you cannot rely on the data. (Is it a zoo or a circus?) You also can't search the data with confidence. (I'll miss Blackford if I look for all operatives in Lower Volta, because he's listed as being in Lower *Votla*.) If you look carefully, you notice that I misspelled "sabotage." It will be very difficult to find everywhere this word is misspelled and fix them all.

Problem with the Operation Information

There's another problem with this database. If for some reason Agent Rahab were dropped from the database (maybe she was a double agent all along), the information regarding Operation Raging Dandelion would be deleted along with her record, because the only place it is stored is as a part of her record. The operation's data somehow needs to be stored separately from the agent data.

Problems with Listed Fields

The specialty field brings its own troubles to the database. This field can contain more than one entity, because spies should be able to do more than one thing.

(My favorite combination is explosives and flower arranging.) Fields with lists in them can be problematic.

- It's much harder to figure out what size to make a field that may contain several entities. If your most talented spy has 10 different skills, you need enough room to store all 10 skills in every spy's record.
- Searching on fields that contain lists of data can be difficult.

You might be tempted to insert several different skill fields (maybe a `skill1`, `skill2`, and `skill3` field, for example), but this doesn't completely solve the problem. It is better to have a more flexible system that can accommodate any number of skills. The flat file system in this `badSpy` database is not capable of that kind of versatility.

Designing a Better Data Structure

The `spy` master database isn't complicated, but the `badSpy` database shows a number of ways even a simple database can go wrong. This database is being used to save the free world, so it deserves a little more thought. Fortunately, data developers have come up with a number of ways to think about data structure.

It is usually best to back away from the computer and think carefully about how data is used before you write a single line of code.

Defining Rules for a Good Data Design

Data developers have come up with a list of rules for creating well-behaved databases:

- Break your data into multiple tables.
- Make no field with a list of entries.
- Do not duplicate data.
- Make each table describe only one entity.
- Create a single primary key field for each table.

A database that follows all these rules will avoid most of the problems evident in the `badSpy` database. Fortunately, there are some well-known procedures for improving a database so it can follow all these rules.

Normalizing Your Data

Data programmers try to prevent the problems evident in the `badSpy` database through a process called *data normalization*. The basic concept of normalization is to break down a database into a series of tables. If each of these tables is designed correctly, the database is less likely to have the sorts of problems described so far. Entire books have been written about data normalization, but the process breaks down into three major steps, called *normal forms.*

First Normal Form: Eliminate Listed Fields

The goal of the first normal form (sometimes abbreviated *1NF*) is to eliminate repetition in the database. The primary culprit in the `badSpy` database is the `specialty` field. Having two different tables, one for agents and another for specialties, is one solution.

Data designers seem to play a one-string banjo. The solution to almost every data design problem is to create another table. As you see, there is quite an art form to what should be in that new table.

The two tables would look somewhat like those shown in Tables 11.1 and 11.2.

TABLE 11.1 AGENT TABLE IN 1NF

Agent ID	Name	Assignment	Description	Location
1	Rahab	Raging Dandelion	Plant Crabgrass	Sudan
2	Gold Elbow	Dancing Elephant	Infiltrate suspicious zoo	London
3	Falcon	Dancing Elephant	Infiltrate suspicious circus	London

TABLE 11.2 SPECIALTY TABLE IN 1NF

Specialty ID	Name
1	electronics
2	counterintelligence
3	sabotage

Note that I did not include all data in these example tables, but just enough to give you a sense of how these tables would be organized. Also, you learn later in this chapter a good way to reconnect these tables.

Second Normal Form: Eliminate Redundancies

Once all your tables are in the first normal form, the next step is to deal with all the potential *redundancy* issues. These mainly occur because data is entered more than one time. To fix this, you need to (you guessed it) build new tables. The `agent` table could be further improved by moving all data about operations to another table. Figure 11.3 shows a special diagram called an Entity Relationship diagram, which illustrates the relationships between these tables.

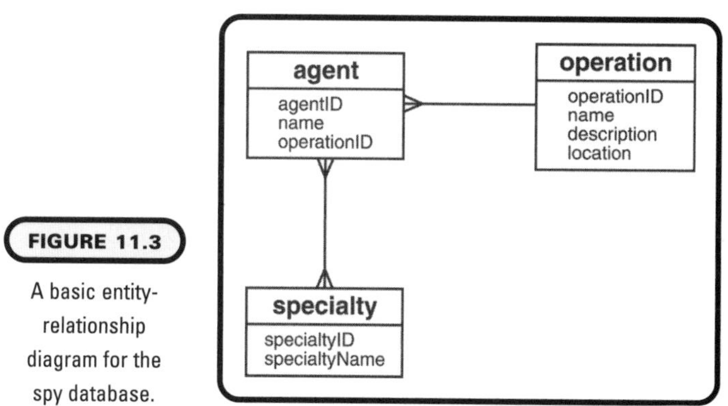

FIGURE 11.3

A basic entity-relationship diagram for the spy database.

An Entity Relationship diagram (ER diagram) reveals the relationships between data elements. In this situation, I thought carefully about the data in the `spy` database. As I thought about the data, three distinct entities emerged. By separating the `operation` data from the `agent` data, I have removed redundancy: The user enters operational data only one time. This eliminates several of the problems in the original database. It also fixes the situation where an operation's data was lost because a spy turned out to be a double agent. (I'm still bitter about that defection.)

Third Normal Form: Ensure Functional Dependency

The third normal form concentrates on the elements associated with each entity. For a table to be in the third normal form, that table must have a single primary key and every field in the table must relate only to that key. For example, the `description` field is a description of the *operation*, not the *agent*, so it belongs in the `operation` table.

In the third phase of normalization you look through each piece of table data and ensure that it directly relates to the table in which it's placed. If not, either move it to a more appropriate table or build a new table for it.

In the Real World

You might notice that my database fell into third normal form automatically when I put it in second normal form. This is not unusual for very small databases, but rare with the large complex databases used to describe real-world enterprises. Even if your database seems to be in the third normal form already, go through each field to see if it relates directly to its table.

Defining Relationship Types

The easiest way to normalize your databases is with a stylized view of them such as the ER diagram. ER diagrams are commonly used as a data-design tool. Take another look at the ER diagram for the spy database in Figure 11.4.

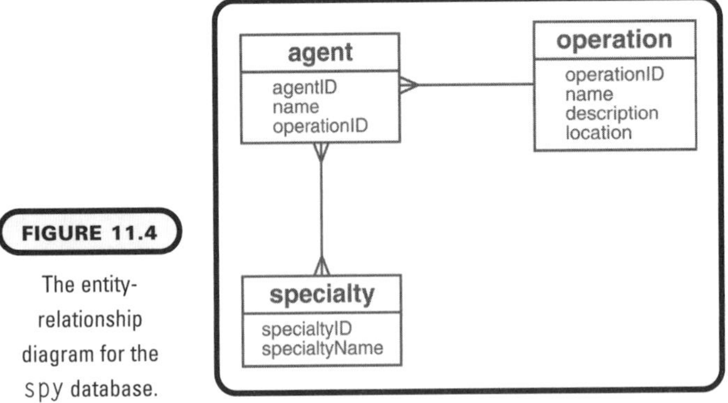

FIGURE 11.4

The entity-relationship diagram for the `spy` database.

This diagram illustrates the three entities in the `spy` database (at least up to now) and the relationships between them. Each entity is enclosed in a rectangle, and the lines between each represent the relationships between the entities. Take a careful look at the relationship lines. They have crow's feet on them to indicate some special relationship characteristics. There are essentially three kinds of relationships (at least in this overview of data modeling).

Recognizing One-to-One Relationships

One-to-one relationships happen when each instance of entity A has exactly one instance of entity B. A one-to-one entity is described as a simple line between two entities with no special symbols on either end.

One-to-one relationships are rare, because if the two entities are that closely related, usually they can be combined into one table without any penalty. The `spy` ER diagram in Figure 11.4 has no one-to-one relationships.

Describing Many-to-One Relationships

One-to-many (and many-to-one) relationships happen when one entity can contain more than one instance of the other. For example, each operation can have many spies, but in this example each agent can only be assigned to one mission at a time. Thus the agent-to-operation relationship is considered a many-to-one relationship, because a spy can have only one operation, but one operation can relate to many agents. In this version of ER notation, I'm using crow's feet to indicate the many sides of the relationship.

There are actually several different kinds of one-to-many relationships, each with a different use and symbol. For this overview I treat them all the same and use the generic crow's feet symbol. When you start writing more-involved databases, investigate data diagramming more closely by looking into books on data normalization and software engineering. Likewise, data normalization is a far more involved topic than the brief discussion in this introductory book.

Recognizing Many-to-Many Relationships

The final type of relationship shown in the `spy` ER diagram is a many-to-many relationship. This type of relationship occurs when each entity can have many instances of the other. Agents and skills have this type of relationship, because one agent can have any number of skills, and each skill can be used by any number of agents. A many-to-many relationship is usually shown by crow's feet on each end of the connecting line.

It's important to generate an ER diagram of your data including the relationship types, because different strategies for each type of relationship creation exist. These strategies emerge as I build the SQL for the improved `spy` database.

Building Your Data Tables

After designing the data according to the rules of normalization, you are ready to build sample data tables in SQL. It pays to build your tables carefully to avoid problems. I prefer to build all my tables in an SQL script so I can easily rebuild my database if (okay, when) my programs mess up the data structure. Besides, enemy agents are always lurking about preparing to sabotage my operations.

In the Real World

Professional programmers often use expensive software tools to help build data diagrams, but you don't need anything more than paper and pencil to draw ER figures. I do my best data design with a partner drawing on a white board. I like to talk through designs out loud and look at them in a large format. Once I've got a sense of the design, I usually use a vector-based drawing program to produce a more formal version of the diagram.

This type of drawing tool is useful because it allows you to connect elements together, already has the crow's feet lines available, and allows you to move elements around without disrupting the lines between them. Dia is an excellent open-source program for drawing all kinds of diagrams. I used it to produce all the ER figures in this chapter. A copy of Dia is on the CD that accompanies this book.

I also add plenty of sample data in the script. You don't want to work with actual data early on, because you are guaranteed to mess up somewhere during the process. However, it is a good idea to work with sample data that is a copied subset of the actual data. Your sample data should anticipate some of the anomalies that might occur in actual data. (For example, what if a person doesn't have a middle name?)

My entire script for the `spy` database is available on the book's CD as `buildSpy.sql`. All SQL code fragments shown in the rest of this chapter come from that file and use the MySQL syntax. If you can't use MySQL or want to try an alternative, check out appendix B for information on SQLite, an intriguing alternative to MySQL. SQLite scripts and database files for all the database examples in the book are packaged on the CD that accompanies this book.

Setting Up the System

I began my SQL script with some comments that describe the database and a few design decisions I made when building the database:

```
######################################
# buildSpy.sql
# builds and populates all databases for spy examples
# uses mysql - should adapt easily to other rdbms
# by Andy Harris for PHP/MySQL for Abs. Beg
######################################
```

```
########################################
# conventions
########################################
# primary key = table name . ID
# primary key always first field
# all primary keys autonumbered
# all field names camel-cased
# only link tables use underscore
# foreign keys indicated although mySQL does not enforce
# every table used as foreign reference has a name field
########################################

########################################
#housekeeping
########################################

use chapter11;
DROP TABLE IF EXISTS badSpy;
DROP TABLE IF EXISTS agent;
DROP TABLE IF EXISTS operation;
DROP TABLE IF EXISTS specialty;
DROP TABLE IF EXISTS agent_specialty;
DROP TABLE IF EXISTS spyFirst;
```

Notice that I specified a series of conventions. These self-imposed rules help make my database easier to manage. Some of the rules might not make sense yet (because I haven't identified what a foreign key is, for instance), but the important thing is that I have clearly identified some rules that help later on.

The code then specifies the `chapter11` database and deletes all tables if they already existed. This behavior ensures that I start with a fresh version of the data.

Creating the agent Table

The normalized agent table is quite simple. The actual table is shown in Table 11.3.

The only data remaining in the agent table is the agent's name and a numerical field for the operation. The `operationID` field is used as the glue that holds together the `agent` and `operation` tables.

I've added a few things to improve the SQL code that creates the `agent` table.

TABLE 11.3 THE AGENT TABLE

Agent ID	Name	Operation ID
1	Bond	1
2	Falcon	1
3	Cardinal	2
4	Blackford	2

These improvements enhance the behavior of the agent table, and simplify the table tremendously.

```
CREATE TABLE agent (
  agentID int(11) NOT NULL AUTO_INCREMENT,
  name varchar(50) default NULL,
  operationID int(11) default NULL,
  PRIMARY KEY  (agentID),
  FOREIGN KEY (operationID) REFERENCES operation (operationID)
);
```

Recall that the first field in a table is usually called the `primary key`. Primary keys must be unique and each record must have one.

- I named each primary key according to a special convention. Primary key names always begin with the table name and end with `ID`. I added this convention because it makes things easier when I write programs to work with this data.
- The `NOT NULL` modifier ensures that all records of this table must have a primary key.
- The `AUTO_INCREMENT` identifier is a special tool that allows MySQL to pick a new value for this field if no value is specified. This will ensure that all entries are unique.
- I added an indicator at the end of the `CREATE TABLE` statement to indicate that `agentID` is the primary key of the `agent` table.

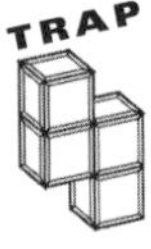

Not all databases use the `AUTO_INCREMENT` feature the same way as MySQL, but most offer an alternative. You might need to look up some other way to automatically generate key fields if you aren't using MySQL. Check the Help system for whatever DBMS you're using to learn any specific quirks.

Creating a Reference to the operation Table

Take a careful look at the operationID field. This field contains an integer, which refers to a particular operation. I also added an indicator specifying operationID as a foreign key reference to the operation table. The operationID field in the agent table contains a reference to the primary key of the operation table. This type of field is referred to as a *foreign key.*

Some DBMS systems require you to specify primary and foreign keys. MySQL currently does not require this, but it's a good idea to do so anyway for two reasons. First, it's likely that future versions of MySQL will require these statements, because they improve a database's reliability. Second, it's good to specify in the code when you want a field to have a special purpose, even if the DBMS doesn't do anything with that information.

Inserting a Value into the agent Table

The INSERT statements for the agent table have one new trick made possible by the primary key's AUTO_INCREMENT designation.

```
INSERT INTO agent VALUES(
  null, 'Bond', 1
);
```

The primary key is initialized with the value null. This might be surprising because primary keys are explicitly designed to never contain a null value. Since the agentID field is set to AUTO_INCREMENT, the null value is automatically replaced with an unused integer. This trick ensures that each primary key value is unique.

Building the operation Table

The new operation table contains information referring to an operation.

TABLE 11.4 THE OPERATION TABLE

Operation ID	Name	Description	Location
1	Dancing Elephant	Infiltrate suspicious zoo	London
2	Enduring Angst	Make bad guys feel really guilty	Lower Volta
3	Furious Dandelion	Plant crabgrass in enemy lawns	East Java

Each operation gets its own record in the operation table. All the data corresponding to an operation is stored in the operation record. Each operation's data is stored only one time. This has a number of positive effects:

- It's necessary to enter operation data only once per operation, saving time on data entry.
- Since there's no repeated data, you won't have data inconsistency problems (like the circus/zoo problem).
- The new database requires less space, because there's no repeated data.
- The operation is not necessarily tied to an agent, so you won't accidentally delete all references to an operation by deleting the only agent assigned to that mission. (Remember, this could happen with the original data design.)
- If you need to update operation data, you don't need to go through every agent to figure out who was assigned to that operation. (Again, you would have had to do this with the old database design.)

The SQL used to create the operation table is much like that used for the agent table:

```
CREATE TABLE operation (
  operationID int(11) NOT NULL AUTO_INCREMENT,
  name varchar(50) default NULL,
  description varchar(50) default NULL,
  location varchar(50) default NULL,
  PRIMARY KEY  (`OperationID`)
);

INSERT INTO operation VALUES(
  null, 'Dancing Elephant',
  'Infiltrate suspicious zoo', 'London'
);
```

As you can see, the operation table conforms to the rules of normalization, and it also is much like the agent table. Notice that I'm being very careful about how I name things. SQL is (theoretically) case-insensitive, but I've found that this is not always true. (I have found this especially in MySQL, where the Windows versions appear unconcerned about case, but UNIX versions treat operationID and OperationID as different field names.) I specified that all field names will use camel-case (just like you've been doing with your PHP variables). I also named the key field according to my own formula (table name followed by ID).

Using a Join to Connect Tables

The only downside to disconnecting the data tables is the necessity to rejoin the data when needed. The user doesn't care that the operation and the agent are in different tables, but he will want the data to look as if they were on the same table. The secret to reattaching tables is a tool called the *inner join*. Take a look at the following `SELECT` statement in SQL:

```
SELECT agent.name AS agent, operation.name AS operation
FROM agent, operation
WHERE agent.operationID = operation.operationID
ORDER BY agent.name;
```

At first glance this looks like an ordinary query, but it is a little different. It joins data from two different tables. Table 11.5 illustrates the results of this query.

Table 11.5 Combining Two Tables

Agent	Operation
Blackford	Enduring Angst
Bond	Dancing Elephant
Cardinal	Enduring Angst
Falcon	Dancing Elephant
Rahab	Furious Dandelion

Creating Useful Joins

An SQL query can pull data from more than one table. To do this, follow a few basic rules.

- Specify the field names more formally if necessary. Notice that the `SELECT` statement specifies `agent.name` rather than simply `name`. This is necessary because both tables contain a field called `name`. Using the `table.field` syntax is much like using a person's first and last name. It's not necessary if there's no chance of confusion, but in a larger environment the more complete naming scheme can avoid confusion.
- Use the `AS` clause to clarify your output. This provides an alias for the column and provides a nicer output.

- Modify the FROM clause so it indicates both of the tables you're pulling data from. The FROM clause up to now has only specified one table. In this example, it's necessary to specify that data will be coming from two different tables.
- Indicate how the tables will be connected using a modification of the WHERE clause.

Examining a Join without a WHERE Clause

The WHERE clause helps clarify the relationship between two tables. As an explanation, consider the following query:

```
SELECT
  agent.name AS 'agent',
  agent.operationID as 'agent opID',
  operation.operationID as 'op opID',
  operation.name AS 'operation'
FROM agent, operation
ORDER BY agent.name;
```

This query is much like the earlier query, except it includes the operationID field from each table and it omits the WHERE clause. You might be surprised by the results, which are shown in Table 11.6.

The results of this query are called a *Cartesian join*, which shows all possible combinations of agent and operation. Of course, you don't really want all the combinations—only those combinations where the two tables indicate the same operation ID.

Adding a WHERE Clause to Make a Proper Join

Without a WHERE clause, all possible combinations are returned. The only concern-worthy records are those where the operationID fields in the agent and operation tables have the same value. The WHERE clause returns only these values joined by a common operation ID.

The secret to making this work is the operationID fields in the two tables. You've already learned that each table should have a primary key. The primary key field is used to uniquely identify each database record. In the agents table, agentID is the primary key. In operations, operationID is the primary key. (You might note my unimaginative but very useful naming convention here.)

Table 11.6 Joining agent and operation without a WHERE clause

Agent	Agent Op ID	Op Op ID	Operation
Blackford	1	1	Dancing Elephant
Blackford	1	2	Enduring Angst
Blackford	1	3	Furious Dandelion
Bond	1	1	Dancing Elephant
Bond	1	2	Enduring Angst
Bond	1	3	Furious Dandelion
Cardinal	2	2	Enduring Angst
Cardinal	2	3	Furious Dandelion
Cardinal	2	1	Dancing Elephant
Falcon	1	1	Dancing Elephant
Falcon	1	2	Enduring Angst
Falcon	1	3	Furious Dandelion
Rahab	3	1	Dancing Elephant
Rahab	3	2	Enduring Angst
Rahab	3	3	Furious Dandelion

Op = operation

I was able to take all data that refers to the operation out of the `agent` table by replacing those fields with a field that points to the `operations` table's primary key. A field that references the primary key of another table is called a `foreign key`. Primary and foreign keys cement the relationships between tables.

Adding a Condition to a Joined Query

Of course, you can still use the `WHERE` clause to limit which records are shown. Use the `AND` structure to build compound conditions. For example, this code returns the code name and operation name of every agent whose code name begins with `B`:

```
SELECT
  agent.name AS 'agent',
```

```
  operation.name AS operation
FROM agent, operation
WHERE agent.operationID = operation.operationID
  AND agent.name LIKE 'B%';
```

THE TRUTH ABOUT INNER JOINS

You should know that the syntax I provided here is a convenient shortcut supported by most DBMS systems. The inner join's formal syntax looks like this:

```
SELECT agent.name, operation.name
FROM
  agent INNER JOIN operation
  ON agent.OperationID = operation.OperationID
ORDER BY agent.name;
```

Many data programmers prefer to think of the join as part of the `WHERE` clause and use the `WHERE` syntax. A few SQL databases (notably many offerings from Microsoft) do not allow the `WHERE` syntax for inner joins and require the `INNER JOIN` to be specified as part of the `FROM` clause. When you use this `INNER JOIN` syntax, the `ON` clause indicates how the tables will be joined.

Building a Link Table for Many-to-Many Relationships

Once you've created an ER diagram, you can create new tables to handle all the one-to-many relationships. It's a little less obvious what to do with many-to-many relationships such as the link between agents and skills. Recall that each agent can have many skills, and several agents can use each skill. The best way to handle this kind of situation is to build a special kind of table.

Enhancing the ER Diagram

Figure 11.5 shows a new version of the ER diagram that eliminates all many-many relationships.

The ER diagram in Figure 11.5 improves on the earlier version shown in Figure 11.4 in a number of ways.

- I added `(PK)` to the end of every primary key.
- I added `(FK)` to the end of every foreign key.

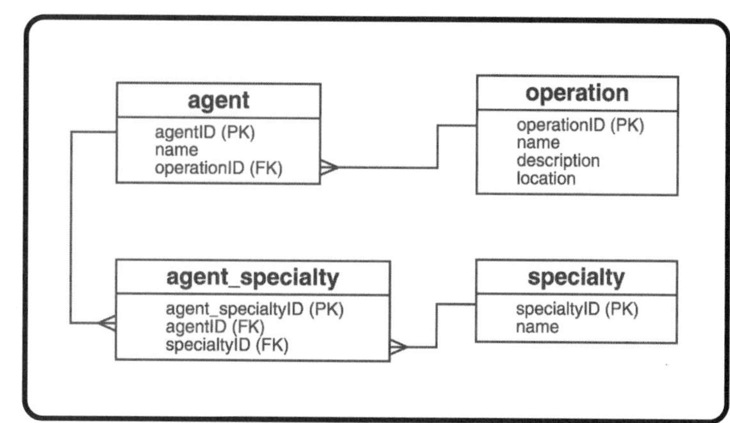

FIGURE 11.5

This newer ER diagram includes a special table to handle the many-many relationship

- The placements of the lines in the diagram are now much more important. I now draw a line only between a foreign key reference and the corresponding primary key in the other table. Every relationship should go between a foreign key reference in one table and a primary key in the other.
- The other main improvement is the addition of the `agent_specialty` table. This table is interesting because it contains nothing but primary and foreign keys. Each entry in this table represents one link between the `agent` and `specialty` tables. All the actual data referring to the agent or specialty are encoded in other tables. This arrangement provides a great deal of flexibility.

Most tables in a relational database are about entities in the data set, but link tables are about *relationships* between entities.

Creating the specialty Table

The `specialty` table is simple, as shown in Table 11.7.

As you can see, there is nothing in the `specialty` table that connects it directly with any particular agent. Likewise, you find no references to specialties in the `agent` table. The complex relationship between these two tables is handled by the new `agent_specialty` table.

This is called a *link table* because it manages relationships between other tables. Table 11.8 shows a sample set of data in the `agent_specialty` table.

TABLE 11.7 THE SPECIALTY TABLE

Specialty ID	Name
0	Electronics
1	Counterintelligence
2	Sabotage
3	Doily Design
4	Explosives
5	Flower Arranging

TABLE 11.8 THE AGENT_SPECIALTY TABLE

Agent Specialty ID	Agent ID	Specialty ID
1	1	2
2	1	3
3	2	1
4	2	6
5	3	2
6	4	4
7	4	5

Interpreting the agent_specialty Table with a Query

Of course, the `agent_specialty` table is not directly useful to the user, because it contains nothing but foreign key references. You can translate the data to something more meaningful with an SQL statement:

```
SELECT agent_specialtyID,
       agent.name AS 'agent',
       specialty.name AS 'specialty'
FROM agent_specialty,
     agent,
     specialty
```

```
WHERE agent.agentID = agent_specialty.agentID
  AND specialty.specialtyID = agent_specialty.specialtyID;
```

It requires two comparisons to join the three tables. It is necessary to forge the relationship between `agent` and `agent_specialty` by common `agentID` values. It's also necessary to secure the bond between `specialty` and `agent_specialty` by comparing the `specialtyID` fields. The results of such a query show that the correct relationships have indeed been joined, as you can see in Table 11.9.

Table 11.9 Query Interpretation of agent_specialty Table

Agent Specialty ID	Agent	Specialty
1	Bond	Sabotage
2	Bond	Doily Design
3	Falcon	Counterintelligence
5	Cardinal	Sabotage
6	Blackford	Explosives
7	Blackford	Flower Arranging

The link table provides the linkage between tables that have many-to-many relationships. Each time you want a new relationship between an agent and a specialty, you add a new record to the `agent_specialty` table.

Creating Queries That Use Link Tables

Whenever you want to know about the relationships between agents and specialties, the data is available in the `agent_specialty` table. For example, if you need to know which agents know flower arranging, you can use the following query:

```
SELECT
  agent.name
FROM
  agent,
  specialty,
  agent_specialty
WHERE agent.agentID = agent_specialty.agentID
  AND agent_specialty.specialtyID = specialty.specialtyID
  AND specialty.name = 'Flower Arranging';
```

This query looks a little scary, but it really isn't bad. This query requires data from three different tables. The output needs the `name` from the `agent` table. I don't want to remember what specialty number is associated with `Flower Arranging`, so I let the query look that up from the `specialty` table. Since I need to know which agent is associated with a particular specialty, I use the `agent_specialty` table to link up the other two tables. The `WHERE` clause simply provides the joins.

The following phrase cements the relationship between `agents` and `agent_specialty`:

```
agents.agentID = agent_specialty.agentID
```

Likewise, the following ensures the connection between `specialties` and `agent_specialty`:

```
agent_specialty.specialtyID = specialties.specialtyID
```

The last part of the `WHERE` clause is the actual conditional part of the query that only returns records where the specialty is flower arranging. (You know, flower arrangement can be a deadly art in the hands of a skilled practitioner.)

It might be helpful to imagine the ER diagram when building queries. If two tables have lines between them, use a `WHERE` clause to represent each line. To replicate a one-to-many join (with one line and two tables) you need one `WHERE` line to handle the connection. If creating a many-to-many join with a link table, you need a compound condition to handle connecting each table to the link table. You can then add any other conditions that help you narrow the query.

Summary

In this chapter you move beyond programming to an understanding of data, the real fuel of modern applications. You learn how to take a poorly designed table and convert it into a series of well-organized tables that can avoid a lot of data problems. You learn about three stages of normalization and how to build an Entity Relationship diagram. You can recognize three kinds of relationships between entities and build normalized tables in SQL, including pointers for primary and foreign keys. You can connect normalized tables with `INNER JOIN SQL` statements. You know how to simulate a many-to-many relationship by building a link table. The civilized world is safer for your efforts.

CHALLENGES

1. Locate ER diagrams for data you work with every day. (Check with your company's Information Technology department, for example.) Examine these documents and see if you can make sense of them.
2. Examine a database you use regularly. Determine if it follows the requirements stated in this chapter for a well-designed data structure. If not, explain what might be wrong with the data structure and how it could be corrected.
3. Diagram an improved data structure for the database you examined in Question 2. Create the required tables in SQL and populate them with sample data.
4. Design a database for data you use every day. (Be warned, most data problems are a lot more complex than they first appear.) Create a data diagram; then build the tables and populate with sample data.

Building a Three-Tiered Data Application

This book begins by looking at HTML pages, which are essentially static documents. It then reveals how to generate dynamic pages with the powerful PHP language. The last few chapters show how to use a database management system such as MySQL to build powerful data structures. This chapter ties together the PHP programming and data programming aspects to build a full-blown data-management system for the spy database. The system you learn can easily be expanded to any kind of data project you can think of, including e-commerce applications. Specifically, you learn how to:

- Design a moderate-to-large data application
- Build a library of reusable data functions
- Optimize functions for use across data sets
- Include library files in your programs

There isn't really much new PHP or MySQL code to learn in this chapter. The focus is on building a larger project with minimum effort.

Introducing the SpyMaster Program

The `SpyMaster` program is a suite of PHP programs that allows access to the spy database created in chapter 11, "Data Normalization." While the database created in that chapter is flexible and powerful, it is *not* easy to use unless you know SQL. Even if your users do understand SQL, you don't want them to have direct control of a database, because too many things can go wrong.

You need to build some sort of front-end application to the database. In essence, this system has three levels.

- The client computer handles communication with the user.
- The database server (MySQL) manages the data.
- The PHP program acts as interpreter between the client and database. PHP provides the bridge between the client's HTML language and the database's SQL language.

This kind of arrangement is frequently called a *three-tier architecture*. As you examine the `SpyMaster` program throughout this chapter, you learn some of the advantages of this particular approach.

Viewing the Main Screen

Start by looking at the program from the user's point of view as shown in Figure 12.1.

The main page has two sections. The first is a series of data requests. Each of these requests maps to a query.

Viewing the Results of a Query

When the user selects a query and presses the Submit button, a screen like the one in Figure 12.2 appears.

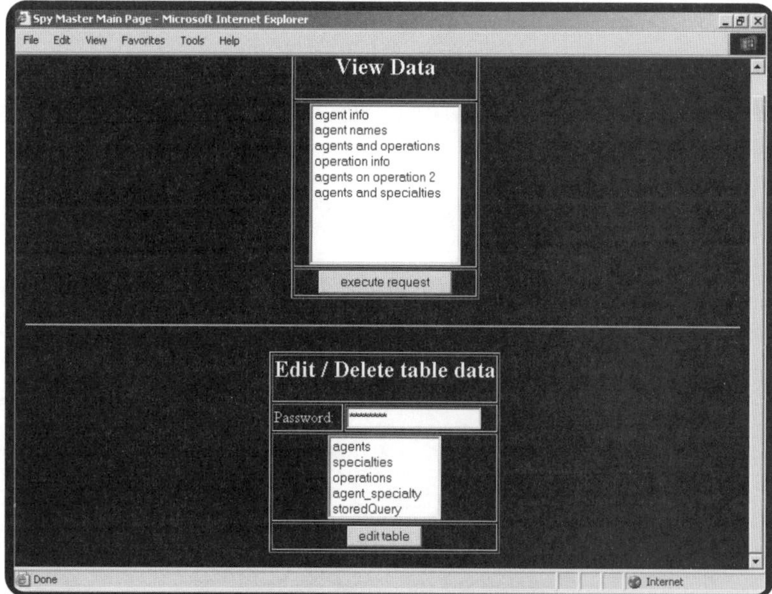

FIGURE 12.1

The entry point to the SpyMaster database is clean and simple.

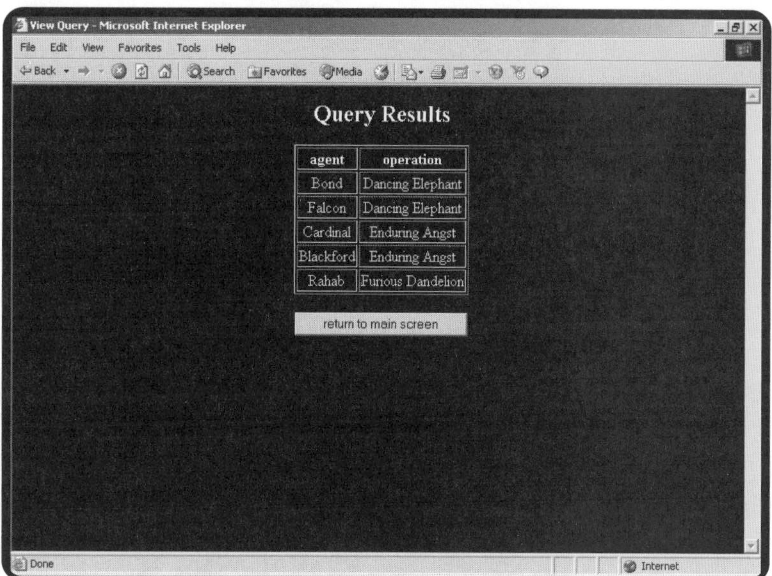

FIGURE 12.2

The results of the query are viewed in an HTML table.

The queries are all prebuilt, which means the user cannot make a mistake by typing in inappropriate SQL code. It also limits the usefulness of the database. Fortunately, you can add new queries.

Viewing Table Data

The other part of the main screen (shown again in Figure 12.3) allows the user to directly manipulate data in the tables. Since this is a more powerful (and thus dangerous) enterprise, access to this part of the system is controlled by a password.

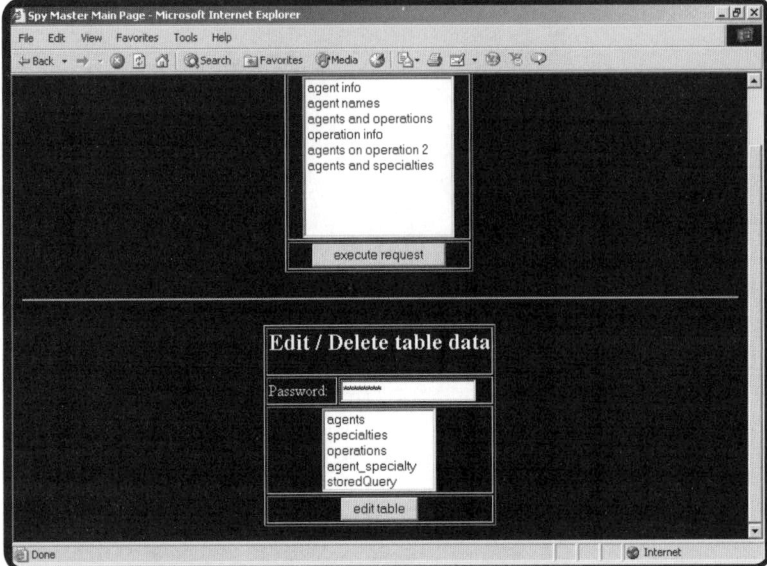

FIGURE 12.3

From the main screen you can also access the table data with a password.

As an example, by selecting the `agent` table I see a screen like Figure 12.4.

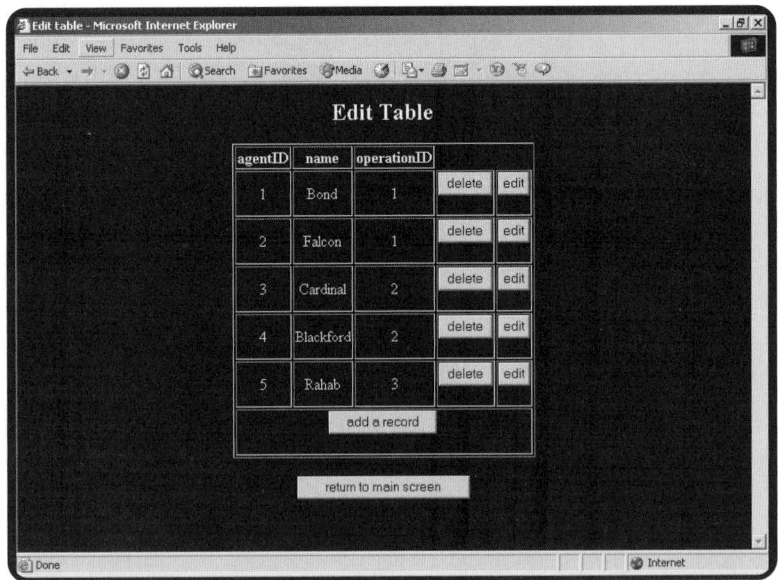

FIGURE 12.4

The `editTable` screen displays all the information in a table.

From this screen, the user can see all the data in the chosen table. The page also gives the user links to add, edit, or delete records from the table.

Editing a Record

If the user chooses to edit a record, a screen similar to Figure 12.5 appears.

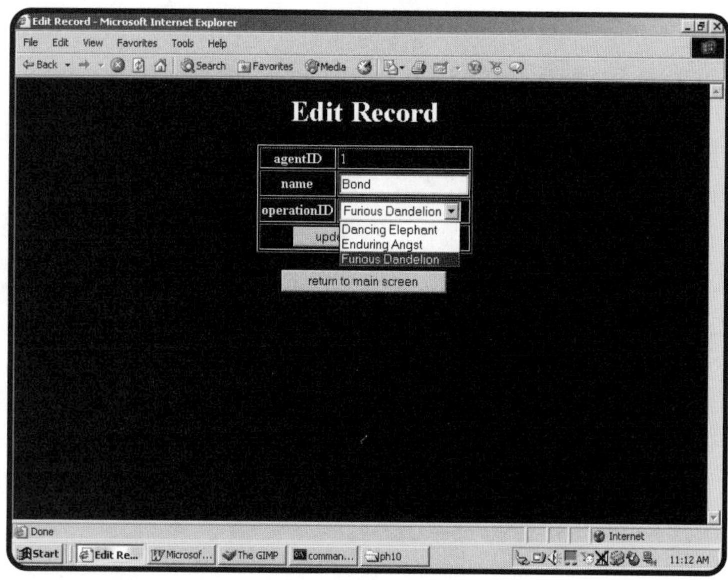

FIGURE 12.5

The user is editing a record in the `agent` table.

The Edit Record page has some important features. First, the user cannot directly change the primary key. If she could do so, it would have profound destabilizing consequences on the database. Also note the way the `operationID` field is presented. The field itself is a primary key with an integer value, but it would be very difficult for a user to directly manipulate the integer values. Instead, the program provides a drop-down list of operations. When the user chooses from this list, the appropriate numerical index is sent to the next page.

Confirming the Record Update

When the user clicks the button, a new screen appears and announces the successful update as in Figure 12.6.

Deleting a Record

The user can also choose to delete a record from the Edit Table page. This action results in the basic screen shown in Figure 12.7.

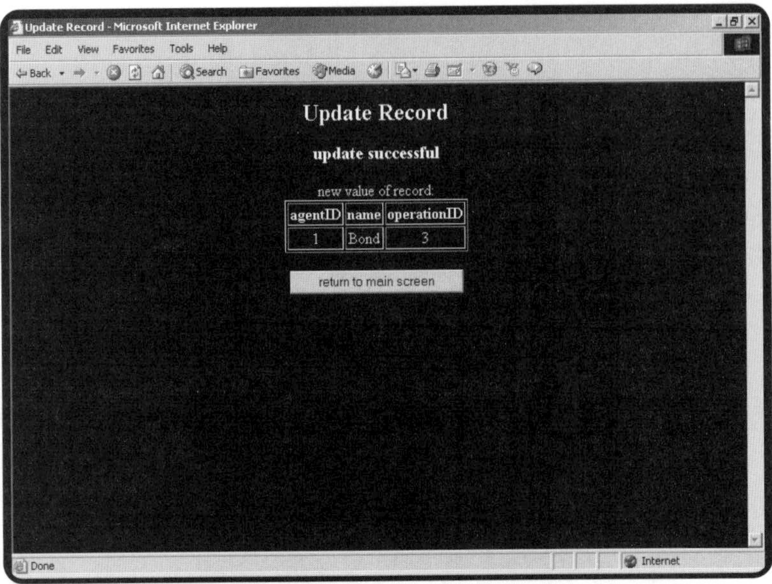

FIGURE 12.6

The user can see the newly updated record.

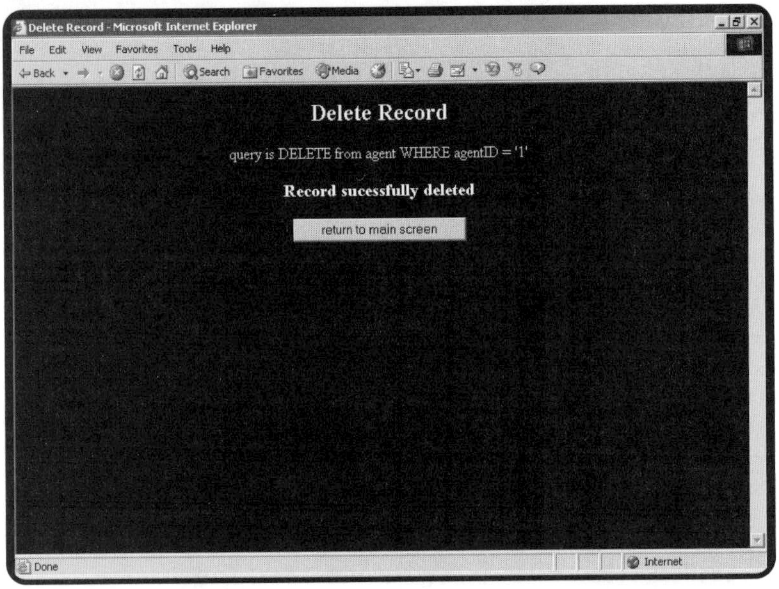

FIGURE 12.7

It's very easy to delete a record.

You can tell from this example why it's so important to have a script for generating sample data. I had to delete and modify records several times when I was testing the system. After each test I easily restored the database to a stable condition by reloading the `buildSpy.sql` file with the MySQL `SOURCE` command.

Adding a Record

Adding a record to the table is a multistep process, much like editing a record. The first page (shown in Figure 12.8) allows you to enter data in all the appropriate fields.

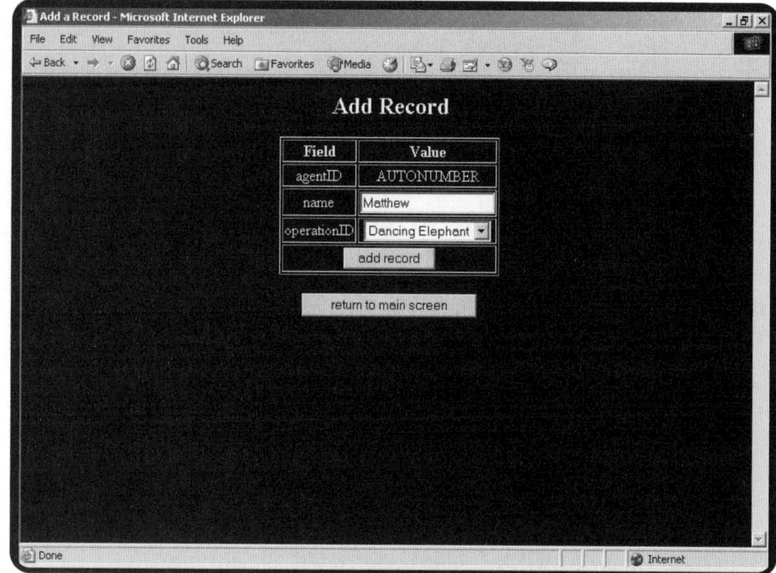

FIGURE 12.8

The add screen includes list boxes for foreign key references.

Like the Edit Record screen, the Add Record page does not allow the user to directly enter a primary key. This page also automatically generates drop-down `SELECT` boxes for foreign key fields like `operationID`.

Processing the Add

When the user chooses to process the add, another page confirms the add (or describes the failure, if it cannot add the record). This confirmation page is shown in Figure 12.9.

Building the Design of the SpyMaster System

It can be intimidating to think of all the operations in the `SpyMaster` system. The program has a lot of functionality. It could be overwhelming to start coding this system without some sort of strategic plan.

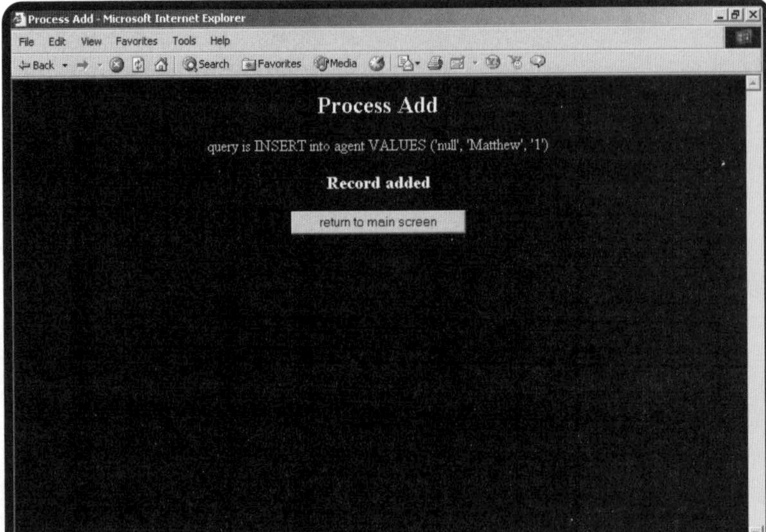

FIGURE 12.9

The user has successfully added an agent.

Creating a State Diagram

Complex programming problems have many approaches. For this particular problem I decided to concentrate on the flow of data through a series of modules. Figure 12.10 shows my overall strategy.

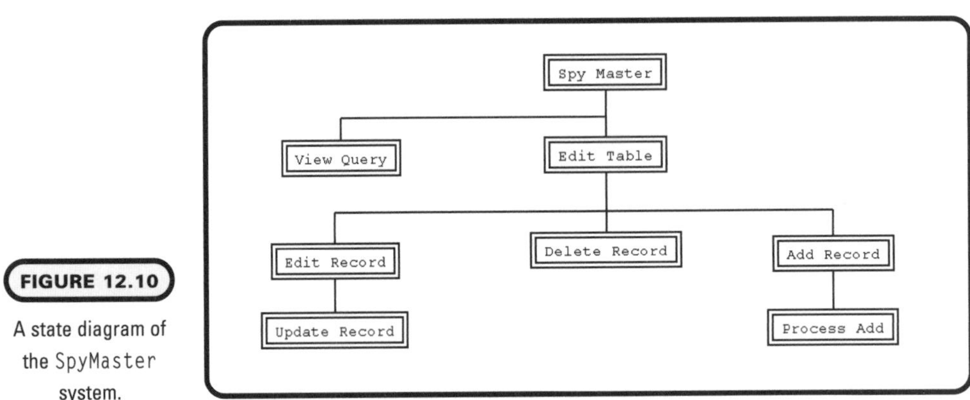

FIGURE 12.10

A state diagram of the `SpyMaster` system.

The illustration in Figure 12.10 is sometimes called a *state diagram*. This kind of illustration identifies what particular problems need to be solved and indicates modules that might be able to solve these problems.

I began the process by thinking about everything that a data-management system should be able to do. Each major idea is broken into a module. A *module* often represents a single screen. A PHP program often (although not always) supports each model.

The View Query Module

Obviously, users should be able to get queries from the database. This is one of the most common tasks of the system. I decided that the View Query module should be able to view any query sent to it and display an appropriate result.

The Edit Table Module

The other primary task in a data system is *data definition,* which includes adding new records, deleting records, and updating information. This kind of activity can be destructive, so it should be controlled using some kind of access system. All data definition is based on the database's underlying table structure, so it is important to allow the three main kinds of data definition (editing, deletion, and updating) on each table.

The Edit Table module provides the interface to these behaviors. It shows all the current records in a table and lets the user edit or delete any particular record. It also has a button that allows the user to add a new record to this table. It's important to see that Edit Table doesn't actually cause anything to change in the database. Instead, it serves as a gateway to several other editing modules.

The Edit Record and Update Record Modules

If you look back at the state diagram, you see the Edit Table module leading to three other modules. The Edit Record module shows one record and allows the user to edit the data in the record. However, the database isn't actually updated until the user submits changes, so editing a record is a two-step process. After the user determines changes in the Edit Record module, program control moves on to the Update Record module, which actually processes the request and makes the change to the database.

The Add Record and Process Add Modules

Adding a record is similar to editing, as it requires two passes. The first module (Add Record) generates a form that allows the user to input the new record details. Once the user has determined the record data, the Process Add module creates and implements the SQL necessary to incorporate the new record in the table.

The Delete Record Module

Deleting a record is a simple process. There's no need for any other user input, so it requires only one module to process a deletion request.

Designing the System

The state diagram is very helpful, because it allows you to see an overview of the entire process. More planning is still necessary, however, because the basic state diagram leaves a lot of questions unanswered. For example:

- Will the Edit Table module have to be repeated for each table?
- If so, will I also need copies of all other editing modules?
- Can I automate the process?
- What if the underlying data structure is changed?
- What if I want to apply a similar structure to another database?
- How can I allow queries to be added to the system?

It is tempting to write a system specifically to manage the `spy` database. The advantage of such a system is that it will know exactly how to handle issues relevant to the `spy` system. For example, `operationID` is a foreign key reference in the `agent` table, so it should be selected by a drop-down list whenever possible. If you build a specific module to handle editing the `agent` table, you can make this happen.

However, this process quickly becomes unwieldy if you have several tables. It is better to have a smart procedure that can build an edit screen for any table in the database. It would be even better if your program could automatically detect foreign key fields and produce the appropriate user-interface element (an HTML `SELECT` clause) when needed. In fact, you could build an entire library of generic routines that could work with any database. That's exactly the approach I chose.

Building a Library of Functions

Although the `SpyMaster` system is the largest example in this book, most of it is surprisingly simple. The system's centerpiece is a file called `spyLib.php`. This file is not meant to run in the user's browser at all. Instead, it contains a library of functions that simplify coding of any database. I stored as much of the PHP code as I could in this library. All the other PHP programs in the system make use of the various functions in the library. This approach has a number of advantages:

- The overall code size is smaller since code does not need to be repeated.

- If I want to improve a module, I do it once in the library rather than in several places.
- It is extremely simple to modify the code library so it works with another database.
- The details of each particular module are hidden in a separate library so I can focus on the bigger picture when writing each PHP page.
- The routines can be reused to work with any table in the database.
- The routines can automatically adjust to changes in the data structure.
- The library can be readily reused for another project.

Figure 12.11 shows a more detailed state diagram.

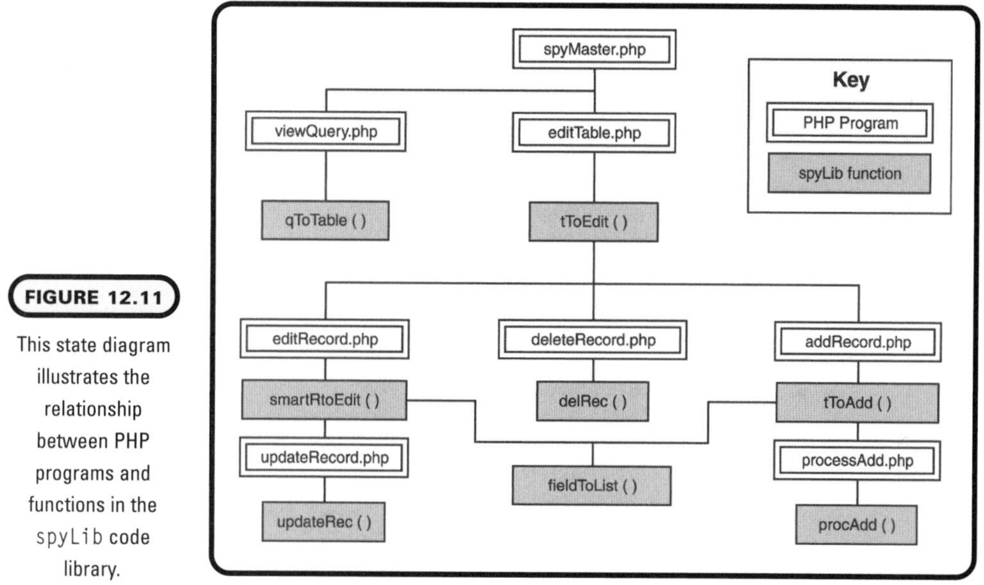

FIGURE 12.11

This state diagram illustrates the relationship between PHP programs and functions in the `spyLib` code library.

When you begin looking at actual code, you'll see most of the PHP programs are extremely simple. They usually just collect data for a library function, send program control off to that function, and then print any output produced by the function.

Writing the Non-Library Code

I begin here by describing all the parts of this project except the library. The library module is driven by the needs of the other PHP programs, so it makes sense to look at the other programs first.

Preparing the Database

The database for this segment is almost the same as the one used in chapter 11, "Data Normalization." I added one table to store queries. All other tables are the same as those in chapter 11. The SQL script that creates this new version of the spy database is available on the CD as buildSpy.sql.

Note I have modified the database slightly from chapter 11, because the new version includes several queries as part of the data! In order to make the program reasonably secure, I don't want typical users to be able to make queries. I also don't want users to be limited to the few queries I thought of when building this system. One solution is to store a set of queries in the database and let appropriate users modify the queries. I called my new table the storedQuery table. It can be manipulated in the system just like the other tables, so a user with password access can add, edit, and delete queries. Here is the additional code used to build the storedQuery table:

```
######################################
# build storedQuery table
######################################

CREATE TABLE storedQuery (
  storedQueryID int(11) NOT NULL AUTO_INCREMENT,
  description varchar(30),
  text varchar(255),
  PRIMARY KEY (storedQueryID)
);

INSERT INTO storedQuery VALUES (
  null,
  'agent info',
  'SELECT * FROM agent'
);
```

The storedQuery table has three fields. The description field holds a short English description of each query. The text field holds the query's actual SQL code.

Examining the spyMaster.php Program

The sypMaster.php program is the entry point into the system. All access to the system comes from this page. It has two main parts. One handles queries from ordinary users, and the other allows more sophisticated access by authorized users. Each segment encapsulates an HTML form that sends a request to a particular PHP program. The first segment has a small amount of PHP code that sets up the query list box.

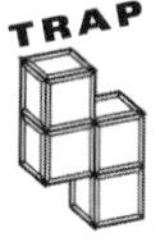

Proper SQL syntax is extremely important when you store SQL syntax inside an SQL database as I'm doing here. It's especially important to keep track of single and double quotation marks. To include the single quotation marks that some queries require, precede the mark with a backslash character. For example, assume I want to store the following query:

```
SELECT * FROM agent WHERE agent.name = 'Bond'
```

I would actually store this text instead:

```
SELECT * FROM agent WHERE agent.name = \'Bond\'
```

This is necessary for storing the single quotation mark characters. Otherwise they are interpreted incorrectly.

In SQLite, the syntax is two single quotation marks together. The SQLite version of the query text reads like this:

```
SELECT * FROM agent WHERE agent.name = ''Bond''
```

Creating the Query Form

```
<html>
<head>
<title>Spy Master Main Page</title>
<?
  include "spyLib.php";
?>

</head>
<body>
<form action = "viewQuery.php"
      method = "post">

<table border = 1
       width = 200>
<tr>
  <td><center><h2>View Data</h2></center></td>
</tr>

<tr>
  <td><center>
    <select name = "theQuery" size = 10>
```

```
<?
//get queries from storedQuery table

$dbConn = connectToSpy();
$query = "SELECT * from storedQuery";
$result = mysql_query($query, $dbConn);
while($row = mysql_fetch_assoc($result)){
  $currentQuery = $row['text'];
  $theDescription = $row['description'];
  print <<<HERE
      <option value = "$currentQuery">$theDescription</option>

HERE;
  } // end while

?>
    </select>
  </center>
</tr>

<tr>
  <td><center>
    <input type = "submit"
        value = "execute request" >
  </center></td>
</tr>
</table>

</form>
```

Most of the code is ordinary HTML. The HTML code establishes a form that calls `viewQuery.php` when the user presses the Submit button. I added some PHP code that generates a special input box based on the entries in the `storedQuery` table.

Including the spyLib Library

The first thing to notice is the `include()` statement. This command allows you to import another file. PHP reads that file and interprets it as HTML. An included file can contain HTML, cascading style sheets (CSS), or PHP code. Most of the functionality for the `spy` data program is stored in the `spyLib.php` library program.

All the other PHP programs in the system begin by including `spyLib.php`. Once this is done, every function in the library can be accessed as if it were a locally defined function. This provides tremendous power and flexibility to a programming system.

Connecting to the spy Database

The utility of the `spyLib` library becomes immediately apparent as I connect to the `spy` database. Rather than worrying about exactly what database I'm connecting to, I simply defer to the `connectToSpy()` function in `spyLib()`. In the current code I don't need to worry about the details of connecting to the database. With a library I can write the connecting code one time and reuse that function as needed.

Notice the `connectToSpy()` function returns a data connection pointer I can use for other database activities.

There's another advantage to using a library when connecting to a database. It's likely that if you move this code to another system you'll have a different way to log in to the data server. If the code for connecting to the server is centralized, it only needs to be changed in one place when you want to update the code. This is far more efficient than searching through dozens of programs to find every reference to the `mysql_connect()` function. Also, if you want to convert the MySQL-based code in this book to SQLite or another database system, you only have to change the `connectToSpy()` function. That's pretty cool, huh?

Retrieving the Queries

I decided to encode a series of prepackaged queries into a table. (I explain more about my reasons for this in the section on the `viewQuery` program.) The main form must present a list of query descriptions and let the user select one of these queries. I use an SQL `SELECT` statement to extract everything from the `storedQuery` table. I then use the description and text fields from `storedQuery` to build a multiline list box.

Creating the Edit Table Form

The second half of the `spyMaster` program presents all the tables in the database and allows the user to choose a table for later editing. Most of the functionality in the system comes through this section. Surprisingly, there is no PHP code at all in this particular part of the page. An HTML form sends the user to the `editTable.php` program.

```
<hr>
<form action = "editTable.php"
      method = "post">

<table border = 1>
<tr>
  <td colspan = 2><center>
    <h2>Edit / Delete table data</h2>
  </center></td>
</tr>

<tr>
  <td>Password:</td>
  <td>
    <input type = "password"
        name = "pwd"
        value = "absolute"><br>
  </td>
</tr>

<tr>
  <td colspan = 2><center>
    <select name = "tableName"
         size = 5>
      <option value = "agent">agents</option>
      <option value = "specialty">specialties</option>
      <option value = "operation">operations</option>
      <option value = "agent_specialty">agent_specialty</option>
      <option value = "storedQuery">storedQuery</option>
    </select>
  </center></td>
</tr>

<tr>
  <td colspan = 2><center>
    <input type = "submit"
        value = "edit table">
  </center></td>
</tr>
</table>
```

```
</form>

</body>
</html>
```

To make debugging easier, I preloaded the `password` field with the appropriate password. In a production environment, you should, of course, leave the password field blank so the user cannot get into the system without the password.

Building the viewQuery.php Program

When the user chooses a query, program control is sent to the `viewQuery.php` program. This program does surprisingly little on its own:

```
<html>
<head>
<title>View Query</title>
</head>
<body>

<center>
<h2>Query Results</h2>
</center>
<?
include "spyLib.php";

$dbConn = connectToSpy();

//take out escape characters...
$theQuery = str_replace("\'", "'", $theQuery);

print qToTable($theQuery);

print mainButton();

?>

</body>
</html>
```

Once `viewQuery.php` connects to the library, it uses functions in the library to connect to the database and print desired results. The `qToTable()` function does most of the actual work, taking whatever query is passed to it and generating a table with add, delete, and edit buttons.

WHY STORE QUERIES IN THE DATABASE?

You might wonder why I chose to store queries in the database. After all, I could have let the user type in a query directly or provided some form that allows the user to search for certain values. Either of these approaches has advantages, but they also pose some risks. It's very dangerous to allow direct access to your data from a Web form. Malicious users can introduce Trojan horse commands that snoop on your data, change data, or even delete information from the database.

I sometimes build a form that has enough information to create an SQL query and then build that query in a server-side program. (Sounds like a good end-of-chapter exercise, right?) In this case, I stored queries in another table. People with administrative access can add new queries to the database, but ordinary users do not. I preloaded the `storedQuery` database with a number of useful queries, then added the capacity to add new queries whenever the situation demands it. Drawbacks remain (primarily that ordinary users cannot build custom queries), but it is far more secure than a system that builds a query based on user input.

The `str_replace()` function is necessary because SQL queries contain single quotation mark (`'`) characters. When I store a query as a `VARCHAR` entity, the single quotation marks embedded in the query cause problems. The normal solution to this problem is to use a backslash, which indicates that the mark should not be immediately interpreted, but should be considered a part of the data. The problem with this is the backslash is still in the string when I try to execute the query. The `str_replace()` function replaces all instances of `\'` with a simple single quote (`'`).

Note that the `qToTable()` function doesn't actually print anything to the screen. All it does is build a complex string of HTML code. The `viewQuery.php` program prints the code to the screen.

If you are using a library, it's best if the library code does not print anything directly to the screen. Instead, it should return a value to whatever program called it. This allows multiple uses for the data. For example, if the `qToTable()` function printed directly to the screen, you could not use it to generate a file. Since the library code returns a value but doesn't actually do anything with that value, the code that calls the function has the freedom to use the results in multiple ways.

The mainButton() function produces a simple HTML form that directs the user back to the spyMaster.php page. Even though the code for this is relatively simple, it is repeated so often that it makes sense to store it in a function rather than copying and pasting it in every page of the system.

Viewing the editTable.php Program

The editTable.php follows a familiar pattern. It has a small amount of PHP code, but most of the real work is sent off to a library function. This module's main job is to check for an administrative password. If the user does not have the appropriate password, further access to the system is blocked. If the user does have the correct password, the very powerful tToEdit() function provides access to the add, edit, and delete functions.

```
<html>
<head>
<title>Edit table</title>
</head>
<body>
<h2>Edit Table</h2>
<?
include "spyLib.php";

//check password

if ($pwd == $adminPassword){
  $dbConn = connectToSpy();
  print tToEdit("$tableName");
} else {
  print "<h3>You must have administrative access to proceed</h3>\n";
} // end if
print mainButton();

?>
</body>
</html>
```

The $pwd value comes from a field in the spyMaster.php page. The $adminPassword value is stored in spyLibrary.php. (The default admin password is *absolute*, but you can change it to whatever you want by editing spyLib.php.)

Viewing the editRecord.php Program

The `editRecord.php` program is called from a form generated by `editTable.php`. (Actually, the `tToEdit()` function generates the form, but `tToEdit()` is called from `editTable.php`.) This program expects variables called `$tableName`, `$keyName`, and `$keyVal`. These variables, automatically provided by `tToEdit()`, help `editRecord` build a query that returns whatever record the user selects. (You can read ahead to the description of `tToEdit()` for details on how this works.)

```
<html>
<head>
<title>Edit Record</title>
</head>
<body>
<h1>Edit Record</h1>
<?

// expects $tableName, $keyName, $keyVal
include "spyLib.php";

$dbConn = connectToSpy();

$query = "SELECT * FROM $tableName WHERE $keyName = $keyVal";
print smartRToEdit($query);

print mainButton();

?>
</body>
</html>
```

The `editRecord.php` program prints the results of the `smartRToEdit()` library function. This function takes the single-record query and prints HTML code that lets the user appropriately update the record.

Viewing the updateRecord.php Program

The `smartRToEdit()` function calls another PHP program called `updateRecord.php`. This program calls a library function that actually commits the user's changes to the database.

```
<html>
<head>
<title>Update Record</title>
</head>
<body>

<h2>Update Record</h2>
<?

include "spyLib.php";

$dbConn = connectToSpy();

$fieldNames = "";
$fieldValues = "";

foreach ($_REQUEST as $fieldName => $value){
  if ($fieldName == "tableName"){
    $theTable = $value;
  } else {

    $fields[] = $fieldName;
    $values[] = $value;
  } // end if
} // end foreach

print updateRec($theTable, $fields, $values);

print mainButton();

?>
</body>
</html>
```

It is more convenient for the updateRec() function if the field names and values are sent as arrays. Therefore, the PHP code in updateRecord.php converts the $_REQUEST array to an array of fields and another array of values. These two arrays are passed to the updateRec() function, which processes them.

Viewing the deleteRecord.php Program

The `deleteRecord.php` program acts in a now-familiar manner. It mainly serves as a wrapper for a function in the `spyLib` library. In this particular case, the program simply sends the name of the current table, the name of the key field, and the value of the current record's key to the `delRec()` function. That function deletes the record and returns a message regarding the success or failure of the operation.

```
<html>
<head>
<title>Delete Record</title>
</head>
<body>
<h2>Delete Record</h2>
<?

include "spyLib.php";

$dbConn = connectToSpy();
print delRec($tableName, $keyName, $keyVal);
print mainButton();
?>

</body>
</html>
```

Viewing the addRecord.php Program

Adding a record, which requires two distinctive steps, is actually much like editing a record. The `addRecord.php` program calls the `tToAdd()` function, which builds a form allowing the user to add data to whichever table is currently selected. It isn't necessary to send any information except the name of the table to this function, because `tToAdd()` automatically generates the key value.

```
<html>
<head>
<title>Add a Record</title>
</head>
<body>
<h2>Add Record</h2>
<?
```

```
include "spyLib.php";

$dbConn = connectToSpy();

print tToAdd($tableName);
print mainButton();

?>

</body>
</html>
```

Viewing the processAdd.php Program

The `tToAdd()` function called by the `addRecord.php` program doesn't actually add a record. Instead, it places an HTML form on the screen that allows the user to enter the data for a new record. When the user submits this form, he is passed to the `processAdd.php` program, which calls `procAdd()` in the library code. The `procAdd()` function generates the appropriate SQL code to add the new record to the table. In order to do this, `procAdd()` needs to know the field names and values. The names and values are passed to the function in arrays just like in `updateRecord.php`.

```
<html>
<head>
        <title>Process Add</title>
</head>
<body>
<h2>Process Add</h2>
<?
include "spyLib.php";

$dbConn = connectToSpy();

$fieldNames = "";
$fieldValues = "";

foreach ($_REQUEST as $fieldName => $value){
  if ($fieldName == "tableName"){
    $theTable = $value;
  } else {
    $fields[] = $fieldName;
```

```
    $values[] = $value;
  } // end if
} // end foreach

print procAdd($theTable, $fields, $values);

print mainButton();


?>
</body>
</html>
```

Creating the spyLib Library Module

Although I have described several PHP programs in this chapter, most of them are simple. The `spyLib` library code does most of the heavy lifting. Having a library like `spyLib` makes data programming pretty easy, because you don't have to know all the `spyLib` details to make it work. All you need is a basic understanding of the functions in the library, what each function expects as input, and what it will produce as output.

Although this library has a good amount of code (over 500 lines, in fact), there are no new concepts in the library code. It's worth looking carefully at this code because it can give you a good idea of how to create your own libraries. You also find there's no better way to understand the library than to dig around under the hood.

Setting a CSS Style

Some of the simplest elements can have profound effects. One example of this maxim is the storage of a CSS style in the library code. Each program in the system operates using the style specified in the library. This means you can easily change the look and feel of the entire system by manipulating one `<style></style>` block.

```
<style type = "text/css">
body{
  background-color: black;
  color: white;
  text-align:center
}

</style>
```

When you include a file, it is interpreted as HTML, not PHP. This means you can place any HTML code in an `include` file and it is automatically inserted in your output wherever the `include` function occurred. I took advantage of this fact to include a CSS block in the library. If you want PHP code in your library file, surround your code with PHP tags (`<?` `?>`) in the library file.

Setting Systemwide Variables

Another huge advantage of a library file is the ability to set and use variables that have meaning throughout the entire system. Since each PHP program in the system includes the library, all have access to any variables declared in the library file's main section. Of course, you need to use the `global` keyword to access a global variable from within a function.

```
<?
//spyLib.php
//holds utilities for spy database

//variables
$userName = "";
$password = "";
$serverName = "localhost";
$dbName = "chapter12";
$dbConn = "";
$adminPassword = "absolute";
$mainProgram = "spyMaster.php";
```

I stored a few key data points in the systemwide variables. The `$userName`, `$password`, and `$serverName` variables set up the data connection. I did this because I expect people to reuse my library for their own databases. They definitely need to change this information to connect to their own copy of MySQL. It's much safer for them to change this data in variables than in actual program code. If you're writing code for reuse, consider moving anything the code adopter might change into variables.

The `$adminPassword` variable holds the password used to edit data in the system. Again, I want anybody reusing this library (including me) to change this value without having to dig through the code.

The `$mainProgram` variable holds the URL of the "control pad" program of the system. In the `spy` system, I want to provide access to `spyMaster.php` in every screen.

The mainButton() function uses the value of $mainProgram to build a link back to the primary screen in every other document produced by the system.

Connecting to the Database

The connectToSpy() function is fundamental to the spy system. It uses system-level variables to generate a database connection. It returns an error message if it is unable to connect to the database. The mysql_error() function prints an SQL error message if the data connection was unsuccessful. This information may not be helpful to the end user, but it might give you some insight as you are debugging the system.

```
function connectToSpy(){
  //connects to the spy DB
  global $serverName, $userName, $password;
  $dbConn = mysql_connect($serverName, $userName, $password);
  if (!$dbConn){
   print "<h3>problem connecting to database...</h3>\n";
  } // end if

  $select = mysql_select_db("chapter12");
  if (!$select){
    print mysql_error() . "<br>\n";
  } // end if
  return $dbConn;
} // end connectToSpy
```

The connectToSpy() function returns a connection to the database that is subsequently used in the many queries passed to the database throughout the system's life span.

Creating a Quick List from a Query

I created a few functions in the spyMaster library that didn't get used in the project's final version. The qToList() function is a good example. This program takes any SQL query and returns a simply formatted HTML segment describing the data. I find this format useful when debugging because no complex formatting gets in the way.

```
function qToList($query){
  //given a query, makes a quick list of data
  global $dbConn;
```

```
  $output = "";
  $result = mysql_query($query, $dbConn);

  //print "dbConn is $dbConn<br>";
  //print "result is $result<br>";

  while ($row = mysql_fetch_assoc($result)){
    foreach ($row as $col=>$val){
      $output .= "$col: $val<br>\n";
    } // end foreach
    $output .= "<hr>\n" ;
  } // end while
  return $output;
} // end qToList
```

Building an HTML Table from a Query

The `qToTable()` function is a little more powerful than `qToList()`. It can build an HTML table from any valid SQL `SELECT` statement. The code uses the `mysql_fetch_field()` function to determine field names from the query result. It also steps through each row of the result, printing an HTML row corresponding to the record.

```
function qToTable($query){
  //given a query, automatically creates an HTML table output
  global $dbConn;
  $output = "";
  $result = mysql_query($query, $dbConn);

  $output .= "<table border = 1>\n";
  //get column headings

  //get field names
  $output .= "<tr>\n";
  while ($field = mysql_fetch_field($result)){
    $output .= "  <th>$field->name</th>\n";
  } // end while
  $output .= "</tr>\n\n";

  //get row data as an associative array
  while ($row = mysql_fetch_assoc($result)){
```

```
      $output .= "<tr>\n";
      //look at each field
      foreach ($row as $col=>$val){
        $output .= "  <td>$val</td>\n";
      } // end foreach
      $output .= "</tr>\n\n";
    }// end while

    $output .= "</table>\n";
    return $output;
} // end qToTable
```

The `viewQuery.php` program calls the `qToTable()` function, but it could be used anytime you want an SQL query formatted as an HTML table (which turns out to be quite often).

Building an HTML Table for Editing an SQL Table

If the user has appropriate access, she should be allowed to add, edit, or delete records in any table of the database. While `qToTable()` is suitable for viewing the results of any SQL query, it does not provide these features. The `tToEdit()` function is based on `qToTable()` with a few differences:

- `tToEdit()` does not accept a query, but the name of a table. You cannot edit joined queries directly, only tables, so this limitation is sensible. `tToEdit()` creates a query that returns all records in the specified table.
- In addition to printing the table data, `tToEdit()` adds two forms to each record.
  - One form contains all the data needed by the `editRecord.php` program to begin the record-editing process.
  - The other form added to each record sends all data necessary for deleting a record and calls the `deleteRecord.php` program.

One more form at the bottom of the HTML table allows the user to add a record to this table. This form contains information that the `addRecord.php` program needs.

```
function tToEdit($tableName){
  //given a table name, generates HTML table including
  //add, delete and edit buttons

  global $dbConn;
```

```
$output = "";
$query = "SELECT * FROM $tableName";

$result = mysql_query($query, $dbConn);

$output .= "<table border = 1>\n";
//get column headings

//get field names
$output .= "<tr>\n";
while ($field = mysql_fetch_field($result)){
  $output .= "  <th>$field->name</th>\n";
} // end while

//get name of index field (presuming it's first field)
$keyField = mysql_fetch_field($result, 0);
$keyName = $keyField->name;

//add empty columns for add, edit, and delete
$output .= "<th></th><th></th>\n";
$output .= "</tr>\n\n";

//get row data as an associative array
while ($row = mysql_fetch_assoc($result)){
  $output .= "<tr>\n";
  //look at each field
  foreach ($row as $col=>$val){
    $output .= "  <td>$val</td>\n";
  } // end foreach
  //build little forms for add, delete and edit

  //delete = DELETE FROM <table> WHERE <key> = <keyval>
  $keyVal = $row["$keyName"];
  $output .= <<< HERE

<td>
  <form action = "deleteRecord.php">
  <input type = "hidden"
         name = "tableName"
         value = "$tableName">
```

```
      <input type= "hidden"
             name = "keyName"
             value = "$keyName">
      <input type = "hidden"
             name = "keyVal"
             value = "$keyVal">
      <input type = "submit"
             value = "delete"></form>
    </td>

HERE;
    //update: won't update yet, but set up edit form
    $output .= <<< HERE
    <td>
      <form action = "editRecord.php"
            method = "post">
      <input type = "hidden"
             name = "tableName"
             value = "$tableName">
      <input type= "hidden"
             name = "keyName"
             value = "$keyName">
      <input type = "hidden"
             name = "keyVal"
             value = "$keyVal">
      <input type = "submit"
             value = "edit"></form>
    </td>

HERE;

    $output .= "</tr>\n\n";

  }// end while

    //add = INSERT INTO <table> {values}
    //set up insert form send table name
    $keyVal = $row["$keyName"];
    $output .= <<< HERE
```

```
    <td colspan = "5">
      <center>
      <form action = "addRecord.php">
      <input type = "hidden"
             name = "tableName"
             value = "$tableName">
      <input type = "submit"
             value = "add a record"></form>
      </center>
    </td>

HERE;

   $output .= "</table>\n";
   return $output;
} // end tToEdit
```

Look carefully at the forms for editing and deleting records. These forms contain hidden fields with the table name, key field name, and record number. This information will be used by subsequent functions to build a query specific to the record associated with that particular table row.

Creating a Generic Form to Edit a Record

The table created in `tToEdit()` calls a program called `editRecord.php`. This program accepts a one-record query. It prints out an HTML table based on the results of that query. The output of `rToEdit()` is shown in Figure 12.12.

The `rToEdit` function produces a very simple HTML table. Every field has a corresponding textbox. The advantage of this approach is that it works with any table. However, the use of this form is quite risky.

- The user should not be allowed to change the primary key, because that would edit some other record, which could have disastrous results.
- The `operationID` field is a foreign key reference. The only valid entries to this field are integers corresponding to records in the `operation` table. There's no way for the user to know what operation a particular integer is related to. Worse, she could enter any number (or any text) into the field. The results would be unpredictable, but almost certainly bad.

I fix these defects in the `smartRToEdit()` function coming up next, but begin by studying this simpler function, because `smartRToEdit()` is built on `rToEdit()`.

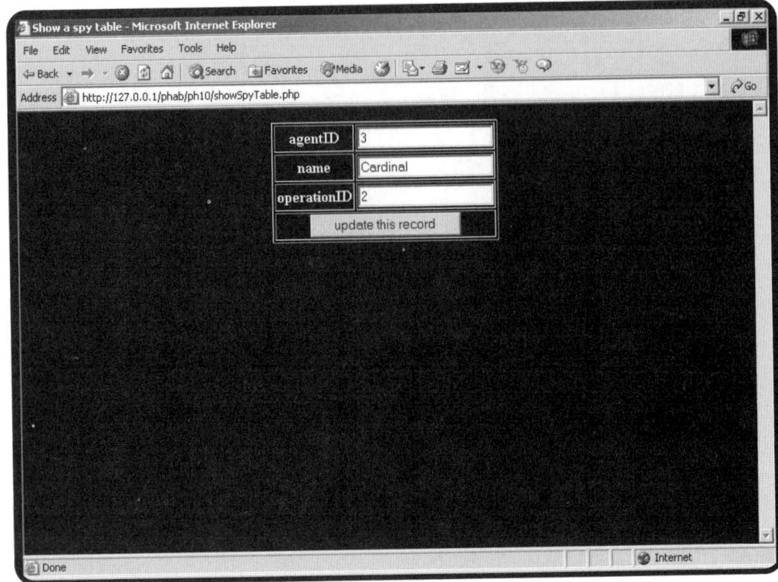

FIGURE 12.12

The rToEdit function is simple but produces dangerous output.

```
function rToEdit ($query){
  //given a one-record query, creates a form to edit that record
  //works on any table, but allows direct editing of keys
  //use smartRToEdit instead if you can

  global $dbConn;
  $output = "";
  $result = mysql_query($query, $dbConn);
  $row = mysql_fetch_assoc($result);

  //get table name from field object
  $fieldObj = mysql_fetch_field($result, 0);
  $tableName = $fieldObj->table;

  $output .= <<< HERE
 <form action = "updateRecord.php"
      method = "post">

 <input type = "hidden"
        name = "tableName"
        value = "$tableName">

 <table border = 1>
```

```
HERE;

   foreach ($row as $col=>$val){
     $output .= <<<HERE
   <tr>
     <th>$col</th>
     <td>
       <input type = "text"
              name = "$col"
              value = "$val">
     </td>
   </tr>

HERE;
   } // end foreach
   $output .= <<< HERE
   <tr>
     <td colspan = 2>
       <center>
       <input type = "submit"
              value = "update this record">
       </center>
     </td>
   </tr>
</table>

HERE;
  return $output;
} // end rToEdit
```

Building a Smarter Edit Form

The `smartRToEdit()` function builds on the basic design of `rToEdit()` but compensates for a couple of major flaws in the `rToEdit()` design. Take a look at the smarter code:

```
function smartRToEdit ($query){
  //given a one-record query, creates a form to edit that record
  //Doesn't let user edit first (primary key) field
  //generates dropdown list for foreign keys
  //MUCH safer than ordinary rToEdit function
```

```
  // --restrictions on table design--
  //foreign keys MUST be named tableID where 'table' is table name
  //  (because mySQL doesn't recognize foreign key indicators)
  // I also expect a 'name' field in any table used as a foreign key
  //   (for same reason)

  global $dbConn;
  $output = "";
  $result = mysql_query($query, $dbConn);
  $row = mysql_fetch_assoc($result);

  //get table name from field object
  $fieldObj = mysql_fetch_field($result, 0);
  $tableName = $fieldObj->table;

  $output .= <<< HERE
<form action = "updateRecord.php"
      method = "post">

<input type = "hidden"
       name = "tableName"
       value = "$tableName">

<table border = 1>

HERE;
  $fieldNum = 0;
  foreach ($row as $col=>$val){
    if ($fieldNum == 0){
      //it's primary key. don't make textbox,
      //but store value in hidden field instead
      //user shouldn't be able to edit primary keys
      $output .= <<<HERE
  <tr>
    <th>$col</th>
    <td>$val
      <input type = "hidden"
             name = "$col"
             value = "$val">
    </td>
  </tr>
```

```
HERE;
      } else if (preg_match("/(.*)ID$/", $col, $match)) {
        //it's a foreign key reference
        // get table name (match[1])
        //create a listbox based on table name and its name field
        $valList = fieldToList($match[1],$col, $fieldNum, "name");

        $output .= <<<HERE
  <tr>
    <th>$col</th>
    <td>$valList</td>
  </tr>

HERE;

      } else {
        $output .= <<<HERE
  <tr>
    <th>$col</th>
    <td>
      <input type = "text"
             name = "$col"
             value = "$val">
    </td>
  </tr>

HERE;
      } // end if
      $fieldNum++;
  } // end foreach
  $output .= <<< HERE
  <tr>
    <td colspan = 2>
      <center>
      <input type = "submit"
             value = "update this record">
      </center>
    </td>
  </tr>
</table>
```

```
</form>

HERE;
  return $output;
} // end smartRToEdit
```

What makes this function smart is its ability to examine each field in the record and make a guess about what sort of field it is. Figure 12.13 shows the result of the `smartRToEdit()` program so you can compare it to the not-so-clever function in Figure 12.12.

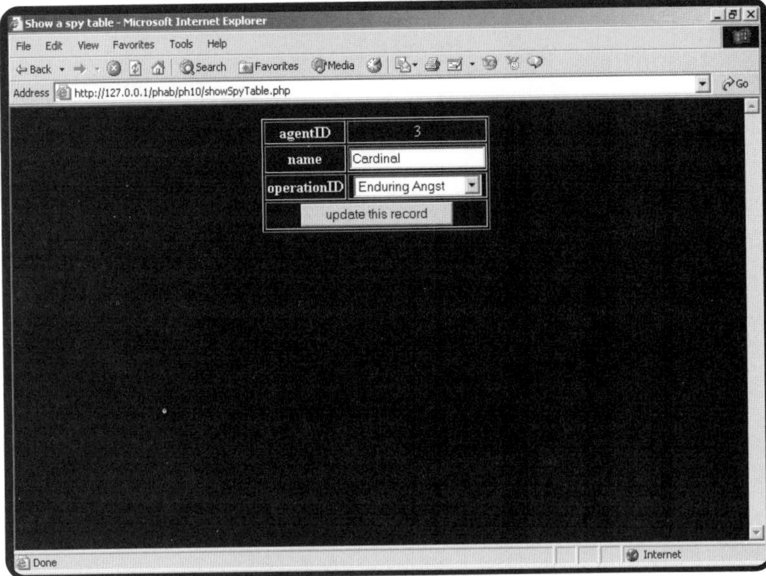

FIGURE 12.13

The smarter function prevents the user from editing the primary key and provides a drop-down list for all foreign key references.

Determining the Field Type

As far as this function is concerned, three field types in a record need to be handled differently.

- **Primary key.** If a field is the primary key, its value needs to be passed on to the next program, but the user should not be able to edit it.
- **Foreign key.** If a field is a foreign key reference to another table, the user should only be able to indirectly edit the value. The best approach is to have a drop-down list box that shows values the user will recognize. Each of these values corresponds to a key in that secondary record. For example, in Figure 12.13 there is a list box for the `operationID` field. The `operationID` field is a foreign key reference in the `agent` table. The ordinary `rToEdit()`

function allows the user to type any index number into the textbox without any real indication what data correlates to that index. This version builds a drop-down list showing operation names. The key value associated with those names is stored in the value attribute of each option. (Details to follow in the `fieldToList()` function.) The user doesn't have to know anything about foreign key references or relational structures—he simply chooses an operation from a list. That list is dynamically generated each time the user chooses to add a record, so it always reflects all the operations in the agency.

- **Neither a primary nor secondary key.** In this case, I print a simple textbox so the user can input the value of the field. In all cases, the output will reflect the current value of the field.

Working with the Primary Key

The primary key value is much more important to the program than it is to the user. I decided to display it, but not to make it editable in any way. Primary keys should not be edited, but changed only by adding or deleting records.

I relied upon some conventions to determine whether a field is a primary key. I assumed that the first field of the record (field number 0) is the primary key. This is a very common convention, but not universal. Since I created the data design in this case, I can be sure that the number 0 field in every table is the primary key. For that field, I simply printed the field name and value in an ordinary HTML table row. I added the key's value in a hidden field so the next program has access to it.

Recognizing Foreign Keys

Unfortunately, there is no way (at least in MySQL or SQLite) to determine if a field is a foreign key reference. I had to rely on a naming convention to make sure my program recognizes a field as a foreign key reference. I decided that all foreign key fields in my database will have the foreign table's name followed by the value `ID`. For example, a foreign key reference to the `operation` table will always be called `operationID` in my database.

This is a smart convention to follow anyway, as it makes your field names easy to remember. It becomes critical in `smartRToEdit()` because it's the only way to tell whether a field is a foreign key reference. I used an `else if` clause to check the name of any field that is not the primary key (which was checked in the `if` clause). The `preg_match()` function lets me use a powerful regular expression match to determine the field's name.

I used this statement to determine whether a field is a foreign key:

```
} else if (preg_match("/(.*)ID$/", $col, $match)) {
```

It uses a simple but powerful regular expression: `/(.*)ID$/`. This expression looks for any line that ends with `ID`. (Recall that the `$` indicates the end of a string.) The `.*` indicates any number of characters. The parentheses around `.*` tell PHP to store all the characters before `ID` into a special array, called `$match`. Since there's only one pattern to match in this expression, all the characters before `ID` contain the table name. So, this regular expression takes the name of a field and determines if it ends with `ID`. If so, the beginning part of the field name (everything but `ID`) is stored to `$match[1]`. If `$col` contains `operationID`, this line returns `TRUE` (because `operationID` ends with `ID`) and the table name (`operation`) is stored in `$match[1]`.

Building the Foreign Key List Box

If a field is a foreign key reference, it is necessary to build a list box containing some sort of meaningful value the user can read. Since I need this capability in a couple of places (and `smartRToEdit()` is already pretty complex), I build a new function called `fieldToList()`. This function (explained in detail later in the "Building a List Box from a Field" section of this chapter) builds a drop-down HTML list based on a table and field name. Rather than worrying about the details of the `fieldToList()` function here, I simply figured out what parameters it would need and printed that function's results.

Working with Regular Fields

Any field that is not a primary or foreign key is handled by the `else` clause, which prints out an `rToEdit()`-style textbox for user input. This textbox handles all fields that allow ordinary user input, but will not trap for certain errors (such as string data being placed in numeric fields or data longer than the underlying field accepts). These would be good code improvement. If the data designer did not name foreign key references according to my convention, those fields are still editable with a textbox, but the errors that could happen with `rToEdit()` are worth concern.

Committing a Record Update

The end result of either `rToEdit()` or `smartRToEdit()` is an HTML form containing a table name and a bunch of field names and values. The `updateRecord.php` takes these values and converts them into arrays before calling the `updateRec()` function. It's much easier to work with the fields and values as arrays than in the somewhat amorphous context they embody after `smartRToEdit()` or `rToEdit()`.

```
function updateRec($tableName, $fields, $vals){
  //expects name of a record, fields array values array
  //updates database with new values

  global $dbConn;

  $output = "";
  $keyName = $fields[0];
  $keyVal = $vals[0];
  $query = "";

  $query .= "UPDATE $tableName SET \n";
  for ($i = 1; $i < count($fields); $i++){
    $query .= $fields[$i];
    $query .= " = '";
    $query .= $vals[$i];
    $query .= "',\n";
  } // end for loop

  //remove last comma from output
  $query = substr($query, 0, strlen($query) - 2);

  $query .= "\nWHERE $keyName = '$keyVal'";

  $result = mysql_query($query, $dbConn);
  if ($result){
    $query = "SELECT * FROM $tableName WHERE $keyName = '$keyVal'";
    $output .= "<h3>update successful</h3>\n";
    $output .= "new value of record:<br>";
    $output .= qToTable($query);
  } else {
    $output .= "<h3>there was a problem...</h3><pre>$query</pre>\n";
  } // end if
  return $output;
} // end updateRec
```

The primary job of updateRec() is to build an SQL UPDATE statement based on the parameters passed to it. It is expecting a table name, an array containing field names, and another array containing field values. The UPDATE statement is primarily a list of field names and values, which can be easily obtained with a for loop stepping through the $fields and $vals arrays.

Once the query has been created, it is submitted to the database. The success or failure of the update is reported back to the user.

Deleting a Record

Deleting a record is actually pretty easy compared to adding or updating. All that's necessary is the table name, key field name, and key field value. The deleteRec() function accepts these parameters and uses them to build an SQL DELETE statement. As usual, the success or failure of the operation is returned as part of the output string.

```
function delRec ($table, $keyName, $keyVal){
  //deletes $keyVal record from $table
  global $dbConn;
  $output = "";
  $query = "DELETE from $table WHERE $keyName = '$keyVal'";
  print "query is $query<br>\n";
  $result = mysql_query($query, $dbConn);
  if ($result){
    $output = "<h3>Record successfully deleted</h3>\n";
  } else {
    $output = "<h3>Error deleting record</h3>\n";
  } //end if
  return $output;
} // end delRec
```

Adding a Record

Adding a new record is much like editing a record. It is a two-step process. The first screen builds a page in which you can add a record. I used techniques from the smartRToEdit() function to ensure the primary and foreign key references are edited appropriately.

```
function tToAdd($tableName){
  //given table name, generates HTML form to add an entry to the
  //table. Works like smartRToEdit in recognizing foreign keys
```

```
  global $dbConn;
  $output = "";

  //process a query just to get field names
  $query = "SELECT * FROM $tableName";
  $result = mysql_query($query, $dbConn);

  $output .= <<<HERE
  <form action = "processAdd.php"
        method = "post">
  <table border = "1">
    <tr>
      <th>Field</th>
      <th>Value</th>
    </tr>

HERE;

  $fieldNum = 0;
  while ($theField = mysql_fetch_field($result)){
    $fieldName = $theField->name;
    if ($fieldNum == 0){
      //it's the primary key field. It'll be autoNumber
      $output .= <<<HERE
      <tr>
        <td>$fieldName</td>
        <td>AUTONUMBER
          <input type = "hidden"
                 name = "$fieldName"
                 value = "null">
        </td>
      </tr>

HERE;
    } else if (preg_match("/(.*)ID$/", $fieldName, $match)) {
      //it's a foreign key reference. Use fieldToList to get
      //a select object for this field

      $valList = fieldToList($match[1],$fieldName, 0, "name");
      $output .= <<<HERE
```

```
      <tr>
        <td>$fieldName</td>
        <td>$valList</td>
      </tr>

HERE;
    } else {
    //it's an ordinary field. Print a text box
    $output .= <<<HERE
      <tr>
        <td>$fieldName</td>
        <td><input type = "text"
                   name = "$fieldName"
                   value = "">
        </td>
      </tr>

HERE;
    } // end if
    $fieldNum++;
  } // end while
  $output .= <<<HERE
    <tr>
      <td colspan = 2>
        <input type = "hidden"
               name = "tableName"
               value = "$tableName">
        <input type = "submit"
               value = "add record">
      </td>
    </tr>
  </table>
  </form>

HERE;

  return $output;

} // end tToAdd
```

The INSERT statement that this function creates uses NULL as the primary key value, because all tables in the system are set to AUTO_INCREMENT. I used the same regular expression trick as in smartRToEdit() to recognize foreign key references. If they exist, I built a drop-down list with fieldToList() to display all possible values for that field and send an appropriate key. Any field not recognized as a primary or foreign key will have an ordinary textbox.

Processing an Added Record

The tToAdd() function sends its results to processAdd.php, which reorganizes the data much like updateRecord.php. The field names and values are converted to arrays, which are passed to the procAdd() function.

```
function procAdd($tableName, $fields, $vals){
  //generates INSERT query, applies to database
  global $dbConn;

  $output = "";
  $query = "INSERT into $tableName VALUES (";
  foreach ($vals as $theValue){
    $query .= "'$theValue', ";
  } // end foreach

  //trim off trailing space and comma
  $query = substr($query, 0, strlen($query) - 2);

  $query .= ")";
  $output = "query is $query<br>\n";

  $result = mysql_query($query, $dbConn);
  if ($result){
    $output .= "<h3>Record added</h3>\n";
  } else {
    $output .= "<h3>There was an error</h3>\n";
  } // end if
  return $output;
} // end procAdd
```

The main job of procAdd() is to build an SQL INSERT statement using the results of tToAdd(). This insert is passed to the database and the user receives a report about the insertion attempt's outcome.

Building a List Box from a Field

Both `smartRToEdit()` and `tToAdd()` need drop-down HTML lists following a specific pattern. In both cases, I needed to build a list that allows the user to select a key value based on some other field in the record. This list should be set so any value in the list can be indicated as the currently selected value. The `fieldToList()` function takes four parameters and uses them to build exactly such a list.

```
function fieldToList($tableName, $keyName, $keyVal, $fieldName){
  //given table and field, generates an HTML select structure
  //named $keyName. values will be key field of table, but
  //text will come from the $fieldName value.
  //keyVal indicates which element is currently selected

  global $dbConn;
  $output = "";
  $query = "SELECT $keyName, $fieldName FROM $tableName";
  $result = mysql_query($query, $dbConn);
  $output .= "<select name = $keyName>\n";
  $recNum = 1;
  while ($row = mysql_fetch_assoc($result)){
    $theIndex = $row["$keyName"];
    $theValue = $row["$fieldName"];
    $output .= <<<HERE
    right now, theIndex is $theIndex and keyVal is $keyVal
  <option value = "$theIndex"
HERE;

    //make it currently selected item
    if ($theIndex == $keyVal){
      $output .= " selected";
    } // end if
    $output .= ">$theValue</option>\n";
    $recNum++;
  } // end while
  $output .= "</select>\n";
  return $output;
} // end fieldToList
```

The `fieldToList()` function begins by generating a query that returns all records in the foreign table. I build an HTML `SELECT` object based on the results of this query. As I step through all records, I see if the current record corresponds to the `$keyVal` parameter. If so, that element is selected in the HTML.

Creating a Button That Returns Users to the Main Page

To simplify navigation, I added a button at the end of each PHP program that returns the user to the program's primary page. The `mainButton()` program creates a very simple form calling whatever program is named in the `$mainProgram` variable, which is indicated at the top of the library.

```
function mainButton(){
  // creates a button to return to the main program

  global $mainProgram;

  $output .= <<<HERE
<form action = "$mainProgram"
      method = "get">
<input type = "submit"
       value = "return to main screen">
</form>

HERE;
  return $output;
} // end mainButton
```

Summary

The details of the `SpyMaster` system can be dizzying, but the overall effect is a flexible design that you can easily update and modify. This system can accept modifications to the underlying database and can be adapted to an entirely different data set with relatively little effort.

Although you didn't learn any new PHP syntax in this chapter, you saw an example of coding for reuse and flexibility. You learned how to use `include` files to simplify coding of complex systems and how to build a library file with utility routines. You learned how to write code that can be adapted to multiple data sets and code that prevents certain kinds of user errors. You learned how to build programs that help tie together relational data structures. The things you have learned in this chapter form the foundation of all data-enabled Web programming, which in turn form the backbone of e-commerce and content-management systems.

CHALLENGES

1. Add a module that lets the user interactively query the database. Begin with a page that allows the user to type in an agent's name and returns data based on that agent.
2. Once the basic functionality of an agent search program is done, add check-boxes that allow certain agent aspects (operation and skills) to be displayed.
3. Build programs that allow searching on other aspects of the data, including skills and operations.
4. Modify the `SpyMaster` database to support another data set or SQLite.

Index

Symbols

A

D

E

F

G

H

I

J

L

P

Q

R

S

T

W

X

License Agreement/Notice of Limited Warranty

By opening the sealed disc container in this book, you agree to the following terms and conditions. If, upon reading the following license agreement and notice of limited warranty, you cannot agree to the terms and conditions set forth, return the unused book with unopened disc to the place where you purchased it for a refund.

License:
The enclosed software is copyrighted by the copyright holder(s) indicated on the software disc. You are licensed to copy the software onto a single computer for use by a single user and to a backup disc. You may not reproduce, make copies, or distribute copies or rent or lease the software in whole or in part, except with written permission of the copyright holder(s). You may transfer the enclosed disc only together with this license, and only if you destroy all other copies of the software and the transferee agrees to the terms of the license. You may not decompile, reverse assemble, or reverse engineer the software.

Notice of Limited Warranty:
The enclosed disc is warranted by Thomson Course Technology PTR to be free of physical defects in materials and workmanship for a period of sixty (60) days from end user's purchase of the book/disc combination. During the sixty-day term of the limited warranty, Thomson Course Technology PTR will provide a replacement disc upon the return of a defective disc.

Limited Liability:
THE SOLE REMEDY FOR BREACH OF THIS LIMITED WARRANTY SHALL CONSIST ENTIRELY OF REPLACEMENT OF THE DEFECTIVE DISC. IN NO EVENT SHALL THOMSON COURSE TECHNOLOGY PTR OR THE AUTHOR BE LIABLE FOR ANY OTHER DAMAGES, INCLUDING LOSS OR CORRUPTION OF DATA, CHANGES IN THE FUNCTIONAL CHARACTERISTICS OF THE HARDWARE OR OPERATING SYSTEM, DELETERIOUS INTERACTION WITH OTHER SOFTWARE, OR ANY OTHER SPECIAL, INCIDENTAL, OR CONSEQUENTIAL DAMAGES THAT MAY ARISE, EVEN IF THOMSON COURSE TECHNOLOGY PTR AND/OR THE AUTHOR HAS PREVIOUSLY BEEN NOTIFIED THAT THE POSSIBILITY OF SUCH DAMAGES EXISTS.

Disclaimer of Warranties:
THOMSON COURSE TECHNOLOGY PTR AND THE AUTHOR SPECIFICALLY DISCLAIM ANY AND ALL OTHER WARRANTIES, EITHER EXPRESS OR IMPLIED, INCLUDING WARRANTIES OF MERCHANTABILITY, SUITABILITY TO A PARTICULAR TASK OR PURPOSE, OR FREEDOM FROM ERRORS. SOME STATES DO NOT ALLOW FOR EXCLUSION OF IMPLIED WARRANTIES OR LIMITATION OF INCIDENTAL OR CONSEQUENTIAL DAMAGES, SO THESE LIMITATIONS MIGHT NOT APPLY TO YOU.

Other:
This Agreement is governed by the laws of the State of Massachusetts without regard to choice of law principles. The United Convention of Contracts for the International Sale of Goods is specifically disclaimed. This Agreement constitutes the entire agreement between you and Thomson Course Technology PTR regarding use of the software.